A native of Germany, Mr. Dietze complements the works of the outstanding foreign observers of the United States in this century: André Siegfried, Harold Laski, and Gunnar Myrdal. He does not, however, share the general opinion that America has a long way to go toward egalitarian democracy, but points out that on the road in that direction she has moved too far away from libertarian values and her constitutional tradition. While emphasizing the tragedy of this development, the author suggests solutions to this political dilemma.

Gottfried Dietze earned doctorates in law from the University of Heidelberg, in philosophy from Princeton University, and in juridical science from the University of Virginia. He is a Professor of Political Science at The Johns Hopkins University, has been a Visiting Professor at the University of Heidelberg and at the Brookings Institution, and is the author of several books and articles in leading professional journals. He was elected a member of the Academy of Human Rights.

AMERICA'S POLITICAL DILEMMA

FROM LIMITED TO UNLIMITED DEMOCRACY

AMERICA'S POLITICAL DILEMMA

FROM LIMITED TO UNLIMITED DEMOCRACY

BY

GOTTFRIED DIETZE

THE JOHNS HOPKINS PRESS, BALTIMORE

Cover Illustration Courtesy of Bettman Archives

For
P. F. G.
Friend of Liberty
Skeptic of Power

Posterity may know we have not loosely

through silence permitted things to pass away as in a dream.

RICHARD HOOKER, . . . TO THEM THAT SEEK

(AS THEY TERM IT) THE REFORMATION OF THE LAWS . . .

PREFACE

America's political dilemma is the dilemma of democratic politics. It exists because Americans have been committed so much to popular government that they have tended to accept whatever is done in its name and moved from limited to unlimited democracy.

Democratic growth is basically a good thing. Since self-government is believed to secure freedom, its expansion generally can be expected to result in an increasing emancipation of men. This, at least, was the promise of the American Dream. However, while democracy can be ideal for the realization of freedom, it is not free from the pitfalls that beset other forms of government. The men who founded the American system were well aware of this. Desirous of having reason prevail over popular passion, they established a free government under which the ruling majority was restricted by a rule of law which provided for the protection of the rights of the individual.

The present study examines whether or not American government still measures up to the Founders' standards. Its answer is in the negative. The march of democracy has made government less reasonable, to the detriment of the minority eliminated checks upon the majority, and resulted in a foreign policy which jeopardizes national security. Popular government, having for its rationale the promotion of freedom, instead has restricted essential human rights. In view of America's general commitment to democracy, this means that her democratic challenge has turned into her democratic dilemma. It suggests that Americans may have a rude awakening from their democratic Dream and find themselves in a democratic tragedy.

A book warning of democratic trends runs the risk of being considered an attack upon an American sanctuary. However, one hardly commits sacrilege if the deity is false. And we believe that present democratic tendencies run not only counter to common sense and the wisdom of the ages, but also to the American constitutional tradition. We have a basic trust in democracy. What we object to is the very thing that was rejected by the men who framed the Constitution, namely, an excess of democracy. We feel that the United States, moving into unlimited majority rule, has ventured into something which her Founders tried to abolish and to prevent. We fear that an overdose of democracy may well bring about the end not only of freedom, but of popular government itself—even if America survives Soviet imperialism. Our prognosis that the development from a limited to an unlimited democracy will be followed by a one-man rule, does not stand on weak ground. Aside from corresponding to a classic cycle, this development was envisaged by the great modern author on democracy, who also is the classic observer of democracy in America. Having mentioned the dangers of democratic excesses as Madison described them in *The Federalist,* de Tocqueville marshaled a statement by Jefferson, whom he considered "the most powerful advocate democracy has ever had," in support of his fear lest majoritarianism will lead to despotism: "The tyranny of the legislature is really the danger most to be feared, and will continue to be so for many years to come. The tyranny of the executive will come in its turn, but at a more distant period." Congressional government has been on the wane, and presidential government, ascendent. The latter may well lead to the despotism of one man.

The aims of someone from abroad in discussing the United States must, for obvious reasons, be modest. As the length of this book indicates, it was not intended to provide another comprehensive study of the scope of those written by the outstanding modern observers of the United States, André Siegfried, Gunnar Myrdal, and Harold J. Laski. The present work is merely an introduction into major political problems of American existence. It does not share the general opinion that the United States has a long way to go toward egalitarian democracy, but asserts that on the road in that direction America has moved too much away from libertarian values. The following pages will achieve their purpose if they succeed in making the reader think about this problem. For a vital problem it is. If the United States goes despotic, the Western hemisphere probably will—and the West and the rest of the still free world might follow.

Thanks are due to many American friends, ranging from those with whom I was under adverse conditions in Germany in 1944 and who helped me to study in this country, to those whom I met in happier circumstances and who greatly inspired my work. I am grateful to the Brookings Institution, the Johns Hopkins University, and the Library of Congress for their research facilities. The permission by the University of Chicago Press to reprint from my article, "Will the Presidency Incite Assassination?" which in 1965 I was able to place in ETHICS, AN INTERNATIONAL JOURNAL OF SOCIAL, POLITICAL, AND LEGAL PHILOSOPHY, is appreciated.

Baltimore, Maryland
March 25, 1968

G. D.

CONTENTS

CONTENTS

AMERICA'S POLITICAL DILEMMA

FROM LIMITED TO UNLIMITED DEMOCRACY

1

AMERICA'S DEMOCRATIC CHALLENGE

The march of democracy is so characteristic of American political development that democracy seems to be America's major sanctuary. Significantly, the classic work on the United States is *On Democracy in America*.[1] As was envisaged in that study, American history demonstrates the growth of democracy. For the sake of a "government of the people, by the people, for the people," the United States with iron and blood was made into a nation which later fought two world wars to make the world "safe for democracy." Modern political programs from the New Freedom to the New Deal to the New Frontier were based upon the recognition of the old belief that "there is no retrograde step in the rear of democracy,"[2] and made the United States increasingly democratic. The Great Society is, above all, a democratic society. The *Pax Americana* is said to rest upon the will of the American people. Proper Americans are supposed to believe in the propriety of democracy. The general recognition of democracy has progressed so far that the American coat of arms could contain the words, *Dieu et mon droit: Honi soit qui mal y pense* just as much as *e pluribus unum*.

The acceptance of popular government as a political *forma formarum* is in tune with the American tradition. The struggle between the colonists and Parliament in large measure grew out of the fact that the colonies were not actually represented in that

---

[1] Alexis de Tocqueville, DE LA DÉMOCRATIE EN AMÉRIQUE (Paris, 1835–40). In the following, references are to DEMOCRACY IN AMERICA (Bradley ed.; New York, 1954).

[2] The former statement was made by Woodrow Wilson when he explained the entry of the United States into World War I (65th Cong., 1st Sess., House Doc. No. 1 p. 7), and the latter, by Chancellor James Kent. REPORTS OF THE PROCEEDINGS AND DEBATES OF THE CONVENTION OF 1821, ASSEMBLED FOR THE PURPOSE OF AMENDING THE CONSTITUTION OF THE STATE OF NEW YORK (Albany, N.Y., 1821), 222.

body. The Declaration of Independence denounced a monarch. In the Philadelphia Convention, the adoption of popular government was a foregone conclusion.[3] The classic commentary to the Convention's product, *The Federalist,* leaves no doubt about the republican character of the Constitution. Even Americans who were skeptical about popular government felt that it was appropriate for their country.[4] So generally was the American system identified with republicanism that Simon Bolívar considered the establishment of monarchy in Spanish-America un-American.[5]

Except for the incarnation and death of Christ, the discovery of the New World—at the transition from the Middle Ages to modern times—has been considered the greatest event since the creation of the world.[6] Perhaps the independence of the New World is the most important event in the history of popular government because of its unequivocal preference for that form of government.

The establishment of the American republic, bold and novel as

[3] See Alpheus T. Mason, FREE GOVERNMENT IN THE MAKING (3d ed.; New York, 1965), 185ff.; Charles Warren, THE MAKING OF THE CONSTITUTION (Boston, 1937), 17ff., 43ff., 58, 378f., 436ff., 771.

[4] When Hamilton praised the British constitution the English monarchy had become constitutionalized. When in the Federal Convention he despaired that republican government could remove the shortcomings of the Articles of Confederation, he hastened to add that he "would hold it, however, unwise to change that form of government." Henry Cabot Lodge (ed.), THE WORKS OF ALEXANDER HAMILTON (New York, 1904), I, 401. See also "A Full Vindication"; "The Farmer Refuted"; letter to James Duane of Sept. 3, 1780. WORKS, I, 5f., 64, 113, 213. John Adams wrote: "I cannot say that democracy has been more pernicious, on the whole, than any of the [other forms of government]. Its atrocities have been more transient; those of the others have been more permanent. The history of all ages shows that the caprice, cruelties, and horrors of democracy have soon disgusted, alarmed, and terrified themselves. . . . Democracy, nevertheless, must not be disgraced; democracy must not be despised. Democracy must be respected; democracy must be honored; democracy must be cherished; democracy must be an essential, integral part of the sovereignty, and have control over the whole government, or moral liberty cannot exist, or any other liberty." To John Taylor, April 15, 1814. Charles Francis Adams (ed.), THE WORKS OF JOHN ADAMS (Boston, 1850–56), VI, 477f.

[5] Considering monarchy "impossible," he added: "Wrongs now existing could not be righted, and our emancipation would be fruitless." Vicente Lecuna/Harold A. Bierck, Jr. (eds.), SELECTED WRITINGS OF BOLÍVAR (2d ed.; New York, 1951), I, 115.

[6] "La mayor cosa después de la creación del mundo, sacando la encarnación y muerte del que lo crío, es el descubrimiento de Indias, y así las llaman Mundo Nuevo." Francisco López de Gómara, HISTORIA GENERAL DE LAS INDIAS (Madrid, 1552; 1932), I, 4.

it was, brought to a conclusion a long development toward democracy in the English-speaking world. One of the first manifestations of that development is the Magna Carta. Even if the Great Charter of Liberties resulted from a "barons' revolt," a thesis which is open to doubt because broader segments of the population seem to have been involved, the Magna Carta still would be a demonstration of the quest for popular participation in government.[7] Without this demonstration, Parliament might not have been founded fifty years later. The struggle between Parliament and the Stuarts also turned around popular participation in government, which by then definitely had spread beyond the landed nobility. And yet, far-reaching as the assertions of parliamentary power may have been, they did not result in an abolition of monarchy. Cromwell's republican Instrument of Government was short-lived. The Glorious Revolution limited, but did not abolish, monarchy. This feat was achieved only in the American Revolution. It was in America that popular government came of age, that it came to exist in form as well as substance.

The described steps toward popular government were prompted by the desire to have the freedom of the individual protected, the general feeling being that the people are the best guardians of their liberties. The Great Charter of Liberties, the Petition of Right and the Bill of Rights, brought about by the people, enumerated the rights to be protected from the King and left no doubt that popular government was to secure such protection.[8] The Declaration of Independence states that "all men . . . are endowed by their creator with certain unalienable rights; that among these are life, liberty, and the pursuit of happiness; that to secure these rights governments are instituted among men, deriv-

---

[7] See ch. 61. On the growing applicability of the benefits of the Magna Carta and the growth of popular government after Runnymede, see the author's MAGNA CARTA AND PROPERTY (Charlottesville, Va., 1965), 4f., 61ff. Popular government in the Middle Ages is discussed in Walter Ullmann, PRINCIPLES OF GOVERNMENT AND POLITICS IN THE MIDDLE AGES (London, 1961).

[8] The Petition of Right (1628), a "Petition exhibited to his Majesty by the Lords Spiritual and Temporal, and Commons in this present Parliament assembled," is based upon acts of Parliament and requests "that no man hereafter be compelled to make or yield any gift, loan, benevolence, tax, or such like charge, without common consent by Act of Parliament." The Bill of Rights (1689) blames James II for having acted oppressively "without consent of Parliament." It sees in the latter the guardian of "undoubted rights and liberties."

ing their just powers from the consent of the governed." The protection of the individual's life, liberty, and property is the professed aim of the popular governments set up by the constitutions of the newly independent states.[9] It is the aim of the federal Constitution, an aim confirmed by its Bill of Rights.

The sequence, "life, liberty, and property," does not imply a ranking according to importance. All these demonstrations of freedom were to enjoy almost equal protection. Property rights were evaluated as highly as liberty and life. Standing in the foreground of the Magna Carta, they occupy a prominent position in the Petition of Right and the Bill of Rights.[10] Perhaps their relevance throughout English history prompted John Locke to call life, liberty, and estate by the general term "property," and to consider the protection of property the major end of government.[11] Property rights also played a significant role in the American Revolution. The Declaration of Independence denounces British violations of property rights as much as infringements upon life and liberty, lending credence to the assertion that for Jefferson the "pursuit of happiness" in a large measure consisted in the protection of property rights. The desire to have property protected is evident in the new state constitutions, the Constitution of the United States and its Bill of Rights.[12] While emphasis upon property rights is less an indication of their pre-eminence before life and liberty than of the fact that they were threatened

[9] Cf. the constitutions of Delaware (1792), Georgia (1777), Maryland (1776), Massachusetts (1780), New Hampshire (1776, 1784), New Jersey (1776), New York (1777), North Carolina (1776), Pennsylvania (1776), South Carolina (1776), Vermont (1777, 1786), Virginia (1776), esp. their preambles. According to Art. 5 of the constitution of Maryland, "the right in the people to participate in the Legislature is the best security of liberty, and the foundation of all free government."

[10] See the author's MAGNA CARTA AND PROPERTY; IN DEFENSE OF PROPERTY (Chicago, 1963), 57ff.

[11] John Locke, TWO TREATISES OF GOVERNMENT (Peter Laslett ed., Cambridge, 1960), 368f., writes that man, leaving the state of nature, "seeks out, and is willing to joyn in Society with others who are already united, or have a mind to unite for the mutual *Preservation* of the Lives, Liberties and Estates, which I call by the general Name, *Property*. The great and *chief end* therefore, of Mens uniting into Commonwealths, and putting themselves under Government, is *the Preservation of their Property*." On the appreciation of property rights prior to Locke, see Carl J. Friedrich, MAN AND HIS GOVERNMENT (New York, 1963), 358.

[12] See *infra*, 64ff.

6

more than other rights, there can be little doubt that their absolute value is on a par with that of life or liberty.[13]

The American Revolution is distinguished from its predecessors not only for its formal abolition of monarchy, but also
because of its protection of the individual from popular government. The English had been content with restricting monarchy
and establishing parliamentary supremacy. Montesquieu's ac-
creditation of their government with a separation of powers was
thus an idealization. The Americans went farther. Realizing Montesquieu's ideal, they abolished monarchy and prevented legislative supremacy. In America, the rights of man were to be as safe
from popular government as from a monarch, from a democratic
legislature as much as from a democratic executive. Institutions
restricting governmental power such as federalism, the separation
of powers, and judicial review, were to secure these rights. While
accepting the Lockean-Blackstonean idea that the protection of
life, liberty, and property is the major end of government, Americans—unable to follow Locke's and Blackstone's beliefs in legislative supremacy in a unitary nation as the best device for securing that end[14] because they had experienced the fallibility of
Parliament and of some of their state legislatures—adopted Montesquieu's guarantees for free government, i.e., institutional and
territorial separations of power, and topped them off with a contribution of their own—judicial review.[15] Democratic aberrations
which occurred in England after Coke had left the scene and

[13] The thesis that the people's struggle for a particular liberty and the final
guarantee of that liberty result from its oppression by the government, is advanced
by Georg Jellinek, DIE ERKLÄRUNG DER MENSCHEN—UND BÜRGERRECHTE (3d ed. by
Walter Jellinek; Leipzig, 1919). The vital importance of property is discussed in
the author's IN DEFENSE OF PROPERTY, 48ff.

[14] Locke's and Blackstone's high appreciation of the legislature derived from the
consideration that the legislature would be the safest depository of life, liberty, and
property, not from a belief that it should have arbitrary power over the regulation
of those rights. Both felt that the legislature would be guided by older law (natural
or common) which protected human rights.

[15] See William S. Carpenter, "The Separation of Powers in the Eighteenth
Century," AMERICAN POLITICAL SCIENCE REVIEW, XXII (1928), 32; Edward S.
Corwin, THE DOCTRINE OF JUDICIAL REVIEW (Princeton, N. J., 1914); "The Progress
of Constitutional Theory between the Declaration of Independence and the
Meeting of the Philadelphia Convention," AMERICAN HISTORICAL REVIEW, XXX
(1925), 511.

which were evident in the shift of power from the monarch to Parliament as a result of Parliament's victory over the Crown, were corrected. *Lex, rex.*[16] Abiding by the rule of law, Americans brought popular government back on the right track of constitutionalism that leads from the Magna Carta to Coke's revival of that charter to James Harrington. The latter named his work *Oceana* perhaps because he sensed that the limitation and salvation of popular government through the "empire of laws" would occur beyond the ocean.[17]

With all the novelties it produced, the American Revolution was thus, in a strict sense, no real revolution. It did not overthrow a legitimate order, but restored the rule of law and its protection of the individual against the machinations of human lawmakers whose acts, while often legal, were not always legitimate. In his famous showdown with James I, Lord Coke had contested the King's claim that the King controls the law, insisting that the law controls the King and that its artificial reason, accumulated by jurists over the ages, was superior to the natural reason of the living.[18] After a century and a half of further democratic development, the Americans, having become aware that the natural reason of elected representatives is as fallible as that of a hereditary king, provided against the dangers flowing from the natural reason of democracy. While admitting that this reason might contribute to the growth and perfection of the law, they stipulated that it ought not to be employed arbitrarily but according to the rule of law and its protection of freedom. They made clear that it had better be a constitutionalist reason, respectful of traditional values and similar to Coke's artificial reason of the law. The latter was transmuted into the Constitution. The American Revolution

---

[16] Cf. [Samuel Rutherford], LEX, REX: THE LAW AND THE PRINCE (London, 1644). The rule of law was defended not only by the Roundheads, but also by the Royalists. Cf. Charles I's SPEECH MADE UPON THE SCAFFOLD (London, 1649).

[17] James Harrington, THE COMMON-WEALTH OF OCEANA (London, 1656), 2, wrote that "Government (to define it [*de jure*] or according to *ancient Prudence*) is an Art whereby a Civil Society of men is instituted and preserved upon the foundation of common right or interest, or (to follow *Aristotle* and *Livy*) it is the *Empire* of *Lawes* and not of *Men*."

[18] See Carl J. Friedrich, CONSTITUTIONAL GOVERNMENT AND DEMOCRACY (rev. ed.; Boston, 1950), 103ff.

was thus an evolutionary rather than revolutionary event.[19] Designed to preserve rather than to overthrow a traditional constitutionalist order, it was an eighteenth century equivalent of the
diffidatio of 1215, and of later attempts at restricting the monarchy, significantly started by the modern revivalist of the Magna
Carta, Lord Coke.[20]

Popular government as established in the American Revolution
was novel mainly because of its abolition of monarchy. It included nothing new as far as its ingredients and their relation-
ships are concerned. The democratic principle of popular participation in government was to guarantee the liberal principle of
protection of the individual from the government. Popular government was considered a means for the protection of the individual under a Constitution embodying a rule of law which had been
cherished for centuries. The American Revolution was in the
mainstream of the constitutionalist development of the common
law. It provided popular government with no license to define—and thus to restrict—freedom, but entrusted it with the
protection of freedom by stipulating that it observe the rule of
law. Popular government, often called republican government by
the Founding Fathers, meant *free government,* under which the
popular majority while ruling, was, for the sake of the protection
of the individual, restricted under the Constitution. "Free government" thus is not some vague, general concept, but a *terminus
technicus* with a specific meaning. While it implies popular government and majority rule, it is not identical to them. Under a
mere popular government, or democracy, the majority can be unre-

---

[19] See Charles H. McIlwain, THE AMERICAN REVOLUTION, A CONSTITUTIONAL
INTERPRETATION (New York, 1923), and Friedrich Gentz, "Der Ursprung und die
Grundsätze der Amerikanischen Revolution, verglichen mit dem Ursprunge und den
Grundsätzen der Französischen," HISTORISCHES JOURNAL, II (1800), 3. (The English
translation of the latter work by John Quincy Adams has been re-edited by Russell
Kirk, THE FRENCH AND AMERICAN REVOLUTIONS COMPARED [Chicago, 1955]). Mod-
ern conservative and liberal historians agree. See Clinton Rossiter, SEEDTIME OF
THE REPUBLIC (New York, 1953), 440, 448; Louis Hartz, THE LIBERAL TRADITION IN
AMERICA (New York, 1955), chs. 2–4.

[20] See Sir Edward Coke's SECOND INSTITUTE (London, 1641); William S. McKech-
nie, MAGNA CARTA: A COMMENTARY ON THE GREAT CHARTER OF KING JOHN (2d
ed.; Glasgow, 1914), 133, 178f., 385; J. G. A. Pocock, THE ANCIENT CONSTITUTION
AND THE FEUDAL LAW (Cambridge, 1957), 44f., 53.

stricted and can oppress the minority. Under a free government, the majority is not free to rule the way it sees fit; it is free only to keep and make the individual free. Freedom is the beginning and the end. Freedom makes popular government possible, but also limits it for the sake of freedom.[21] The democratic challenge emerging from the American Revolution was a challenge of limited, constitutional, democracy—a challenge of free government.

This challenge brought forth general enthusiasm. The idea that "civil liberty" implied not "a government of laws, made agreeable to charters, bills of rights or compacts, but a power existing in the people at large, at any time, for any cause, or for no cause, but their own sovereign pleasure, to alter or annihilate both the mode and essence of any former government, and to adopt a new one in its stead,"[22] may have enjoyed some popularity shortly after Independence as a result of restrictions of executive power.[23] However, it mainly reflected radical beliefs that often come to the fore in the beginning of revolutions. Most Americans agreed with Jefferson that the fight for independence was not a fight for an "elective despotism," but for a free government,[24] and were optimistic about the prospects of the latter. Their appreciation was matched by foreigners. Dr. Richard Price, the English clergyman and moralist, admired "the revolution in favour of universal liberty which has taken place in America;—a revolution which opens a new prospect in human affairs." To him, this was "a revolution by which *Britons* themselves will be the greatest gainers, if wise

[21] See the author's THE FEDERALIST (Baltimore, 1960), esp. 69, 117f., 148. Cf. Justice Stone: "The Constitution expresses more than the conviction of the people that democratic processes must be preserved at all costs. It is also an expression of faith and a command that freedom of mind and spirit must be preserved, which government must obey, if it is to adhere to that justice and moderation without which no free government can exist." *Minersville School District* v. *Gobitis,* 310 U.S. 586, 606–7 (1940). Just as free government implies democracy, the latter usually implies the protection of the freedom of the individual. Therefore, when in the following free government is distinguished from democracy or popular government or majority rule and the latter are denounced for curtailing freedom, it should be kept in mind that they could still contain sufficient liberal elements, which in the eyes of many people qualify them to be considered free governments.

[22] Speech of Benjamin Hichborn in Boston, 1777. Hezekiah Niles (ed.), PRINCIPLES AND ACTS OF THE REVOLUTION (Baltimore, 1822), 27, 30.

[23] See Allan Nevins, THE AMERICAN STATES DURING AND AFTER THE REVOLUTION, 1775–1789 (New York, 1924), chs. 3–4. Carpenter, "Separation of Powers in the Eighteenth Century."

[24] See *infra,* 145f.

enough to improve properly the check that has been given to the despotism of their ministers, and to catch the flame of virtuous liberty which has saved their American brethren." Following this remark against despotism under the parliamentary type of popular government, Price, obviously distinguishing between parliamentary legality and constitutional legitimacy, wrote that the War of Independence "did great good by disseminating just sentiments of the rights of mankind, and the nature of legitimate government; by exciting a spirit of resistance to tyranny . . . and by occasioning the establishment in America of forms of government more equitable and more liberal than any the world has yet known." While leaving no doubt as to his republican inclinations, Price, whose arguments are based upon "reason, as well as tradition and revelation," believed that America has demonstrated that "the members of a civil community are *confederates,* not *subjects;* and their rulers, *servants,* not *masters.*—And that all legitimate government consists in the dominion of equal laws made with common consent; that is, in the dominion of men over *themselves;* and not in the dominion of communities over communities, or of any men over other men."[25] Published shortly after the Treaty of Paris, Price's ideas were matched by Condorcet two years later. The Frenchman admired popular government in America because it protected the rights of man. He saw a great future for it.[26]

[25] Richard Price, OBSERVATIONS ON THE IMPORTANCE OF THE AMERICAN REVOLUTION (Boston, 1784), 3ff., 7. To Price, American independence provided "a place of refuge for opprest men in every region of the world"; it laid "the foundation . . . of an empire which may be the seat of liberty, science and virtue, and from whence there is reason to hope these sacred blessings will spread, till they become universal . . ." *Ibid.,* 4. To him, "next to the introduction of Christianity among mankind, the American revolution may prove the most important step in the progressive course of human improvement. It is an event which may produce a general diffusion of the principles of humanity, and become the means of setting free mankind from the shackles of superstition and tyranny, by leading them to see and know that nothing is *fundamental* but impartial enquiry, an honest mind, and virtuous practice . . ." *Ibid.,* 7.

[26] Condorcet called the Declaration of Independence a "simple and sublime exposition" of "rights so sacred and so long forgotten," and added that in "no nation, have they been so well known and so well preserved in such a perfect integrity." While considering America's "republican sages" . . . "attached to some remains of English prejudices," he wrote that they are "the only people with whom one finds neither maxims of Machiavellism established into political principles, nor, among the leaders, the . . . opinion that it is impossible to make the social order

The enthusiasm displayed toward American institutions prior to the Federal Convention at Philadelphia, grew after the Constitution improved free government by correcting some of its democratic flaws. Condorcet, while wondering whether the Constitution improved things, gladly acknowledged the high caliber of the men who made it.[27] A generation later, Friedrich Gentz lauded the legitimate character of the American Revolution. He was happy that its popular government was in the constitutionalist tradition.[28] Americans were even more enthusiastic. Washington praised the "new and free Government" established by the "Great Constitutional Charter" which regards "the eternal rules of order and right, which Heaven itself has ordained."[29] Feeling that "no government before introduced among mankind ever contained so many checks and such efficacious restraints to prevent it from degenerating into any species of oppression," he was "convinced . . . that the balances arising from the distribution of the Legislative, Executive, and Judicial powers are the best that have been instituted."[30] He anticipated "the sweet enjoyment of partaking . . . the benign influence of good Laws under a free Government."[31] His ideas were shared by Federalists and Republicans alike. *The Federalist* emphasized that the government under the Constitution was a free government with great prospects.[32] Jefferson agreed.[33]

---

perfect and to reconcile public prosperity with justice." He felt that "in a few generations, America, by producing nearly as many men who can add to knowledge as all of Europe, will at least double progress . . ." and improve the lot of humanity. Marie Jean Antoine de Condorcet, "De l'influence de la Révolution d'Amérique sur l'Europe" (written in 1786, published in 1788). A. Condorcet O'Connor and M. F. Arago (eds.), OEUVRES DE CONDORCET (Paris, 1847), VIII, 11ff., 29f.

[27] *Ibid.*, 104. While Condorcet admitted the dangers inherent in Shays's Rebellion, he emphasized that it was an exceptional event.

[28] "Der Ursprung und die Grundsätze der Amerikanischen Revolution."

[29] First Inaugural Address (1789). John C. Fitzpatrick (ed.), THE WRITINGS OF GEORGE WASHINGTON (Washington, 1931–44), XXX, 293, 294.

[30] Proposed Address to Congress of 1789. WORKS, XXX, 300, 301.

[31] Farewell Address (1796). WORKS, XXXV, 238. Washington wished "that your Union and brotherly affection may be perpetual; that the free constitution . . . may be sacredly maintained; . . . that, in fine, the happiness of the people of these States, under the auspices of liberty, may be made complete, by so careful a preservation and so prudent a use of this blessing as will acquire to them the glory of recommending it to the applause, the affection, and adoption of every nation which is yet a stranger to it." *Ibid.*, 218.

[32] Cf. the author's FEDERALIST, esp. chs. 4–6.

[33] In his first Inaugural Address of 1801, Jefferson considered republican govern-

12

Evident in these praises is the hope that American achievements, important as they were as an act of liberation from the past, would be the beginning of further emancipations. The American Revolution was conceived not as a static but a dynamic event, the blessings of which would expand.[34] An enlargement of popular participation in government through a broadening of the suffrage, it was hoped, would bring about an increased protection of the rights of the individual. However, while a greater quantity of democracy would result in a greater quantity of freedom, the quality of free government, implying the subordination of the democratic principle of popular participation in government as a means to the liberal principle of the protection of the individual from the government as the end, would not be changed. Irrespective of how much popular participation in government would grow, it would still remain a mere means for the protection of the individual from the government. Irrespective of how the ruling majority would increase, it would still have to respect the rights of the minority, however small the latter might become. An overwhelming majority would have no license to overwhelm any minority.[35]

---

ment as it existed under the Constitution "the world's best hope," the "strongest government on earth." He believed that "it is the only one where every man, at the call of the laws, would fly to the standard of the law, and would meet invasions of the public order as his own personal concern." On March 6, 1801, he wrote John Dickinson: "A just and solid republican government maintained here, will be a standing monument and example for the aim and imitation of the people of other countries; and I join with you in the hope and belief that they will see, from our example, that a free government is of all others the most energetic; that . . . our revolution and its consequences, will ameliorate the condition of man over a great portion of the globe." Andrew A. Lipscomb (ed.), THE WRITINGS OF THOMAS JEFFERSON (Washington, 1903–04), III, 319f.; X, 217. Cf. also his statements in the sources given *infra*, 16n., 68, 210f., 271f.

[34] On the "permanent" revolution, see Benjamin Rush's letter to Richard Price of May 25, 1786, in Lyman H. Butterfield (ed.), LETTERS OF BENJAMIN RUSH (Princeton, N.J., 1951), 388, and Rush's speech of January, 1787, in Niles, PRINCIPLES AND ACTS OF THE REVOLUTION, 402. Cf. the author's "Benjamin Rush and the American Revolution," in Dickinson College (ed.), THE BOYD LEE SPAHR LECTURES IN AMERICANA (Harrisburg, Pa., 1961), III, 75. On July 4, 1787, Joel Barlow took a similar position. Niles, PRINCIPLES AND ACTS OF THE REVOLUTION, 386. The idea was also advanced by Price and Condorcet. For a modern view, see U.S.A. THE PERMANENT REVOLUTION (New York, 1951), by the editors of FORTUNE Magazine.

[35] Washington, after having stated that "The basis of our political systems is the right of the people to make and to alter their Constitutions of Government," warned: "Towards the preservation of your Government and the permanency of your present happy state, it is requisite, not only that you steadily discountenance irregular oppositions to its acknowledged authority, but also that you resist with

Since the American Revolution was a *diffidatio* based upon the rule of law and its inherent protection of freedom, the prospects that the quality of free government would not suffer from its quantitative expansion appeared to be good. On the other hand popular government, being as human as any other form of government—and quantitatively certainly more human if not necessarily more humane—was not immune from the corruption that tends to come with power. An expansion of popular power, probably inevitable as a result of the increase of popular participation in government, could bring about despotism as much as had the expansion of monarchical power as a result of the decrease of such participation. In a word, the growth of democracy could conceivably reduce the protection of the individual. It could pervert free government into a sheer majority rule which considered democracy an end in itself.

It testifies to the wisdom of the Founding Fathers that they recognized this danger. The oppressive acts of Parliament and of some state legislatures had brought home to them a democratic dilemma which was expressed by Elbridge Gerry's remark in the Federal Convention: "The evils we experience flow from the excess of democracy."[36] The recognition that American government had to be democratic was accompanied by the realization that democracy could degenerate into a majoritarian despotism. To prevent this, democracy was bridled. While men were deemed worthy of self-government, they were not considered so perfect as to be trusted absolutely. They were not given free reign. Since power only "tends to corrupt and absolute power corrupts abso-

---

care the spirit of innovation upon its principles however specious the pretexts . . . In all the changes to which you may be invited, remember that time and habit are at least as necessary to fix the true character of Governments, as of other human institutions; that experience is the surest standard, by which to test the real tendency of the existing Constitution of a country; that facility in changes upon the credit of mere hypotheses and opinion exposes to perpetual change, from the endless variety of hypotheses and opinion." Farewell Address, WRITINGS, XXXV, 224, 225f.

[36] Max Farrand (ed.), THE RECORDS OF THE FEDERAL CONVENTION (New Haven, Conn., 1911), I, 48. Edmund Randolph said: "Our chief danger arises from the democratic parts of our constitutions . . . None of the constitutions have provided sufficient checks against democracy." *Ibid.*, 26. See also *ibid.*, 48, 132. In these statements, the basic acceptance of popular government is as evident as the fear of democratic excesses.

lutely,"[37] the natural reason of democracy was subordinated to its constitutional reason, as it was reflected in the Constitution. The *demos* was limited by what Americans thought they had discovered of the *ratio dei*.

Good as the forecasts for popular government were, they were cautious. The Constitution was evaluated as good, not perfect.[38] It was considered an "experiment."[39] Since the Constitution's aim was constant—protection of the rights of the individual—that experiment basically turned around popular government and its ability to protect those rights. The First Inaugural of the first President expressed this fact when it stated that "the preservation of the sacred fire of liberty, and the destiny of the Republican model of Government, are justly considered as *deeply,* perhaps as *finally* staked, on the experiment entrusted to the hands of the

[37] Lord Acton to Bishop Creighton, April 5, 1887. John N. Figgis and Reginald V. Lawrence (eds.), HISTORICAL ESSAYS AND STUDIES (London, 1907), 504. Jakob Burckhardt stated: "Now power is of its nature evil, whoever wields it. It is not stability but a lust, and *ipso facto* insatiable, therefore unhappy in itself and doomed to make others unhappy." REFLECTIONS ON HISTORY (London, 1943), 86. Americans had expressed similar ideas. John Adams wrote that "power is always abused when unlimited and unbalanced, whether it be permanent or temporary," that "absolute power intoxicates alike despots, monarchs, aristocrats, and democrats, and jacobins, and *sans culottes*." "Defence of the Constitutions of Government of the United States of America," WORKS, VI, 73, 477. According to James Madison, "All power in human hands is liable to be abused," and "Power wherever lodged is liable more or less to abuse." To Thomas Ritchie, Dec. 18, 1825, and to Thomas Lehre on Aug. 2, 1828. Gaillard Hunt (ed.), THE WRITINGS OF JAMES MADISON (New York, 1900–10), IX, 232, 315. They followed Montesquieu. Cf. Bk. XI of THE SPIRIT OF THE LAWS (Thomas Nugent trans., Franz Neumann, ed.; New York, 1949), I, 149ff.

[38] According to Madison, "a faultless plan was not to be expected." As compared with the Articles of Confederation, the Constitution provided for "the GREATER, not the PERFECT, good." Hamilton, not expecting "to see a perfect work from imperfect man," wrote that its "system, though it may not be perfect in every part, is, upon the whole, a good one; is the best that the present views and circumstances of the country will permit." Edward M. Earle (ed.), THE FEDERALIST (New York, 1937) Nos. 37, 41, 85. Washington stated: "Although the agency I had in forming this system, and the high opinion I entertained of my Colleagues for their ability and integrity may have tended to warp my judgment in its favour; yet I will not pretend to say that it appears absolutely perfect to me, or that there may not be many faults which have escaped my discernment." Proposed Address to Congress, WRITINGS, XXX, 299. To Jefferson the Constitution was "a good canvass, on which some strokes only want retouching." To James Madison on July 31, 1788. WRITINGS, VII, 96. See also his letters to James Madison of Dec. 20, 1787, to Washington of May 2, 1788, and to David Humphreys of March 18, 1789. WRITINGS, VI, 386ff., 454; VII, 322f.

[39] THE FEDERALIST, No. 14.

American people."[40] Liberty, something to be preserved, was known; the destiny of republican government was not.

That destiny depended upon how the American people would handle popular government. There was nothing "manifest" about it. It could turn either way. The Founders had performed a "great rehearsal."[41] It was up to the American people to perform the show and to keep it running without adulterating it. While Washington hoped that the government "entrusted to the hands of the American people" would protect freedom, he was aware that it might not, and even felt that this failure would not be unnatural. "Should, hereafter, those who are intrusted with the management of this government, incited by the lust of power and prompted by the Supineness or venality of their Constituents, overleap the known barriers of this Constitution and violate the unalienable rights of humanity," he wrote, "it will only serve to shew, that no compact among men . . . can be pronounced everlasting and inviolable . . . that no Wall of words, that no mound of parchmt. can be so formed as to stand against the sweeping torrent of boundless ambition on the one side, aided by the sapping current of corrupted morals on the other."[42]

In the opinion of the Founding Fathers, then, Americans could enter a millennium if they could make popular government work by keeping it free. Through a continuous growth of democracy, men could become freer and freer under a Constitution that embodied cherished liberties. Here was America's democratic challenge; here was the American Dream.

What happened to that dream will be examined in the following chapters. These chapters will discuss how free government fared before and after the Civil War, which was not only the most tragic event in American history, but also a turning point of American democracy.

[40] WRITINGS, XXX, 294f.
[41] Carl C. van Doren, THE GREAT REHEARSAL (New York, 1948).
[42] Proposed Address to Congress, WRITINGS, XXX, 302. Jefferson wrote to Joseph Priestley on June 19, 1802, that the United States "furnishes hopeful implements for the interesting experiment of self-government; and we feel that we are acting under obligations not confined to the limits of our own society. It is impossible not to be sensible that we are acting for all mankind; that circumstances denied to others, but indulged to us, have imposed on us the duty of proving what is the degree of freedom and self-government in which a society may venture to leave its individual members." WRITINGS, X, 324f.

2

LINCOLN'S CONSTITUTIONAL DILEMMA

INTRODUCTION

The Civil War must have convinced many people that the American Dream was just a dream. It must have come as a terrible shock. The Dream held out hope that the Revolution's "sacred blessings will spread, till they become universal and the time arrives when kings and priests shall have no more power to oppress"; it had considered American independence "one of the steps ordained by Providence" to introduce a "universal empire . . . of reason and virtue, under which the gospel of peace (better understood) *shall have free course and be glorified.*"[1] Now not only was there no perpetual peace among nations, but there was a bitter war within the United States. International wars during the past decades could still be blamed upon the presence of kings and priests; the Civil War—a war within a republic in which political power was wielded by the people—could not. It had to question popular government itself. It had to question the democratic dream. Here was a war more cruel than all of the wars ever fought since America became independent, the first total war in modern times. Many Americans now saw that to be is to be not in a dream, but in reality. They saw that to be is to exist in tragedy—even under popular government.

Lincoln probably realized this. Perhaps the forlorn look, often noted in contemporary photographs, expressed a yearning for what had been, as if gone with the wind. Perhaps he saw his administration as the beginning of the end of the American Dream. Our inquiry into this administration will go beyond orthodox evaluations which have been content with seeing the tragedy of that administration confined to the duration of Lincoln's presi-

[1] Price, OBSERVATIONS ON THE AMERICAN REVOLUTION, 4, 7.

17

dency and thereafter diminishing. The fact that the wounds of that war are not healed to this day, prompts the question whether the tragic aspects of the Lincoln administration, rather than diminishing, actually remained or even increased as we progressed toward the present day.

On the face of it, one is inclined to answer that question in the negative. Tragic as the administration of Lincoln was, it is usually considered to have been a blessing for the United States, in spite of all deprivations and sacrifices under it. These sacrifices are said not to have been in vain. The Union survived; moreover, it survived without what came to be looked upon more and more as a blot upon its honor—slavery. Like the phoenix from the ashes, the United States emerged from the Civil War to become a world power. High as the price for the preservation of the Union may have been, it is usually believed to have been worth paying. Perhaps even the assassination of Lincoln was not as tragic as it is often depicted. Renowned for having put his personal interests behind those of the Nation, Lincoln—who probably would have gladly given the supreme sacrifice he demanded of his soldiers—had, unlike many of them, the satisfaction of seeing the cause of the Union prevail and of knowing that the sacrifices of the war had not been in vain. Besides, the assassination secured him martyrdom. Thus the tragedy of his administration seems to have been confined to the Civil War.

But did Lincoln consider the successful conclusion of the war a victory with all the attributes of victory? We do not think so, and ask whether the tragedy of his administration stretches beyond the years of the war and even those of Reconstruction. We ask whether the war actually generated a decline of free government, much as on the surface it seems to have heralded a victory for that government. Lincoln, able though he was as a politician who knew how to master existing situations, was also a statesman.[2] As

2 "The Master Politician of the Ages"—so another genius in that art whispered as Lincoln was being laid to rest in Springfield. Quoted by George F. Milton, THE USE OF PRESIDENTIAL POWER (Boston, 1944), 128. For Lincoln the politician, see also *ibid.*, 128, 131ff.; T. Harry Williams, "Abraham Lincoln: Pragmatic Democrat," in Norman A. Graebner (ed.), THE ENDURING LINCOLN (Urbana, Ill., 1959), 23. Lincoln the statesman is evident in James G. Randall, LINCOLN THE LIBERAL STATESMAN (New York, 1947).

such, he, who "thought more than any man in his sphere in America," who "had a feeling for the pace of history . . . calculating closely the major trends of the age,"[3] must not only have thought about how to save the Union, but also about the future of his country beyond the decades following the war. There are indications that he did.[4] A look at photographs taken of him shortly before the war and shortly thereafter, suggests the truth of John Hay's observation that Lincoln's face in the latter photograph had "a look as of one on whom sorrow and care had done their worst without victory."[5] Indeed, Lincoln the statesman did not indicate traces of victory, as would have been expected of Lincoln the politician after re-election and after the successful termination of the war. Did the problems he foresaw for generations to come overshadow the joy of his recent victories at the polls and on the battlefield? Did Lincoln, in spite of victory, recognize the tragedy of his administration not only for his contemporaries but also for future generations of Americans? We think he might have.

FREE GOVERNMENT AND LINCOLN PRIOR TO THE CIVIL WAR

When Lincoln became President, the American system of government had basically proved itself. The Founders' hope that the

[3] Norman A. Graebner, "Abraham Lincoln: Conservative Statesman," in Graebner, ENDURING LINCOLN, 82.

[4] See First Annual Message, Dec. 3, 1861: "The struggle of today, is not altogether for today—it is for a vast future also." Roy P. Basler (ed.), THE COLLECTED WORKS OF ABRAHAM LINCOLN (New Brunswick, N.J., 1953), V, 53; message to Congress, May 26, 1862; speech at Frederick, Md., Oct. 4, 1862; letters to Alexander Reed, Feb. 22, 1863, and to James C. Conkling, Aug. 26, 1863. WORKS, V, 241, 450; VI, 114, 410. In a speech to the 166th Ohio regiment, Lincoln stated on Aug. 22, 1864: "It is not merely for to-day, but for all time to come that we should perpetuate for our children's children this great and free government, which we have enjoyed all our lives . . . It is in order that each one of you may have through this free government which we have enjoyed, an open field and a fair chance for your industry, enterprise and intelligence . . ." WORKS, VII, 512. In a response to a serenade of Nov. 8, 1864, Lincoln said: ". . . all who have labored to-day in behalf of the Union organization, have wrought for the best interests of their country and the world, not only for the present, but for all future ages." WORKS, VIII, 96.

[5] Quoted in James G. Randall, LINCOLN THE LIBERAL STATESMAN, under a reproduction of photographs opposite p. 65.

New World would demonstrate the success of free government, had not been repudiated. Though foreign observers of the United States might take exception to some aspects of American life, they usually praised the American experiment with democracy.[6] American principles of government were adopted by other nations in the Old and New Worlds.[7] In a large measure, this success can be attributed to the Americans' continued belief in the political ideas of the formative period as they became reflected in the Constitution which embodied the principle that majority rule, while accepted, was for the sake of the individual restrained by law.

Unburdened by a absolutist heritage,[8] the United States, unlike Europe, was spared attempts at a revival of principles derived from the age of absolutism. Where there had been no *ancien régime,* that regime could not very well be restored. In the first half of the nineteenth century the United States experienced no Restoration. Unlike Europeans, Americans did not fall under the spell of the organic theory of society, a theory which tends to blur the distinction between the individual and the state and to suggest that the individual is a subject rather than a citizen. Theirs remained a belief in the contractual origin of society and government, a belief which clearly delineated the rights of men from those of the government, and left no doubt that men were citizens rather than subjects. For Americans who, unlike Europeans, did not recognize the state as a quasi-divine institution, the individual remained the vital center of society and its government. American dreams—be they concerned with liberty or equality—kept centering around man and his rights, not so much around society and not at all around the state.

In so far as it existed, American romanticism differed basically from its European counterpart. It was not revolutionary and did not constitute a reaction against the age of reason. Rather, it preserved the achievements of that age through a steady evolution. Americans, continuing to believe in the spirit of the laws of

---

[6] Cf. de Tocqueville, DEMOCRACY IN AMERICA; Robert von Mohl, DAS BUNDES-STAATSRECHT DER VEREINIGTEN STAATEN VON NORD-AMERIKA (Stuttgart, 1824).

[7] Notably the constitutions of Switzerland (1848), and Argentina (1853).

[8] Cf. Louis Hartz, THE LIBERAL TRADITION IN AMERICA.

the Enlightenment, were not recaptured by emotional doctrines, as were many Europeans. Their romantic notions were reflected in the individualistic idea that the free man could make the most of his opportunities and thereby contribute to the good of society. By contrast, European romanticism, resulting in the group idol of nationalism, implied the basic absorption of the individual by society. Neither belief in a divine right of kings or the people, nor in the idea that the state is the march of God in the world, nor in nationalism, characterized American thought prior to 1860. Rather, it was the humble recognition of a rule of law as the soul of American laws, a belief in a spirit of the laws under which the individual was free in the pursuit of happiness. Such a philosophy excluded concentration of governmental power. It was based upon the political system created by the Founding Fathers, under which political harmony and equilibrium were secured among society's various interests, through checks and balances among people and institutions rather than through their amalgamation.

In view of this orientation, it is not surprising that the principles of the Constitution were not seriously jeopardized by an outstanding feature in the political development from the administration of Jefferson to that of Lincoln: the march of democracy. That march, mainly reflected in a broadening of the suffrage in the states and in the election of Andrew Jackson to the presidency, hardly challenged existing ideas on the purpose of government or existing governmental institutions.[9]

Fears, expressed in state constitutional conventions, that an abolition of property qualifications for the right to vote would result in an insecurity of property rights, proved to be unfounded. The argument of some of the reformers, that in America the desire of acquiring property is a universal passion,[10] from which follows that everybody, and not just the rich, were interested in the protection of property rights, became generally accepted. While Chief Justice Taney's decision in the Charles River Bridge case was more community-conscious than previous decisions rendered by John Marshall, it still favored the protection of private

[9] Cf. however, David Donald, AN EXCESS OF DEMOCRACY (Oxford, 1960).
[10] Mason, FREE GOVERNMENT IN THE MAKING, 407.

property.[11] The Taney court probably protected property rights as much as the Marshall court.[12] "The Jacksonian movement grew out of expanding opportunities and a common desire to enlarge these opportunities still further by removing restrictions and privileges that had their origin in acts of government." While it was "a phase in the expansion of democracy," it was "essentially a movement of laissez-faire."[13] This basic orientation did not change under Jackson's successors, when perhaps the principles of limited government were even more evident.

By and large, the march of democracy also did not substantially affect existing institutions of government. These institutions remained in a fair balance. Whereas a "tribune of the people"[14] like General Jackson emphasized the importance of the presidency, his successors refrained from doing so. The years between Jackson and Lincoln have been described as a period during which the presidency was "at low ebb."[15] During that period, Congress was certainly a match for the presidency—the forum for the "great debates" which discussed the major issues of the day. The preponderant issue of that time probably was federalism. Here again, provisions made by the Founders prevailed. The ambiguity inherited from them concerning the nature of the Union was as evident during the period under consideration as it had been in *The Federalist*.[16] States righters as well as nationalists advanced cogent arguments in favor of their respective positions. As a result, American federalism was characterized by a fair balance between states rights and national power, among various sections of the Union, and among the various states.

In spite of a diversity of interests which were pursued relatively freely by individuals as well as groups, the rule of law

[11] "While the rights of private property are sacredly guarded, we must not forget that the community also have rights, and that the happiness and wellbeing of every citizen depends on their faithful preservation." *Charles River Bridge* v. *Warren Bridge,* 11 Pet. 420, 548 (1837).

[12] See Benjamin F. Wright, THE CONTRACT CLAUSE OF THE CONSTITUTION (Cambridge, Mass., 1938), 63.

[13] Richard Hofstadter, THE AMERICAN POLITICAL TRADITION AND THE MEN WHO MADE IT (New York, 1954), 56.

[14] The term is used by Wilfred E. Binkley, AMERICAN POLITICAL PARTIES: THEIR NATURAL HISTORY (New York, 1947), 135.

[15] Milton, USE OF PRESIDENTIAL POWER, 96.

[16] See the author's FEDERALIST, 125f., 154f., 260ff., 271f.

provided for peace and harmony in the body politic. Great jurists, be they, like Marshall and Taney, chief justices, or, like Story and Kent, commentators on the Constitution, helped to spread the idea that this was a government of laws and not of men. In the decades before Lincoln, respect for the laws and for those who were trained in them was such a universal feature of the American way of life that it impressed the outstanding foreign observer of democracy in America.[17] That democracy basically had remained within the confines of free government, in as much as it had remained a majority rule under which the individual, on account of constitutional limitations upon the government, was free in his legal pursuit of happiness.

However democracy, though remaining within the framework of constitutionalism, had entered a dimension in which there existed a good possibility that the rule of law would be replaced by the dogma *vox populi vox dei,* that democratic power would become concentrated, that the rights of the individual would fall prey to the majority or the executor of its will. This possibility, feared by Americans, was also recognized by foreign observers such as de Tocqueville and von Mohl. With political issues sharpening as the election of Lincoln approached, the basic harmony and equilibrium which characterized the American political scene in the first half of the nineteenth century could, in view of the growth of democracy, conceivably become disturbed. The Lincoln administration became the first demonstration of this possibility.

When Lincoln became President, there was good reason to believe that his administration would not bring about drastic changes in the accepted forms of government. His whole career had indicated that he considered the system established by the Founding Fathers a good one, a system that had proven itself and was to prevail.

Significantly, Lincoln's first major address on the United States was not, as one would perhaps expect from a young man addressing young men, on innovation, but on *"the perpetuation of our political institutions,"* and contained strong polemics against the

---

[17] De Tocqueville, DEMOCRACY IN AMERICA, I, 256ff., 282ff.

urge toward political change.[18] This speech, characterized by a note of pessimism which was probably rare among Americans of that day and perhaps foreshadows the later tragedy of Lincoln's presidency, entered a strong plea for obedience to the law. While Lincoln did not want to "be understood as saying there are no bad laws, nor that grievances may not arise, for the redress of which, no legal provisions have been made," and while he proposed that "bad laws, if they exist, should be repealed as soon as possible" and thus showed an awareness of the value of legal flexibility for a realization of the rule of law, he emphasized that while bad laws "continue in force, for the sake of example, they should be religiously observed."[19]

Denouncing mob-rule as expressed in lynch justice, Lincoln complained about "the increasing disregard for law which pervades the country; the growing disposition to substitute the wild and furious passions, in lieu of the sober judgment of Courts; and the worse than savage mobs, for the executive ministers of justice."[20] Considering transgressions upon legal procedures as dangerous as transgressions upon substantive law and thus indicating the importance of procedural as well as substantive law for a realization of the rule of law, Lincoln demonstrated the inevitability of continuous increases of violations of the law once seemingly minor violations are permitted:

When men take it in their heads to day, to hang gamblers, or burn murderers, they should recollect, that, in the confusion usually attending such transactions, they will be as likely to hang or burn some one, who is neither a gambler nor a murderer [as] one who is; and that, acting upon the [exam]ple they set, the mob of to-morrow, may, an[d] probably will, hang or burn some of them, [by th]e very same mistake. And not only so; the innocent, those who have ever set their faces against violations of law

---

[18] Address Before the Young Men's Lyceum of Springfield, Illinois, of Jan. 27, 1838, WORKS, I, 108. Albert A. Woldman, LAWYER LINCOLN (Boston, 1936), 11, relates that even earlier Lincoln had written "a composition on the necessity of preserving the Constitution and perpetuating the Union."

[19] WORKS, I, 112. Lincoln added: "So also in unprovided cases. If such arise let proper legal provisions be made for them with the least possible delay; but, till then, let them if not too intolerable, be borne with." *Ibid.*, 112f.

[20] *Ibid.*, 109. It is interesting that following this passage the man who later saved the Union stated that disregard for the law can be found in the whole American "community," that it has "pervaded the country, from New England to Louisiana," that its cause "is common to the whole country."

in every shape, alike with the guilty, fall victims to the ravages of mob law; and thus it goes on, step by step, till the walls erected for the defence of the persons and property of individuals, are trodden down, and disregarded. But all this even, is not the full extent of the evil. By such examples, by instances of the perpetrators of such acts going unpunished, the lawless in spirit, are encouraged to become lawless in practice; and having been used to no restraint, but dread of punishment, they thus become, absolutely unrestrained. Having ever regarded Government as their deadliest bane, they make a jubilee of the suspension of its operations; and pray for nothing so much, as its total annihilation. While, on the other hand, good men, men who love tranquility, who desire to abide by the laws, and enjoy their benefits, who would gladly spill their blood in the defence of their country; seeing their property destroyed; their families insulted, and their lives endangered; their persons injured; and seeing nothing in prospect that forebodes a change for the better; become tired of, and disgusted with, a Government that offers them no protection; and are not so much averse to a change in which they imagine they have nothing to lose. Thus, then, by the operation of this mobocratic spirit, which all must admit, is now abroad in the land, the strongest bulwark of any Government, and particularly those constituted like ours, may effectually be broken down and destroyed—I mean the *attachment* of the People.[21]

In spite of the fact that "the American People are *much* attached to their Government," and "would suffer *much* for its sake," Lincoln felt that "if the laws be continually despised and disregarded, if their rights to be secure in their persons and property, are held by no better tenure than the caprice of a mob, the alienation of their affections from the Government is the natural consequence; and to that, sooner or later, it must come." He proposed a "simple" solution to the problem:

Let every American, every lover of liberty, every well wisher to his posterity, swear by the blood of the Revolution, never to violate in the least particular, the laws of the country; and never to tolerate their violation by others. As the patriots of seventy-six did to the support of the Declaration of Independence, so to the support of the Constitution and Laws, let every American pledge his life, his property, and his sacred honor;—let every man remember that to violate the law, is to trample on the blood of his father, and to tear the character [charter?] of his own, and his children's liberty. Let reverence for the laws, be breathed by every American mother, to the lisping babe, that prattles on her lap—let it be taught in schools, in seminaries, and in colleges;—let it be written

---

[21] *Ibid.*, 110f.

in Primmers, spelling books, and in Almanacs;—let it be preached from the pulpit, proclaimed in legislative halls, and enforced in courts of justice. And, in short, let it become the *political religion* of the nation; and let the old and the young, the rich and the poor, the grave and the gay, of all sexes and tongues, and colors and conditions, sacrifice unceasingly upon its altars.[22]

As the preceding quotation shows, Lincoln, when advocating obedience to the laws, meant obedience to "the Constitution and Laws" making up the American system of government, "which for the last half century, has been the fondest hope, of the lovers of freedom, throughout the world."[23] Favoring "cold, calculating, unimpassioned reason," he put a *"reverence for the constitution and laws"* side by side with *"general intelligence"* and sound *"morality,"* and admonished his audience to strive toward these values.[24] Obedience to the Constitution and the laws was to be expected from "every American," from rulers and ruled alike. Lincoln warned that some "towering genius" might want to bring about innovations by "pulling down" established forms of government. He entreated his countrymen "to be united with each other, attached to the government and laws, and generally intelligent, to successfully frustrate his designs."[25]

Since these designs would be directed against the existing constitutional order, Lincoln's plea for obedience to the law was a plea for *"the perpetuation of our political institutions."* It was a plea for the Constitution, for the primary values it embodied and the institutions it established for the protection of those values. In a word, it was a plea for free government as it existed with the aid of constitutionalist institutions such as federalism and the separation of powers and the checks and balances deriving from them. Lincoln again and again referred to what he considered the end of American government, namely, the freedom of the individual and its various aspects, be they in the "civil" or "religious" sphere. He was happy to note that Americans find themselves "under the government of a system of political institutions, conducive more essentially to the end of civil and religious liberty, than any of

[22] *Ibid.,* 112.
[23] *Ibid.,* 112.
[24] *Ibid.,* 115.
[25] *Ibid.,* 112, 114.

which the history of former times tells us." Emphasizing the need for a protection of the individual's life, liberty, and property, he expressed satisfaction with the existing "political edifice of liberty and equal rights."[26] Also, he approved of the established popular government designed to secure freedom for all, and was happy to note that the American experiment, trying to prove *"the capability of a people to govern themselves,"*[27] had been successful. Although he did not mention federalism, the separation of powers and the checks and balances ensuing from them, it may be assumed that he accepted these institutions as much as he did popular government for the sake of the freedom of the individual. For he accepted the Constitution and the "system of political institutions" established under it.[28]

This is borne out by statements Lincoln made in the years following. While these statements show that his values remained basically those expressed in 1838 and demonstrate how he continued to advocate a popular government in which the majority was, for the sake of the individual's freedom, restricted under law, they leave no doubt about the essential role he attributed to federalism and the separation of powers for the realization of free government.[29] Having voted for the presidential candidate of the Whig party from 1832 to 1852,[30] Lincoln opposed a concentration

[26] *Ibid.,* 108.
[27] *Ibid.,* 113.
[28] *Ibid.,* 108.
[29] For Lincoln's evaluation of federalism, see his speeches at Chicago, July 10, 1858, and Carlinville, Aug. 31, 1858. WORKS, II, 493; III, 78; his debate, Jonesboro, Sept. 15, 1858. WORKS, III, 120f. On Dec. 28, 1860, he wrote Duff Green: "[T]he maintenance inviolate of the rights of the States, and especially the right of each state to order and control its own domestic institutions according to its own judgment exclusively, is essential to that balance of powers on which the perfection, and endurance of our political fabric depends—and I denounce the lawless invasion, by armed force, of the soil of any State or Territory, no matter under what pretext, as the gravest of crimes." WORKS, IV, 162. For Lincoln's evaluation of the separation of powers, see his memorandum of March, 1848, WORKS, I, 454; his speech in Congress, July 27, 1848. WORKS, I, 501. As late as Feb. 15, 1861, he said in Pittsburgh: "By the constitution, the executive may recommend measures which he thinks proper; and he may veto those he thinks improper; and it is supposed he may add to these, certain indirect influences to affect the action of congress. My political education strongly inclines me against a very free use of any of these means, by the Executive, to control the legislation of the country. As a rule, I think it better that congress should originate, as well as perfect its measures, without external bias." WORKS, IV, 214.
[30] During his debates with Douglas, Lincoln reminded his audiences of his Whig

of power in the national government as much as in the executive.[31]

It has been said that Lincoln was no philosopher. There is some truth in this, for he was not a philosopher in the continental meaning of the term.[32] Like the Founding Fathers and his predecessors in the presidency, Lincoln was basically a "pragmatist."[33] However, it would be wrong to deny that he had firm and definite ideas on government.[34] Able though he was as a politician, he was not an opportunist as far as his political credo is concerned. He had received his legal training mainly from reading Blackstone,[35] who had maintained that Parliament, powerful as it was as the representative of the people, was still limited by the rights of Englishmen.[36] Blackstone's ideas had a strong impact upon Lincoln, the more so since these ideas had become institutionalized into American constitutional law, a law for which Lincoln had much admiration. Lincoln was a firm believer in free government.[37]

---

past: "In '32, I voted for Henry Clay, in '36 for the Hugh L. White ticket, in '40 for 'Tip and Tyler.' In '44 I made the last great effort for 'Old Harry of the West.' . . . Taylor was elected in '48, and we fought nobly for Scott in '52." Quoted by David Donald, "Abraham Lincoln: Whig in the White House," in Graebner, ENDURING LINCOLN, 56.

[31] See *ibid.*, 57ff. Stating that the Whigs, as heirs of the Federalists, were at heart strong nationalists, Donald admits that their nationalism did not go beyond that of the Federalists, i.e., a nationalism tempered by federalism. Donald's statement that one important current of Whig thought did not resent a strong executive in times of war does not deny that in general Whigs resented a strong executive, especially in times of peace.

[32] See T. Harry Williams, "Abraham Lincoln: Pragmatic Democrat," in Graebner, ENDURING LINCOLN, 24f.; Stanley Pargellis, "Lincoln's Political Philosophy," THE ABRAHAM LINCOLN QUARTERLY, III (1945), 275ff.

[33] Williams, "Lincoln: Pragmatic Democrat," 26; see also Pargellis, "Lincoln's Political Philosophy," 279.

[34] Williams, "Lincoln: Pragmatic Democrat"; Pargellis, "Lincoln's Political Philosophy"; Andrew C. McLaughlin, "Lincoln, the Constitution, and Democracy," ETHICS, XLVII (1936), 1.

[35] See McLaughlin, *ibid.*, 4f.; Pargellis, "Lincoln's Political Philosophy," 289; Woldman, LAWYER LINCOLN, 7, 14f.; Frederick T. Hill, LINCOLN THE LAWYER (New York, 1906), 50.

[36] William Blackstone, COMMENTARIES ON THE LAWS OF ENGLAND (19th ed.; New York, 1847), Introduction, 38ff.; Bk. I, 121ff.; Bk. II, 1ff.

[37] On Lincoln's concept of free government, cf. McLaughlin, "Lincoln, the Constitution, and Democracy"; Allan Nevins, "Lincoln's Ideas of Democracy," in Nevins and Irving Stone (eds.), LINCOLN: A CONTEMPORARY PORTRAIT (Garden City, N.Y., 1962), 1; Williams, "Lincoln: Pragmatic Democrat." For Lincoln's advocacy of the protection of property, see Graebner, "Lincoln: Conservative Statesman," 84; Williams, "Lincoln: Pragmatic Democrat," 25f.

His political philosophy rejected extremes.[38] It was a philosophy of measure. Being a "bundle of compromises,"[39] the Constitution held for Lincoln a promise that free government could be best secured through compromise. Consequently he, who by temperament and upbringing tended to shun extremist action which he considered the result of passion rather than reason, strove for compromise whenever he could. He opposed the free states' lording it over the slave states, the majority's lording it over the minority.[40] He opposed concentration of power in the presidency.[41] Like most of his contemporaries, Lincoln felt that a fair balance among states and groups of states, between nation and states, complemented by a balance among the institutional branches of government, would ideally secure an order enabling the individuals freely to develop their abilities. Lincoln has been called a "Whig," a "conservative," a "liberal."[42] His conservatism consisted in preserving liberalism as it was conceived by the Whigs. Lincoln could well be called a "constitutionalist."[43]

As he resented extremes,[44] Lincoln was highly cautious about changes in the law.[45] This is especially evident in his attitude to-

[38] See *ibid.,* 27f., 35ff.; T. Harry Williams, LINCOLN AND THE RADICALS (Madison, Wisc., 1941).

[39] The term is used by Alpheus T. Mason, "The Nature of Our Federal Union Reconsidered," POLITICAL SCIENCE QUARTERLY, LXV (1950), 503. Jefferson, said to be an ideological ancestor of Lincoln (Randall, LINCOLN THE LIBERAL STATESMAN, 179), wrote to Madison on Dec. 20, 1787, concerning the Constitution: "I am captivated by the compromise of the opposite claims of the great and little States, of the last to equal, and the former to proportional influence." WRITINGS, VI, 387.

[40] Cf. his letter to Duff Green, Dec. 28, 1860, WORKS, IV, 162.

[41] See Donald, "Lincoln: Whig in the White House," 55ff.; Williams, "Lincoln: Pragmatic Democrat," 32.

[42] Donald, "Lincoln: Whig in the White House"; Graebner, "Lincoln: Conservative Statesman," 67; Pargellis, "Lincoln's Political Philosophy," 288f.; Lyman Bryson, "Lincoln in Power," POLITICAL SCIENCE QUARTERLY, LXI (1946), 165; Randall, LINCOLN THE LIBERAL STATESMAN, 175ff.

[43] Kenneth A. Bernard, "Lincoln and Civil Liberties," ABRAHAM LINCOLN QUARTERLY, VI (1951), 393. McLaughlin, "Lincoln, the Constitution, and Democracy," 5, calls Lincoln an "archconstitutionalist."

[44] Lincoln lauded "the SPIRIT of COMPROMISE; . . . of mutual concession—that spirit which first gave us the constitution." Speech at Peoria, Ill., Oct. 16, 1854. WORKS, II, 272. In that speech, he admonished his audience to favor the restoration of the Missouri Compromise and to oppose the repeal of the fugitive slave law: "In both cases you oppose [expose?] the dangerous extremes. In both you stand on middle ground and hold the ship level and steady. In both you are national, and nothing less than national. This is good old Whig ground." *Ibid.,* 273. See Pargellis, "Lincoln's Political Philosophy," 280.

[45] See McLaughlin, "Lincoln, the Constitution, and Democracy," 9, who consid-

ward changing the Constitution. He shared the Founders' opinion that the Constitution was not perfect but good, feeling that a perfect work could not come from imperfect man.[46] Consequently, he was not absolutely opposed to changing it. Even so, he who admonished his countrymen to obey the Constitution and the laws,[47] expressed himself consistently against amending the Constitution even in the manner permitted by it, although such a change would have been consistent with his belief that the Constitution and the laws were to be obeyed. When in 1848 Lincoln submitted "a few remarks on the general proposition of amending the Constitution," he said as a general rule, "I think we would [do] much better [to] let it alone. No slight occasion should tempt us to touch it. Better not take the first step, which may lead to a habit of altering it. Better, rather, habituate ourselves to think of it, as unalterable. It can scarcely be made better than it is." He continued: "New provisions, would introduce new difficulties, and thus create, and increase appetite for further change. No, sir, let it stand as it is. New hands have never touched it. The men who made it, have done their work, and have passed away. Who shall improve on what *they* did?"[48] Six years later, he said:

---

ers two "salient principles" to have been Lincoln's: "Law must be continuous; and yet it must be changeable. A fluctuating law is a misnomer; a law not adapted to social need is an anachronism." Cf. also Lincoln's statement quoted *supra,* 23ff. In a speech at Springfield on June 26, 1857, Lincoln stated: "We believe, as much as Judge Douglas, (perhaps more) in obedience to, and respect for the judicial department of government. We think its decisions on Constitutional questions, when fully settled, should control, not only the particular cases decided, but the general policy of the country, subject to be disturbed only by amendments of the Constitution as provided in that instrument itself. More than this would be revolution. But we think the Dred Scott decision is erroneous. We know the court that made it, has often over-ruled its own decisions, and we shall do what we can to have it over-rule this. We offer no *resistance* to it." WORKS, II, 401. Comp. also his remark on the Supreme Court in his First Inaugural Address. WORKS, IV, 268. Lincoln favored "adherence to the old and tried, against the new and untried." Address at Cooper Institute, Feb. 27, 1860. WORKS, III, 537.

[46] On Aug. 15, 1863, Lincoln, in an opinion on draft law which was never published, wrote: "It has been said, and I believe truly, that the Constitution itself is not altogether such as any one of its framers would have preferred. It was the joint work of all, and certainly the better that it was so." John C. Nicolay and John Hay (eds.), COMPLETE WORKS OF ABRAHAM LINCOLN (memorial ed.; New York, 1905), IX, 78. See also Williams, "Lincoln: Pragmatic Democrat," 33f.; Graebner, "Lincoln: Conservative Statesman," 81.

[47] Speech, Bloomington, May 29, 1856. Arthur B. Lapsley (ed.), THE WRITINGS OF ABRAHAM LINCOLN (New York, 1905), II, 273. Basler, WORKS, II, 341, doubts whether the actual speech was the same as the one printed in the Lapsley edition.

[48] Speech in Congress, June 20, 1848. WORKS, IV, 488.

"I do not . . . propose to destroy, or alter, or disregard the constitution. I stand to it, fairly, fully and firmly."[49] In 1856 he added: "Don't interfere with anything in the Constitution. That must be maintained, for it is the only safeguard of our liberties."[50] Toward the end of 1860, he wrote, while admitting that he would not feel justified or inclined to withhold from the American people the right to amend the Constitution: "I do not desire any amendment of the Constitution."[51] In February, 1861, he sponsored a resolution of the Illinois legislature that "the people of Illinois do not desire any change in our federal constitution."[52]

Lincoln's belief in free government as it existed under the Constitution is also evident in his First Inaugural Address. That address, made in an explosive political situation shortly before the Civil War, is not in discord with the stream of thought that had emanated from him since his early manhood. In distinction to some campaign speeches,[53] it is similar to his speech at the Springfield Lyceum. Like that speech, it advocates the preservation of American institutions and stresses the need for the protection of life, liberty, and property. As to the latter, Lincoln went so far as to reiterate: "I have no purpose, directly or indirectly, to interfere with the institution of slavery in the States where it exists. I believe I have no lawful right to do so, and I have no inclination to do so." He confirmed "that the property, peace and security of no section are to be in anywise endangered by the now incoming Administration," that "all the protection which, consistently with the Constitution and the laws, can be given, will be cheerfully given to all the States when lawfully demanded."[54]

The idea of the protection of the individual is also evident in statements concerning popular government. Lincoln left no doubt that he considered that form of government a mere means for the achievement of freedom. He admitted that, "[if,] by the mere force of numbers, a majority should deprive a minority of any clearly written constitutional right, it might, in a moral point of

---

[49] Speech, Peoria, Ill., Oct. 16, 1854. WORKS, II, 269.
[50] Speech, Kalamazoo, Mich., Aug. 27, 1856. WORKS, II, 366.
[51] To Duff Green, Dec. 28, 1860. WORKS, IV, 162.
[52] Resolution, Illinois Legislature, Feb. 1, 1861. Emanuel Hertz, ABRAHAM LINCOLN: A NEW PORTRAIT (New York, 1931), II, 809.
[53] Notably his "House Divided" speeches. See *infra,* 42.
[54] WORKS, IV, 263.

view, justify revolution—certainly would, if such right were a vital one," but was glad that "[a]ll the vital rights of minorities, and individuals, are so plainly assured to them, by affirmations and negations, guarranties and prohibitions, in the Constitution, that controversies never arise concerning them." To him only a "majority, held in restraint by constitutional checks, and limitations, and always changing easily, with deliberate changes of popular opinions and sentiments," was the "true sovereign of a free people."[55]

Lincoln also left no doubt about his belief in federalism. Although he emphasized that the American Union was older than the Constitution and that it had continually matured after its formation under the Articles of Association of 1774, he still considered the United States under the Constitution, much as the latter was designed *"to form a more perfect Union,"* a *federal* union. And while he denied to any state the right to secede,[56] he emphasized that "the maintenance inviolate of the rights of the States, and especially the right of each State to order and control its own domestic institutions according to its own judgment exclusively, is essential to that balance of power on which the perfection and endurance of our political fabric depend."[57]

The First Inaugural Address also does not indicate any intention toward diminishing the separation of powers. When Lincoln indicated that the Supreme Court be subject to the will of the people, he refrained from suggesting that it ought to be under the will of the President, and did not refrain from paying his respects to the nation's highest tribunal.[58] His statement that he entered his office "for the brief constitutional term of four years," indicates no desire of becoming a dictator. After saying that "the power confided to me, will be used to hold, occupy, and possess the property, and places belonging to the government, and to collect duties and imposts," Lincoln added that he would refrain from exercising legal rights of the executive to enforce the exercise of federal office, where such an exercise would be irritating to the local community. He stressed that "the Chief Magistrate

[55] *Ibid.,* 267, 268.
[56] *Ibid.,* 265.
[57] *Ibid.,* 263.
[58] *Ibid.,* 268. See also Woldman, LAWYER LINCOLN, 296.

derives all his authority from the people," and that by "the frame of the government under which we live, this same people have wisely given their public servants but little power for mischief; and have, with equal wisdom, provided for the return of that little to their own hands at very short intervals. While the people retain their virtue, and vigilance, no administration, by any extreme wickedness or folly, can very seriously injure the government, in the short space of four years."[59]

Aside from emphasizing the protection of the individual from and his mode of participation in government, as well as the value of spatial and institutional separations of powers, the First Inaugural Address stresses the need for obedience to the law. It speaks of "universal law, and of the Constitution"—perhaps indicating the close connection between the two and that the former may have become transmuted into the latter—and of "the Constitution and the laws," and leaves no doubt that rulers and ruled alike are bound by the law. Members of Congress "swear their support to the whole Constitution" and are bound by all its provisions. It is the duty of the chief executive "to administer the present government, as it came to his hands, and to transmit it, unimpaired by him, to his successor." Feeling that he was enjoined by the Constitution to see to it "that the laws of the Union be faithfully executed in all the States," Lincoln promised not to "construe the Constitution or laws, by any hypercritical rules." He was glad to note that no "right, plainly written in the Constitution, has been denied," and asked rulers and ruled alike to obey the laws: "I do suggest, that it will be much safer for all, both in official and private stations, to conform to, and abide by, all those acts which stand unrepealed, than to violate any of them, trusting to find impunity in having them held unconstitutional." While he recognized that the people, "whenever they shall grow weary of the existing government . . . can exercise their *constitutional* right of amending it," and while he favored "a fair opportunity being afforded the people to act upon it," he made "no recommendation of amendments."[60] He thus confirmed his belief in the Constitution as it stood.

[59] WORKS, IV, 264, 266, 270.
[60] *Ibid.*, 263, 264, 267, 269, 270.

In summary, it may be said that the Lincoln of the First Inaugural Address was basically the same man as the Lincoln of the preceding decades. Perhaps it was this continuity in his attitude that brought about Lincoln's emergence as a national leader. At a time when incipient crises must have generated a desire for order, people were likely to look for guidance to someone who consistently had advocated obedience to the letter as well as the spirit of the laws, feeling that observance of the former was a prerequisite for the existence of the latter.[61] Since in his private law practice Lincoln had demonstrated that he put justice above material success,[62] people could trust that he would act similarly as President, that he would put obedience to the form and substance of the Constitution above personal ambitions. When Lincoln became President, there was good reason to believe that American government would continue to be a government of law rather than of men.

LINCOLN'S WAR MEASURES
AND DEMOCRATIC ACTIVITY

A few months later, people had good reason to wonder whether their government had not only become a government of men, but of one man—the President. "In the interval between April 12 and July 4, 1861, a new principle . . . appeared in the constitutional system of the United States, namely, that of a temporary dictatorship. All the powers of government were virtually concentrated in a single department, and that the department whose energies were directed by the will of a single man."[63] Delaying the meeting of a special session of Congress until July 4 because he "intended to take the first steps himself,"[64] Lincoln (1) called out the militia of the several states;[65] (2) decreed a blockade of the

---

[61] See, however, James G. Randall, "Lincoln in the Rôle of Dictator," SOUTH ATLANTIC QUARTERLY, XXVIII (1929), 245.

[62] See Hill, LINCOLN THE LAWYER, ch. 21; Woldman, LAWYER LINCOLN, ch. 16.

[63] William A. Dunning, ESSAYS ON THE CIVIL WAR AND RECONSTRUCTION AND RELATED TOPICS (New York, 1898), 20f.

[64] Milton, USE OF PRESIDENTIAL POWER, 109.

[65] Proclamation of Apr. 15, 1861. WORKS, IV, 331.

seceded states, a measure hitherto regarded as permitted only if the country was in a state of war with a foreign nation;[66] (3) ordered nineteen vessels to be added to the navy for purposes of public defense;[67] (4) appealed for volunteers, enlarged the regular army and navy[68] and thus "passed well beyond the most latitudinarian construction of his constitutional powers and entered into one of the hitherto (and ever since) most jealously guarded fields of congressional power;"[69] (5) advanced two million dollars of unappropriated funds to private citizens unauthorized to receive it for military and naval measures necessary for the defense and support of the government[70] in spite of the constitutional provision that "no money shall be drawn from the Treasury but in consequence of appropriations made by law;"[71] (6) offered a temporary loan and pledged the credit of the United States for a quarter of a billion dollars;[72] (7) authorized, in spite of the prevalent opinion that under the Constitution only Congress could suspend the writ of habeas corpus, the suspension of that writ and disregarded a decision by Chief Justice Taney which denied the President the right to suspend the writ;[73] (8) directed in a clear "deviation from established and constitutional American practice,"[74] the Post Office to be closed to "treasonable

[66] Proclamations of Apr. 19 and 27, 1861. WORKS, IV, 338, 346.

[67] Cf. his message to Congress of May 26, 1862. James D. Richardson, MESSAGES AND PAPERS OF THE PRESIDENTS (Washington, 1897–1927), VI, 78.

[68] Proclamation of May 3, 1861. WORKS, IV, 353.

[69] Clinton L. Rossiter, CONSTITUTIONAL DICTATORSHIP (Princeton, N.J., 1948), 226. See also Rossiter's THE AMERICAN PRESIDENCY (2d ed., New York, 1960), 98ff.; Donald, "Lincoln: Whig in the White House"; Randall, "Lincoln in the Rôle of Dictator"; Bryson, "Lincoln in Power." The most elaborate general discussion can be found in James G. Randall, CONSTITUTIONAL PROBLEMS UNDER LINCOLN (rev. ed.; Urbana, Ill., 1951).

[70] Quoted by Rossiter, CONSTITUTIONAL DICTATORSHIP, 226. Lincoln directed Secretary of the Treasury Chase to advance the money on April 20, 1861, but did not adequately recount and elucidate that measure until a letter to Congress of May 26, 1862. Richardson, MESSAGES AND PAPERS OF THE PRESIDENTS, VI, 77.

[71] Art. I, sec. ix, clause 6.

[72] Rossiter, CONSTITUTIONAL DICTATORSHIP, 227.

[73] To the Commanding General of the Army of the United States on Apr. 27 and July 2, 1861; Proclamation of May 10, 1861. WORKS, IV, 347, 364, 419. Cf. S. G. Fisher, "The Suspension of Habeas Corpus during the War of the Rebellion," POLITICAL SCIENCE QUARTERLY, III (1888), 454. Taney's decision was in *Ex parte Merryman*, FED. CASES, No. 9487 (1861). On Lincoln's relationship to Taney, see Woldman, LAWYER LINCOLN, ch. 24.

[74] Rossiter, CONSTITUTIONAL DICTATORSHIP, 228.

correspondence" and "caused persons who were represented to him as being or about to engage in disloyal and treasonable practices to be arrested by special civil as well as military agencies and detained in military custody when necessary to prevent them or deter others from such practices."[75]

These actions, decried as dictatorial at the time they occurred,[76] have been considered "radical, dictatorial, and constitutionally questionable" ever since.[77] Lincoln himself was well aware of their dubious nature. He reputedly said in the first days of the war: "These rebels are violating the Constitution to destroy the Union. I will violate the Constitution if necessary to save the Union; and I suspect . . . that our Constitution is going to have a rough time of it before we get done with this row."[78] In his message to Congress of July 4, 1861, he admitted doubts as to the legality of some of his measures.

Timed to a day when national emotions were likely to run high, this message sounds like a Machiavellian oration delivered by an authoritarian democrat. Cleverly framed by respectful references to the Constitution[79] and thus given an aura of constitutionalism, the message negates essential features of the Constitution, such as the separation of powers and the protection of the individual's freedom. It defends unconstitutionalist acts, such as the concentration of power in the hands of the President and suspension of the writ of habeas corpus.

Unlike messages made by Lincoln's predecessors, it confronted

[75] *Ibid.* See also executive order of Secretary Stanton of Feb. 14, 1862, in Richardson, MESSAGES AND PAPERS OF THE PRESIDENTS, VI, 102.

[76] See Charles Warren, "Lincoln's Despotism as Critics Saw It in 1861," NEW YORK TIMES (May 12, 1918), sec. 5; Benjamin R. Curtis, EXECUTIVE POWER (Boston, 1862).

[77] Rossiter, CONSTITUTIONAL DICTATORSHIP, 228. See also *infra,* 39f.; James F. Rhodes, HISTORY OF THE UNITED STATES FROM THE COMPROMISE OF 1850 (New York, 1893–1906) IV, 234f.; Randall, "Lincoln in the Rôle of Dictator," 237.

[78] James Bryce, THE AMERICAN COMMONWEALTH (2d ed.; London, 1891), 289n. The quotation is considered dubious.

[79] The message starts out with the words: "Having been convened on an extraordinary occasion, as authorized by the Constitution . . ." and ends saying that the Executive "hopes that your [Congress's] views, and your action, may so accord with his, as to assure all faithful citizens, who have been disturbed in their rights, of a certain, and speedy restoration to them, under the Constitution, and the laws. And having thus chosen our course, without guile, and with pure purpose, let us renew our trust in God, and go forward without fear, and with manly hearts." WORKS, IV, 421, 440f.

Congress with accomplished facts. And while Lincoln invited whatever congressional ratification was deemed necessary to legalize his acts, he neither indicated that he particularly cared about such ratification, nor that he felt it was relevant, nor that he would revoke any of his measures in case it was not forthcoming. Introducing the idea of the "war power of the Government," which to him meant power of the national executive, Lincoln asserted that power unequivocally. In his message, Lincoln (1) did not bother to offer any apology or even an explanation of why he had postponed convening Congress for as long as he did; (2) maintained that his calling out the militia and establishing a blockade had been legal; (3) defended his legally most dubious actions, i.e., actions of a legislative nature such as enlarging the armed forces and financial transactions, measures of which he doubted whether they were "strictly legal or not," on the grounds of "popular demand and public necessity;" (4) doubted whether the power to suspend the writ of habeas corpus actually belonged to Congress.[80]

The design of the message is shrewd. By telling Congress at the very outset that they were "convened . . . as authorized by the Constitution," Lincoln posed as a legalist and enabled himself to omit an explanation as to why he had convened them as late as he did. An attempt to lull his audience is also evident in the sequence of his remarks on his various measures. By first mentioning acts he considered "strictly legal," such as calling out the militia and establishing a blockade, Lincoln not only precluded arguments over the legality of those acts, but also put himself in a position of respectability from which he could more easily make the legislators swallow measures of which he had doubts whether they were "strictly legal or not," measures that infringed upon the legislative domain, such as the increase of the armed forces and financial measures. Or, to look at it from another angle, perhaps he chose to mention the smaller evil—measures taken under the war power which in his opinion were legal—first, in order to prepare his audience for more severe measures of which he did not know

---

[80] For comments on Lincoln's message, see Rossiter, CONSTITUTIONAL DICTATORSHIP, 228f.; Milton, USE OF PRESIDENTIAL POWER, 109f., 115; Randall, "Lincoln in the Rôle of Dictator," 239.

whether they were "strictly legal or not" because they were within legislative competence. And, while the latter bad news was still being digested, he mentioned his most serious infringements upon habeas corpus which to Congress must have appeared a mere anticlimax because these infringements did not concern a right specifically reserved to them.

Lincoln had his way. Congress, "faced by a *fait accompli* that was in its nature irrevocable,"[81] approved "all the acts, proclamations, and orders of the President respecting the army and navy of the United States and calling out or relating to the militia or volunteers from the United States."[82] Congress not only sanctioned what had been done, but provided authorization for future action. Its appetite for power whetted by the presidential example, Congress itself claimed dictatorial power[83] which became reflected in its enactments. These enactments, executed as they were by the President, enhanced executive power further. Thus, in spite of a congressional assertion of power, the power of the President was never seriously challenged, criticized as it may have been. Especially after the failure of the radicals in Congress to work a readjustment of the cabinet in December, 1862, "the success of the President's assertion of power could no longer be doubted."[84] The Supreme Court also fell into line. In a 5–4 decision which sanctioned Lincoln's blockade of the South, it gave the President far-reaching authority.[85]

With the uncertainties concerning the legality of some of his acts prior to July 4, 1861, dispelled, Lincoln became increasingly convinced that the use of dictatorial force was in large measure an executive affair.[86] "[A]s commander-in-chief of the army and

[81] Rossiter, CONSTITUTIONAL DICTATORSHIP, 230.

[82] Act of Aug. 6, 1861.

[83] Rossiter, CONSTITUTIONAL DICTATORSHIP, 230ff.

[84] *Ibid.*, 232.

[85] In the *Prize Cases,* the Court stated: "Whether the President in fulfilling his duties, as Commander-in-Chief, in suppressing an insurrection, has met with such armed hostile resistence, and a civil war of such alarming proportions as will compel him to accord to them the character of belligerents, is a question to be decided by him, and this court must be governed by the decisions and acts of the Political Department of the government to which this power is entrusted. 'He must determine what degree of force the crisis demands!' " 2 Black 635, 670 (1862). Three of the five judges sustaining Lincoln had been appointed by him.

[86] Commenting upon the war power, Milton, USE OF PRESIDENTIAL POWER, 109, writes: "This concept began as a transition device, to be validated by Congress when it assembled. In less than two years it grew into an independent power under

navy, in time of war, I suppose I have a right to take any measure which may best subdue the enemy," he stated.[87] "After 1861 he never doubted that his power to preserve the Union had no limits."[88]

While, as the war progressed, many of the President's extraordinary measures, such as confiscations of rebel property[89] and suspensions of the writ of habeas corpus, were executory of the will of Congress, Lincoln continued to exercise unprecedented authority by broadly interpreting his war powers. He was not content with using his powers as Commander in Chief extensively by exercising considerable control and direction of the military prosecution of the war.[90] In a "revolutionary and unique reading of the war clauses" of the Constitution, not only "did he do things that were regarded . . . as within the exclusive field of Congress's power, but he went further and asserted his competence to do things in an emergency that Congress could never do at all, maintaining that his designation as Commander in Chief allowed him to adopt measures that in normal times could only be effected by an amendment to the Constitution."[91]

Abolition of slavery is probably the most outstanding case in point. Feeling that Congress could provide for emancipation only by way of compensation, Lincoln waited until it had adjourned and then issued the Emancipation Proclamation. That proclamation, which has been called "as absolute an exercise of power as the ukase of the Czar which freed the serfs of Russia,"[92] and "the most stupendous act of sequestration in the history of Anglo-Saxon jurisprudence,"[93] proclaimed slaves to be free without compensation to their owners.[94] Later, Lincoln through presidential

---

which he felt authorized to suspend the execution of the writ of habeas corpus, issue the Emancipation Proclamation, and restore reoccupied States."

[87] Reply to a Chicago church committee, Sept. 13, 1862. WORKS, V, 421.

[88] Rossiter, CONSTITUTIONAL DICTATORSHIP, 233.

[89] See Randall, THE CONFISCATION OF PROPERTY DURING THE CIVIL WAR (Indianapolis, 1913).

[90] For Lincoln's role in military matters, see Donald, "Lincoln: Whig in the White House," 49f.; Milton, USE OF PRESIDENTIAL POWER, 112ff.; Richardson, MESSAGES AND PAPERS OF THE PRESIDENTS, VI, 100f.

[91] Rossiter, CONSTITUTIONAL DICTATORSHIP, 234.

[92] Henry J. Ford, THE RISE AND GROWTH OF AMERICAN POLITICS (New York, 1898), 280.

[93] Quoted by Donald, "Lincoln: Whig in the White House," 50.

[94] Rather than basing this measure upon the Confiscation Acts, he based it on the presumed powers of the Commander in Chief under the Constitution.

order instituted the first national program of conscription in United States history.[95] Disregarding the constitutional provision that Congress shall "make rules for the Government and regulation of the land and naval forces," he asked Francis Lieber to draw up and General Halleck to proclaim a code on the legal rules of war.[96] Without consulting Congress, the President set up military and even permanent governments in conquered territories.[97] Without approval of Congress, he established provisional courts in conquered Southern states, giving them "the unlimited power of determining every question that could be the subject of judicial decision."[98] Without congressional authorization, he created offices unknown to the Constitution by naming military governors for Louisiana, Arkansas, and Tennessee. These officials were not obliged to observe normal legal procedures. Lincoln himself directed them to "follow forms of law as far as convenient . . ."[99] It is perhaps no exaggeration to say that no other American President has "found so many new sources of executive power, nor so expanded and perfected those others already had used."[100]

Unlike the French Revolution, the Civil War did not witness the establishment of a Committee of Public Safety. The question is whether the presidency under a man like Lincoln, who considered himself the executor of the popular will, was perhaps an American equivalent of that committee.[101] Lincoln's statement of 1863, that "by degrees" he had come to realize that "strong measures" were "indispensable to the public Safety,"[102] ought to give us pause. Viewed from the American tradition, a tradition characterized by freedom, the curtailments of the liberties of the

[95] Militia Act of 1862. Richardson, MESSAGES AND PAPERS OF THE PRESIDENTS, VI, 120. See Donald, "Lincoln: Whig in the White House," 49; Rossiter, CONSTITUTIONAL DICTATORSHIP, 234.

[96] "Lieber's Code" can be found in General Orders, No. 100, OFFICIAL RECORDS, WAR OF REBELLION, Series 3, vol. III. See Donald, "Lincoln: Whig in the White House," 49; Rossiter, CONSTITUTIONAL DICTATORSHIP, 234.

[97] See A. H. Carpenter, "Military Government of Southern Territory, 1861–1865," REPORTS, AMERICAN HISTORICAL ASSOCIATION, I (1900), 465; Rossiter, CONSTITUTIONAL DICTATORSHIP, 234.

[98] Donald, "Lincoln: Whig in the White House," 50f.

[99] Quoted ibid., 51.

[100] Milton, USE OF PRESIDENTIAL POWER, 107.

[101] See ibid., 114; Randall, "Lincoln in the Rôle of Dictator;" Bernard, "Lincoln and Civil Liberties."

[102] Quoted by Donald, "Lincoln: Whig in the White House," 48f.

individual during the Civil War[103] were perhaps as drastic as Jacobin terror, viewed from the authoritarian French tradition.

It has been maintained that the Lincoln administration was a comparatively mild dictatorship, perhaps no dictatorship at all.[104] It has also been said that even after Lincoln entered the White House, he retained his Whig philosophy, as is borne out by the fact that he imposed his will on neither Congress nor the Supreme Court, both of which continued to function independently.[105] Furthermore, it has been emphasized that Lincoln kept his distance from the radicals in his own party, that throughout his administration he remained an example of moderation,[106] that whatever infringements upon the rights of individuals may have occurred, they were of a mild nature, as compared with oppressions in other dictatorships.[107]

All this is true. However, comparisons with situations in other nations are risky. They tend to blur the perspective. A fair evaluation of the Lincoln administration appears to be possible only by seeing it within the framework of the American tradition, a tradition from which it sprang and which it tried to save. To evaluate otherwise would be unfair to Lincoln himself. For he seems to have been thinking in terms of the American tradition as it had come to exist in the Union. Viewed from that tradition, his administration, by concentrating power in the national executive and by infringing upon the rights of individuals in a manner hitherto unknown, was out of tune with accepted standards of constitutionalism. Violation of good constitutional provisions by the man who had exhorted his fellow-citizens that even "bad laws . . . should be religiously observed" looked peculiar indeed.

---

[103] See Bernard, "Lincoln and Civil Liberties," 375; George F. Milton, ABRAHAM LINCOLN AND THE FIFTH COLUMN (New York, 1942); S. G. Fisher, "The Suspension of Habeas Corpus"; Randall, CONSTITUTIONAL PROBLEMS UNDER LINCOLN; Thomas F. Carroll, "Freedom of Speech and of the Press during the Civil War," VIRGINIA LAW REVIEW, IX (1923), 516; Randall, LINCOLN THE LIBERAL STATESMAN, 118ff.

[104] See *ibid.*, 129ff.; Bernard, "Lincoln and Civil Liberties," 379f., 385ff., 393ff.; Randall, "Lincoln in the Rôle of Dictator."

[105] See Donald, "Lincoln: Whig in the White House"; Rossiter, CONSTITUTIONAL DICTATORSHIP, 230ff.

[106] See Williams, LINCOLN AND THE RADICALS; Carl Sandburg, ABRAHAM LINCOLN: THE WAR YEARS (New York, 1939), I, 636ff.

[107] See Randall, "Lincoln in the Rôle of Dictator."

From the point of view of constitutional law, the only excuse that could be offered for many of Lincoln's acts is that they were required to save the traditional constitutional order. It could be argued that his measures, while they may not have been "strictly legal," were legitimate. Lincoln justified his behavior on exactly these grounds. He maintained that his actions were prompted by the desire to maintain free government as provided for by the Constitution. In order to do so, he felt it was necessary to save the Union.

It has been emphasized that Lincoln's policy during his administration was prompted mainly by a desire to save the Union.[108] A good many arguments can be marshaled in support of this assertion. Before he became President, Lincoln never seems to have swerved from his belief in the Union. His statements perhaps stress the importance of the Union more than anything else. The preservation of the Union seemed to overshadow even moral considerations such as slavery. "Much as I hate slavery," he said in 1854, "I would consent to the extension of it rather than see the Union dissolved, just as I would consent to any GREAT evil, to avoid a GREATER one."[109] The same thought is evident in his famous "House Divided" speech four years later.[110] In 1860, he wrote that the Union must be maintained at all hazards.[111]

In tune with his attitude prior to his accession to the presidency, Lincoln stressed the importance of the preservation of the Union throughout his administration. This is obvious in his First Inaugural Address,[112] as well as in his special message to Congress

---

[108] Rossiter, CONSTITUTIONAL DICTATORSHIP, 224; Williams, "Lincoln: Pragmatic Democrat," 44; Graebner, "Lincoln: Conservative Statesman," 92. Hofstadter, AMERICAN POLITICAL TRADITION, 126, writes concerning Lincoln's role in the Civil War: "From the beginning, then, everything was subordinate to the cause of the Union." On the other hand, he states on p. 124 that "the Union itself was a means to an end."

[109] Speech, Peoria, Ill., Oct. 16, 1854. WORKS, II, 270.

[110] " 'A house divided against itself cannot stand.' I believe this government cannot endure, permanently half *slave* and half *free*. I do not expect the Union to be dissolved—I do not expect the house to *fall*—but I *do* expect it will cease to be divided. It will become *all* one thing or *all* the other." Speech, Springfield, June 16, 1858. WORKS, II, 461. The speech was repeated several times in 1858. In a letter to George Robertson of Aug. 15, 1855, Lincoln had expressed similar feelings. WORKS, II, 318.

[111] To Governor A. G. Curtin, Dec. 21, 1860. WORKS, IV, 158.

[112] WORKS, IV, esp. 264ff.

of July 4, 1861. In that message, Lincoln, after having discussed Southern attempts to frustrate the functioning of the federal government, stressed that he had taken whatever steps he deemed necessary for the preservation of the Union. "Believing it to be an imperative duty upon the incoming Executive, to prevent . . . the consummation of . . . an attempt to destroy the Federal Union, a choice of means to that end became indispensable." That choice in the beginning amounted to "the exhaustion of all peaceful measures," and, later on, to "a resort to . . . stronger ones." In the end, "no choice was left but to call out the war power of the Government," and to order measures that appeared dubious to his contemporaries and not "strictly legal" to Lincoln himself.[113]

The importance Lincoln attributed to the preservation of the Union is evident also in some of his later statements. In his First Annual Message of December 3, 1861, he considered "the integrity of the Union prominent as the primary object of the contest." Feeling that "[t]he Union must be preserved, and hence, all indispensable means must be employed," he made it plain that "radical and extreme measures, which may reach the loyal as well as the disloyal, are indispensable."[114] Preservation of the Union was above the solution of moral issues, such as slavery.[115] In the middle of the war, he wrote: "I would save the Union. I would save it the shortest way under the Constitution. The sooner the national authority can be restored; the nearer the Union will be 'the Union as it was' . . . My paramount object in this struggle *is* to save the Union, and is *not* either to save or to destroy slavery. If I could save the Union without freeing *any* slave I would do it, and if I could save it by freeing *all* the slaves, I would do it; and if I could save it by freeing some and leaving others alone I would also do that. What I do about slavery, and the colored race, I do because I believe it helps to save the Union; and what I forbear, I forbear because I do *not* believe it would help to save the Union."[116]

[113] WORKS, IV, 423, 426, 429. Lincoln also stated that "the Executive found the duty of employing the war-power, in defence of the government [of the Union], forced upon him." *Ibid.*, 440.

[114] First Annual Message, Dec. 3, 1861. WORKS, V, 49.

[115] See Lincoln's interview with James R. Gilmore of April 13, 1861. James R. Gilmore, PERSONAL RECOLLECTIONS OF ABRAHAM LINCOLN AND THE CIVIL WAR (Boston, 1898), 19.

[116] To Horace Greeley, Aug. 22, 1862. WORKS, V, 388.

The preliminary Emancipation Proclamation of a month later was clearly prompted by the desire to save the Union. Preservation of the Union was more important to him than the abolition of slavery even after he had issued that Proclamation.[117] In 1864, he told Governor Randall: "My enemies pretend I am now carrying on this war for the sole purpose of abolition. So long as I am President, it shall be carried on for the sole purpose of restoring the Union."[118] He admitted that "the administration accepted the war . . . for the sole avowed object of preserving our Union; and it is not true that it has since been, or will be, prosecuted by this administration for any other object."[119] During the final year of the war, Lincoln's aim was to reconstruct the Union spiritually as well as physically.[120] This aim did not change after victory had been won. In his last speech Lincoln directed the North to accept peace without recrimination, and emphasized the need for "restoring the proper practical relations" between the Southern states and the Union without delay.[121] The day he was assassinated he planned "to restore the Union, so as to make it . . . a Union of hearts and hands as well as of States."[122]

If there cannot be much doubt that Lincoln's statements often made the Union appear to be an end in itself, it would be wrong to believe that he considered mere preservation of the Union as the end of the war. For him, saving the Union was nothing but a means for saving a popular government that protected the individual's life, liberty, and property.

Lincoln, who had left no doubts about his belief in popular government and majority rule before he became President,[123] remained a staunch adherent of that belief thereafter. Statements

[117] See his letter to A. G. Hodges of Apr. 4, 1864. WORKS, VII, 281.
[118] Interview with John T. Mills, Aug. [15?], 1864. WORKS (mem. ed.), X, 191.
[119] Unfinished letter to Isaac M. Schermerhorn, Sept. 12, 1864. WORKS (mem. ed.), X, 221.
[120] Graebner, "Lincoln: Conservative Statesman," 92.
[121] WORKS, VIII, 403.
[122] To Gen. Van Alen, Apr. 14, 1865. WORKS, VIII, 413.
[123] Cf. for instance, the following statement: "I have said, very many times . . . that no man believed more than I in the principle of self-government; that it lies at the bottom of all my ideas of just government from beginning to end . . . I deny that any man has ever gone ahead of me in his devotion to the principle, whatever he may have done in efficiency in advocating it." Speech, Chicago, July 10, 1858. WORKS, II, 493.

he made during his administration reveal not only a firm belief in popular government, but also a conviction that the cause of the Union was the cause of popular government; perhaps even a conviction that the preservation of the Union was a prerequisite for the preservation of self-government. This is evident during his eleven-week "dictatorship."[124] It is also evident in what can be considered the outstanding defense of the President's war powers, namely, the special message to Congress of July 4, 1861. In that message, Lincoln, while justifying his exercise of war powers by the exigencies of Union, also stressed that the preservation of the Union was conducive to, and perhaps a necessity for, the survival of popular government. He defended his war measures from considerations of popular government rather than from those of Union. Considering the war basically a people's contest, he praised "the patriotic instinct of the plain people" for recognizing that the fight for the Union was one for self-government. "They understand, without argument, that destroying the government, which was made up by Washington, means no good to them." "Our popular government has often been called an experiment," he added. "Two points in it, our people have already settled—the successful *establishing*, and the successful *administering* of it. One still remains—its successful *maintenance* against a formidable . . . attempt to overthrow it."[125] To prove the viability of popular government beyond doubt, one last hurdle had to be taken: The attempt of the Southern states—a minor-

---

[124] On May 7, 1861, Lincoln told the Regent Captains of San Marino: "You have kindly adverted to the trial through which this republic is now passing . . . It involves the question whether a Representative republic, extended and aggrandized so much as to be safe against foreign enemies can save itself from the dangers of domestic faction." WORKS, IV, 360. To John Hay he wrote the same day: "I consider the central idea pervading this struggle is the necessity that is upon us, of proving that popular government is not an absurdity. We must settle this question now, whether in a free government the minority have the right to break up the government whenever they choose. If we fail it will go far to prove the incapability of the people to govern themselves. . . . Taking the government as we found it we will see if the majority can preserve it." Tyler Dennett (ed.), LINCOLN AND THE CIVIL WAR IN THE DIARIES AND LETTERS OF JOHN HAY (New York, 1939), 19f.

[125] WORKS, IV, 438f. Lincoln added: "It is now for them to demonstrate to the world, that those who can fairly carry an election, can also suppress a rebellion—that ballots are the rightful, and peaceful, successors of bullets; and that when ballots have fairly, and constitutionally, decided, there can be no successful appeal, back to bullets; that there can be no successful appeal, except to ballots themselves, at succeeding elections." *Ibid.*, 439.

ity—to destroy the Union had to be frustrated by the successful effort of the Northern majority to maintain the Union. No clearer indication of the importance of the Union for self-government could have been given. Later on, more statements showing the relevance of the Union for self-government were made.[126]

In view of Lincoln's unequivocal praise for popular government,[127] supplemented as it was by occasional advocacies of a seemingly unrestricted majority rule, and in view of the fact that often he lauded popular government without stating what it actually stood for, one is tempted to think that he wanted popular government or majority rule merely for their own sake. One gains the impression that Lincoln justified his war measures on the ground that they were necessary for the preservation of popular government as an end in itself, i.e., for the survival of something that in the last analysis was as value-free as the Union. At best, such a defense of his disputed actions was shallow. It was likely to arouse rather than quiet fears, the more so since Lincoln's dictatorship, prompted as it was by "a popular demand, and a public necessity,"[128] had convinced many people that popular government could be quite oppressive.

However, to evaluate Lincoln's conception of popular government this way would do him injustice. For he did not believe in popular government for the sake of popular government, or in majority rule for the sake of majority rule. As one author put it, for Lincoln "popular government is something deeper and more valuable than a mere system of political organization: it is a

---

[126] In his First Annual Message of Dec. 3, 1861, Lincoln stated that "the insurrection is largely, if not exclusively, a war upon the first principle of popular government—the rights of the people." WORKS, V, 51. To border-state congressmen, he said on July 12, 1862: "As you would perpetuate popular government for the best people in the world, I beseech you that you do in no wise omit this [compensated emancipation]. WORKS, V, 319. The idea of self-government is evident in his Gettysburg Address.

[127] In a speech in Peoria of Oct. 16, 1854, Lincoln had gone so far as to say: "The doctrine of self government is right—absolutely and eternally right." WORKS, II, 265. In his First Inaugural Address, he asked: "Why should there not be a patient confidence in the ultimate justice of the people? Is there any better, or equal hope, in the world? If the Almighty Ruler of nations, with his eternal truth and justice, be on your side of the North, or on yours of the South, that truth, and that justice, will surely prevail, by the judgment of this great tribunal, the American people." WORKS, IV, 270. Compare, however, Williams, "Lincoln: Pragmatic Democrat," 33f.

[128] Special message to Congress, July 4, 1861. WORKS, IV, 429.

system of social life that gives the common man a chance" because it secures "the stupendous value to mankind of the free-labor system."[129] For Lincoln, popular government was a means to further men's freedom to make the most of their opportunities, and that freedom was secured best by their participation in government. In a word, the popular government Lincoln cherished was a free government.

The message of July 4, 1861, defended his war measures primarily on the grounds of freedom to be achieved through popular government in the Union. "This is essentially a People's contest," it stated. "On the side of the Union, it is a struggle for maintaining in the world, that form, and substance of government, whose leading object is, to elevate the condition of men—to lift artificial weights from all shoulders—to clear the paths of laudable pursuit for all—to afford all, an unfettered start, and a fair chance, in the race of life. Yielding to partial, and temporary departures, from necessity, this is the leading object of the government for whose existence we contend."[130] The central position of freedom vis-à-vis the auxiliary roles of popular government and the Union, is even more convincingly stated in the following passage:

. . . this issue embraces more than the fate of these United States. It presents to the whole family of man, the question, whether a constitutional republic, or a democracy—a government of the people, by the same people—can, or cannot, maintain its territorial integrity, against its own foes. It presents the question, whether discontented individuals, too few in numbers to control administration, according to organic law, in any case, can always, upon the pretences made in this case, or on any other pretences, or arbitrarily, without any pretence, break up their Government, and thus practically put an end to free government upon the earth. It forces us to ask: 'Is there, in all republics, this inherent, and fatal weakness?' 'Must a government, of necessity, be too *strong* for the liberties of its own people, or too *weak* to maintain its own existence?' So viewing the issue, no choice was left but to call out the war power of the Government; and so to resist force, employed for its destruction, by force, for its preservation.[131]

On July 4, 1861, Lincoln asserted the legitimacy of measures which many people considered illegal if not revolutionary, just as

---

[129] Hofstadter, AMERICAN POLITICAL TRADITION, 124.
[130] WORKS IV, 438.
[131] *Ibid.*, 426.

Jefferson on July 4, 1776, had asserted the legitimacy of the colonists' behavior. But whereas Jefferson had appealed to older, natural, and common law, Lincoln based his claim merely upon the Constitution.[132] He maintained that his exercise of the war power was justified because it could save the Constitution, which established popular government in a more perfect Union in order to secure freedom. The values emphasized were thus the same as those for which the soldiers he honored at Gettysburg a few years later had given their lives, namely, the values of "government of the people, by the people, for the people." The sequence of this enumeration is significant. Lincoln first mentioned government "of the people" because he considered the people the original source of American government. He then mentioned government "by the people" because he felt that a legitimate popular government was ideally one run by the people themselves. Finally, he spoke of government "for the people" to indicate the end of popular government. The construction is quite logical: the legitimate source of government is followed by a definition of the legitimate form of government which, in turn, is succeeded by a description of the legitimate end of government. The formal institution of government is symbolically confined by the legitimate source of, as well as by the legitimate limitation upon, its authority. To Lincoln, legitimate popular government implied that people participate in government in order to protect themselves. Popular government was a means—he felt the ideal means—for the achievement of freedom. As he did in his Gettysburg Address, Lincoln left no doubt in his 4th of July message that the people are the legitimate fountain of a Constitution which established popular government in the more perfect Union in order to secure freedom. Throughout his administration, he made clear his high evaluation of the Constitution as a document of free government.[133]

---

[132] In a speech made at Springfield on Aug. 26, 1852, Lincoln made plain that the Constitution ought not to be violated on grounds of 'higher law.' WORKS, II, 156. In his First Inaugural Address, he seems to identify "universal law" and the Constitution. WORKS, IV, 264. Williams, "Lincoln: Pragmatic Democrat," 32, writes that Lincoln "thought the Constitution approximated the spirit of divine law and embodied the best experience of man in government," that "Lincoln accepted the principle of higher law, but he refused to give it logical extension, logical in theory, that some opponents of slavery gave it."

[133] Lincoln's feeling that the Constitution, by creating the Union, furthered free

Lincoln's defense of his war measures, then, whether at times it seemed to be based upon the necessity of preserving the Union, or popular government, or freedom, was always based upon his desire to protect the Constitution. He claimed that his war measures, illegal as they may have been, were justified because the Constitution as supreme law gave him, the Supreme Executive, the supreme command to do all he could to preserve it. As he said in his First Inaugural Address, he felt bound by "the most solemn" oath "registered in Heaven" to " 'preserve, protect and defend' " the Constitution.[134] From this paramount duty he derived the right to disregard particular provisions of the Constitution. "Are all the laws [i.e., all the constitutional provisions], *but one,* to go unexecuted, and the government itself go to pieces, lest that one be violated?" he asked when he asserted that a disregard for the constitutional provision protecting habeas corpus would be justified if it served to save the rest of the Constitution.[135] For Lincoln, this represented a general principle on what in an emer-

---

government, i.e., a popular government legitimized by its protection of freedom, is evident in his Proclamation of May 8, 1863, which states that "no service can be more praiseworthy and honorable than that which is rendered for the maintenance of the Constitution and Union, and the consequent preservation of free government." WORKS VI, 203. Cf. also his speech to the 164th Ohio regiment of Aug. 18, 1864: "We have, as all will agree, a free Government, where every man has a right to be equal with every other man. In this great struggle, this form of Government and every form of human rights is endangered if our enemies succeed." WORKS, VII, 505. Four days later, he elaborated further on the theme of free government in a speech to the 166th Ohio regiment: "It is not merely for to-day, but for all time to come that we should perpetuate for our children's children this great and free government, which we have enjoyed all our lives . . . It is in order that each one of you may have through this free government which we have enjoyed, an open field and a fair chance for your industry, enterprise and intelligence; that you may all have equal privileges in the race of life, with all its desirable human aspirations. . . . The nation is worth fighting for, to secure such an inestimable jewel." WORKS, VII, 512.

[134] Lincoln, addressing his "dissatisfied fellow countrymen" in the South, actually said: "*You* have no oath registered in Heaven to destroy the government, while *I* shall have the most solemn one to 'preserve, protect and defend' it." WORKS, IV, 271. On Jan. 8, 1863, he wrote Gen. McClernand: "I never did ask more, nor ever was willing to accept less, than for all the States, and the people thereof, to take and hold their places, and their rights, in the Union, under the Constitution of the United States. For this alone have I felt authorized to struggle; and I seek neither more nor less now." On Jan. 19, 1863, he told workers of Manchester: "Whatever might have been the cause [of the Civil War], or whosoever the fault, one duty paramount to all others was before me, namely, to maintain and preserve at once the Constitution and the integrity of the federal republic." WORKS, VI, 48, 63.

[135] WORKS, IV, 430.

49

gency situation was permissible for the preservation of the constitutional order. He felt "that measures, otherwise unconstitutional, might become lawful, by becoming indispensable to the preservation of the constitution, through the preservation of the nation."[136] While Lincoln believed in the doctrine of reason of state, his was a belief in constitutional reason of state.[137]

Lincoln confirmed his desire to protect the Constitution throughout his administration. He also made clear that after victory he would adhere to the Constitution. Thus his defense of his war measures has the same keynote as his first major political address of 1838: obedience to the Constitution and the laws. To judge by that defense, one is inclined to believe that the Whig who entered the White House remained exactly that throughout his administration, that President Lincoln did not camouflage his political ambitions under a Whig's wig.

GUILT AND TRAGEDY

The preceding pages portrayed Lincoln's attitude toward the Constitution. They depicted that attitude before the Civil War, described his war measures, and stated his defense of those measures. It remains to examine whether the Lincoln administration was tragic for the development of American government.

Since tragedy often presupposes guilt, we shall first ask whether the man who was, and who claimed to be, the responsible leader of the United States during the period under consideration, was guilty of violating the Constitution. Basically, this amounts to asking whether Lincoln wanted to be a constitutional innovator; whether he decreed his controversial war measures mainly out of ambition, not necessity. An answer to that question could help us to determine and appreciate properly not only Lincoln's role, but also the tragic aspects of his administration on account of, or in spite of, that role. Furthermore, such an answer seems to be required out of fairness to Lincoln himself. For in view of the

[136] To A. G. Hodges, April 4, 1864. WORKS, VII, 281.

[137] Carl J. Friedrich, CONSTITUTIONAL REASON OF STATE (Providence, R.I., 1957), does not mention Lincoln. For Friedrich's skepticism toward Lincoln's constitutional dictatorship, see his CONSTITUTIONAL GOVERNMENT AND DEMOCRACY, 578.

novel if not revolutionary character of his measures, people have been reluctant to accept unequivocally his defense of those measures, a defense which makes a master politician[138] appear as an unselfish protector of the status quo under the Constitution, and not at all as an ambitious innovator, let alone revolutionary. Since defenses of political behavior are indeed often of a political rather than a legal nature, and especially since a behavior that is dubious on constitutional grounds has often been defended by twisting the law for political ends, the skepticism toward Lincoln's defense of his war measures could well be justified.

The document burdening Lincoln the most is probably his first major political speech, delivered in 1838. As shown in that speech, Lincoln admonished his countrymen in North and South to abide by the Constitution and the laws. He also made some other intriguing statements. Concerned with *"the perpetuation"* of American *"political institutions,"* he was rather pessimistic as to the chances of such perpetuation. Human nature, he felt, always made men look for innovations. The Founding Fathers had "aspired to display before an admiring world, a practical demonstration of the truth of a proposition, which had hitherto been considered . . . problematical; namely, *the capability of a people to govern themselves.*" In the formative period, "all that sought celebrity and fame, and distinction, expected to find them in the success of that experiment. Their *all* was staked upon it:—their destiny was *inseparably* linked with it." He added: "If they succeeded, they were to be immortalized; their names were to be transferred to counties and cities, and rivers and mountains; and to be revered and sung, and toasted through all time." After stating that the experiment had been successful and that "thousands have won their deathless names in making it so," Lincoln came to the conclusion that no further laurels could be earned with the government they set up. For "the game is caught; and . . . with the catching, end the pleasures of the chase. This field of glory is harvested, and the crop is already appropriated." And then, looking into the future, he continued:

But new reapers will arise, and *they*, too, will seek a field . . . [M]en of ambition and talents will . . . continue to spring up amongst us. And,

[138] See *supra,* 18n.

51

when they do, they will as naturally seek the gratification of their ruling passion, as others have *so* done before them . . . [Can] that gratification be found in supporting and maintaining an edifice that has been erected by others? Most certainly it cannot. Many great and good men sufficiently qualified for any task they should undertake, may ever be found, whose ambition would aspire to nothing beyond a seat in Congress, a gubernatorial or a presidential chair; *but such belong not to the family of the lion, or the tribe of the eagle,* [.] What! think you these places would satisfy an Alexander, a Caesar, or a Napoleon? Never! Towering genius disdains a beaten path. It seeks regions hitherto unexplored. It sees *no distinction* in adding story to story, upon the monuments of fame, erected to the memory of others. It *denies* that it is glory enough to serve under any chief. It *scorns* to tread in the footsteps of *any* predecessor, however illustrious. It thirsts and burns for distinction; and, if possible, it will have it, whether at the expense of emancipating slaves, or enslaving freemen. Is it unreasonable then to expect, that some man possessed of the loftiest genius, coupled with ambition sufficient to push it to its utmost stretch, will at some time, spring up among us? And when such a one does, it will require the people to be united with each other, attached to the government and laws, and generally intelligent, to successfully frustrate his designs.
Distinction will be his paramount object; and although he would as willingly, perhaps more so, acquire it by doing good as harm; yet, that opportunity being past, and nothing left to be done in the way of building up, he would set boldly to the task of pulling down.[139]

Thus spoke Lincoln decades before his contemporary Nietzsche wrote *Thus Spake Zarathustra*. His speech on the preservation of American institutions was also a speech on innovating those institutions. And whereas it left no doubt about the value of preservation and the danger of innovation, it also demonstrated that distinction does not so much depend on preserving as it does on innovating; not as much on maintaining the existing constitutional order by observing its laws as upon innovating, revolutionizing, or even overthrowing that order by disregarding its laws. The speech thus appears to have a split personality. On the one hand, it admonishes people to obey the laws; on the other, it admits that obedience to the laws will usually prevent people from achieving distinction.[140] Distinction does not so much derive

---

[139] WORKS, I, 113f.

[140] On account of Lincoln's use of the word "many" in the sentence beginning "Many great and good men sufficiently qualified for any task they should undertake," it is believed that "distinction" to him meant "greatness" and "goodness." Even if this was not so, the validity of the following arguments would hardly be affected.

from legal, as from illegal behavior. While it is good to obey the laws, it is distinguished to disobey them.

Students critical of Lincoln could make the most of his remarks. They could assert that a man who spoke of distinction as Lincoln did was likely to possess a drive for distinction and to be torn between the basically moral idea of obeying the laws, and the basically value-free idea of becoming immortal. In view of Lincoln's war measures—the emancipation of slaves, given in the Springfield speech as an example of distinction, was one of them—they could suspect that Lincoln adopted those measures mainly from a desire to innovate in order to become immortal, even if it meant to "set boldly to the task of pulling down" the existing order; that Lincoln's frequent—perhaps all too frequent—statements on the necessity of preserving the Constitution derived from a regret over a self-revealing slip concerning distinction and innovation, and was motivated by a desire to paint over that slip; that his emphasis on that necessity was mere window-dressing, a hypocritical attempt at concealing his ambition of becoming immortal through innovation; that his assertion that his war "measures, whether strictly legal or not, were ventured upon, under what appeared to be a popular demand, and a public necessity,"[141] reveals a democratic Machiavellian whose latent desire to achieve immortality broke forth at the first opportunity offered by the unique situation of the Civil War.[142]

On the other hand, defenders of Lincoln could doubt whether a recognition of political distinction necessarily results, even in the case of a master politician like Lincoln, in a drive for such distinction. They could argue that in his Lyceum speech Lincoln pointed to the *dangers* of innovation and the *dangers* resulting from designs of ambitious men, clearly indicating his opposition toward innovation and his skepticism of ambitious designs.[143] If these arguments were not accepted, they could maintain that Lincoln's consistent advocacy of obedience to the Constitution and the laws refute the idea that he desired to be an innovator for the sake of

[141] Special message of July 4, 1861. WORKS, IV, 429.

[142] Cf. Edmund Wilson, "Abraham Lincoln: The Union as Religious Mysticism," in that author's EIGHT ESSAYS (Garden City, N.Y., 1954), 181, 190f., 202; Harry V. Jaffa, CRISIS OF THE HOUSE DIVIDED (Garden City, N.Y., 1959), esp. ch. 9.

[143] On the unambitious Lincoln, see Roy P. Basler, "Abraham Lincoln: An Immortal Sign." Graebner, ENDURING LINCOLN, 18ff.

immortality; that it was the mature Lincoln that counted, not the young man, that it was foolish to measure the behavior of Lincoln in the sixties by a remark he had made in the thirties. As to his war measures, Lincoln's defenders could deny that he was eager to introduce innovations by pointing to his confession that during the war he had not controlled events, but events had controlled him;[144] they could add that Lincoln was prompted by the desire to save the constitutional order and was thus a preserver and not an innovator, let alone a revolutionizer; that it was unfair to suspect a man who assumed many personal sacrifices for the common good of being willing to sacrifice the public interest to some selfish purpose such as immortality.

Although the arguments of the first group ought not to be taken lightly, on the face of the bulk of Lincoln's statements one could be inclined to believe that basically he was a conserver, not an innovator. Consequently, one would be reluctant to accuse him of being eager to introduce measures of a legally dubious character. Certainly, it would be hard to prove his guilt in that respect. He at least deserves the benefit of the doubt. *In dubio pro reo.* Lincoln, who considered himself the supreme guardian of the supreme law, must be acquitted of being guilty of the supreme crime a man in his position could commit—contempt of the Constitution.

For the question whether Lincoln's administration involved constitutional tragedy, however, his guilt does not really matter so much. Even if we deny the idea that constitutional innovations during the Civil War were in large measure due to the dubious machinations of an ambitious democratic demagogue, those innovations would still exist. Absence of constitutional guilt may exonerate Lincoln; it does not imply an absence of constitutional tragedy. It perhaps even enhances that tragedy. For it could be argued that American constitutional development was tragic because, in spite of the leadership of an "archconstitutionalist,"[145] the Constitution did not escape the "rough time" he had envisaged for it at the beginning of his administration;[146] that in spite of Lincoln's Whig orientation, of his desires to adhere by existing

---

[144] To A. G. Hodges on Apr. 4, 1864. WORKS, VII, 282.
[145] McLaughlin, "Lincoln, the Constitution, and Democracy," 5.
[146] See *supra,* 36.

laws, he was caught in a current of events that mastered him and forced him into illegal actions. That current was a democratic current, a current which Jakob Burckhardt, worried on account of the French Revolution over the freedom of the individual in democratic society, suspected of an everlasting desire to innovate.[147] Such a current was unlikely to respect liberal inhibitions. It was likely to sweep away such inhibitions. Perhaps this is what occurred. While Lincoln can hardly be called a descendant of the French Revolution, perhaps that revolution descended upon him. Perhaps Lincoln, who as a Whig was interested not only in the protection of the individual, but also in popular government and majority rule, became so impressed by the democratic ingredient of free government that he permitted that ingredient to gain the upper hand over its liberal counterpart, concerned with the protection of the individual, and let himself be carried away by the democratic tide. Though he spoke out against radicals[148] and was thus not midstream in the democratic current, he was unable to stay out of it altogether. Had Lincoln followed the radicals, the Constitution would, of course, have fared worse than it did. As it was, the Constitution fared ill enough, considering the measures taken against its letter, if not spirit.

We showed what these measures were. We shall now attempt to point out to what degree they turned out to be tragic. In doing so, we do not so much have in mind the hardship they involved at the time they were undertaken, great as that hardship was in view of the fact that the Civil War probably was the first modern total war and perhaps constituted the most authoritarian era Americans had experienced since the founding of their Republic. We have in mind the period after Lincoln when it became evident that the constitutionalist idyll of pre-war days was gone, that the war had initiated a new phase of American constitutionalism. In that phase, the "Father of Waters," fed from the democratic heartland of democratic America, indeed again could go "unvexed to the sea,"[149] a symbol of a victorious and untrammeled democracy

---

[147] Jakob Burckhardt, HISTORISCHE FRAGMENTE (Stuttgart, 1942), 205.

[148] See the chapter "The Unpopular Mr. Lincoln" in Randall, LINCOLN THE LIBERAL STATESMAN, 65, and the works cited *supra*, 41n.

[149] To J. C. Conkling, Aug. 26, 1863. WORKS, VI, 409.

in a new nation. But did that democracy perhaps come to vex the Constitution and free government?

As far as the immediate and most obvious results of the Lincoln administration are concerned, no major constitutional tragedy seems to be evident. By his war measures Lincoln achieved about everything he set out to do. Considering himself the executor[150] of the will of the people, he succeeded in saving cherished features of constitutional government. He preserved majority rule, popular government, and the Union. They continued under the Constitution. The problem of constitutional tragedy arises only when we ask whether Lincoln succeeded in preserving the Constitution in its original meaning, its kind of Union, its kind of popular government and majority rule, for generations to come. Here the answer is perhaps less comforting. We arrive at it by examining the kind of popular government that emerged from his administration. Since Lincoln defended his war measures on grounds of "popular demand" and "public necessity," it is hardly to be expected that popular government decreased. As a matter of fact, the government emerging from the Civil War certainly was more "popular" than that prior to the war. The emancipation of slaves broadened the popular base of government.

Majority rule was confirmed by the victory of the Northern majority over the Southern minority. These features were, on the face of it, quite in line with American thought. From the point of view of constitutional, or limited, government, however, they were not without problems; for they could possibly result in a democratic challenge to free government.

This problem becomes acute, for instance, in the case of institutions that were designed to check democratic excesses for the sake of freedom, such as federalism and the separation of powers. As to the former, the Lincoln administration, representing a majority of the people as well as of the states, achieved a major war aim when it succeeded in saving the Union. On the face of it, there was no constitutional tragedy involved in this achievement. However, on looking more closely, it appears doubtful whether the Union that emerged from the Civil War was up to the standards

[150] Carl Schmitt, DIE DIKTATUR (München, 1921), 136, called Lincoln a *kommissarischer Diktator* who suspended the Constitution in order to save it.

of federalism that had prevailed in the pre-war period. The new Union was obviously more "perfect" than the "more perfect Union" which according to Lincoln had been established by the Constitution.[151] The United States became more of a Nation.[152] This was not to be without consequences. The trend toward nationalism was likely to continue. As a result, any particular state or minority of states and their people were likely to become dependent upon the national government as the representative of the national majority. This meant that a state or a minority of states and their people could conceivably be oppressed by the national government. Federalism as a means of constitutionalism, a means for the protection of the minority, could be challenged.

A similar situation presents itself with respect to the separation of powers. Lincoln, it will be remembered, subscribed to that separation before he became President. Even later on, he did not openly denounce it.[153] On the surface, again, there was, as far as the separation of powers is concerned, nothing constitutionally problematic about his administration. Upon closer inspection, however, things appear less assuring. Lincoln's exercise of emergency powers was unlikely to leave the traditional separation of powers unaffected. It was likely to lay the groundstone for executive emergency government in the future.[154] In view of the vagueness of the concept of emergency and the obvious executive discretion in defining that concept, the exercise of emergency power could conceivably not remain confined to emergencies like war or civil war. It could possibly be claimed by a President in times that were more normal, or, by objective standards, quite normal. In the end, the state of emergency possibly could become the rule

---

[151] In his First Inaugural Address, Lincoln stated: "The Union is much older than the Constitution. It was formed in fact, by the Articles of Association in 1774. It was matured and continued by the Declaration of Independence in 1776. It was further matured and the faith of all the then thirteen States expressly plighted and engaged that it should be perpetual, by the Articles of Confederation in 1778. And finally, in 1787, one of the declared objects for ordaining and establishing the Constitution, was '*to form a more perfect union.*' " WORKS, IV, 265.

[152] See Mason, "The Nature of Our Federal Union Reconsidered," 520f.

[153] See Randall, LINCOLN THE LIBERAL STATESMAN, 125ff.; Rossiter, CONSTITUTIONAL DICTATORSHIP, 230ff.

[154] See Rossiter, AMERICAN PRESIDENCY, 101. William B. Hesseltine, LINCOLN AND THE WAR GOVERNORS (New York, 1948), and LINCOLN'S PLAN OF RECONSTRUCTION (Tuscaloosa, Ala., 1960).

rather than the exception. Under the pretense of executing the will of the people, a President could thus emerge as a rather permanent dictator. While the possibility of executive dictatorship could, as was demonstrated in Lincoln's administration, exist even in the presence of an antagonistic and competing Congress, it could, *a fortiori,* exist whenever there was substantial agreement between the executive and the other branches of government, whenever the President would emerge as a legislative and perhaps even judicial leader, something that was not improbable in democratic evolution.[155]

Concentrations of power in the national and executive branches of government, brought about by Lincoln in the name of the people, were processes that conceivably complemented each other to the detriment of free government. Lincoln's administration thus opened the way for the development of an omnipotent national executive who as a spokesman for the people might consider himself entitled to do whatever he felt was good for the Nation, irrespective of the interests and rights of states, Congress, the judiciary, and the individual.

Aside from initiating challenges to institutional safeguards of freedom, Lincoln, acting upon "popular demand" and "public necessity," also brought about infringements upon freedom by curtailing habeas corpus, freedom of the press and of speech, and property rights. Again, from the point of view of constitutionalism, these curtailments would not have been too bad had they been confined to the war emergency. What makes them appear more tragic is that they set a precedent. Once certain rights had been curtailed under a certain emergency, there was no reason why other rights could not be curtailed in other emergencies. Furthermore, in view of the vague nature of the concept of emergency and the President's discretion to define that concept, it was conceivable that the rights of the individual could be suspended in any situation which was considered an emergency situation by the President, normal as it may appear to more objective observers. Thus it was conceivable that infringements upon the rights of the individual would become the rule rather than the exception.

In summary, it may be said that the tragedy of the Lincoln

[155] See *infra,* 182ff.

administration probably lies in its *Relativierung,* in the name of the people, of the Constitution. As we had seen, Lincoln suspended parts of the Constitution in order to save the whole. From the point of view of constitutional government, such a procedure is perhaps defensible as long as it succeeds in re-establishing the major values of the Constitution with a good chance of permanency.[156] On the other hand, the undertaking is risky in view of the fact that "all breaches of the law are destructive of the general belief in law upon which constitutionalism rests."[157] Making values relative often will result in the elimination of those values. If federalism is relativized by an undue increase of national power, it is likely to be eliminated. If the separation of powers is relativized by an undue increase of executive power, it could well be abolished. If it is maintained that some rights of the individual are not as important as others, these rights are likely to pass away. What is worse, once certain rights (of states, Congress, or the individual) are considered less important than others, not only are *they* likely to be eliminated, but other constitutional values will probably follow suit. In the end no constitutional values may be left and free government eliminated. Making the rule of law relative marks the beginning of its elimination.

In view of Lincoln's affirmation of popular government and majority rule, future *Relativierungen* of the Constitution were likely to be determined by the national majority. Thus any existing majority could conceivably replace the Constitution at any time for any purpose by its own will, unreasonable and passionate as that will might be. Arbitrary majority rule, despotic democracy, could come into existence. The rule of law could be replaced by the rule of men, temporary as the latter might be.

To an "archconstitutionalist"[158] like Lincoln, who from his early days admonished his fellow-citizens to observe the Constitution and the laws, this would—if he was sincere in his admonitions—have appeared as a tragic development indeed. When or-

[156] On the different value of constitutional provisions, see the author's FEDERALIST, 276, 279; "Unconstitutional Constitutional Norms? Constitutional Development in Postwar Germany," VIRGINIA LAW REVIEW, XLII (1956), 1.

[157] Friedrich, CONSTITUTIONAL GOVERNMENT AND DEMOCRACY, 578. Randall, LINCOLN THE LIBERAL STATESMAN, 124, writes about the "noticeable lack of legal precision" which characterized the Lincoln administration.

[158] See also Bernard, "Lincoln and Civil Liberties," 393ff.

dering his war measures, Lincoln perhaps was comforted by John Marshall's dictum that a broad interpretation of the Constitution was in order because a constitution is "intended to endure for ages to come, and, consequently, to be adopted to the various *crises* of human affairs."[159] Probably Lincoln felt that once the crisis of the Civil War was over, the Constitution would lastingly re-emerge as it was conceived by the Founders, by Marshall, and by himself: a document of free government, with all the original trimmings and safeguards of that form of government. Perhaps he did not think that in view of his own *Relativierung* of the Constitution later democratic generations might look upon Marshall's statement as a green light for democratic rather than constitutional interpretations of the Constitution, interpretations which would replace constitutional restraint by democratic action, substitute sheer majority rule for free government, and a rule of laws and regulations for the rule of law.

CONCLUSION

In *The Trial of the Constitution*,[160] a book which has been considered an "eloquent statement of the powers of emergency and self-preservation inherent in the Constitution and government,"[161] it was observed in 1863: "If the Union and the Government cannot be saved out of this terrible shock of war constitutionally, *a* Union and *a* Government must be saved unconstitutionally."[162] It has been suggested that Lincoln might have felt that way.[163] However, in view of his repeated confirmations of the Constitution, it seems more likely that he wanted to save the kind of Union and government he had admired from the days of his youth. Be this as it may, it can hardly be denied that a Union and a government emerged from the Civil War that were different from those that had existed.[164] Perhaps this was a constitutional

---

[159] *McCulloch* v. *Maryland,* 4 Wheat. 316, 515 (1819).
[160] Sidney G. Fisher, THE TRIAL OF THE CONSTITUTION (Philadelphia, 1862).
[161] Rossiter, CONSTITUTIONAL DICTATORSHIP, 224.
[162] Fisher, TRIAL OF THE CONSTITUTION, 199.
[163] Rossiter, CONSTITUTIONAL DICTATORSHIP, 224.
[164] See Graebner, "Lincoln: Conservative Statesman," 93.

tragedy. Perhaps Lincoln aged as much as he did during the war years because he recognized that the American system would never be the same, that the supposedly temporary tragedy of the war years might endure.

That possibility was most immediately obvious in the era of Reconstruction, a demonstration of the idea of *vae victis* which Americans had never known before and had probably not thought possible. It will always be a fascinating question whether Lincoln could have prevented the cruelties of that era.[165] While the outcome of the war kept the Union formally intact, it in many respects tore it apart. It was a case of a lost victory, and this is why the Civil War could be called the only war America ever lost.[166] "Out of its agonies, losses, confusion, and moral debasement it seemed difficult to create anything ennobling."[167] As President Taylor's son wrote in his war record, the Civil War was a war not of construction, but of destruction and reconstruction.[168] That reconstruction, being highly questionable in the era of Reconstruction, perhaps remained questionable in the following generations, although this may have been veiled to most people on account of the stupendous development of the United States, as it became reflected in such phenomena as the westward movement, the industrial revolution, and the emergence as a world power.

It is true that after Reconstruction free government, showing its enormous survival power, recovered. The sad 'sixties, characterized by a toll in lives, liberty and property, as well as by a tenuous existence of institutional guarantees of freedom, such as federalism, the separation of powers, and judicial review, were

---

[165] In his message of July 4, 1861, Lincoln said: "Lest there be some uneasiness in the minds of candid men, as to what is to be the course of the government, towards the Southern States, *after* the rebellion shall have been suppressed, the Executive deems it proper to say, it will be his purpose then, as ever, to be guided by the Constitution, and the laws; and that he probably will have no different understanding of the powers, and duties of the Federal government, relatively to the rights of the States, and the people, under the Constitution, than that expressed in the inaugural address." WORKS, IV, 439. Similar conciliatory statements were made by Lincoln throughout the war. Cf. John Hope Franklin, RECONSTRUCTION: AFTER THE CIVIL WAR (Chicago, 1961); J. G. Randall and David Donald, THE CIVIL WAR AND RECONSTRUCTION (2d ed.; Boston, 1961).

[166] In his address of Jan. 27, 1838, Lincoln said: "If destruction be our lot, we must ourselves be its author and finisher. As a nation of freemen, we must live through all time, or die by suicide." WORKS, I, 109.

[167] Allan Nevins, THE STATESMANSHIP OF THE CIVIL WAR (New York, 1953), 12.

[168] Quoted *ibid.*, 12f.

followed by decades in which a more genuine balance of powers, coupled with a better protection of the rights of the individual, was restored. Nevertheless, what had occurred in the 'sixties was likely to leave its traces.

The following chapters will investigate whether it has done so by examining the most characteristic features of American government—federalism, the separation of powers, and judicial review. Since under the Constitution all these features were instituted for the protection of life, liberty and property, the discussion will reveal how freedom has fared in the American democracy.

3

ECONOMIC RIGHTS AND FEDERALISM
SUBMERGENT

INTRODUCTION

The civil rights issue focused attention not only on so-called civil rights, but also on economic freedom and federalism.[1] It thus revived the debate about two characteristic features of American government, a debate that flared up again and again during the past decades. Whereas proponents of civil rights legislation favor the protection by the national government of those rights, its opponents maintain that such legislation involves undue increases of national power and unjustified restrictions of economic freedom and private property. The remarkable showing which Governor Wallace of Alabama, campaigning for property and states' rights rather than for segregation, made in the primaries of non-segregationalist states like Wisconsin, Indiana, and Maryland; the reluctance of Northern senators to halt the Southern filibuster against the Civil Rights Bill of 1964; the many amendments attached to the original bill before its passage became possible—all show how mixed feelings were. Throughout the Senate debate, uneasiness hung over the nation. When the Act was finally

[1] The distinction made between "civil rights" and "economic freedom" follows a modern usage which appears to be unwarranted. Economic rights are as civil as any other rights. They were traditionally so considered. Robert E. Cushman, "Civil Liberties," ENCYCLOPEDIA OF THE SOCIAL SCIENCES (New York, 1930–34), III, 509, includes economic freedom. The article thus expresses what had been the prevalent opinion since the days of Blackstone. However, Cushman, CIVIL LIBERTIES IN THE UNITED STATES (n.p., 1956), no longer mentions economic freedom or property rights. This shift is characteristic of the exclusion of economic rights from the civil rights category which has come about since the New Deal. The official proclamation of the new doctrine can probably be found in Chief Justice Stone's footnote 4, in *U.S.* v. *Carolene Products Co.*, 304 U.S. 144, 152 (1938). See, also, *West Virginia School Board* v. *Barnette*, 319 U.S. 624 (1943); *Thomas* v. *Collins*, 323 U.S. 516 (1944). See *infra*, 132f., 140ff.

passed before a deadline set by Negro leaders, many people felt that it was passed reluctantly because there was no alternative to preventing violence and bloodshed. The Civil Rights Bill of 1966 was not enacted at all.

Passage of civil rights legislation would hardly have been as complicated as it was had that legislation been concerned merely with giving equal rights to all. That idea is so much a part of the American credo that few politicians can afford to oppose it. Doubts about civil rights measures can only be explained by the fact that these measures challenge principles of constitutionalism. The urgency with which it was maintained that civil rights legislation would topple foundations of American government such as economic freedom and federalism makes us wonder about the position of these values today. Clearly, acts of Congress alone can hardly topple foundations of a system as venerated as the American, which is generally considered a bulwark of constitutionalism, unless these foundations already have become eroded away. In this chapter, we wish to investigate whether or not they have.

Remarks on the Founders' attitude toward federalism and economic rights will be followed by an examination of how these values have fared and how, with the advance of democracy, they became challenged. The chapter will conclude with a discussion of the implications of these trends for free government.

PROTECTION OF ECONOMIC RIGHTS THROUGH FEDERALISM UNDER TRADITIONAL CONSTITUTIONAL GOVERNMENT

The American Revolution was in a large measure a federal effort for the protection of economic freedom. Already prior to independence, the inhabitants of the colonies demonstrated their resentment of English mercantilist restrictions by vigorously denouncing taxation and regulation of trade. The Declaration of Independence speaks of the "unalienable rights" of life, liberty, and the pursuit of happiness, which also included economic rights.[2] Thus, the very year in which *The Wealth of Nations* was published in the Old World, when Europe began theorizing about freedom of economic liberties, Americans took action for the protection of those liberties. The New World was first to shed its blood for the new world of economic freedom. It also recognized the value of federalism for the achievement of that aim. To further the war effort, the thirteen states entered "into a firm league of friendship with each other, for . . . the security of their liberties"—including economic ones—under the Articles of Confederation.[3]

The Americans' desire for economic freedom, demonstrated before and during the War of Independence, contributed to the framing and adoption of the federal Constitution. Although that war had eliminated mercantilistic restrictions imposed by the British, curtailments of trade continued to exist among the thirteen states. Economic conditions prompted the various states to adopt tariff policies which resulted in impediments to commerce, as did regulations concerning shipping on the Mississippi. Different currencies, weights and measures contributed to commercial and financial difficulties. In order to bring about greater economic freedom, Massachusetts led an effort as early as 1783 toward federal liberalization of trade. Restrictions on trade between Maryland and Virginia furnished the immediate cause for the calling of the Annapolis Convention whose task it was to liberalize trade and commerce.[4]

The desire for free trade was matched by the demand for the

---

[2] For the fact that Jefferson, when speaking of "the pursuit of happiness," had in mind the protection of property, see Edward Dumbauld, THE DECLARATION OF INDEPENDENCE (Norman, Okla., 1950), 60ff., and the author's IN DEFENSE OF PROPERTY, 31f. The Declaration blames the King for having "sent hither swarms of officers to harass our people, and eat out their substance," for "cutting off our trade with all parts of the world," for "imposing taxes on us without our consent," for having "plundered our seas, ravaged our coasts, burnt our towns."

[3] Art. 3. According to Merrill Jensen, THE ARTICLES OF CONFEDERATION (Madison, Wisc., 1940), the quest for a loose confederacy like that established by the Articles of Confederation rather than a more consolidated federal state derived from the fact that the Americans, having become aware of oppressions by the unitary government of Britain, did not want to take a chance with a strong American national government for fear it would be as oppressive as its English predecessor.

[4] See Allan Nevins, THE AMERICAN STATES DURING AND AFTER THE REVOLUTION, 544ff.

protection of vested rights and private property. Just as English mercantilist regulations were followed by state restrictions upon commerce and trade, English infringements upon property were followed by those committed by the states. Laws infringing upon the obligation of contracts and upon property were passed in many states where a "rag money" party, composed of debtors, artisans, and small farmers, had won control of the legislature over a "hard money" faction composed of creditors, merchants, and large planters. This situation aroused severe criticism. The leaders in the struggle for independence who had previously denounced parliamentary infringements upon property, now did not hesitate to attack the democratic legislatures of the states. They advocated a federal government that could protect the individual's property from oppression by the states.[5]

State regulations of economic freedom—including free trade as well as property rights—resulted in bitter feeling among the states. Thus, when the Annapolis Convention proposed a federal convention "to render the constitution of the Federal Government adequate to the exigencies of the Union,"[6] its delegates were to a large degree prompted by the desire to bring about a greater protection of economic rights.[7]

In the Philadelphia Convention the desire to protect these rights was obvious. The Constitution framed by that convention liberalized commerce and trade by depriving the states of the right to impose tariffs, issue currency, define weights and measures, and to regulate commerce with other states or foreign nations or tribes. Property was protected in so far as the states were prohibited from passing laws interfering with the obligation of contracts. The more perfect Union was established not merely for the sake of security from foreign nations and peace among the

[5] See Corwin, "Progress of Constitutional Theory," 534ff.

[6] "Proceedings of the Commissioners to Remedy Defects of the Federal Government," in Jonathan Elliot (ed.), THE DEBATES IN THE SEVERAL STATE CONVENTIONS ON THE ADOPTION OF THE FEDERAL CONSTITUTION (Washington, 1876), I, 118. According to the Resolution of Congress of Feb. 21, 1787, the Federal Convention was proposed to "render the federal constitution adequate to the exigencies of Government and the preservation of the Union": Farrand, RECORDS OF THE FEDERAL CONVENTION, III, 14.

[7] See the author's "Das Problem der Demokratie bei den amerikanischen Verfassungsvätern," ZEITSCHRIFT FÜR DIE GESAMTE STAATSWISSENSCHAFT, CXIII (1957), 301.

member states, but also—and mainly—for the protection of the rights of the individual, among which economic rights ranked high.[8] Most delegates favored laissez faire and shared John Adams's opinion that "property is surely a right of mankind as really as liberty . . . The moment the idea is admitted into society that property is not as sacred as the laws of God, and that there is not a force of law and public justice to protect it, anarchy and tyranny commence."[9]

Economic freedom and federalism thus became major features of the original Constitution of the United States—the former an end, the latter a means to that end. The importance of federalism as a means of constitutionalism ought not to be overlooked. Federalism, instituted to enable the federal government to check oppressions by the governments of the states, and vice versa, appears to be a supreme principle of the Constitution.[10] Characteristically, *The Federalist* is a classic treatise on federalism and free government. Its exposition of federalism as a means of protection for the individual is in a large measure concerned with economic rights.[11]

The quality of federalism as a protector of economic rights was not changed when the first ten amendments were adopted on the prompting of those who feared that the rights of the individual might be curtailed by the federal government. The Bill of Rights, while establishing further guarantees for economic rights,[12] also reconfirms the federal principle: Whereas the preamble to the original Constitution states that the people of the United States ordain the Constitution in order to form a more perfect Union

---

[8] Charles A. Beard, AN ECONOMIC INTERPRETATION OF THE CONSTITUTION (New York, 1913), advances the thesis that the framers of the Constitution were to a large degree prompted by self-interest. It is here believed that their desire to protect property derived in a large measure from the fact that they believed the protection of property to be a prerequisite for freedom and public order, conducive to progress, justice, and the individual's as well as society's welfare and happiness. See Robert E. Brown, CHARLES BEARD AND THE CONSTITUTION (Princeton, N.J., 1956) ; Forrest McDonald, WE, THE PEOPLE (Chicago, 1958).

[9] WORKS, VI, 8f.

[10] It could even be argued that federalism is *the* supreme principle of the Constitution: Of all constitutional provisions, only the provision that "no State without its consent, shall be deprived of its equal suffrage in the Senate" is immune from amendment (Art. V).

[11] See the author's FEDERALIST.

[12] Amendments Three, Four, Five, and Seven.

and to secure the blessings of liberty, the Tenth Amendment stresses that "the powers not delegated to the United States by the Constitution or prohibited by it to the States, are reserved to the States respectively, or to the people." Having created a more perfect Union for the protection of the rights of the individual, the people hastened to stress the importance of the states for that protection, thus putting beyond doubt the limited character of the new system of government, characterized by a genuine balance between federal power and states' rights. Having ratified the original Constitution in their desire to protect freedom through federalism, the people emphasized their claim to be the guardians of federalism for the sake of freedom.

The author of the Declaration of Independence, impressed by the federal design of Philadelphia, could, after his desire for a Bill of Rights had been fulfilled,[13] well be satisfied with the new government, for which he had ample praise in his First Inaugural Address. In that address he also stressed the need for the protection of economic rights when he said: "With all these blessings, what more is necessary to make us a happy and prosperous people? Still one thing more, fellow citizens, a wise and frugal government, which shall restrain men from injuring one another, shall leave them otherwise free to regulate their own pursuits of industry and improvement and shall not take from the mouth of labor the bread it has earned. This is the sum of good government, and this is necessary to close the circle of our felicities."[14] Spoken by the Republican antagonist and successor of the Federalist John Adams, these words indicate that, as far as economic freedom is concerned, Republicans and Federalists were in general agreement. Also, both parties considered federalism a means for the protection of the rights of the individual, including his economic rights.

Made in 1801, Jefferson's statement cast its spell over the nineteenth century, when American federalism was characterized by a general and generous protection of economic rights. Depending upon the quarter from which threats to these rights would

[13] See Jefferson's letter to Madison of Dec. 20, 1787. WRITINGS, VI, 387.
[14] WRITINGS, III, 320f.

arise, state or national measures would be declared unconstitutional.

John Marshall the Federalist who, in order to protect freedom, consolidated the federal structure after having initiated national judicial review, was a strong defender of property rights.[15] Having deemed the clause prohibiting the states from making laws impairing the obligation of contracts to be of "high value" when the Constitution was up for ratification,[16] later, "by employing a far broader conception of contract than had been prevalent in 1787, and by combining this conception with the principles of eighteenth-century natural law, he was able to make of the contract clause a mighty instrument for the protection of the rights of private property."[17] That protection was continued by his successor, the Republican and advocate of states' rights Roger B. Taney.[18]

The broad protection of property under the contract clause was later broadened under the provision that no person could be deprived of his life, liberty, and property without due process of law. And just as Marshall, in his desire to protect property, had interpreted the contract clause broadly, the Court, motivated by the same desire, enlarged the due process clause by shifting from its traditional procedural interpretation to a substantive one.[19] That interpretation which under the Fifth Amendment limited only the federal government, after the passage of the Fourteenth Amendment also limited the states.

When, toward the end of the nineteenth century, free enter-

---

[15] It ought not to be overlooked that Marshall advanced the doctrine of implied powers in *McCulloch* v. *Maryland,* 4 Wheat. 316 (1819), and that he gave the commerce clause a wide interpretation in *Gibbons* v. *Ogden,* 9 Wheat. 1 (1824), only *after* having established judicial review as an effective means of protecting the rights of the individual in *Marbury* v. *Madison,* 1 Cranch 137 (1803) and *after* having given the contract clause a broad interpretation for the sake of those rights in *Fletcher* v. *Peck,* 6 Cranch 87 (1810). This is perhaps symbolic of the fact that Marshall preferred the rights of the individual to those of the national government and that he considered the latter as a mere means to secure the former.

[16] Quoted by Edward S. Corwin, JOHN MARSHALL AND THE CONSTITUTION (New Haven, Conn., 1919), 151.

[17] Wright, CONTRACT CLAUSE OF THE CONSTITUTION, 28.

[18] *Ibid.,* 62f. For the thesis that Taney's interpretation of the contract clause fundamentally differed from that of Marshall, see Carl B. Swisher, ROGER B. TANEY (New York, 1935), chs. 17, 18.

[19] See the author's IN DEFENSE OF PROPERTY, 81f.

prise became challenged, the Court used the due process clauses not only for the protection of claims to, and ownership of, physical objects. Justice Peckham expressed a general view when he stated that "liberty" (as used in the Fifth and Fourteenth Amendments) "means, not only the right of the citizen to be free from the mere physical restraint of his person, as by incarceration, but the term is deemed to embrace the right of the citizen to be free in the enjoyment of all his faculties; to be free to use them in all lawful ways; to live and work where he will; to earn his livelihood by any lawful calling; to pursue any livelihood or avocation, and for that purpose to enter into all contracts which may be proper, necessary, and essential to his carrying out to a successful conclusion the purposes above mentioned."[20]

To conclude, we may say that during the nineteenth century broad bases were laid for the protection of economic rights. The Founders, perhaps taking for granted the right to the free acquisition of property, had confined themselves to expressly protecting physical property and claims thereto. However, when attempts to restrict such acquisition created doubts as to whether it was protected under the contract clause and the provision that no one could be deprived of his property without due process of law, the Supreme Court hastened to protect free enterprise by broadly interpreting the provision that no one can be deprived of his liberty without due process of law.[21]

The Court's protection of economic rights often demonstrated the usefulness of federalism. Wherever regulation of those rights would appear, it would be put in its place. When the states unduly interfered with economic rights, their acts were declared invalid on the grounds that they went beyond what the states were authorized to do under the Constitution; when the federal government unduly interfered with these rights, its acts would be declared invalid on the ground that they went beyond what the

---

[20] *Allgeyer* v. *Louisiana,* 165 U.S. 578, 589, 590 (1897). Nine years earlier, the Court had stated that the individual has the right to "his enjoyment upon terms of equality with all others in similar circumstances of the privilege of pursuing an ordinary calling or trade, and of acquiring, holding, and selling property": *Powell* v. *Pennsylvania,* 127 U.S. 678, 684 (1888).

[21] See Edward S. Corwin, THE CONSTITUTION AND WHAT IT MEANS TODAY (12th ed.; Princeton, N.J., 1958), 218f.

federal government was authorized to do. One often has the feeling that in their desire to protect economic freedom, the judges were literally fishing for a federal basis upon which to put their declaration of unconstitutionality. Dubious as such a procedure may have been at times, it should never be forgotten that it was a *constitution* they were expounding, that they stretched a constitutional means rather than the end in order to achieve the purpose of constitutional government—the freedom of the individual. To make sure that people would remain aware of the limited nature of American government, the Court would go out of its way to emphasize federalism as a limitation upon government. In this endeavor, it would not shy away from coining a redundant doctrine such as that of "dual federalism."[22]

However, the coining of that doctrine was indicative of the twilight of federalism. Had federalism remained strong, there would hardly have been a need for emphasizing "dual" federalism, since federalism implies dualism. As a matter of fact, when the doctrine of dual federalism was created, federalism was already about to wither away. The term "dual federalism" was used to prolong the life of a concept which was receiving mortal blows in its duel with nationalism. But this propping up of a dying concept was of no avail. Soon, "The Passing of Dual Federalism" was announced.[23]

Since originally federalism was to a large extent conceived as a means for the protection of economic rights, the question arises whether its decline was connected with a decrease of the desire for a protection of those rights from governmental control. This was, indeed, the case. During the twentieth century, the American outlook upon freedom and government changed. Whereas previously Americans had considered that government best which governed least, they increasingly desired active government. Traditional freedom, implying no interference with economic life, was replaced by a "New Freedom," suggesting such interference.[24]

[22] See Alfred H. Kelly and Winfred A. Harbison, THE AMERICAN CONSTITUTION—ITS ORIGINS AND DEVELOPMENT (rev. ed.; New York, 1963), 689ff., 744f., 790f., 794.

[23] Edward S. Corwin, "The Passing of Dual Federalism," VIRGINIA LAW REVIEW, XXXVI (1950), 1.

[24] Woodrow Wilson, THE NEW FREEDOM (New York, 1913). Cf. also the author's IN DEFENSE OF PROPERTY, 4, 199.

This new trend decreased the popularity of federalism with its weak, passive type of government. The "New Freedom" became matched by a new federalism, characterized by an increasing abolition of the balance between states' rights and federal power through the co-operation of state and national governments and the consolidation of power in the latter.

REGULATION OF ECONOMIC RIGHTS UNDER THE NEW FEDERALISM OF MODERN DEMOCRATIC GOVERNMENT

Although the nineteenth century was characterized by a protection of economic rights, the forces favoring a regulation of those rights had remained alive. Madison's statement in the tenth essay of *The Federalist,* that "the most common and durable source of factions has been the various and unequal distribution of property," augured ill for the protection of property, indicating, as it was, that the United States would not be spared factions along economic lines. Taney's decision in the *Charles River Bridge* case could conceivably support the argument of those who favored a more restricted protection of vested rights for the sake of the community.[25] By the end of the century, the far-reaching protection of property which was part of the common-law tradition had decreased.[26] Legislation providing for an income tax was passed. Infringements upon property were matched by those upon free enterprise. From the 1840s, state laws regulating child labor and the employment of women were passed. Later on, such laws restricted the employment of men.[27] Owing to economic, political and social changes,[28] pressure for governmental control over the

---

[25] See *supra,* 21f.

[26] Cf. for instance the shift in adjudication concerning spite walls and spite fences from *Rideout* v. *Knox,* 148 Mass. 368, 19 N.E. 390 (1889) to *Bordeaux* v. *Greene,* 22 Mont. 254, 56 Pac. 218 (1899). William L. Prosser, HANDBOOK OF THE LAW OF TORTS (St. Paul, Minn., 1941), 33, contains a list of state laws against spite fences and spite walls.

[27] See Edwin E. Witte, "Labor Legislation," ENCYCLOPEDIA OF THE SOCIAL SCIENCES, VIII, 660.

[28] The impact of immigration since the 1890s ought not to be overlooked. It is interesting to note that in the wake of this new immigration there was discarded, aside from federalism, another American institution for the protection of the rights

economy mounted. By the end of the nineteenth century, there was a general awareness that free property and free enterprise were in for serious challenges.

Under these conditions federalism, conceived as a bulwark for the protection of economic freedom, lost much of its *raison d'être*. It could hardly fulfill its function to protect economic rights in an atmosphere that no longer seemed to care for protection of those rights, the more so since during the nineteenth century it had become weakened as an institution owing to a continuous decrease of states' rights. That decrease already can be discerned before the Civil War when the nature of American federalism was still a subject of debate. The outcome of the Civil War ended that debate. The nationalists emerged as victors. National power increased as the twentieth century approached.[29] In that century, America entered another "critical period" of her history. Unlike the critical period of which John Fiske wrote,[30] that period is not critical on account of the sovereignty of the states, but on account of the disappearance of states' rights. Like its predecessor prior to the adoption of the Constitution, it is characterized by an increasing interference with economic freedom. It constitutes a constitutional revolution that can well be termed a reversal of the revolution of 1787.

In 1819, John Marshall suggested a flexible interpretation of the Constitution.[31] Nationalists during the "Progressive Era" made the most of this passage, overlooking the fact that the Federalist Marshall was interested in strengthening the national government mainly in order to protect property.[32] When American

---

of the individual, namely, judicial review. Characteristically, Justice Oliver W. Holmes, one of the originators of sociological jurisprudence, while opposed to testing laws that corresponded "with the actual feelings and demands of the community" (THE COMMON LAW [Boston, 1881], 41ff.), favored the exercise of judicial review for the sake of national unity: "I do not think the United States would come to an end if we lost our power to declare an Act of Congress void. I do think the Union would be imperiled if we could not make that declaration as to the laws of the several States." ("Law and the Court," COLLECTED LEGAL PAPERS [New York, 1920], 295f.). Holmes's attitude favoring the will of the majority over the individual is thus matched by one favoring national power over states' rights. Cf. *infra*, 153ff., 265.

[29] Cf. Mason, "The Nature of the Union Reconsidered," 502.
[30] John Fiske, THE CRITICAL PERIOD OF AMERICAN HISTORY (Boston, 1888).
[31] *McCulloch* v. *Maryland*, 4 Wheat. 316, 407, 515 (1819).
[32] See *supra*, 69. Characteristically, Albert J. Beveridge, THE LIFE OF JOHN

popular government, traditionally favoring the individual, became one favoring the masses, when the United States came to be considered a democracy rather than a republic, the ethnical melting pot was complemented by a federal one in which the protection of economic rights melted away.[33] Economic rights and federalism, considered an end of government and a means for achieving that end ever since the adoption of the Constitution, declined. Whereas "during the 65 years following the Civil War, economic liberty emerged as a star set high in the constellation of judicial values,"[34] later, that liberty became submerged by a flood of legislation which was prompted by the everlasting American desire to help the weak. The decline of economic rights can be noted quite generally on the state and federal levels, as a few examples concerning price control, working hours and wages, private property, and vested interests, will show.

Ever since the decision in *Munn v. Illinois* (1876) permitted state price control of business affected with a public interest, the Supreme Court, by substituting its own standard of reasonableness for that of legislatures bent on regulation, narrowed down controls and virtually confined them to public utilities. Although after 1876 more and more businesses came under price control—another demonstration of how regulation spreads if permitted once[35]—it cannot be denied that control was the exception. The case of *Nebbia* v. *New York,* decided in 1934, completely changed this situation. "The whole structure of economic freedom built on judicial interpretation of *Munn* v. *Illinois* collapsed with

---

MARSHALL (Boston, 1916–19), concludes his biography with a chapter entitled "The Supreme Conservative" rather than "The Supreme Nationalist." Marshall's desire to protect property rights was evident throughout his life, from Shays's Rebellion to the Virginia Constitutional Convention. He wanted a strong national government for the protection of those rights. See Edward S. Corwin, JOHN MARSHALL AND THE CONSTITUTION, 147ff., 173ff. Considering the more perfect Union a means for the protection of property, Marshall thus is a follower of Hamilton. Cf. the author's "Hamilton's Concept of Free Government," NEW YORK HISTORY, XXXVIII (1957), 351.

[33] There is a familiar ring to the term "federal republic" which is absent from the term "federal democracy."

[34] Paul G. Kauper, FRONTIERS OF CONSTITUTIONAL LIBERTY (Ann Arbor, Mich., 1956), 33.

[35] Cf. the author's IN DEFENSE OF PROPERTY, ch. 4.

a thud."[36] The Court not only upheld a statute fixing a minimum retail price in an industry that by accepted standards did not qualify as a public utility, but also diluted the test of reasonableness as a limitation upon regulation by holding that the legislative standard of reasonableness ought to be accepted. It "in effect rejected the whole theory of the limits imposed on governmental price control by the due process clauses which had been gradually developed during a period of more than fifty years."[37] It "calmly discarded its decisions of fifty years," protecting economic freedom, even without paying "those decisions the obsequious respect of a funeral oration."[38] "The statement that one has dedicated his property to a public use" was said to be "merely another way of saying that if one embarks in a business which public interest demands shall be regulated, he must know regulation will ensue," since "an industry, for adequate reason, is subject to control for the public good," as defined by the legislature.[39]

The *Nebbia* decision permitted not only state control of retail prices, soon to be complemented by the admission of the states' right to fix fees, regulate rates, etc.,[40] but also opened the way for national legislation to that effect. After the *Nebbia* case, the federal government regulated the dairy industry with a plan similar in purpose and method to that of New York, a plan which it later applied to the bituminous coal industry. Both types of national regulation were held not to violate the due process clause of the Fifth Amendment.[41]

The Court's acquiescence in legislation regulating prices, fees,

[36] Kauper, FRONTIERS OF CONSTITUTIONAL LIBERTY, 34.

[37] Henry Rottschaefer, THE CONSTITUTION AND SOCIO-ECONOMIC CHANGE (Ann Arbor, Mich., 1948), 158.

[38] The Hon. James M. Beck. CONGRESSIONAL RECORD, Mar. 24, 1934, p. 5480 (unofficial paging), as quoted by Edward S. Corwin, THE CONSTITUTION AND WHAT IT MEANS TODAY, 255.

[39] *Nebbia* v. *New York*, 291 U.S. 502, 534, 536 (1934). Cf. also Henry Rottschaefer, "The Field of Governmental Price Control," YALE LAW JOURNAL, XXXV (1926), 438; Walton H. Hamilton, "Affection with Public Interest," YALE LAW JOURNAL, XXXIX (1930), 1089; Robert L. Hale, "The Constitution and the Price System: Some Reflections on *Nebbia* v. *New York*," COLUMBIA LAW REVIEW, XXXIV (1934), 401.

[40] See Kauper, FRONTIERS OF CONSTITUTIONAL LIBERTY, 35ff; Rottschaefer, THE CONSTITUTION AND SOCIO-ECONOMIC CHANGE, 160ff.

[41] *United States* v. *Rock Royal Co-op, Inc.*, 307 U.S. 533 (1939); *Sunshine Anthracite Coal Co.* v. *Adkins*, 310 U.S. 381 (1940).

rates, etc., was complemented by its admission of laws regulating working hours and wages. Justice Holmes's assertion that "the Fourteenth Amendment does not enact Mr. Herbert Spencer's Social Statics,"[42] expressed in dissent to a decision invalidating a New York statute limiting working hours on the grounds that it deprived employers and employees of freedom of contract, augured ill for freedom of contract. After a decade the Court sustained without apparent effort a general ten-hour law of the state of Oregon.[43] In the same year, the Court upheld the Adamson Act enacted by Congress which established the standard workday at eight hours. The due process clauses no longer could be relied upon for protection of freedom of contract as far as working hours were concerned.

The same is true with respect to minimum wage laws. Whereas such laws were generally declared incompatible with the due process clauses until the coming of the New Deal,[44] the situation changed after 1933. In 1923, an act of Congress providing for minimum wages for women was held to be an unconstitutional restriction of freedom of contract.[45] Similarly, the Court as late as 1936 invalidated a New York statute on the grounds that the state was "without power by any form of legislation to prohibit, change or nullify contracts between employers and adult women workers as to the amount of wages to be paid."[46] However, the year after, the Supreme Court—under threat of being packed—sustained a minimum wage law for women and redefined liberty to mean "liberty in a social organization which requires the protection of law against the evils which menace the health, safety, morals and welfare of the people."[47] A few years later, the Court upheld the Fair Labor Standards Act providing for minimum wages for adults and minors, as well as men and women, stating that "it is no longer open to question that the fixing of a minimum

---

[42] Lochner v. New York, 198 U.S. 45, 75–6 (1905).

[43] Bunting v. Oregon, 243 U.S. 426 (1917).

[44] Rottschaefer, THE CONSTITUTION AND SOCIO-ECONOMIC CHANGE, 170.

[45] Adkins v. Children's Hospital of District of Columbia, 261 U.S. 525 (1923).

[46] Moorhead v. New York, 298 U.S. 587, 611 (1936).

[47] West Coast Hotel Company v. Parrish, 300 U.S. 379, 391 (1937). The Court continued: "Liberty under the Constitution is thus necessarily subject to the restraints of due process, and regulation which is reasonable in relation to its subject and is adopted in the interests of the community is due process."

wage is within the legislative power and that the bare fact of its exercise is not a denial of due process under the Fifth more than under the Fourteenth Amendment."[48]

Restrictions of the freedom of contract were complemented by laws infringing upon property and vested rights. As a result of the Depression, quite a few laws affecting the fulfillment of contracts were passed. For instance, state moratory laws as well as the first and second Frazier-Lemke Acts sought to relieve a particular class of debtors. These laws were attacked as interfering with the contract clause, respectively the due process clause of the Fifth Amendment. However, the Court decided that the state had "authority to safeguard the vital interests of its people" even though this involved the modification or abrogation of existing contracts. It maintained that there is implied in every contract a clause reserving to the state the right to protect those interests and stressed the need for preventing "the perversion of the [contract] clause through its use as an instrument to throttle the capacity of the States to protect their fundamental interests,"[49] interests that were those of the public power rather than those of the individual. The Court also decided that federal moratory laws were constitutional.[50] This admission was later complemented by decisions concerning the federal power of eminent domain which for all practical purposes eliminated the "public use" concept as a limitation upon the power of condemnation,[51] and by the Gold Clause Cases which marked a further subordination of property rights to the fiscal powers of the federal government.[52]

In summary, it may be said that during the New Deal, attempts to restrict economic freedom, which had increased since the end of the nineteenth century, had become crowned by suc-

[48] *U.S.* v. *Darby,* 312 U.S. 100, 125 (1941).
[49] *Home Building & Loan Assn.* v. *Blaisdell,* 290 U.S. 398, 434, 444 (1934). This is, indeed, a far cry from John Marshall's broad interpretation of the contract clause in *Fletcher* v. *Peck,* 6 Cranch 87 (1810), where he invoked the doctrine of implied contract in order to protect the individual's rights against the legislature.
[50] *Wright* v. *Vinton Branch of the Mountain Trust Bank of Roanoke,* 300 U.S. 440 (1937).
[51] *U.S. ex rel. T.V.A.* v. *Welch,* 327 U.S. 546 (1946); *Berman* v. *Parker,* 348 U.S. 26 (1955).
[52] *Norman* v. *Baltimore & Ohio R.R. Co.,* 294 U.S. 240 (1935); *Perry* v. *U.S.,* 294 U.S. 300 (1935). Cf. Rottschaefer, THE CONSTITUTION AND SOCIO-ECONOMIC CHANGE, 197ff.

cess that was perhaps greater than was desired by those who during the "Progressive Period" had advocated certain controls over economic rights and proclaimed a "New Freedom." With a good deal of justification, one author expressed doubts whether the Supreme Court could any longer be considered a bulwark against arbitrary infringements upon property, saying that "whether completely illegitimized or still claiming some modicum of protection as a stepchild, the laissez-faire philosophy as epitomized in the concept of economic liberty is no longer a substantial factor in constitutional interpretation," and that there was "ground to suppose that economic liberty has been completely blotted out of the category of protected constitutional rights."[53] Constitutional provisions for the protection of economic freedom were reinterpreted. Their individualistic meaning was replaced by a more collectivistic one. An unequivocal protection of property under the contract clause was denounced as "perverted"[54] because it appeared to be incompatible with the right of the majority to provide for its own good. The protection of free property and free enterprise under the due process clauses was considered out of tune with the right of the majority to give due process "an affirmative thrust"—a thrust toward the control of economic rights.[55]

As was shown, the regulation of those rights was admitted on the state and federal levels. The distinction between the state and federal governments became blurred. Once the protection of economic freedom had become undesirable, the means for such protection—federalism—could hardly be expected to survive. Attempts to stop economic regulation by invoking the federal principle were doomed as is demonstrated by the treatment of the Tenth Amendment. In 1918, the Court, outlawing federal legislation regulating child labor under the commerce clause, admonished

---

[53] Kauper, FRONTIERS OF CONSTITUTIONAL LIBERTY 36, 37. Cf. also Justice Douglas's opinion for the Court in *Olsen v. Nebraska ex rel. Western Reference & Bond Association, Inc.*, 313 U.S. 236 (1941) and Justice Black's opinion for the Court in *Lincoln Federal Labor Union v. Northwestern Iron & Metal Co.*, 335 U.S. 525 (1949).

[54] See the quotation in the *Blaisdell* case, *supra*, 77.

[55] Cf. Arthur S. Miller, "An Affirmative Thrust to Due Process of Law?" GEORGE WASHINGTON LAW REVIEW, XXX (1962), 399.

the people that "it must never be forgotten that the nation is made up of States . . . and to them and to the people the powers not expressly delegated to the national government are reserved."[56] This doctrine of dual federalism was invoked in a series of decisions upsetting New Deal legislation. But the battle was lost. Justice Stone, after having denounced what his biographer referred to as a "judicial perversion"[57] of American federalism[58] and after having received a negative answer from—of all people!—Charles A. Beard to his question whether the framers of the Tenth Amendment "intended to reserve powers of the States to constitute a limitation of the power of Congress,"[59] wrote in 1941 for a unanimous Court that the Tenth Amendment did not deprive the national government of the power to regulate economic rights.[60] The regulation of these rights had reached its final stage. Having started out in the states, it soon began in the nation, growing on both levels. This development could hardly have been different in view of the fact that on the state as well as the federal level, American government had become more and more democratic.

The founders of the United States had provided that state and federal governments had to be republican. Identical forms of government, they felt, would facilitate the achievement of the general aim of the protection of the rights of the individual, including his economic rights. They overlooked the fact that similarity of institutions can also have its drawbacks. Although it is probable that factions in one part of a federal state will be neutralized by those in other parts—as Madison had hoped in the tenth essay of *The Federalist*—this need not be so. In our time of easy communication and mass democracy there is a good chance that a similarity of forms of government will facilitate the spreading of factions from one part of the federation to others until these factions control the whole. This has happened in the United

---

[56] *Hammer* v. *Dagenhart,* 247 U.S. 251, 275 (1918).

[57] Alpheus T. Mason, "Must We Continue the States Rights Debate?" RUTGERS LAW REVIEW, XVIII (1963), 70.

[58] Dissent in *United States* v. *Butler,* 297 U.S. 1, 78 (1936).

[59] Letter of Apr. 15, 1936. Quoted in Alpheus T. Mason, HARLAN FISKE STONE (New York, 1956), 410.

[60] *United States* v. *Darby,* 312 U.S. 100, 123–24 (1941).

States with respect to economic rights. The quest for their regulation first gripped a few states, where in the beginning it was checked by the Supreme Court, which acted as the representative of the Union and of the majority of the states. Once that quest had spread to more and more states, it became harder and harder for the Court to annul state regulation, even though as the representative of the Union it could still do so. Under increasing pressure from a growing number of states, the Court was likely to permit such regulation. Once that step had been taken, regulation of economic rights on the federal level could hardly be denied. Democracy, having become palatable to the American people,[61] made obstruction of the general will which was in favor of regulating economic rights improbable. The states and the federal government, instead of checking one another for the sake of the protection of economic freedom, more or less unconsciously came to collaborate in the regulation of that freedom. And whereas their collaboration was originally unplanned and not institutionalized, the awareness that their respective regulations pursued identical aims soon resulted in a desire for planned and institutionalized co-operation.

The rise of "co-operative federalism" thus occurred at the time when the regulation of economic rights came to the fore.[62] Since state as well as federal operations were to a large extent concerned with the regulation of those rights, it is not surprising that co-operative federalism became concerned with such regulation.

Although some co-operation between the state and federal governments—going beyond that expressly prescribed by the Constitution—had existed since the founding of the Republic,[63] co-operative federalism as we know it, oriented primarily toward economic rights,[64] came about "in the 1930's with the inauguration

[61] The word "democracy" had for a long time the connotation it had for the Founding Fathers, namely, that of radical democracy or unlimited majority rule.
[62] The first comprehensive study of "Federal–State Cooperation in the United States" is Jane P. Clark, THE RISE OF A NEW FEDERALISM (New York, 1938). A recent article on the subject is Richard H. Leach, "Intergovernmental Cooperation and American Federalism," in Dietze (ed.), ESSAYS ON THE AMERICAN CONSTITUTION (Englewood Cliffs, N.J., 1964), 125.
[63] See Clark, RISE OF A NEW FEDERALISM; Louis W. Koenig, "Federal and State Cooperation under the Constitution," MICHIGAN LAW REVIEW, XXXVI (1938), 752.
[64] M. J. C. Vile, THE STRUCTURE OF AMERICAN FEDERALISM (London, 1961), 194,

of the great new range of social security and social welfare services operated jointly by the Federal and State governments."[65] It
came about on a large scale, ranging from medical care and aid to
the aged, the blind, dependent children, and disabled persons, to
employment security, the building of hospitals and schools, and
low-cost housing.

One would assume that "co-operative" federalism implies participation by the state and federal governments as about equal
partners. However, this is hardly the case. The federal government has considerably greater weight in the undertaking on account of grants-in-aid it pays to the states for certain projects.
Most of these grants are conditional. This resulted in the establishment of a set of interrelationships between state and federal administrative machineries, with the federal administration
setting up standards to which the states must conform and requir-
ing state personnel engaged in such programs to be chosen and
controlled according to federal civil service standards. Although
federal officials on the whole have approached their supervisory
task "as a co-operative one,"[66] and have cared for "substantial
conformity" with federal requirements rather than detailed com-
pliance,[67] even permitting the states to retain practices that were
strongly disapproved by the federal agency,[68] it can be said that
the program of federal grants-in-aid and subsidies has resulted in a
certain dependence of the states upon the federal government.
Even though many people will not admit that "federal subsidies
are a vicious influence that may ultimately ruin the nation,"[69] it
can hardly be denied that co-operative federalism, being another

---

writes: "The term 'co-operative federalism' comes from an emphasis upon the new
common programmes of Federal and State governments particularly in the fields of
social legislation. It is to some extent a misleading term, because it emphasizes one
new aspect of federalism and ignores the still important areas of American
government which are not co-operative in this way."

[65] *Ibid.*, 160.

[66] *Ibid.*, 162.

[67] R. Raup, INTERGOVERNMENTAL RELATIONS IN SOCIAL WELFARE (Minneapolis,
1952), 84f.

[68] Francis E. Rourke, INTERGOVERMENTAL RELATIONS IN EMPLOYMENT SECURITY
(Minneapolis, 1952), 30ff.

[69] Leonard D. White, THE STATES AND THE NATION (Baton Rouge, La., 1953), 78,
quoting Governor William M. Tuck in a dispatch from Los Angeles, Sept. 29,
1948.

example of "the march of power to Washington,"[70] has been a step toward the elimination of federalism.[71]

In 1938, when much regulation of economic rights had become accepted and more was still to come, a member of the Supreme Court of Switzerland wrote that if the fight of American libertarians was a death-struggle, it was also a death-struggle of the federal state.[72] A year later, Harold Laski, the ideologist of the British Labour Party and modern English observer of the United States, told Americans: "The epoch of federalism is over . . . It is insufficiently positive in character; it does not provide for sufficient rapidity of action; it inhibits the emergence of the necessary standards of uniformity; it relies upon compacts and compromises which take insufficient account of the urgent category of time; it leaves the backward areas in restraint, at once parasitic and poisonous, on those which seek to move forward; at least its psychological results, especially in an age of crisis, are depressing to a democracy that needs the drama of positive achievement to retain its faith."[73] These statements indicate the changes that have come about in the United States as a result of the advance of democratic, as distinguished from republican, government. Whereas the latter, a limited popular government of reasoned compacts and compromises which refrained from regulating economic rights, had been prevalent from the founding of the Republic to the twentieth century, the former, an unrestricted majority rule of organic growth which is filled with emotion and out to regulate these rights, became characteristic of the twen-

---

[70] White, THE STATES AND THE NATION, 1.

[71] Roscoe Drummond, "Are We Maintaining Our Federal System?" STATE GOVERNMENT, XXII (Special Supplement, Jan., 1949), 1, writes: "In point of fact, our federal system no longer exists and has no more chance of being brought back into existence than an apple pie can be put back on the apple tree." Although White, THE STATES AND THE NATION, 3, takes issue with Drummond, he voices concern: "A federal system implies a partnership, all members of which are effective players on the team and all of whom retain the capacity for independent action. It does not imply a system of collaboration in which one of the collaborators is annihilated by the other." Cf. Austin F. Macdonald, FEDERAL AID (New York, 1928); Henry J. Bittermann, STATE AND FEDERAL GRANTS-IN-AID (New York, 1938).

[72] Hans Huber, "Ueber Foederalismus," NEUE SCHWEIZER RUNDSCHAU, VI (N.S., 1938), 243.

[73] Harold J. Laski, "The Obsolescence of Federalism," NEW REPUBLIC, XCVIII (1939), 367.

tieth century. Governmental passivity, evident throughout the period when power was fundamentally divided between the state and federal governments, became replaced by governmental activity when power became concentrated in Washington. The combination of federalism and economic freedom has become replaced by one of national power and what has been called the "D.D.T. of federalism"[74]—planning.

THE DECLINE OF ECONOMIC FREEDOM AND FEDERALISM AS A CHALLENGE TO FREE GOVERNMENT

The wane of cherished principles such as economic freedom and federalism poses a dilemma for many Americans who feel that their way of life is being turned upside down. To the position advanced by the advocates of democratic action for the sake of the masses that the "negative" state of the past century, characterized by laissez faire, must be replaced by a positive one, characterized by regulation of the economy, those favoring constitutional restraint for the sake of the individual reply that *laissez faire* is better than *faîtes faire,* maintaining that a positive and progressive government can only be one that permits the free exercise of economic rights, that governmental activity in the regulation of those rights is something negative because it induces people to be passive.[75] The argument that the national government should promote social welfare by regulating economic freedom is countered by the assertion that more power for the protection of that freedom ought to be left to the states. A constitutional drama is taking place today in the United States, the importance

[74] Quoted by Vile, STRUCTURE OF AMERICAN FEDERALISM, 185. Vile states that "economic planning may be the 'D.D.T. of federalism,' but not the type of economic planning at present operated in the United States." With these words of an English observer, Americans—having grown up in a federal rather than unitary tradition—might take issue. Cf. George C. S. Benson, THE NEW CENTRALIZATION (New York, 1941); James Jackson Kilpatrick, THE SOVEREIGN STATES (Chicago, 1957); Felix Morley, FREEDOM AND FEDERALISM (Chicago, 1959); Walter Thompson, FEDERAL CENTRALIZATION (New York, 1923).

[75] These positions are taken, respectively, by modern and classical liberals. Cf. Mason, FREE GOVERNMENT IN THE MAKING (1949), ch. 16 entitled "Liberal Variations." In the 3d ed. (1965), that title is no longer used.

and complexity of which should not be underestimated. In a way, it has a familiar ring to the student of American constitutionalism. Just as in 1787 federalism—implying a more *perfect* Union, i.e., a stronger federal government—was desired by those favoring economic freedom because that freedom was restricted by democratic majorities in the states, today federalism—implying a more *federal* Union, i.e., a weaker national government—is desired by them because economic rights are curtailed by the democratic majority of the nation. And whereas the advocates of economic freedom scored a victory in 1787 when the forces of egalitarian democracy had taken hold of some states, it is doubtful whether they can make their ideas prevail today when those forces are running the whole nation. In modern America, the advocates of economic freedom, federalism, and constitutional government seem to fight a losing battle. For them, no happy ending seems to be in sight this time.

It is against this background that we must view the civil rights issue. That issue is not merely due to racial prejudices. Living in an ethnical melting pot, Americans are probably less prejudiced than many other nations which, not confronted with a similar problem, are all too ready to criticize the United States. Robert von Mohl once said that slavery was America's misfortune rather than her fault.[76] The same could be said of today's segregation. The "American Dilemma" of which Myrdal spoke twenty years ago[77] goes beyond the problem of racial equality. It includes such problems as economic freedom and federalism.[78] All these values, federalism and economic freedom as well as racial equality, are dear to Americans. It is the conflict between those values rather than racial prejudice that makes the civil rights issue delicate and complicated. Traditional, cherished ideals seem to be pitted against one another. Many opponents of civil rights laws are

[76] "German Criticism of Mr. Justice Story's Commentaries on the Constitution of the United States," AMERICAN JURIST, XV (1836), 8f. This is a translation of Mohl's review in KRITISCHE ZEITSCHRIFT FÜR RECHTSWISSENSCHAFT UND GESETZGEBUNG DES AUSLANDES, VII (1835), 1.

[77] Gunnar Myrdal, AN AMERICAN DILEMMA, THE NEGRO PROBLEM AND MODERN DEMOCRACY (New York, 1944).

[78] Myrdal's second book on the United States is called CHALLENGE TO AFFLUENCE (New York, 1963). Restrictions upon economic freedom, as they are suggested by Myrdal, constitute too dangerous a challenge to affluence to be ventured upon.

not opposed to desegregation. They are merely afraid of a further increase of national power and of further curtailments of economic rights.[79] In view of the traditional prestige of these factors in American life, their attitude can hardly surprise us.

A hundred years ago, the classic, *A Treatise on the Constitutional Limitations which Rest upon the Legislative Power of the States of the American Union,* was published.[80] Defending economic freedom against democratic majorities in the states, this book reasserted the ideals of the Philadelphia Convention. In view of the increase of national power since the Civil War and the increasing curtailments of economic freedom by the national government, one is tempted to argue that the limitations of which it spoke would apply to Congress *a fortiori.* However, no classic on the constitutional limitations which rest upon the power of the national government of the American Union has so far come forth, and in view of the enormous powers that government has assumed, it appears doubtful whether it ever will.

The American disposition to help the weak, traditionally a matter of private concern, has become institutionalized. Voluntary action has been replaced by governmental activity. But governmental activity is governmental command: care for the masses, achieved through social legislation, implies infringements upon the individual's rights, especially those of an economic nature.[81] Having become a major end of government, care-taking resulted in the decline of federalism. Whether, as Laski thought, this democratic drama has mastered the crisis of our age or whether it has brought about a constitutional crisis of the first order, is the question. We ask this question not only out of an awareness that democratic government is not necessarily constitutional government, but also out of doubts whether in a modern

[79] Cf. Senator Goldwater's statement on the Civil Rights Bill of June 18, 1964. CONGRESSIONAL RECORD, CX (1964), 13825. See also *supra,* 63f., *infra,* 108ff.

[80] Thomas M. Cooley, A TREATISE ON THE CONSTITUTIONAL LIMITATIONS WHICH REST UPON THE LEGISLATIVE POWER OF THE STATES OF THE AMERICAN UNION (Boston, 1868).

[81] William E. Rappard, DIE BUNDESVERFASSUNG DER SCHWEIZERISCHEN EIDGENOSSENSCHAFT 1848–1948 (Zürich, 1948), 428, comments on National Socialism: "This experience has shown us the abyss into which humanity is pushed by the State, if the State is burdened by the individual with all functions, duties and social responsibilities, but reciprocates by assuming all rights, of which it deprives men under the pretense of serving and being of use to them."

nation, genuine democracy can exist without federalism. We wonder whether the democratic drama of which Laski spoke, implying an abolition of federalism, has resulted not only in a constitutional crisis, but also in a democratic tragedy.

Leonard D. White, one of the few American scholars who try to halt the increase of national power, favors a strengthening of the states because "traditional forms of democracy are jeopardized by the tendency to remove decisions on public policy and its application from the localities and states to Washington."[82] White, when saying that traditional forms of democracy are jeopardized, does not specify whether he is worried over the survival of freedom or over that of popular government. He is right in either case.

Let us consider the former alternative first. It is indeed an important question whether freedom can exist in modern nations without federalism or some kind of decentralization. Americans gave a classic answer in the negative when they founded their Republic. A loose confederation like that under the Articles of Confederation was all the revolutionaries were willing to risk, feeling that only a high degree of decentralization would secure freedom under popular government. Even when the Philadephia Convention, reacting against democratic excesses and their resultant oppressions of property rights in the states, established a more perfect Union, it did not establish a unitary, but only a federal form of government. The former was felt to be incompatible with free government.

The French pursued a different course in their democratic revolution. Instead of continuing to permit a certain degree of local and regional independence as it had persisted under the *ancien régime*,[83] they abolished such independence in what was referred to as the first demonstration of radical democracy in Europe.[84] In 1789, the National Assembly dealt a death-blow to the provinces. After the establishment of the Republic in 1792,

---

[82] White, THE STATES AND THE NATION, 5.

[83] See Hedwig Hintze, STAATSEINHEIT UND FÖDERALISMUS IM ALTEN FRANKREICH UND IN DER REVOLUTION (Stuttgart, 1928), 9ff., 48ff. The survival of viable political centers, especially in the provinces, prompts her to state that France on the eve of the Revolution was a "territorially united" rather than a "centralized" state. *Ibid.*, 60.

[84] Anton Philipp von Segesser, POLITIK DER SCHWEIZ (Zürich, 1937), 30.

the last remnants of autonomy which had managed to survive in the communes were done away with.[85] The plan of Abbé Sieyès, first voiced at the beginning of the Revolution,[86] was realized. Bertrand Barère expressed a general feeling when in 1793 he told the Convention: "Unity is your basic maxim. Unity is your defense. Unity is your blessing."[87]

If we compare the French Revolution, characterized by democratic radicalism[88] with its quest for centralization, by bloodshed and infringements upon liberty and property, with the American Revolution, characterized by democratic restraint with its desire for federalism, and a protection of the individual's life, liberty and property, then the value of federalism for freedom suggests itself strongly.[89] This impression is enhanced by a comparison between the turbulent political development in France which often challenged the rights of the individual, and the quiet evolution in America which in general has been conducive to a protection of those rights.

The radically democratic and anti-federalist[90] French Revolution did not only result in an insecurity to life, liberty and prop-

---

[85] See Hintze, STAATSEINHEIT UND FÖDERALISMUS, 172ff.

[86] Significantly, the author of QU'EST-CE QUE LE TIERS-ÉTAT? advocated centralization under a monarch. Contesting the arguments advanced by Brissot and Condorcet, that the will of the French people ought to be distinguished from the will of their representatives, Sieyès voiced fear that France might be split up into "innumerable small democracies which, like the thirteen or fourteen American States, would join a general confederation. France is no democracy and ought not to be made into one. She is no federal state, composed of a variety of republics . . . France is one single whole and shall remain so." DIRE DE L'ABBÉ SIEYÈS (Paris, n.d.), 10, as quoted in Hintze, STAATSEINHEIT UND FÖDERALISMUS, 182f. Perhaps here is a classic indication of the theory that egalitarianism can best be promoted through centralization and one-man rule, a principle many socialists believe in.

[87] He added that whereas the Republic was unitary and indivisible, the kings hostile to her were, to their disadvantage, federated [fédéralisés]. MONITEUR, XVIII, 516ff., as quoted by Hintze, STAATSEINHEIT UND FÖDERALISMUS, 473.

[88] European authors often use the term "democratism" for "radical democracy." Cf. Gonzague de Reynold, LA DÉMOCRATIE ET LA SUISSE (Bienne, Switzerland, 1934), xxvii. For a recent use of the term "radical democracy" see Carl J. Friedrich, "Nationaler und Internationaler Föderalismus in Theorie und Praxis" POLITISCHE VIERTELJAHRESSCHRIFT, V (1964), 174.

[89] Cf. Wilhelm Röpke, CIVITAS HUMANA (English trans.; London, 1948), 23f.; JENSEITS VON ANGEBOT UND NACHFRAGE (Zürich, 1958), 192f., 312; Martin Usteri, THEORIE DES BUNDESSTAATES (Zürich, 1954), 347; see also, H. Nef, "Demokratie und Richtigkeit des Rechts," ZENTRALBLATT FÜR STAATS–UND GEMEINDEVERWALTUNG (1947), 377.

[90] See Georg Messmer, FOEDERALISMUS UND DEMOKRATIE (Zürich, 1946), 131ff.

erty, but also in a replacement of republican by monarchical government. In contrast to the American development which never seriously challenged popular government, that of France was bare of democratic continuity.[91] It has been asserted that during the Revolution the French Assembly followed "the monarchical tradition and the old royal policy toward levelling and centralization."[92] Perhaps it ought to be examined whether centralization has been destructive not only of freedom with its inherent recognition of the distinctive features of the human being, but also of popular government.

To begin with, it appears doubtful whether or not the modern state, large as it is, can be a democracy in the original sense where the rulers are about identical with the ruled. This kind of democracy existed from antiquity to the French Revolution, in the Greek city states as well as in the rural and urban communities of the Middle Ages. As late as the eighteenth century, writers, irrespective of whether they were leaning toward constitutional government or sheer majority rule, maintained that the more direct democracy was, the more genuine it was. Montesquieu felt that a truly democratic government was possible only in small communities.[93] Rousseau, generally considered the father of modern democracy, agreed with him.[94]

Similar ideas were accepted in America. The Mayflower Compact under which but a handful of men set up government for themselves, to this day has been cherished as an example of genuine self-government. The spirit of the frontier kept alive the idea that direct democracy was genuine democracy.[95] The introduction of representation did not change that opinion. After Inde-

[91] See Maurice Hauriou, PRÉCIS DE DROIT CONSTITUTIONNEL (2d ed.; Paris, 1929), 293ff.

[92] Hintze, STAATSEINHEIT UND FÖDERALISMUS, 184.

[93] See SPIRIT OF THE LAWS, I, xliii, 120f.; Emile Durkheim, MONTESQUIEU AND ROUSSEAU (Ann Arbor, Mich., 1960), 26; Werner Stark, MONTESQUIEU (London, 1960), 70ff. Cf. Werner Kaegi, "Der Typus des Kleinstaates im europäischen Denken," NEUE SCHWEIZER RUNDSCHAU, VI (N.S., 1938), 257.

[94] CONTRAT SOCIAL, Bk. II, ch. 9; Bk. III, chs. 2 and 4; GOUVERNEMENT DE POLOGNE, ch. 5. C. E. Vaughan (ed.), THE POLITICAL WRITINGS OF JEAN-JACQUES ROUSSEAU (New York, 1962), II, 56ff., 69ff., 72ff., 442f. See Alfred Cobban, ROUSSEAU AND THE MODERN STATE (London, 1934), 95ff., 110; Durkheim, MONTESQUIEU AND ROUSSEAU, 125.

[95] Cf. Frederick Jackson Turner, THE FRONTIER IN AMERICAN HISTORY (New York, 1920).

pendence, the feeling that the probability of popular government decreased with the growth of society persisted. In spite of the emergency ensuing from the war with Britain, the thirteen states refrained from giving up their sovereignty when in 1781 they entered "the perpetual Union between the States of New Hampshire, Massachusetts Bay, Rhode Island and Providence Plantations, Connecticut, New York, New Jersey, Pennsylvania, Delaware, Maryland, Virginia, North Carolina, South Carolina, and Georgia."[96] Also, that feeling played an important role when the more perfect Union was formed under the present Constitution. Unimpressed by the argument that representation could secure self-government even in large states—an attitude understandable in view of the general absence of the imperative mandate—the Founding Fathers created not a unitary, but a federal republic. The latter proved to be an asset to self-government.[97]

The usefulness of federalism for popular government can even be seen in a small nation like Switzerland. That nation not only demonstrates that foreigners have learned from America, but also that they can increase the awareness of the value of federalism. Although the Swiss, who count Rousseau among their native sons, live in an area smaller than West Virginia, they adopted federalism as a prerequisite for popular government. However, they did not consider federalism alone a sufficient guarantee for democracy. Although their territory did not grow after the adoption of their Constitution, the Swiss adopted such devices as popular initiative and referendum in order to make sure that popular government would prevail. On the other hand the United States,

---

[96] Articles of Confederation, Preamble.

[97] The idea that federalism is a prerequisite for democracy has been generally accepted even in the smallest of federal states, namely, Switzerland. Already Jakob Burckhardt had stated that only in a small state "the largest possible proportion of the inhabitants are citizens in the fullest sense of the word." REFLECTIONS ON HISTORY, 37. Contemporary Swiss authors agree with him. Werner Kaegi writes that in a small community democracy is "more personal" because the voter has a more intimate knowledge of public affairs and issues. "Vom Sinn des Föderalismus," JAHRBUCH DER NHG (1944), 58. Messmer states that "since the sovereign people are unable to supervise large-scale conditions . . . democracy has by its very nature, by its spiritual structure, the form of a small State" FOEDERALISMUS UND DEMOKRATIE, 143ff. Messmer acknowledges following Philipp Etter, DIE SCHWEIZERISCHE DEMOKRATIE (Olten, Switzerland, 1934), 37 and "Der schweizerische Staatsgedanke" SCHWEIZERISCHE RUNDSCHAU, XXXIII (1933), 6; See also Röpke, DIE GESELLSCHAFTSKRISIS DER GEGENWART (5th ed.; Zürich, 1948), 145f.

although she has enormously expanded ever since her Constitution was adopted and although she extends over a much bigger area and counts considerably more inhabitants than Switzerland, never complemented federalism through a national popular initiative and referendum. In the United States, popular government thus appears to be more exclusively staked upon federalism.[98] Consequently, an abandonment of federalism is likely to constitute a more serious threat to popular government than it would in Switzerland.

To summarize, it may be said that federalism has proved its value not only for freedom, but also for popular government. It is therefore not surprising that it has been proposed by the advocates of various types of popular government, be they interested mainly in constitutional, or in sheer, democracy. As a matter of fact, while some authors, conceiving of democracy in an absolute sense, speak of an irreconcilable conflict between federalism and democracy,[99] it is often hard to find out whether writers propose federalism as a means to secure the individual's freedom from democratic rule, or as a device to secure democratic rule itself. Often, federalism appears as a prerequisite for both. It has been described both as a check upon, as well as a complement of, democracy for the sake of freedom.[100] Rousseau, when proposing

[98] For the idea that federalism is conducive to popular government, see THE FEDERALIST, Nos. 9, 10, 14, 39, 46.

[99] See Franz L. Neumann, "Federalism and Freedom: A Critique," in Arthur W. Macmahon (ed.), FEDERALISM, MATURE AND EMERGENT (Garden City, N.Y., 1955), 44. Friedrich, "Nationaler und Internationaler Föderalismus," 174, writes that Neumann's opinion is "characteristic of the attitude of many 'radical' democrats among European socialists." P. J. Proudhon, a French socialist and anarchist, writes: "As much as the people feel themselves to be innumerable, irresistible, immense, as much they have an horror of divisions, schisms, minorities. Their ideal, their most delightful dream is unity, identity, uniformity, concentration; they condemn as an outrage to their Majesty everything that can divide their will, cut down their mass, create in them diversity, plurality, divergence . . . Democracy never has understood the trinominal revolutionary slogan, Liberty–Equality–Fraternity . . . Its confessed and definitely adopted motto is, in one single term, Unity. . . . Democracy has for its principle unity; its end is unity; its means, unity; its law,—always unity. Unity is its alpha and omega, its supreme formula, its last reason. It is all united and nothing but united, as is proved by its discourses and acts." DU PRINCIPE FÉDÉRATIF ET DE LA NÉCESSITÉ DE RECONSTITUER LE PARTI DE LA RÉVOLUTION (Paris, 1863), 94, 133, 136.

[100] This is especially evident with Swiss authors. Messmer, while acknowledging an anti-federalist democratism, also demonstrates how federalism and democracy complement one another. (FOEDERALISMUS UND DEMOKRATIE, 124ff., 138ff.) Similar

federalism, appears to see it primarily as a means for the promotion of popular government, although he was certainly interested in the protection of the individual.[101] Montesquieu, while favoring popular government, felt that federalism was primarily a means for securing freedom.[102] *The Federalist* emphasizes the value of federalism for the protection of the rights of the individual, especially those of property. However, irrespective of that work's emphasis on the freedom of the individual from popular government, it leaves no doubt about the value of federalism for popular government.[103] From all this we may well conclude that the desire of radical democrats to abolish federalism because it supposedly hinders the majority in realizing its will—a will that more and more has become bent on restricting economic rights—is likely to be detrimental not only to the freedom of the individual, but also to popular government.

The experience of Germany ought to be a warning not only to those interested in freedom, but also to the friends of popular government. In that nation, freedom as well as popular government seem to have been secure only as long as they were aligned with federalism. Under the federal system of the Empire, the freedom of the individual, including his economic rights, enjoyed a great deal of protection.[104] Also, popular government was pro-

---

Röpke, JENSEITS VON ANGEBOT UND NACHFRAGE, 91f.; Usteri, THEORIE DES BUNDESSTAATES, 346ff.; Hans Haug, "Föderalismus und Demokratie," NEUE SCHWEIZER RUNDSCHAU, XII (N.S., 1944), 131, esp. 135ff., 141. See, also, the Swiss authors mentioned *supra,* 89n. All these authors use the term "democracy" in the sense of "limited" or "constitutional" democracy. Friedrich writes: "The tensions between federalism and democracy disappear if we choose a constitutional rather than an absolutist democracy as a starting point for theoretical analysis and practical procedure." "Nationaler und Internationaler Föderalismus," 175.

[101] CONTRAT SOCIAL, Bk. III, ch. 15. Significantly, the passage in which Rousseau proposes a *confédération* which can *"réunir la puissance extérieure d'un grand Peuple avec la police aisée et le bon ordre d'un petit État,"* concludes his argument against representation. While he considers representation incompatible with self-government, he considers it also incompatible with liberty: *"À l'instant qu'un peuple se donne des Représentants, il n'est plus libre; il n'est plus."* POLITICAL WRITINGS, II, 98.

[102] See SPIRIT OF THE LAWS, I, 126ff., 149ff.

[103] See the author's FEDERALIST, chs. 4–6, *passim.* Cf. Haug, "Föderalismus und Demokratie," 141: "Federalism and democracy are destined to form a synthesis. Where they combine, springs the well of liberty."

[104] See Georg Meyer/Gerhard Anschütz, LEHRBUCH DES DEUTSCHEN STAATSRECHTS (7th ed.; München, 1914–19), 946ff.; Georg Meyer, DER STAAT UND DIE ERWORBENEN RECHTE (Leipzig, 1895).

gressing.[105] This changed under the Weimar Constitution which, while retaining some federal features, created a unitary state.[106] Drafted and adopted by the general will of "the German people united,"[107] it promoted democracy, but qualified the protection of the individual, especially with respect to his economic rights.[108] This policy, accompanied as it was by an abolition of federalism, proved to be detrimental not only to freedom, but also to popular government. And whereas toward the end of the Weimar Republic there was at first perhaps some justification in calling "constitutional" a dictatorship which was exercised by a democratically elected President and sanctioned by the Constitution in cases of emergency,[109] the conflict between Prussia and the Reich in which the Reich government disregarded a court decision rendered in favor of the Land Prussia (significantly a conflict involving a remnant of federalism!) convinced many observers that the dictatorship was no longer deserving of the adjective "constitutional."[110] Hitler walked away with the powers which the constitution-makers of Weimar had vested in the executive in the naïve belief that an executive elected by the people constituted no liability. Taking advantage of democratic trends toward centralization and dictatorship, he abolished the last remnants of federalism and did away with freedom and popular government.[111] The

[105] See Fritz Hartung, DEUTSCHE VERFASSUNGSGESCHICHTE (5th ed.; Stuttgart, 1950), 287ff., 303ff.; Ernst Rudolf Huber, DEUTSCHE VERFASSUNGSGESCHICHTE SEIT 1789 (Stuttgart, 1957–63), III, 773ff., 860ff.

[106] See Anschütz, DREI LEITGEDANKEN DER WEIMARER REICHSVERFASSUNG (Tübingen, 1923), 12ff. For a federal interpretation of the Weimar Constitution, see Hans Nawiasky, DIE GRUNDGEDANKEN DER REICHSVERFASSUNG (München, 1920), 25, 36ff.; GRUNDPROBLEME DER REICHSVERFASSUNG. ERSTER TEIL: DAS REICH ALS BUNDESSTAAT (Berlin, 1928). The Weimar Republic was also called a "decentralized unitary state."

[107] Preamble to the Weimar Constitution.

[108] Whereas in Imperial Germany most state constitutions contained provisions similar to that of Art. 9 of the Prussian Constitution, "property is inviolable," the Weimar Constitution stated in Art. 153: "Property is guaranteed by the Constitution. Its content and limits follow from the laws . . . Property implies duties. Its use shall be determined by what is best for the community." Cf. Gerhard Anschütz, DIE VERFASSUNG DES DEUTSCHEN REICHS VOM 11. AUGUST 1919 (13th ed.; Berlin, 1930), 606f., 612, 620; Martin Wolff, "Reichsverfassung und Eigentum," BERLINER FESTGABE FÜR KAHL (Tübingen, 1923), 10ff.

[109] Art. 48. See Carl Schmitt, DIE DIKTATUR (München, 1928); Rossiter, CONSTITUTIONAL DICTATORSHIP, 29ff.

[110] See PREUSSEN CONTRA REICH VOR DEM STAATSGERICHTSHOF (n.p., 1932), with a preface by Arnold Brecht.

[111] After the *Anschluss,* Hans Huber stated: "The German Reich . . . is a

reestablishment of free government in West Germany after World War II was undertaken under the banner of federalism which was considered a guarantee for the freedom of the individual as well as for popular government.[112] Aside from other liberties, those of an economic nature received a far-reaching protection.[113] The situation in the West German Federal Republic stands in striking contrast to that in the East German Democratic Republic. The latter, a unitary state, is characterized by an oppression of freedom, especially of economic freedom, and by the absence of popular government.[114]

CONCLUSION

It is hoped that in the United States the growing disregard for economic rights and federalism will not have the consequences it had in Germany. In view of America's democratic tradition, the

---

unitary state. Federalism is through in Germany. Even without National Socialism would it eventually have become abolished. National Socialism only sped up the process because the federal structure is an impediment to dictatorship." "Ueber Foederalismus," 241. The outstanding commentator on the Weimar Constitution, Anschütz, who advocated a "further evolution of Germany into a unitary state" (LEITGEDANKEN DER WEIMARER REICHSVERFASSUNG, 18) as early as 1923, suffered persecution under the Hitler regime. True, Anschütz emphasized that he did not want centralization, but, like Treitschke, a "national unitary state with a strong self-administration of autonomous provinces" (ibid., 21). Still, as soon as the Länder were reduced to mere provinces, centralization was dangerously close. The German development shows that once genuine federalism is abolished, there is no halting the drift toward centralization.

[112] See the author's "The Federal Republic of Germany: An Evaluation after Ten Years," JOURNAL OF POLITICS, XXII (1960), 123, 126ff., 134f.

[113] The Basic Law not only provides for a protection of the rights of the individual from the legislature, but also from the amending power (Arts. 19, 79). While according to the Basic Law, which proclaims the Federal Republic to be a "social" state (Arts. 20, 28), economic rights appear to be less secure than under the Weimar Constitution, the practice has shown a far-reaching protection of economic rights because the legislature did not restrict these rights, but rather freed them from existing restrictions. Cf. Erich Fechner, FREIHEIT UND ZWANG IM SOZIALEN RECHTSSTAAT (Tübingen, 1953); Helmut Rumpf, DER IDEOLOGISCHE GEHALT DES BONNER GRUNDGESETZES (Karlsruhe, 1958), 27.

[114] The names of the two German states are indicative of different meanings of democracy. If we take "republic" to mean "democracy," then the term "Democratic Republic" means "democratic democracy." Obviously such a super-democracy is, to the detriment of the individual, too democratic. On the other hand, "Federal Republic" means a democracy qualified, for the sake of the individual, by federalism.

process is likely to be slower.[115] However, due to her greater extension and population, the end result could also be more disastrous. If, as we believe, federalism is a safeguard against big government and its minimization of the individual,[116] then centralization in the American colossus might well be more detrimental to free government than centralization in the German semi-colossus. The American argument, "it can't happen here," ought to be considered with skepticism. It ought to give us concern that even in the smallest of federal states, Switzerland, people have become frightened by the experience of their neighbor to the north in spite of the fact that their country is only a fraction the size of Germany and that, consequently, the probability of despotism appears to be more remote. More and more Swiss authors have raised their voice against the increasing abolition of federalism and the growing interference by the federal government in private affairs, especially in those of an economic nature.[117] One of them even concluded quite generally that a federal state can exist only where free government is possible—that "it is as much incompatible with the political principle of totalitarianism as it is with the economic principle of a centrally administered economy or any kind of despotic principle."[118] The attitude of Swiss writers

[115] Having observed centralization under the Third Reich from his vantage point in Switzerland, Hans Huber wrote in 1938: "Although in North America one counts by decades rather than months as one does in Germany on account of the fact that democratic mills grind more slowly than authoritarian ones, he must prophesy also for the former country a diminution of the member states, if not the arrival of a unitary state." "Ueber Foederalismus," 242.

[116] Cf. Huber, "Ueber Foederalismus," 141: "Federalism is the protest against the cult of the colossal and the chimera of big spaces which leads to nothing better than the deprivation of man of his rights. Federalism, while it is opposed to an isolation of the individual, is the only steadfast rampart against the evil of totalitarianism."

[117] Cf. Huber, *ibid.*, 287: "When William Rappard, viewing the future at the end of his book, L'INDIVIDU ET L'ÉTAT DANS L'ÉVOLUTION CONSTITUTIONELLE DE LA SUISSE, considers a return to individual freedom as essential to the survival of democracy, one might add that also the survival of the federal structure of our state depends upon the possibility of greater individual freedom, especially in the economic sphere. Just as modern State intervention paralyzes or falsifies democratic institutions and makes the democratic spirit sick, in a like manner statism is a threat to federalism. However, even on the farthest horizon no possibility of a return to the original and healthy relationship between individual freedom and State intervention and authority is discernible. Perhaps there is no return. This is part of the tragedy mentioned." Cf. also William E. Rappard, DIE BUNDESVERFASSUNG DER SCHWEIZERISCHEN EIDGENOSSENSCHAFT 1848–1948, 427f., 429ff.

[118] Usteri, THEORIE DES BUNDESSTAATES, 348f.

stands in striking contrast to that of their American colleagues, among whom the proponents of federalism and economic rights have dwindled down to a small minority. This is perhaps not surprising in view of the fact that unlike Switzerland, the United States is not close to Germany, and thus has had less opportunity to observe the democratic causes and aspects of despotism at close range. In their splendid isolation across the Atlantic, Americans can perhaps not be expected to be as aware of the pitfalls of democracy as can the Swiss, surrounded as they are by nations which amply demonstrated these pitfalls. However, this only increases the danger that confronts free government in the United States. If people permit themselves to be lulled by the democratic dogma that the voice of the people is the voice of God, they might not wake up from their dream until it is too late and they find themselves living under some form of centralized socialism.

The aspects of federalism may be many. Its basic mission for free government is constant. As its new dimensions develop, care must be taken not to accept variations that might make out of a new federalism an untrue federalism, by destroying the genuine balance between national power and states' rights and by depriving federalism of its quality as a means of constitutionalism. As are the aspects of federalism, those of the freedom of the individual are many. A distinction, as arbitrary as it is out of tune with tradition, is often drawn today between civil and economic rights.[119] It is here believed that the moment the latter are forsaken, freedom will suffer, no matter how much the former will be expanded. Federalism and economic freedom were reliable companions of the United States in her rise to the most powerful nation on earth. Whether or not America will continue without these companions remains to be seen.

[119] See *supra,* 63; *infra,* 132f.

4

NATIONAL POWER AND "CIVIL" RIGHTS EMERGENT

INTRODUCTION

It will be argued that the decline of economic rights and federalism amounts neither to a disappearance of freedom nor of democracy, because the increase of national power was matched by one of civil rights. The national government has been credited with having promoted civil rights to a degree that more than made up for the decline of economic rights and states' rights. Democrats and Republicans alike have emphasized that there are no states' rights, but only human rights.[1] Just as at the beginning of the nineteenth century there seemed to exist no basic difference between the major parties with respect to federalism and economic rights,[2] so today Democrats and Republicans seem to agree on the need for expanding civil rights through national power. Recent literature is as full of praise for what the national government has done in expanding civil rights as of regrets for what that

---

[1] Their arguments overlook that states rights are designed to ensure the protection of human rights, and that the adoption of a federal, as distinguished from a unitary, government, is usually due to the recognition of this fact. In the United States, this was emphasized not only be advocates of states rights like John Taylor (CONSTRUCTION CONSTRUED, AND CONSTITUTIONS VINDICATED [Richmond, Va., 1820], TYRANNY UNMASKED [Washington, 1822], NEW VIEWS OF THE CONSTITUTION OF THE UNITED STATES [Washington, 1823]), and John C. Calhoun (A DISQUISITION ON GOVERNMENT, AND A DISCOURSE ON THE CONSTITUTION AND GOVERNMENT OF THE UNITED STATES [Charleston, S.C., 1851]), but also in THE FEDERALIST.

[2] See *supra,* 68. In his First Inaugural Address, Jefferson stated that "every difference of opinion is not a difference of principle. We have called by different names brethren of the same principle. We are all republicans—we are federalists. If there be any among us who would wish to dissolve this Union or to change its republican form, let them stand undisturbed as monuments of the safety with which error of opinion may be tolerated where reason is left free to combat it." WRITINGS, III, 319.

government has not yet been able to achieve. The expansion of civil rights through national power is considered part of the American tradition.[3]

No doubt the national government has done much for the advancement of civil rights in recent decades. The Supreme Court became a "civil rights court." Before World War II, a Civil Liberties Unit was established in the executive branch of the national government for "the aggressive protection of fundamental rights" and a "vigilant action in the prosecution of infringements of these rights."[4] After the war, President Truman, feeling that it was "essential that all possible steps be taken to safeguard our civil rights," established a Committee on Civil Rights.[5] Congress passed Civil Rights Acts in 1957, 1960, 1964, and the Voting Rights Act in 1965.

These activities seem to be in the American tradition. Recent civil rights acts seem to be the successors of the national Civil Rights Acts of 1866, 1870, 1871, and 1875. The concern of modern Presidents for today's underdog seems to carry on Lincoln's concern for the slaves. The attitude of the modern Supreme Court seems to be in line with that Court's traditional protection of life, liberty, and property. Furthermore, it could be argued that just as the Constitution originally was adopted in order to prevent the states' encroachment upon civil rights, so it was amended after the Civil War from a similar motive. It could be claimed that national power—restricted as it is by the Constitution and the Bill of Rights—cannot hinder, but only advance,

---

[3] Bibliographies are supplied by Kelly/Harbison, AMERICAN CONSTITUTION, 1051ff., and Leo Pfeffer, THE LIBERTIES OF AN AMERICAN (n.p., 1956), 288ff. More recent works include Edward Dumbauld, THE BILL OF RIGHTS AND WHAT IT MEANS TODAY (Norman, Okla., 1957); Learned Hand, THE BILL OF RIGHTS (Cambridge, Mass., 1958); Milton R. Konvitz and Theodore Leskes, A CENTURY OF CIVIL RIGHTS (New York, 1961); Paul G. Kauper, CIVIL LIBERTIES AND THE CONSTITUTION (Ann Arbor, Mich., 1962); Walter Gellhorn, AMERICAN RIGHTS (New York, 1963); Arthur E. Sutherland, APOLOGY FOR UNCOMFORTABLE CHANGE 1865–1965 (New York, 1965).

[4] Statement by Attorney General Frank Murphy when making public the Order of the Attorney General, No. 3204. (NEW YORK TIMES, Feb. 4, 1939). Cf. Henry A. Schweinhaut, "The Civil Liberties Section of the Department of Justice," BILL OF RIGHTS REVIEW, I (1941), 206. In 1941, the name was changed to "Civil Rights Section."

[5] Executive Order 9808, Establishing The President's Committee on Civil Rights, Dec. 5, 1946.

civil rights. The idea, "civil rights through national power" seems to be as fashionable today as it appeared to be in Hamilton's writings.[6]

However, the present situation is not without problems. If it were, civil rights would hardly constitute an "issue." That issue exists because there are doubts about the way the national government has pushed civil rights as well as about the kind of civil rights that have been advocated. Recent civil rights measures have come under attack. This is probably due not so much to an outright rejection of civil rights—something unlikely to occur in the United States—but to different evaluations and appreciations of these rights and the modes of their advancement. The modern concept of civil rights and their implementation by the national government are considered to be out of tune with traditional free government.

In the following pages, we shall deal with these arguments. Remarks concerning the original concept of civil rights and the role the national government was supposed to play in its promotion will be followed by observations on what has become of these rights and their national promotion. It will be examined whether, as a result of the march of democracy, civil rights and their advancement by the national government have undergone change. The chapter will conclude with a discussion of the implications for free government.

PROTECTION OF CIVIL RIGHTS THROUGH FEDERAL POWER UNDER TRADITIONAL CONSTITUTIONAL GOVERNMENT

The American Revolution was a federal effort for the protection of civil rights. This is not surprising if we consider its historical roots. Many of the colonists came to America in order to escape persecution under the Tudors and Stuarts. It was the New World of America rather than such new worlds as Massachusetts or Maryland that attracted immigrants. Although there

[6] Cf. the author's FEDERALIST, 168.

was intolerance toward certain rights in some places, it was balanced by the tolerance displayed by other colonies. Roger Williams, persecuted in Massachusetts for his beliefs, could well move into another part of America where he could enjoy the liberty he desired.[7] When Madison advanced his theory on the balance of factions,[8] that theory had already proved its value in colonial America. The colonies were civil rights laboratories. If people did not like living in one colony, they could move to another which was better suited to them. To the European, America appeared as a haven for civil rights, irrespective of how these rights fared in any particular section. While the conditions in one colony might disappoint the immigrant, America as a whole was likely to fulfill his dreams. A big laboratory of civil rights, profiting from the experiences of her parts, she was the New World of Freedom.[9]

In view of this identification between freedom and America, it is not surprising that the struggle for Independence was an American effort. While it should never be forgotten that the sparks of the American Revolution were kindled in particular colonies and that the various colonies decided on a united course against England, it was the two Continental Congresses which took stock of English oppressions. Since England had infringed not only upon the rights of any particular colony but upon the rights of all, it was natural that all colonies should take concerted action against her. The Declaration of Independence and the Articles of Confederation reflect this fact. The former is a *unanimous* declaration of the thirteen *united* states of America, which defends the

[7] See Georg Jellinek, DIE ERKLÄRUNG DER MENSCHEN–UND BÜRGERRECHTE; B. Katherine Brown, "Freemanship in Puritan Massachusetts," AMERICAN HISTORICAL REVIEW, LIX (1954), 865; Perry Miller, ROGER WILLIAMS: HIS CONTRIBUTION TO THE AMERICAN TRADITION (Indianapolis, 1953); Ola E. Winslow, MASTER ROGER WILLIAMS (New York, 1957).

[8] THE FEDERALIST, No. 10.

[9] See James T. Adams, PROVINCIAL SOCIETY 1690–1763 (New York, 1936); Merle Curti, THE GROWTH OF AMERICAN THOUGHT (3d ed.; New York, 1964), chs. 2–5; Robert A. Rutland, THE BIRTH OF THE BILL OF RIGHTS 1776–1791 (Chapel Hill, N.C., 1955), ch. 2; Arthur E. Sutherland, CONSTITUTIONALISM IN AMERICA (New York, 1965), ch. 8. J. B. McMaster, THE ACQUISITION OF POLITICAL, SOCIAL AND INDUSTRIAL RIGHTS OF MAN IN AMERICA (Cleveland, 1903) and Albert E. McKinley, THE SUFFRAGE FRANCHISE IN THE THIRTEEN ENGLISH COLONIES IN AMERICA (Boston, 1905), emphasize the democratic development.

"unalienable rights" of men, and the latter in an effort to secure civil rights, unites the thirteen states into a confederation.[10]

After Independence the value of the Union for civil rights continued to be recognized. To secure these rights, the newly independent states adopted constitutions containing bills of rights and providing for the separation of powers.[11] However, their hopes soon proved to have been in vain. In several states, governmental power became concentrated in the legislatures which often did not respect civil rights. As a result, the friends of freedom, who previously had advocated common American action for the protection of civil rights from the British, now advocated a more perfect Union in order to protect those rights from democratic majorities in the states.[12] In an all-American effort, a constitutional convention was called[13] which drafted a Constitution creating a more perfect Union and providing for the protection of civil rights from the state governments.[14] In another all-American effort, that Constitution was ratified by conventions of all the states.

America's image as a haven for civil rights was enhanced not only because the Constitution prohibits the states from impairing certain rights, but also because it protects those rights from the federal government. The powers of that government are few and defined, and as originally conceived, unlikely to challenge civil rights. The federal government is expressly forbidden from suspending the writ of habeas corpus, except in cases of rebellion or invasion where the public safety may require it; to pass bills of attainder or *ex post facto* laws; to impose (with a few exceptions) per capita or direct taxes or taxes or duties on articles exported from any state.[15] These features prompted Hamilton, in essay

---

[10] Cf. Jensen, ARTICLES OF CONFEDERATION, and his later history of the United States from 1781–83, THE NEW NATION (New York, 1950).

[11] See Kelly/Harbison, AMERICAN CONSTITUTION, 93ff. Nevins, THE AMERICAN STATES DURING AND AFTER THE REVOLUTION, 117ff. Carpenter, "The Separation of Powers in the Eighteenth Century."

[12] See *supra*, 7, 64ff.; *infra*, 145f. and the author's FEDERALIST, 55ff.

[13] See Corwin, "Progress of Constitutional Theory."

[14] Esp. Art. I, sec. x, clause 1. Chief Justice Marshall called this provision "a bill of rights for the people of each state." *Fletcher* v. *Peck*, 6 Cranch 87, 138 (1810).

[15] Art. I, sec. ix, clauses 2–5.

eighty-four of *The Federalist,* to consider the original Constitution a bill of rights, and the addition of a separate Bill of Rights to be not only superfluous but dangerous.

Still, a formal Bill of Rights was added to quell fears lest its absence result in federal infringements upon freedom.[16] The Bill of Rights explicitly protects freedom of religion, of speech, of the press, of assembly, of petition; of the right to bear arms; of the right to be protected from the quartering of soldiers; of the right to secure one's person, house, papers, effects, etc., against unreasonable searches and seizures. It prohibits certain forms of indictment, excessive bail, fines as well as cruel and unusual punishment; it guards against double jeopardy, self-incrimination, deprivation of life, liberty, and property without due process of law, and confiscation of property without just compensation; it guarantees the right to a speedy, public, and fair trial by jury in criminal prosecutions, as well as the right to trial by jury in suits at common law. An implicit protection of civil rights—leaving no doubt that the freedom of the individual is the rule, and infringements upon it are the exception—is evident in the Ninth Amendment: "The enumeration in the Constitution of certain rights shall not be construed to deny or disparage others retained by the people."[17] Finally, the Tenth Amendment provides that "the powers not delegated to the United States by the Constitution, or prohibited by it to the States, are reserved to the States respectively, or to the people."

With the adoption of the Constitution and the Bill of Rights, the United States basically remained the haven for civil liberties it was during the colonial period. Whereas state infringements upon civil rights were restricted, they were not absolutely restricted. The states could no longer make anything but gold and silver coin tender in payment of debts. They could pass no bills of attainder, *ex post facto* laws, and laws impairing the obligation of contracts. On the other hand, they could—each to its liking— infringe upon other civil rights, such as freedom of religion, of

[16] See Rutland, THE BIRTH OF THE BILL OF RIGHTS; Dumbauld, BILL OF RIGHTS, ch. 1; Irving Brant, THE BILL OF RIGHTS (Indianapolis, 1965).

[17] Bennett B. Patterson, THE FORGOTTEN NINTH AMENDMENT (Indianapolis, 1955).

speech and the press, and the right to trial by jury. This did not necessarily detract from America's quality as a haven for freedom. As a matter of fact, it probably enhanced that quality. For as a practical matter, an absolute standard of civil rights is a contradiction in terms. Just as the risk of prescribing a specific civil rights standard increases with the size of the community, diversity in civil rights standards is a guarantee of the enjoyment of those rights. Since civil rights—being *rights*—cannot well be imposed upon communities which enjoy self-government, diverse civil rights standards in the United States are perhaps as desirable as they are natural. For instance, some people might not want to live in a state in which there exists absolute freedom of speech, but would prefer to live in a state which prohibits libel. Others might like to be in a state in which trial by jury is not compulsory, feeling that their interests would be served better by a judge trained in the law than by twelve laymen. Others still might prefer a "dry" over a "wet" state, a state that prohibits polygamy to one that does not, or a state that punishes adultery to one that does not. Like the stars, the rights of men are myriad and inscrutable, and men would act in *hybris* if they claimed to know the right standard of civil rights. It testifies to the wisdom of the Founding Fathers that while they saw to the protection of a certain nationally recognized minimum of civil rights, they were cautious in maximizing that minimum, recognizing that the people in the states were perhaps better judges of civil rights in their respective ways of life. Also, while the Founders provided for a civil rights barrier to the federal government, they did not make that barrier absolute.

By the Constitution and the Bill of Rights, a certain minimum of civil rights had now received sanction throughout the continent. America's image as a haven for freedom was institutionalized. Institutionalizations have their advantages, but they are not devoid of danger. Important as the institutionalization of civil rights is, it can be dangerous if it amounts to an over-imposition of those rights. The fact that even a great compromiser like Madison was unable to bring about prohibitions upon the states beyond those provided by the Constitution indicates that even after the more perfect Union had been established, the danger of imposing the observation of too many civil rights upon the states was recognized.[18] It obviously was felt that such an imposition would unduly hinder the small community from determining its own way of life, that it would restrict experimentation with civil rights, and curtail the individual's freedom of choice as to the relative importance of those rights.

The Supreme Court's implementation of civil rights was in line with this thinking. Whereas explicit constitutional restrictions upon the states were honored, these restrictions were not unduly enlarged. True, Chief Justice Marshall, known for his desire to protect property through federal power, gave the contract clause a broad scope.[19] And yet, whereas he stretched that clause to the limit of the permissible, he refrained from stretching it beyond that limit. His reluctance to impose upon the states the observance of additional civil rights is evident in his attitude toward the applicability of the federal Bill of Rights. Whereas the First Amendment clearly guards civil rights from the federal government, the other amendments that make up the Bill of Rights are more vague on this point. And although "the legislative history of these amendments leaves little doubt that they were directed exclusively against the central government,"[20] it would have been conceivable that the "nationalist" Marshall would have applied these amendments to the states. Instead, he destroyed whatever doubts may have existed by stating that "these amendments con-

---

[18] In the First Congress, Madison proposed an amendment that no state shall violate the equal rights of conscience, freedom of speech and the press, and trial by jury in criminal cases. This proposal was approved by the House, but rejected in the Senate. ANNALS OF CONGRESS (Washington, 1834) I, 76, 755; JOURNAL OF THE FIRST SESSION OF THE SENATE (New York, 1789, reprinted 1820), 121. Dumbauld, BILL OF RIGHTS, 47n., writes: "The fact that Jefferson approved all of Madison's proposals . . . shows that he, like Madison, was more interested in human rights than in States' rights." It ought to be added that neither Jefferson nor Madison was generally opposed to states rights, because they recognized the basic value of the states for the protection of human rights. For a recent recognition of the value of states rights in the area of civil rights, see Justice John M. Harlan, "The Bill of Rights and the Constitution," address of Aug. 9, 1964, in New York; his opinions in *Roth* v. *United States,* 354 U.S. 476, 503–8 (1957); *Hoag* v. *New Jersey,* 356 U.S. 464, 465–73 (1958); *Reynolds* v. *Sims,* 377 U.S. 533, 589–625 (1964); *Pointer* v. *Texas,* 380 U.S. 400, 408–9 (1965).

[19] See *supra,* 69.

[20] Robert K. Carr, FEDERAL PROTECTION OF CIVIL RIGHTS: QUEST FOR A SWORD (Ithaca, N.Y., 1947), 6f.

tain no expression indicating an intention to apply them to the state governments."[21]

The Court's attitude did not change under Marshall's successor. Taney was as reluctant to stretch the Constitution's prohibitions upon the states as he was to apply restrictions of the federal government to the states. While favoring the protection of private property as an important liberal right, he made it plain that no local community should be restricted by the federal government through an unduly broad interpretation of the contract clause, which limited state interference.[22] As to the applicability of the federal Bill of Rights to the states, Taney shared his predecessor's opinion.

In the preceding pages, what was referred to as "civil rights" are the individual's rights *from* the government, i.e., his liberal rights as specifications of his general freedom from governmental interference. As did its English predecessor and French successor, the American Revolution aimed at the security of the individual's freedom, or liberties, from the government. Like the English Petition of Right and Bill of Rights and the French Declaration of the Rights of Man and Citizen, the American Declaration of Independence and the constitutions adopted in the formative period leave no doubt about this fact.[23] Like its English and French

[21] *Barron* v. *Baltimore,* 7 Peters 243, 250 (1833). Thirteen years earlier, Jefferson had complained of Marshall's nationalism: "The judiciary of the United States is the subtle corps of sappers and miners constantly working under ground to undermine the foundations of our confederate fabric. They are construing our Constitution from a co-ordination of a general and special government to a general and supreme one alone." To Thomas Ritchie on Dec. 25, 1820. WRITINGS, XV, 297. Cf. Julian Boyd, "The Chasm that Separated Thomas Jefferson from John Marshall," in Dietze (ed.), ESSAYS ON THE AMERICAN CONSTITUTION, 3. For the fact that Marshall considered national power a means for the protection of civil rights, see *supra,* 69, 73f.

[22] *Charles River Bridge Co.* v. *Warren Bridge,* 11 Pet. 420, 548 (1837). See *supra,* 22.

[23] See the author's IN DEFENSE OF PROPERTY, ch. 2; Carr, FEDERAL PROTECTION OF CIVIL RIGHTS, 5f., 33. When in the following the word "freedom" is used without qualification, it refers to the general freedom of the individual *from* the government, i.e., the sum of the various liberal rights of man, of liberties which specify parts of freedom, such as freedom of religion, of assembly, of association, of contract, etc. Cf. the author's ÜBER FORMULIERUNG DER MENSCHENRECHTE (Berlin, 1956), 36ff., 42ff. This freedom, while constituting a freedom from the government, can, of course, be enforced not only against the government, but also be sanctioned by the government against inroads by private persons. It is to be distinguished

counterparts, the American Revolution was nourished by the idea that the civil institution of government was a trust, and that its end was the protection of the individual's liberties or civil rights.

The term "civil rights" was not used arbitrarily in the preceding pages. Already Locke's *Second Treatise of Government,* "An Essay Concerning the True Original, Extent, and End of Civil Government," maintains that the protection of the individual's life, liberty, and property is the end of all civil government.[24] Blackstone's commentaries on the law of England speak of "civil privileges" that fall into "three principal or primary articles; the right of personal security, the right of personal liberty, and the right of private property."[25] This meaning of civil rights prevailed during the American Revolution and thereafter.[26] It should be noted that whereas the term "civil rights" as originally understood in America comprises *all liberal* rights of the individual, it does not comprise *democratic* rights, i.e., the rights to participate in government.[27]

Since according to American thought civil rights are inalienable rights which those who establish government as a trust wish to protect for themselves and posterity, it is not surprising that the constituent act would be not of a simple, but of a qualified, majority. The Declaration of Independence was a "unanimous declaration" for the protection of civil rights. For the same purpose, the Articles of Confederation and the Constitution were adopted by all the states. The Constitution perpetuated the origi-

from the pseudo-freedom which is imposed by the government on some people for the sake of others, a freedom which approaches bills of attainder. The latter freedom also has different aspects. While it gives men the right to contract, to assemble, to associate with people with whom they do not want to contract, assemble, and associate, it also imposes upon them the duty to do so thus transforming a right into a duty.

[24] Locke, TWO TREATISES OF GOVERNMENT, esp. 294, 307, 325, 339, 341ff., 347ff., 352, 355, 368, 370f., 373, 375ff., 425, 430, 433. Although Locke often identifies "civil" with "political" society, he considered government, i.e., civil or political power, a trust for the protection of the individual's rights.

[25] Blackstone, COMMENTARIES, Bk. I, 129.

[26] See *supra,* 5ff., 10f.

[27] Whereas Locke often identified civil with political liberty, Blackstone drew a distinction between "civil and political liberty." COMMENTARIES, Bk. I, 126f. In America, "civil" rights were distinguished from "political" rights, the latter being rights to participate in government, in *Amy* v. *Smith,* 11 Kentucky 327 (1822), as well as in James Kent's COMMENTARIES ON AMERICAN LAW (3d ed.; New York, 1836), II, 257n.

nal constituent power in a qualified majority of Congress and the states. It was this qualified majority that adopted the Bill of Rights as a complement to the Constitution. While enumerating certain rights and generally not leaving their implementation to Congress,[28] the Bill of Rights emphasizes in the Tenth Amendment that further federal guarantees of civil rights could be effected only by the constituent power—the states and the people. The last words of the Bill of Rights are thus in tune with the first words of the Constitution. And just as the people of the United States, as the original constituent power, did ordain the more perfect Union for the protection of civil rights through ratifying state conventions, the same people, acting as the constituent power established by the Constitution through the qualified majorities of Congress and the states, made sure that civil rights would remain protected from the federal government.

That government, it should be emphasized, was based upon the recognition that the small community was a good judge and guardian of civil rights. This did not detract from the Union's reputation as a haven of freedom. On the contrary, it added to it. Since, unlike Great Britain and France, the United States emerged from her democratic revolution as a federal—as distinguished from unitary—state, she had a better chance of experimenting with these rights in each one of her constituent parts, the states. She thus secured a greater potential of freedom than did England or France. Whereas Englishmen and Frenchmen were bound by their respective national government's monopolistic conception of civil rights, the American was not under the civil rights monopoly of any one particular state but free to move to states with different civil rights standards. He was bound, of course, by the federal Constitution's conception of civil rights. However, since under that Constitution the bulk of civil rights had remained with the states, he was not restricted too much. His was a greater freedom of choice—perhaps the most important

---

[28] Only the Third Amendment, permitting the quartering of soldiers in time of war "in a manner to be prescribed by law," seems to admit congressional legislation. The wording of Amendments Four–Six is less clear. It is doubtful whether they permit regulations by statute or by common law. Amendment Seven is explicit in stating that regulations are permissible only "according to the rules of the common law."

civil right.[29] It has been said that modern civil rights originated with Roger Williams's fight for freedom of conscience,[30] the ideal dimension of freedom of choice. Freedom of choice, it could be added, was enhanced in America because its actual implementation was facilitated by the absence of centralization.

By the time of the Civil War, the hopes of the American Founders proved not to have been in vain. As America, divided up into colonies, did previously, now the United States of America, composed of states, became known as a haven for freedom.[31] While it should not be overlooked that this status in large measure was due to the fact that under the Constitution the United States constituted a federal rather than a national republic, there is little doubt that America's image as a haven for civil rights also existed because the states were united.

PROTECTION OF "CIVIL" RIGHTS
THROUGH NATIONAL POWER UNDER
MODERN DEMOCRATIC GOVERNMENT

The promotion of the traditional concept of civil rights by the federal Union in time was replaced by the promotion of a new concept of civil rights by a democratic nation. The Civil War made the Union appear to be the promoter of civil rights. No matter how much freedom of choice may have existed prior to the war, that freedom did not exist for a substantial part of the population—the slaves. The Civil War changed that situation. On September 22, 1862, Lincoln issued a preliminary proclamation which stated that on January 1, 1863, he would name the states that were in rebellion and declare all slaves in those states free. From this proclamation, "it was clear that Lincoln desired to put the Confederate States on notice that he intended to free their Negro slaves exactly one hundred days later, and that he would

---

[29] The freedom to move around has been taken for granted so much in the United States that it is not mentioned in the Constitution. European constitutions usually mention this freedom, as well as the freedom to emigrate. Perhaps freedom of movement is taken for granted in the United States because it is, in a way, natural in a nation of immigrants. Locke recognized the importance of this freedom in TWO TREATISES, 363ff.

[30] See *supra*, 100.

[31] Gilman Ostrander, THE RIGHTS OF MAN IN AMERICA, 1606–1861 (Columbia, Mo., 1960), emphasizes the development of popular government.

not extend his effort at emancipation to reach the slaves in loyal states—a state that would rejoin the Union would not have its slaves freed."[32] The Emancipation Proclamation designated Alabama, Arkansas, Florida, Georgia, Louisiana, Mississippi, North Carolina, South Carolina, Texas, and Virginia in rebellion and emancipated slaves in those states as "a fit and necessary war measure for suppressing" the rebellion, "an act of justice, warranted by the Constitution, upon military necessity."[33] While emancipation was thus motivated by a desire to save the Union rather than to free the slaves, the Union was bound together with emancipation and likely to be celebrated as a protagonist of civil rights.

Shortly before Lee's surrender a Freedmen's Bureau, headed by a Union commissioner and Union assistant commissioners in the Southern states, was established. It was designated to provide for the needs of freedmen.[34] The apparent quality of the Union government as a promoter of civil rights was confirmed by measures following the war—by constitutional amendments as well as acts of Congress. Two years after the Emancipation Proclamation, Congress proposed the Thirteenth Amendment. It provided that neither slavery nor involuntary servitude shall exist within the United States, and gave Congress the power to enforce this provision by appropriate legislation. Ratification was completed in December, 1865.

Early in 1866, a new Freedmen's Bureau Bill was passed by Congress. This bill, asking the President to extend protection to all Negroes discriminated against in their "civil rights or immunities" in consequence of any state or local law, ordinance, police or other regulation, custom, or prejudice,[35] was successfully vetoed

[32] Konvitz/Leskes, A CENTURY OF CIVIL RIGHTS, 41. The preliminary proclamation can be found in WORKS, V, 433.

[33] WORKS, VI, 29, 30.

[34] For a general study of the Bureau, see Paul S. Peirce, THE FREEDMEN'S BUREAU (Iowa City, Iowa, 1904).

[35] The bill defined "civil rights" as "any of the civil rights or immunities belonging to white persons, including the right to make and enforce contracts, to sue, be parties, and give evidence, to inherit, purchase, lease, sell, hold and convey real and personal property, and to have full and equal benefit of all laws and proceedings for the security of person and estate, including the constitutional right of bearing arms." The bill can be found in Edward McPherson, POLITICAL HISTORY OF THE UNITED STATES DURING THE PERIOD OF RECONSTRUCTION (2d ed.; Washington, 1875), 72.

by President Johnson because it was "not warranted by the Constitution" and because it failed to define "civil rights and immunities."[36] On April 9, 1866, however, Congress passed, over the President's veto, "An Act to protect all Persons in the United States in their Civil Rights, and furnish the Means of their Vindication." Aimed at outlawing the "Black Codes" which restricted the movement and occupation of Negroes, it declared all persons born in the United States to be citizens who—whatever their race or color, without regard to any previous condition of slavery or involuntary servitude—shall have the same rights in every state or territory as those enjoyed by white citizens. The Slave Kidnapping Act of May 21, 1866, designed to implement the Thirteenth Amendment, made it a federal crime to kidnap or carry away a person with the intention of placing him in slavery or involuntary servitude. On July 16, 1866, Congress passed the second Freedmen's Bureau Act over the President's veto. Speaking of "personal liberty, personal security," the "free enjoyment" of "immunities and rights," this act provided that the bureau should care for freedmen "to enable them to become self-supporting citizens of the United States, and to aid them in making the freedom conferred . . . available to them and beneficial to the Republic."[37] On March 2, 1867, the Peonage Abolition Act, which also implemented the Thirteenth Amendment, was passed.

President Johnson's veto of the Civil Rights Act of 1866 prompted Congress to prepare the Fourteenth Amendment. However, in late 1866 and early 1867 all the Southern states but Tennessee rejected that amendment. Following this rejection, the first Reconstruction Act was passed on March 2, 1867, whereupon all the "reconstructed" legislatures of the Southern states ratified the amendment. It outlawed any state action which might abridge the privileges and immunities of citizens of the United States, deprive any person of life, liberty, or property without due process of law, or deny to any person the equal protection of the laws. It gave Congress the power to enforce the amendment by

[36] See *infra,* 116.
[37] See Walter L. Fleming, DOCUMENTARY HISTORY OF RECONSTRUCTION (Cleveland, Ohio, 1906–7), I, 321.

appropriate legislation. The latter provision was also part of the Fifteenth Amendment, which stated that "the right of citizens of the United States to vote shall not be denied or abridged by the United States or by any State on account of race, color, or previous condition of servitude." Passed by Congress in February, 1869, this amendment was ratified a year later.

These amendments were followed by further civil rights acts. The second Civil Rights, or Enforcement Act of May 31, 1870, was amended by an act of February 28, 1871. Both were designed to make the Fourteenth and Fifteenth Amendments effective. They provided for federal supervision of elections in the states, prohibited restrictions (because of race or color) on suffrage in federal or state elections, as well as interference with the free exercise by any citizen of the rights granted to him by the laws or the Constitution. On April 20, 1871, Congress passed an act to enforce the provisions of the Fourteenth Amendment, also known as the Ku Klux Klan, or Anti-lynching Act. It penalized actions which, under the cloak of law, deprive persons of their rights under the Constitution and laws of the United States, as well as conspiracy to overthrow the government of the United States or to prevent the execution of its laws. It authorized the President to use military force against unlawful acts if the states did not prevent obstructions of the citizen's rights or of federal processes. Finally, Congress passed on March 1, 1875, "An Act to protect all citizens in their civil and legal rights." It guaranteed Negroes equal accommodation with white citizens in "inns, public conveyances on land or water, theaters, and other places of public amusement." Persons who denied such accommodations were made guilty of a misdemeanor. Injured persons were entitled to damages.[38]

The preamble to the last act has been considered "notable for its echo of some phrases of the Declaration of Independence."[39] This brings up the question of whether the civil rights measures of the Civil War and Reconstruction periods are a harmonious

[38] Cf. Samuel S. Cox, UNION–DISUNION–REUNION: THREE DECADES OF FEDERAL LEGISLATION, 1855–1885 (Washington, 1885).
[39] Konvitz/Leskes, A CENTURY OF CIVIL RIGHTS, 62.

sequence to the documents that were adopted when the American republic was founded. On the face of it, similarities exist between the laws of the two periods. Like the Declaration of Independence, the Articles of Confederation, the Constitution and its Bill of Rights, the measures of the Civil War and Reconstruction eras were designed to protect civil rights. The outward similarity of the substance of the two series of laws is matched by a similarity of circumstances from which they originated. Both came about in emergency situations; the first, in an effort to become and remain free from Britain; the second, from an effort to decrease the chances of foreign dominance over America under the principle of divide and conquer. Both series issued from the same source—the United States. Constitution-making in the two periods also shows similarities. Just as the Constitution and its Bill of Rights restrict state and federal governments, so do the Thirteenth, Fourteenth, and Fifteenth Amendments. According to their wording, the Thirteenth Amendment is directed to the United States; the Fourteenth, to the states; the Fifteenth, to the United States as well as to the individual states. A balance between restrictions of the state and federal governments, similar to the one existing in the Constitution and the Bill of Rights, seems to exist.

However, these similarities ought not to conceal important differences between the two series of civil rights measures. The balance just mentioned may exist in the wording of the Civil War amendments; actually, it does not. For those amendments primarily restrict the states, depriving them of important aspects of their jurisdiction. Thus, whereas the Constitution and its Bill of Rights provided for a balance between restrictions of the state and federal governments, the Civil War amendments, mainly curtailing state discretion on civil rights, shifted that balance in favor of the United States. Also, post-Civil War constitution-making did not result so much from the desire to make the United States secure against foreign powers as from the necessity of preventing the destruction of the Union. Furthermore, the Union of the states, basically undisputed throughout the formative period, was now split into majority and minority factions. The unanimity or near-unanimity which had characterized constitution making during the formative period was replaced by mere majoritarianism, by the rule of a formally qualified majority which had been created artificially by the Reconstruction, and its exercise of duress upon the Southern minority.

The degradation of civil rights through amendments of dubious procedural validity was complemented by the amendments' provisions that Congress had the power to pass enforcement legislation, whereas previously the sphere of civil rights had been reserved basically to the constituent power. It has been pointed out that the "significance of the nearly simultaneous action of Congress in passing the three Amendments and seven statutes implementing them cannot be overlooked."[40] Indeed, it cannot, for that action demonstrates that jurisdiction over civil rights was transferred from the constitution-maker to the ordinary law-maker. It shows that the constituent power, i.e., the people and the states, a power that in principle had enjoyed exclusive jurisdiction over civil rights, was superseded by the constituted power—Congress—a power that in addition represented only the victorious Northern majority. It demonstrates that the power of Congress to implement civil rights, exceptionally permitted by the Third Amendment only in time of war, had become more generally admitted for normal times. Considering that congressional regulation of civil rights previously had been permitted only for the exceptional emergencies of war and rebellion,[41] the transfer of power to Congress amounted to a novelty indeed. Having been non-existent in normal times, Congress' power to legislate on civil rights was increased immensely. Since the United States government was now permitted to do in normal times what previously had been permitted only in an emergency, the thought occurs that the United States from now on would be as much—and in view of the increased congressional power over civil rights perhaps even more—in a state of emergency as in the case of war or rebellion. This raises the question of whether the civil rights measures of

---

[40] Carr, FEDERAL PROTECTION OF CIVIL RIGHTS, 36. Carr refers to Horace E. Flack, THE ADOPTION OF THE FOURTEENTH AMENDMENT (Baltimore, 1908) and Carl B. Swisher, AMERICAN CONSTITUTIONAL DEVELOPMENT (Boston, 1943), ch. 15, to support his contention that the framers of the Civil War amendments meant them to serve as a basis for a positive, comprehensive, federal program. He admits that this contention has been the subject of much controversy.

[41] Art. I, sec. ix, clause 2; Third Amendment.

the Civil War and Reconstruction suggest that the American haven of civil rights, in which people could move among peaceful states as in a quiet harbor among safely anchored ships, had become a stormy sea in which the states and groups of states were pitted against one another, making it difficult for individuals to move until Congress restored the calm through "enforcement" acts which appeared to be enabling acts.[42]

The lowering of the civil rights guarantor from the constituent to a constituted power was accompanied by a protection of rights that were not on a par with traditional civil rights. As we have shown, civil rights were rights of the individual *from* the government, liberal rights which constituted a barrier to governmental action. They were not rights to participate in government—or democratic rights. In distinction to the Constitution and the Bill of Rights, the new civil rights measures not only protected classic civil rights, but also democratic rights. The amendments seemed to do so reluctantly. As if haunted and impeded by the orientation of the Bill of Rights toward classic civil rights, these amendments introduced democratic rights only slowly, step by step. Whereas the Thirteenth Amendment, since it did not expressly provide for the individual's participation in government, still appears to protect liberal rights exclusively, the other amendments go a little further. The Fourteenth Amendment, while providing for the protection of liberal rights, already points toward a protection of the individual's participation in government when it protects "the privileges and immunities of citizens of the United States"—voting and running for public office being such privileges. The Fifteenth Amendment is exclusively concerned with democratic rights: "The right of citizens of the United States to vote shall not be denied or abridged by the United States or by any State on account of race, color, or previous condition of servitude." Congressional legislation shows similar trends. Its protection of liberal rights was increasingly matched by that of democratic rights. The first Reconstruction Act granted suffrage to Negroes. The Civil Rights Act of 1870 was officially called "An

[42] We do not want to compare the acts with the Enabling Act of 1933 which gave Hitler far-reaching power toward *Gleichschaltung*, although such a comparison comes to mind in view of the Reconstruction's "equalization" by force rather than consensus.

Act to enforce the Right of Citizens of the United States to vote in the several States of this Union, and for other Purposes."[43] Democratic rights were protected in the Civil Rights Acts of 1871 and 1875.

While the introduction of democratic rights into the framework of civil rights was not without risk because it raised democratic rights—a means—to the level of civil rights—an end—it could be defended on the ground that it was not out of tune with the American tradition of free government, a tradition based upon the belief that popular participation in government is the best means of protecting the individual from the powers of government. However, the new concept of civil rights differs from that of the Bill of Rights not only because it includes democratic rights, but also because it introduces a new category of rights which not only restrict the government but also private individuals. That introduction, again, seems to have been done cautiously, step by step. Whereas the amendments appear to protect several classic civil rights, the Civil Rights Acts also protect the new category when they provide penalties for infringements by private individuals. Since such infringements are punished even if they are prompted by the desire to protect other civil rights, the Reconstruction measures in a new manner also favor some rights over others.[44]

Summing up, it can be said that the measures discussed were dubious on procedural as well as substantive grounds. The procedures under which the amendments were adopted were at best legal, but hardly legitimate. The amendments were made by a dubious constitution-changer in an emergency situation rather than by a normal constituent power. Their new origin was matched by their new regulations of civil rights. Their enforcement was left to Congress. Congress was made a civil rights legislator, a capacity that previously had been reserved to the

[43] Konvitz/Leskes, A CENTURY OF CIVIL RIGHTS, 57, comment: "The act dealt with voting rights and with civil rights," and thus draw a distinction between democratic and civil rights. However, their concept of civil rights is not identical to our concept of classic civil rights = liberal rights = protection of the individual from the government. Cf. Norman Dorsen, Thomas I. Emerson and David Haber, POLITICAL AND CIVIL RIGHTS IN THE UNITED STATES (3d ed.; Boston, 1967).

[44] The rights that were probably most hurt by those measures were those of property. Cf. *infra,* 132.

constituent or amending power—the people and the states. The new amendments provided for democratic as well as for liberal rights, and the Civil Rights Acts in addition provided for rights that were valid against private individuals as well as against the government. Some rights were favored over others. New "civil rights" were made equal—if not superior to—classic civil rights.

The questionable nature of the Civil War and Reconstruction measures was recognized from the beginning. While the amendments survived, most legislation was declared unconstitutional, or made ineffective by the Supreme Court, or revoked by Congress.

President Johnson who, like his predecessor, favored a conciliatory policy toward the South and the traditional equilibrium between national power and states rights once hostilities had ended,[45] opposed some of these measures from the beginning. Vetoing the Freedmen's Bureau Bill early in 1866, he contended that it was "not warranted by the Constitution." He opposed national aid for the Negro. For instance, the national government was not to provide for Negro schools, since under the Constitution education was reserved to the states, local communities, private persons, or associations. Nor was the national government to provide for homes. Johnson was confident that Negroes "will distinguish themselves by their industry and thrift, and soon show the world that in a condition of freedom they are self-sustaining, capable of selecting their own employment and their own places of abode, of insisting for themselves on a proper remuneration." If freedmen did not like conditions in one place, they could move to another.[46] In his veto of the Civil Rights Act of 1866, President Johnson resented national jurisdiction over "the internal policy and economy of the respective States," and denounced what he considered "another step, or rather stride, towards centralization of all legislative power in the national Government." He criticized the bill for trying "to settle questions of political economy through the agency of numerous officials, whose interest it will be to foment

---

[45] He pleaded with Congress to seat Southern representatives and vetoed the Reconstruction Act of Mar. 2, 1867. McPherson, HISTORY DURING RECONSTRUCTION, 68, 166.

[46] *Ibid.*, 68.

discord between the two races," instead of leaving the relationship between white capital and colored labor to the market.[47]

Johnson was not alone in his opposition. The civil rights measures were by no means easily adopted. Congress was unable to pass the first Freedmen's Bureau Bill over the President's veto. The Fourteenth Amendment was rejected early in 1867 not only by Confederate States, but also by Delaware, Kentucky, and Maryland. New Jersey, Ohio, and Oregon withdrew their ratifications in 1868. California, Iowa, and Nebraska originally failed to act on the amendment. In the end, California rejected—and the other two ratified it. The Fifteenth Amendment also was denied ratification by states not subject to the Reconstruction Acts. It took the Civil Rights Act of 1875 five years to get through Congress.[48]

Court decisions circumscribed the amendments, invalidated legislation, or made it ineffective. While holding that the Fifteenth Amendment protects the right to vote against state interference and authorizes Congress to provide such protection against interferences on account of the voter's race, color, or previous condition of servitude, the Supreme Court struck down important parts of the Civil Rights Act of May 31, 1870, because they were directed also against other types of interference.[49] Stating that under the Fourteenth and Fifteenth Amendments Congress could safeguard rights from state governments but not from private persons, it invalidated the Civil Rights Act of 1875.[50] Admitting that the Thirteenth Amendment entitled Congress to protect freedom from slavery and involuntary servitude against private as well as public interference, the Court maintained that this freedom must be defined narrowly and does not include freedom from discrimination based upon color. It invalidated part of the Act of May 31, 1870.[51] In other decisions, the Court restricted civil rights legislation by insisting that the Constitution does not establish a major body of civil rights on a federal level

---

[47] *Ibid.*, 74.
[48] See Konvitz/Leskes, A CENTURY OF CIVIL RIGHTS, 51ff., 57, 90ff.
[49] *United States* v. *Reese*, 92 U.S. 214 (1876).
[50] *Civil Rights Cases*, 109 U.S. 3 (1883).
[51] *Hodges* v. *United States*, 203 U.S. 1 (1906). The three cases just mentioned were complemented by *United States* v. *Harris*, 106 U.S. 629 (1883); *Baldwin* v. *Franks*, 120 U.S. 678 (1887); *James* v. *Bowman*, 190 U.S. 127 (1903).

which Congress may protect. It held that the "privileges and immunities clause" of the Fourteenth Amendment did not "federalize"[52] the great body of civil rights, or place any large group of rights under the protection of the national government against infringements by the states let alone those by private persons. Civil rights were primarily to be protected by state law.[53] The Court also took a narrow view of the rights provided by the Act of May 31, 1870.[54]

Since the Court's attitude was acclaimed by the public,[55] it is not surprising that Congress became more and more lukewarm in pushing civil rights. We remarked that it took the last Civil Rights Act five years to pass through Congress. During that period, civil rights legislation was rearranged in the official *Revised Statutes* and, in this pursuit, lost its drive.[56] In 1877, Congress repealed much of the federal enforcement program. In 1894, it repealed about four-fifths of the sections of all enforcement acts. In 1909, it reduced civil rights and suffrage enactments still further.[57]

In view of the adverse decisions of the Supreme Court and the repeal of civil rights legislation by Congress, it is not surprising that the executive branch of the national government became less enthusiastic about enforcing whatever provisions had remained on the books. While the Department of Justice for a while tried to enforce these provisions, it soon gave up. "By the last decade of the nineteenth century it had lost heart, and thereafter only sporadic attempts were made to enforce the remnants of the civil rights legislation."[58]

In summary: A generation after they came into existence, the

[52] The expression is used by Carr, FEDERAL PROTECTION OF CIVIL RIGHTS, 44.
[53] *Slaughterhouse Cases,* 16 Wallace 36 (1873).
[54] *United States* v. *Cruikshank,* 92 U.S. 542 (1876).
[55] For a survey, see Charles Warren, THE SUPREME COURT IN UNITED STATES HISTORY (Boston, 1937) II, chs. 32–34.
[56] According to Francis Biddle, "Civil Rights and the Federal Law," in SAFEGUARDING CIVIL LIBERTY TODAY (Edward L. Bernays Lectures; Ithaca, N.Y., 1945), 131, this action "effectively concealed the whole scheme for the protection of rights established by the three amendments and five acts by separating their provisions under unrelated chapters of the *Revised Statutes.*"
[57] See William W. Davis, THE FEDERAL ENFORCEMENT ACTS (New York, 1914).
[58] Carr, FEDERAL PROTECTION OF CIVIL RIGHTS, 46f., referring to Homer Cummings and Carl McFarland, FEDERAL JUSTICE (New York, 1937), ch. 12, and to SAFEGUARDING CIVIL LIBERTY TODAY, 109, 131f.

new civil rights provisions were no longer effective. With the restoration of normal times, a no longer "reconstructed" Congress came to recognize the abnormality of most congressional civil rights norms and repealed them. Its action was prompted by a—never "reconstructed"—Supreme Court which made civil rights legislation ineffective, interpreted the new amendments narrowly, and favored the traditional federal balance of power over a modern democratic concentration of power. Praised for this attitude by a sobered, no longer war-impassioned public opinion, the Court exercised its traditional function. It scrutinized acts of Congress for their constitutionality, but accepted constitutional amendments—dubious as their origin may have been—and interpreted the latter as it saw fit. In a word, the Court protected the constituent from a constituted power, leaving no doubt about its mission as the natural interpreter of the laws.[59] By invalidating civil rights legislation and accepting amendments to the Constitution, the Court indicated the risk of leaving such legislation to Congress. Congress, by repealing much of what had not been invalidated by the Court, showed that it concurred. Thus the jurisdiction over civil rights was in principle handed back to the power where it originally had been vested—the constituent power, or the people and the states. The implementation of civil rights in the states was basically entrusted to their respective governments. Whereas the addition of democratic rights to civil rights was not contested, the idea that rights were to be protected from private individuals was questioned.

Considerable as congressional and judicial restrictions of the civil rights measures may have been, they were not absolute. While the new category of rights was restricted, it was not abolished; while the states were basically entrusted with the implementation of civil rights within their respective boundaries, they were not totally trusted; while congressional civil rights legislation was curtailed, it was not abolished altogether. National potentials for the regulation of civil rights thus remained. Possibilities of further guaranteeing liberal rights against private actions; of increasing the protection of civil rights within the

[59] Cf. Hamilton's defense of judicial review in THE FEDERALIST, No. 78.

states; of expanding congressional civil rights legislation—all these possibilities were left open. Overshadowing everything else was the admission that the growth of democratic rights throughout the states and the nation would aid the advance of the rights of men.

The expansion of democratic rights, combined as it was with an increase of national power, resulted in an American mass democracy that was likely to make use of the possibilities just mentioned. The national mass was to look into what it considered the states' mess.

Unfortunately, the states often failed to protect civil rights. Run, like all governments, by fallible men, state governments often did not fulfill the trust put in them. While the situation in any state can be judged fairly only from the traditions, mores, and special conditions of that state, this failure in many cases has been quite bad.[60] And whereas this was not necessarily as detrimental to America's image as a haven of freedom, as some critics have asserted, because the inhabitants of one state were free to move to another, it did not go unnoticed. As a result, the national government reassumed a role as defender of civil rights. And just as the Supreme Court after the Civil War had initiated restriction of national protection of civil rights within the states, it now paved the way for an expansion of such protection.

We have seen that Chief Justice Marshall held that the Bill of Rights did not apply to the states; that in a series of decisions, beginning with the Slaughterhouse Cases in 1873, the Court refused to regard the liberties of the Bill of Rights as "privileges or immunities of citizens of the United States."[61] As late as 1922, it resisted the argument that the word "liberty" in the clause "nor shall any State deprive any person of life, liberty, or property, without due process of law" included the liberties enumerated in

[60] See the literature listed *supra*, 98n.; also Carr, FEDERAL PROTECTION OF CIVIL RIGHTS, 20ff.

[61] 16 Wallace 36 (1873); *Walker* v. *Sauvinet*, 92 U.S. 90 (1876); *Maxwell* v. *Dow*, 176 U.S. 581 (1900); *Twining* v. *New Jersey*, 211 U.S. 78 (1908). Andrew C. McLaughlin, A CONSTITUTIONAL HISTORY OF THE UNITED STATES (New York, 1935), 730f., is in agreement with this position, Robert E. Cushman, LEADING CONSTITUTIONAL DECISIONS (8th ed.; New York, 1946), 41, is not.

the Bill of Rights.[62] However, in view of the increasing pressure which was partly reflected in dissenting opinions, the Court began to retreat from its position in 1923.[63] In 1931, it invalidated a state statute on the ground that this statute interfered with freedom of the press.[64] In the following years, other liberties enumerated in the Bill of Rights were brought within the orbit of the Fourteenth Amendment.[65] And while the Court in 1937 stated that not all the liberties mentioned in the Bill of Rights were to be safeguarded against state action, but only "those fundamental principles of liberty and justice which lie at the base of all our civil and political institutions,"[66] it was plain that at the Court's discretion all the liberties of the Bill of Rights could be enforced by the national government against the states. In 1947, it could well be maintained that in spite of the Court's failure to use the "due process" clause of the Fourteenth Amendment for the protection of *"all* of the items in the Bill of Rights, nationalization of civil liberty against state infringements is now pretty much an established fact. The function of the Constitution as a shield which protects our fundamental civil rights against interference resulting from *governmental* activity has thus been rendered complete."[67]

Segregation in the states was increasingly abolished under the equal protection clause of the Fourteenth Amendment. The "Separate but Equal" Case, *Plessy* v. *Ferguson* (1896), had held that that clause required only that a state treat members of different

---

[62] *Prudential Insurance Co.* v. *Cheek,* 259 U.S. 530 (1922).

[63] See, for instance, Justice Harlan's dissenting opinion in *Patterson* v. *Colorado,* 205 U.S. 454, 463 (1907). Cf. also *Meyer* v. *Nebraska,* 262 U.S. 390 (1923); *Pierce* v. *Society of Sisters,* 268 U.S. 510 (1925). In *Gitlow* v. *New York,* 268 U.S. 652, 666 (1925), Justice Edward T. Sanford, while accepting the statute under review as constitutional, stated: "[W]e may and do assume that freedom of speech and of the press—which are protected by the 1st Amendment from abridgement by Congress—are among the fundamental personal rights and 'liberties' protected by the due process clause of the 14th Amendment from impairment by the states."

[64] *Near* v. *Minnesota,* 283 U.S. 697 (1931).

[65] For freedom of religion, see *Cantwell* v. *Connecticut,* 310 U.S. 296 (1940); for the right of assembly, see *DeJonge* v. *Oregon,* 299 U.S. 353 (1937); for the right of petition, see *Bridges* v. *California,* 314 U.S. 252 (1941). A survey is supplied by Dumbauld, THE BILL OF RIGHTS AND WHAT IT MEANS TODAY, 132ff.; see also Osmond K. Fraenkel, OUR CIVIL LIBERTIES (New York, 1944), 46ff.

[66] *Palko* v. *Connecticut,* 302 U.S. 319, 328 (1937).

[67] Carr, FEDERAL PROTECTION OF CIVIL RIGHTS, 14.

races equally, not that it treat them so in the same places.[68] In spite of Justice Harlan's dissent that "our Constitution is color-blind,"[69] the "separate but equal doctrine" prevailed until 1927.[70] Later on, it was gradually abolished. In 1935, the Court held that a state could not select jurors by race.[71] In 1938, it held that a state was denying equal protection of the laws if it refused a Negro admission to a white law school, even though it stood ready to pay his tuition in an appropriate law school in another state.[72] In 1948 it ruled that a state could not enforce a covenant which forbade use of certain real estate "by people of the Negro or Mongolian Race."[73] In 1950 the Court held that a student had to be admitted to a white law school of a state because that school was better than the state's law school for colored students.[74] It also held that a Negro student in a state medical school could not be required to keep to himself in lecture rooms, the cafeteria, and the library.[75] Finally, in 1954, a unanimous Court explicitly ended the "separate but equal doctrine" in *Brown* v. *Board of Education*.[76] These cases were matched by decisions that prevented segregation under the Fifteenth Amendment.[77]

The Supreme Court's protection of civil rights vis-à-vis the states was matched by a protection of those rights against the national government, be it under the original Constitution, the Bill of Rights, or the later amendments. Often, constitutional

---

[68] 163 U.S. 537 (1896).

[69] *Ibid.*, 559. The whole passage reads: "The white race deems itself to be the dominant race in this country. And so it is, in prestige, in achievements, in education, in wealth, and in power. So, I doubt not that it will continue to be for all time, if it remains true to its great heritage and holds fast to the principles of constitutional liberty. But in view of the Constitution, in the eye of the law, there is in this country no superior, dominant, ruling class of citizens. There is no caste here. Our Constitution is color-blind, and neither knows nor tolerates classes among citizens. In respect of civil rights, all citizens are equal before the law. The humblest is the peer of the most powerful. The law regards man as man, and takes no account of his surroundings or of his color when his civil rights as guaranteed by the supreme law of the land are involved."

[70] *Gong Lum* v. *Rice,* 275 U.S. 78 (1927).

[71] *Norris* v. *Alabama,* 294 U.S. 587 (1935).

[72] *Missouri ex rel. Gaines* v. *Canada,* 305 U.S. 337 (1938).

[73] *Shelley* v. *Kraemer,* 334 U.S. 1 (1948).

[74] *Sweatt* v. *Painter,* 339 U.S. 629 (1950).

[75] *McLaurin* v. *Oklahoma State Regents,* 339 U.S. 637 (1950).

[76] 347 U.S. 483; see also *Bolling* v. *Sharpe,* 347 U.S. 497 (1954).

[77] *Smith* v. *Allwright,* 321 U.S. 649 (1944); *Terry* v. *Adams,* 345 U.S. 461 (1953).

provisions were interpreted broadly. "A new era in civil liberties"[78] came about, adorned by a "new liberty."[79] For "liberty" existed not only because the Supreme Court took the liberty of applying the Bill of Rights to the states, but also because it expanded civil liberties and also protected them against the national government.

As things turned out, civil rights soon needed little protection against the national government. For the political branches of that government became ardent advocates of those rights. The "new liberty," brought about by the Supreme Court, encouraged both the President and Congress to become more active in the promotion of civil rights. In 1939, a Civil Liberties Unit was created in the Department of Justice. In 1941, President Roosevelt created a Fair Employment Practices Commission, and Congress appropriated money for its operation until 1945. In 1946, President Truman appointed a Committee on Civil Rights. The Committee's report, while leaving no doubt about the great progress which had been made in the implementation of civil rights, emphasized the serious gap still remaining between the egalitarian ideal and actual practice, and recommended extensive new federal legislation to narrow this gap.[80] In 1948 President Truman asked Congress for such legislation. Similar demands were made by his successors, Eisenhower, Kennedy, and Johnson.[81] These demands led to civil rights acts.

The Civil Rights Act of 1957, to "provide means of further securing and protecting the civil rights of persons within the jurisdiction of the United States," established a Commission on Civil Rights, with which all federal agencies were required to co-operate. That Commission was to investigate allegations that certain citizens were being deprived of "their right to vote and to have that vote counted" on account of color, race, religion, or national origin, and to study and collect information "concerning

[78] Kelly/Harbison, AMERICAN CONSTITUTION (rev. ed., 1955), 790.

[79] The expression is by Charles Warren, "The New 'Liberty' under the Fourteenth Amendment," HARVARD LAW REVIEW, XXXIX (1926), 431.

[80] The report is published under the title TO SECURE THESE RIGHTS (Washington, 1947).

[81] See Kelly/Harbison, AMERICAN CONSTITUTION, 924ff.; Bureau of National Affairs (ed.), THE CIVIL RIGHTS ACT OF 1964 (Washington, 1964), 9ff.

legal developments constituting a denial of equal protection of the laws under the Constitution." The act provided that neither public officials nor private individuals shall intimidate, coerce or threaten another person for the purpose of interfering with the latter's right to vote for any federal office at any general, special, or primary election. The Attorney General of the United States was authorized to enforce the citizen's right to vote.[82] The Civil Rights Act of 1960 strengthened the Act of 1957.[83] The Civil Rights Act of 1964 has been considered "the strongest Civil Rights Act since Reconstruction."[84] It marshals the executive and judicial agencies of the national government to eliminate grievances of those who are denied equal treatment by reason of race, color, religion, national origin, and sex. It recurrently provides for intervention by the Attorney General of the United States in litigation to effect civil rights, whereas hitherto the burden of such court proceedings had mainly rested on private organizations or individuals. In particular, this act strengthens previous legislation protecting the right to vote. It reverses the result of the Civil Rights Cases of 1883, and gives persons equal access to places of "public accommodation" which affect interstate commerce or in which discrimination is supported by state action. The act strengthens desegregation of public facilities, reinforces desegregation in public education, and supports the Commission on Civil Rights. It authorizes the withdrawal of federal support from any activity which discriminates on the basis of race, color, or national origin. It prescribes equal employment opportunity irrespective of race, color, religion, national origin, or sex, and creates a Commission charged with the promotion of these policies. It directs the Secretary of Commerce to compile relevant registration and voting statistics and hints at the utilization of the provision of the Fourteenth Amendment which reduces a state's representation in Congress in proportion to the state's denial of federal electoral participation to qualified citizens. Furthermore, the act facilitates removal to federal courts of state court actions con-

[82] The history and major features of the act are described in Konvitz/Leskes, A CENTURY OF CIVIL RIGHTS, 72ff.

[83] See *ibid.*, 83ff.

[84] Sutherland, CONSTITUTIONALISM IN AMERICA, 518. The most comprehensive work on the act is THE CIVIL RIGHTS ACT OF 1964.

cerning civil rights, and establishes a Community Relations Service to assist communities and persons therein in resolving racial problems.

The modern civil rights measures in many respects are similar to those of the Civil War and Reconstruction periods. President Lincoln's establishment of a Freedmen's Bureau was matched by the establishment under President Roosevelt of a Civil Liberties Unit and of a Fair Employment Practices Commission. As civil rights acts had resulted from the emergency existing after the Civil War, they came about in the emergency situation of the Cold War. The formal source of the civil rights acts of both periods is the same: Congress acting as the representative of the national majority. Also, the content of both series of acts is similar. They protect liberal rights from the actions of public officials as well as from those of private individuals.[85] They also protect democratic rights, securing the individual's participation in government. They provide for sanctions against those who contravene the acts. With justification, the modern civil rights acts were called an "echo" of the Reconstruction Enforcement Acts.[86]

The echo has been magnifying. While the modern civil rights acts show many similarities to their Reconstruction counterparts, they enlarge the civil rights introduced by the latter. They go further in their protection of civil rights against actions of private persons. Their equal accommodation provisions are more comprehensive. The Civil Rights Acts of the Reconstruction period, providing for equal accommodation in "inns, public conveyances on land and water, theaters, and other places of public amusement," basically followed the common law rule.[87] The Civil Rights Act of 1964 goes beyond that when, for instance, it extends the equal accommodation obligation to restaurants. Furthermore, whereas the acts of the Reconstruction period did not provide for equal, or "fair," employment, the Act of 1964 does. As a matter of fact, it does so to a degree that it has been called

---

[85] Cf. Carr, FEDERAL PROTECTION OF CIVIL RIGHTS, 14ff.; Gellhorn, AMERICAN RIGHTS, 163ff.

[86] Konvitz/Leskes, A CENTURY OF CIVIL RIGHTS, 80.

[87] See CIVIL RIGHTS ACT OF 1964, 79f.

"The Fair Employment Practice Act."[88] This quality shows another shift toward "new" rights: the Civil Rights Acts of the Reconstruction period, providing for equal accommodation, had compelled private persons to suffer individuals on their premises on a more-or-less temporary basis. Modern legislation, providing for fair employment, compels private persons to employ others more or less permanently. The demand for a basically *passive* behavior, as in the case of innkeepers or the owners of theaters, was replaced by one for a basically *active* behavior, as in the case of employers. What finally concerns democratic rights, their protection in the new laws also is more comprehensive than in the old ones, complemented as they were by the Voting Rights Act of 1965.

The broadening of the span of civil rights is matched by an enlargement of their applicability and intensification of their sanction. The private persons for whom the earlier acts implied obligations, such as innkeepers, owners of public conveyances, and theaters, were few. "The Civil Rights Act of 1964 affects almost every American."[89] It affects almost every American not only because it secures his rights, but also because it places him under obligations. The enforcement of civil rights also has changed. Whereas formerly only private organizations or individuals could become a party to a suit to effectuate those rights, now the Attorney General of the United States can intervene in litigation: "The United States of America will be an adversary difficult to dislodge."[90]

In general, the new civil rights acts have more thrust than their predecessors. This is not surprising in view of the fact that there was greater force behind their adoption. The civil rights legislation of the Reconstruction period had been imposed by a Northern majority of states upon a Southern minority of states. It was passed by a federal Congress that was just about to become a national Congress at a time when national power basically was still supposed to be balanced by states rights, irrespective of how much the latter may have been belittled as a result of the Union

[88] *Ibid.*, iii, 1.
[89] *Ibid.*, vii.
[90] Sutherland, CONSTITUTIONALISM IN AMERICA, 519.

victory. Emphatic as the "reconstructed" Congress may have been in enacting civil rights laws, its zest was overshadowed by doubts. After all, Congress acted under amendments whose legitimacy was disputed, knowing that the other branches of the government and large segments of the public did not share its views. On the other hand, modern civil rights laws were adopted by a large national majority over the resistance of a small sectional minority. They were made by a Congress that had developed from a federal into a national legislature. Furthermore, Congress acted under constitutional provisions about the validity of which there was not much doubt, such as the commerce clause and the Civil War amendments which had become generally accepted. Congress did not act in spite of presidential and judicial doubts, but in large measure acted upon judicial and presidential proddings.

Concluding, it may be said that the difference between the modern civil rights situation and that of the Reconstruction period is about as notable as the difference between the latter situation and the situation prior to the Civil War. The egalitarian additions to classic civil rights since the Civil War and the recent expansion of these additions brought about greater and greater civil rights obligations. This development is in no small measure due to the basically undisputed growth of democratic rights. This growth, combined as it was with an expansion of national power, created a national democracy which became the proponent of a civil rights program that was broader than ever before, and was accompanied by increasing obligations.

THE GROWTH OF
NATIONAL POWER AND "CIVIL" RIGHTS
AS A CHALLENGE TO FREE GOVERNMENT

We wonder whether the promotion of civil rights through national power has been a blessing. The question is posed by the fact that the legitimacy of the civil rights legislation of the Reconstruction was disputed. Since modern civil rights policy goes beyond that legislation, must it not be dubious *a fortiori?* In the following, an attempt will be made to supply an answer by examining the meaning of modern civil rights policy for free government, a government implying popular government as a means for the protection of the individual.

While the expansion of democratic rights generally is expected to secure the individual's freedom, this need not be so. For while such an expansion does not necessarily imply the emergence of an uninhibited majority rule, it will often result in such a rule. And whereas this rule can promote civil rights, it can also determine those rights and thus eliminate them, for the power to define is the power to destroy. An unrestricted democratic rule can be compared to Rousseau's Legislator. It can do much good for the individual, but also much harm by subjecting him to the will of the majority or the general will.[91] In its desire to create the greatest good of the greatest number—a basically democratic desire—the majority, or greater number (perhaps by accommodating in a given situation merely a relatively small component) can bring about great evil for the small number, or minority, an evil which sooner or later may engulf greater numbers, and, in the end, the majority itself. In the following, it will be examined whether modern civil rights policy, as determined by the American national majority, constitutes such a danger. In this endeavor, personal desires to see discrimination because of race,

---

[91] Cf. Rousseau's CONTRAT SOCIAL, Bk. II, ch. 7: "The Lawgiver must feel himself in a position to change the nature of man; to transform each individual, who in himself is a self-contained and isolated whole, into part of a larger whole, from which he receives, in some sense, his life and his being. He must feel himself able to alter the constitution of man, with a view to giving it greater strength; to put a dependent and moral existence in place of the independent and physical existence which we have received from nature. In a word, he must take from man his natural powers, in order to give him powers which are foreign to him, and of which he can make no use without the help of others. The more completely those natural powers are mortified and annihilated, the greater is the strength and durability of those which he acquires; the more solid and perfect, moreover, is the work of the Lawgiver. It follows that, if the individual citizen is nothing and can do nothing without the aid of all the rest, if the powers acquired by the whole body are equal or superior to the sum of powers belonging by nature to all the individual members, then we are entitled to say that the legislation has reached the highest point of perfection which it can attain." POLITICAL WRITINGS, I, 29. See also the remarks by the editor, *ibid.,* 28ff.

color, religion, national background and sex ended, will be put behind rational arguments that could conceivably promote the continued existence of free government. For the aim must not be some short-range democratic appeasement of certain groups, convenient and expedient as it may be for the time being, but a long-range constitutionalist peace for all, inconvenient and inexpedient as it may appear at present.

In 1939, the Attorney General of the United States stated: "In a democracy, an important function of the law enforcement branch of government is the aggressive protection of fundamental rights inherent in a free people."[92] Later, the word "aggressive" was emphasized by the executive director of the Commission on Civil Rights. He advocated the "nationalization" of civil rights and an aggressive activity of the national government for the advancement of those rights.[93] As the preceding pages have shown, both the "nationalization" of those rights as well as their aggressive protection by the national government have more or less come about. Doubts about modern civil rights policy in large measure derive from this fact, for concepts such as "aggressive protection" and "nationalization" have an authoritarian undertone.

An aggressive civil rights policy seems to be a contradiction in terms. While it is defensible with respect to the execution of the laws,[94] it is dubious as a legislative program because it makes civil rights appear as an imposition by, rather than a restriction upon, the government. President Truman showed that this supposition is not much off the mark: "[We] cannot be content with a civil liberties program which emphasizes only the need of protection against the possibility of tyranny by the Government. We cannot stop there. We must keep moving forward, with new concepts of civil rights to safeguard our heritage. The extension of civil rights

---

[92] NEW YORK TIMES, Feb. 4, 1939.

[93] Carr, FEDERAL PROTECTION OF CIVIL RIGHTS, 1, 10, 14, 203ff.

[94] Hamilton considered "Energy in the Executive . . . essential . . . to the steady administration of the laws; to the protection of property against those irregular and high-handed combinations which sometimes interrupt the ordinary course of justice; to the security of liberty against the enterprises and assaults of ambition, of faction, and of anarchy." THE FEDERALIST, No. 70.

today means, not protection of the people *against* the Government, but protection of the people *by* the government."[95] Civil rights no longer are merely classic civil rights, securing the protection of the individual *from* the government, but include "new concepts of civil rights" such as the protection against actions of private persons, and democratic rights, all of which are promoted by the national government.[96] The latter has been elevated from its original role of a respecter of classic civil rights to a determinant of civil rights, a function which originally was—and should be—reserved to the constituent or amending power. However, even with these innovations an aggressive civil rights policy could still be defensible provided it does not create obligations which are incompatible with classic civil rights. If it imposes such obligations, it would amount to an aggression upon cherished liberties of the individual, and come close to a contradiction in terms.

Modern civil rights policy imposes such obligations. While we hope for the day when discrimination based on race, color, religion, national origin, and sex will no longer be practiced, we would never think of imposing our opinion upon others and are wary if the government tries to do so. This wariness has been shared by others. It is reflected in the refusal to pass the Civil Rights Bill of 1966; in the reluctance to enforce the Civil Rights Act of 1964; in the misgivings with which the latter was passed.[97]

The Bill of 1966 encountered difficulties mainly because of its provisions for "open housing," and for good reason. However much the idea, "my home is my castle," may be denounced, it still is one of the most cherished common law principles securing freedom, dating back to the feudal age. On that account it is not, however, a remnant of feudalism which would impose anachronistic limitations upon modern life. If it were, it should be discarded

---

[95] Address before the National Association for the Advancement of Colored People, June 29, 1947. PUBLIC PAPERS OF THE PRESIDENTS OF THE UNITED STATES: HARRY S TRUMAN (Washington, 1947), 311.

[96] Carr, FEDERAL PROTECTION OF CIVIL RIGHTS, vi, uses the following statement by John Marshall in *Marbury* v. *Madison* as the leitmotif for his work: "The very essence of civil liberty certainly consists in the right of every individual to claim the protection of the laws, whenever he receives an injury. One of the first duties of government is to afford that protection." It is open to doubt whether this use is justified, since Marshall believed in the classic concept of civil liberty. See *supra,* 69, and the author's IN DEFENSE OF PROPERTY, 78f.

[97] See *supra,* 63f.

as were entail and primogeniture.[98] As it is, the principle is as valuable today as it has been in preceding generations. Housing in the United States today is "closed" not because it was so decreed by past generations, but because it is freely desired by the present generation. To force "open housing" would thus amount to intruding into cherished liberal rights—the rights to rent or to sell one's property to whomever one wants, and the right to live however one wants. It would encroach upon a traditionally protected private sphere of the individual. It would subject the law-abiding owner to inconveniences that are conceivably greater than those to which the law-breaking inhabitant is subjected under the Fourth Amendment. It would make a farce not only of the common law principle, "my home is my castle," but also of a provision of the Bill of Rights which reflects that principle.

Whereas doubts concerning housing prevented the passage of the Civil Rights Bill of 1966, doubts concerning equal accommodation and fair employment did not prevent the Civil Rights Act of 1964. Still, such doubts did not disappear after the passage of that act. And whereas laws should be obeyed as long as they are valid in spite of doubts, they must always be subject to criticism, for criticism is the father of progress. The problem of equal accommodation is similar to that of open housing. However, the common law provides for an exception to the principle "my home is my castle" in the case of public accommodations.[99] Some of the accommodations mentioned in the act fall within this exception; others, such as restaurants, do not. In their case, while it must not be forgotten that the common law has been flexible and changed through equity, skepticism ought to prevail against too great an expansion of the concept of public accommodation. For instance, it is probably insufficient merely to exclude from the list of establishments that are forbidden to discriminate because they provide lodging to transient guests, "an establishment located within

---

[98] Today's civil rights legislation cannot well be compared with Prussia's *Befreiungsgesetzgebung* (liberation-legislation) at the beginning of the nineteenth century. The latter abolished remnants of feudalism, whereas today's restrictions upon the sale of real estate in the United States are due to recent contractual agreements.

[99] Blackstone, COMMENTARIES, Bk. III, 144ff. See also THE CIVIL RIGHTS ACT OF 1964, 79f.

a building which contains not more than five rooms for rent or hire and which is actually occupied by the proprietor of such establishment as his residence."[100] Also, it is dubious to make such a building look like an exception, whereas actually public accommodations themselves constitute exceptions to the rule, "my home is my castle." Needless to say, the right to equal accommodation does not only compete with the principle just mentioned, but also with freedom of contract, another traditional liberal right sanctioned by the Constitution.

The latter right bears the brunt of fair employment provisions. While the principle, "my home is my castle," originally often extended to a person's business, business today is usually away from the home. However, in a free society, employment presupposes individuals contracting freely. Fair employment provisions are thus likely to collide with freedom of contract. For this reason, their passage was prevented initially.[101] Freedom of contract is one of the foremost American liberties.[102] For many Americans, it draws the line between the free and the regulated man. The free man wants the government to mind its own business and leave him alone to regulate his business. In matters of employment, he wants to be as open to the appeal of color, race, religion, or national origin as to that of sex—as open as the voter who elects or rejects candidates. The free man wants freedom of contract to be above the color line or similar lines. Governmental attempts to abolish these lines are apt to appear like a line given to conceal steps toward governmental control of business.

Reconsidering the major moot points of modern civil rights policy, it turns out that that policy is above all incompatible with economic rights. Therefore, since civil rights originally included economic rights; since the latter are as civil as other rights; since civilization cannot exist without their protection;[103] the rights

---

[100] Sec. 201.

[101] See Kelly/Harbison, AMERICAN CONSTITUTION, 950ff.

[102] See *supra,* 64ff.; Milton Friedman, CAPITALISM AND FREEDOM (Chicago, 1962). Herbert Hoover, AMERICAN INDIVIDUALISM (Garden City, N.Y., 1922), THE CHALLENGE TO LIBERTY (New York, 1934). In "The Fifth Freedom," ADDRESSES UPON THE AMERICAN ROAD: WORLD WAR II, 1941–45 (New York, 1946), 222, Hoover stated that "there is a Fifth Freedom—economic freedom—without which none of the other four freedoms will be realized."

[103] See the author's IN DEFENSE OF PROPERTY, ch. 1.

pushed today by the national government in a large measure are pseudo-civil rights, or "civil" rights. In its desire to promote civil rights, the democratic majority has used and abused that term for its own purposes, for the advancement of rights that are often interfering with classic liberties.

The pseudo character of "civil" rights also can be seen in the paradox that they impose tolerance and prohibit prejudice. While we feel that prejudice is bad, we also feel that its prohibition is just as bad. The end does not justify the means. A government which penalizes men for entertaining prejudices which do not amount to the kind of intolerance that is evident in the socio-ethically objectionable behavior of criminals,[104] oversteps its legitimate authority. For it basically penalizes disagreement.[105] If the end does not justify the means, then the means must be even less justified if the end's goodness is open to doubt. And whereas we applaud the government for following the Constitution by not providing for privileges because "privilege is the greatest enemy of justice,"[106] we doubt the propriety of its prohibiting prejudice to private individuals.

Prejudice is natural in the form of taste, for which no reason need be given or even exist. If we love someone, we probably are as prejudiced in his favor as we are prejudiced against those whom we do not love; if we hate someone, we probably are as prejudiced against him as we are prejudiced in favor of those whom we do not hate. Love and hatred often make men blind. The same applies to our likes and dislikes. Some people are prejudiced in favor of some, and against other, precious stones; in favor of some and against other animals; in favor of classic and against modern art; in favor of blonds and against brunets, or, as it so happened in the French Revolution, the other way around. These are but a few examples, for there seems to be no end to taste and prejudice, even if people realize that their prejudices are unwar-

---

[104] See Hans Welzel, DAS DEUTSCHE STRAFRECHT (9th ed.; Berlin, 1965), 1.

[105] A slogan of German Marxists was, *"Und willst Du nicht mein Bruder sein, so schlag ich Dir den Schädel ein"*—[if you don't want to be my brother, I'll smash your skull].

[106] *"Der grösste Feind des Rechts ist das Vorrecht."* Marie von Ebner-Eschenbach, as quoted by Gustav Radbruch, RECHTSPHILOSOPHIE (4th ed.; Stuttgart, 1950), 125.

ranted and unreasonable. *Chacun à son goût.* The right to prejudice is part of freedom—another side of freedom of choice.[107]

Like any exercise of freedom, prejudice may be in poor taste.
However, while poor taste is to be deplored, it appears doubtful
whether it should be legislated away. In our opinion, prejudice on
account of race, color, religion, national origin, and sex is in poor
taste. It hurts. But while we feel that such prejudice should be
discouraged, we also feel that it should not be prohibited, especially if it does not assume outrageous proportions. In the United
States—a nation generally characterized by tolerance—such proportions do not exist. The American heritage has precluded them.
While there were some witch burnings here and there, there was
no over-all inquisition. America, having so far been spared a
major social revolution, experienced no equivalent to the French
Revolution in which blond aristocrats had preference in being
executed; or the National Socialist revolution in which blond
beasts took preference as executors; or the Communist revolution
in which the bourgeoisie was singled out for liquidation by a
prejudiced proletariat—revolutions about which so many intelligent people have disagreed with this author's opinion that they
were disastrous displays of prejudice that he often wondered
himself whether his opinion was a prejudiced one. While we
oppose prejudice on account of race, color, religion, national
origin, and sex, we do not know whether our inclination is justified. New truths are continually being discovered in the so-called
exact sciences, brought about by doubts concerning—and prejudices against—existing beliefs. Must not new truths be discov-

---

[107] Montesquieu's remarks on conceptions of liberty in Bk. XI, ch. 2 of his SPIRIT
OF THE LAWS come to mind: "There is no word that admits of more various
significations, and has made more varied impressions on the human mind, than that
of liberty. Some have taken it as a means of deposing a person on whom they had
conferred a tyrannical authority; others for the power of choosing a superior
whom they are obliged to obey; others for the right of bearing arms, and of being
thereby enabled to use violence; others, in fine, for the privilege of being governed
by a native of their own country, or by their own laws. A certain nation for a long
time thought liberty consisted in the privilege of wearing a long beard. Some have
annexed this name to one form of government exclusive of others: those who had a
republican taste applied it to this species of polity; those who liked a monarchical
state gave it to monarchy. Thus they have all applied the name of liberty to the
government most suitable to their own customs and inclinations . . ." SPIRIT OF
THE LAWS, I, 179f.

ered even more so in less exact social sciences? May it not be proven some day that people who are now condemned because of their prejudices toward race, color, religion, national origin, and sex, were right? As an expression of doubt, prejudice can be quite reasonable and a prerequisite for progress.[108]

---

[108] From the aforesaid it follows that prejudice cannot simply be identified with unreasonableness. In the beginning of this century, prejudice was defined as being "in a wider sense, a preliminary judgment preceding an examination of causes, a judgment which (as the so-called judgments of common sense or natural tact show) can nevertheless be true; in a narrower sense, a preconceived judgment made not only prior to the examination of causes, but also rejecting such an examination as a matter of principle in order not to shatter its supposed truth. Such a judgment, be it true or false, will always be an unscientific one, not really worthy of the name." MEYER'S KONVERSATIONS-LEXIKON (6th ed.; Leipzig, 1902–17), XX, 266. Today we are inclined to consider prejudice just in the latter sense. (See ENCYCLOPEDIA AMERICANA [New York, 1963], XXII, 529a.) It is doubtful, however, whether even in that sense, prejudice is always unreasonable, since even then it may be "true or false." What is rational and true has been open to dispute. Even law we know, often considered the embodiment of reason ("reason unaffected by desire"), is not absolutely rational. See my "The Limited Rationality of Law," NOMOS VII (New York, 1964) 67. The doubts concerning truth were shown in John Stuart Mill's ESSAY ON LIBERTY (1859), of which we quote only two passages: "Popular opinions, on subjects not palpable to sense, are often true, but seldom or never the whole truth. They are a part of the truth; sometimes a greater, sometimes a smaller part, but exaggerated, distorted, and disjointed from the truths by which they ought to be accompanied and limited. Heretical opinions, on the other hand, are generally some of these suppressed and neglected truths, bursting the bonds which kept them down, and either seeking reconciliation with the truth contained in the common opinion, or fronting it as enemies, and setting themselves up, with similar exclusiveness, as the whole truth. The latter case is hitherto the most frequent, as, in the human mind, one-sidedness has always been the rule, and many-sidedness the exception. Hence, even in revolutions of opinion, one part of the truth usually sets while another arises. Even progress, which ought to superadd, for the most part only substitutes, one partial and incomplete truth for another; improvement consisting chiefly in this, that the new fragment of truth is more wanted, more adapted to the needs of time, than that which it displaces. Such being the partial character of prevailing opinions, even when resting on a true foundation, every opinion which embodies somewhat of the portion of truth which the common opinion omits, ought to be considered precious, with whatever amount of error and confusion that truth may be blended . . . We have now recognised the necessity to the mental well-being of mankind (on which all their other well-being depends) of freedom of opinion, and freedom of the expression of opinion, on four distinct grounds; which we will now briefly recapitulate. First, if any opinion is compelled to silence, that opinion may, for aught we can certainly know, be true. To deny this is to assume our own infallibility. Secondly, though the silenced opinion be an error, it may, and very commonly does, contain a portion of the truth; and since the general or prevailing opinion on any subject is rarely or never the whole truth, it is only by the collision of adverse opinions that the remainder of the truth has any chance of being supplied. Thirdly, even if the received opinion be not only true, but the whole truth; unless it is suffered to be, and actually is, vigorously and earnestly contested,

Although prejudice should not be promoted, it should be permitted out of respect for the dignity of man. While it may hurt the dignity of those against whom it is exercised, its prohibition is likely to do as much harm to the dignity of those who want to practice it. Being a demonstration of freedom of choice and doubt, prejudice is also a demonstration of freedom of thought, a freedom that ranks so high that in distinction to some of its more concrete forms such as freedom of religion or speech, it is not mentioned in many bills of rights—the American Bill of Rights is one of them—because the government could not curtail it anyway.[109] Thoughts are free even under the most totalitarian regimes. Freedom of prejudice is a shade of freedom of thought, and freedom of religion is a tangible demonstration of prejudice. Therefore, prejudice should be as free as religion. It would be strange indeed if we could be prejudiced against God but not against men. While we would never be prejudiced against our fellow men, we would never think of forcing them not to be prejudiced against us. Our conscience and thinking are not theirs, and may be as wrong as theirs.

The ideas here advanced are confirmed by the Constitution. The original document basically is not opposed to prejudice. Delegating only a few competencies to the federal government, it leaves the bulk of powers to the states—and to their discretion of permitting prejudice. Furthermore, it permits Congress discretion and prejudice in the exercise of whatever powers they possess, with a few exceptions such as the passage of bills of attainder.[110] For instance, Congress regulated some types of commerce, but not

---

it will, by most of those who receive it, be held in the manner of a prejudice, with little comprehension or feeling of its rational grounds. And not only this, but, fourthly, the meaning of the doctrine itself will be in danger of being lost, or enfeebled, and deprived of its vital effect on the character and conduct; the dogma becoming a mere formal profession, inefficacious for good, but cumbering the ground, and preventing the growth of any real and heartfelt conviction, from reason or personal experience." ON LIBERTY AND CONSIDERATIONS ON REPRESENTATIVE GOVERNMENT (R. B. McCallum ed.; Oxford, 1946) 40f., 46f. See also Max Horkheimer and Samuel H. Flowerman (eds.), STUDIES IN PREJUDICE (New York, 1949–   ).

[109] Cf. John B. Bury, A HISTORY OF FREEDOM OF THOUGHT (2d ed.; London, 1952); Anton Rohner, DIE GEWISSENSFREIHEIT (Freiburg, Switzerland, 1940); Heinrich J. Scholler, DIE FREIHEIT DES GEWISSENS (Berlin, 1958).

[110] Art. I, sec. ix. Cf., in this connection, *United States* v. *Darby*, 312 U.S. 100 (1941).

others. It taxed some articles and some people more than others.[111] Students of the legislative process are well aware of the role of prejudice.

Prejudice also is not prohibited by the Bill of Rights. The First Amendment provides that "Congress shall make no law respecting an establishment of religion, or prohibiting the free exercise thereof; or abridging the freedom of speech or of the press," etc. Whereas the government is not permitted to exercise prejudice concerning religion, speech, and the press, it is not permitted to prohibit the exercise of such prejudice by private individuals. For what is freedom of religion but the right of demonstrating not only one's rational conviction, but also one's prejudice in favor of one religion and against others? What is freedom of speech, of the press, of assembly, of petition, or of other liberties mentioned in the Bill of Rights if not the right also to demonstrate inclination and prejudice? Well-reasoned as these exercises of freedom may be, all of them, since they involve interest, will often involve a grain of prejudice. Furthermore, the provisions concerning trial by jury are based upon the idea that a trial by judges is detrimental to the interest of the defendant. That this idea is a prejudice has been shown by the experience of other nations which do not require a jury, and was admitted by American courts.[112] The protection of the individual's liberty in the Fifth Amendment, implying freedom of contract,[113] gives no indication of excluding prejudice or discrimination. The free man must be able to be a discriminating man. And discrimination includes the exercise of prejudice.[114]

[111] Cf. the author's IN DEFENSE OF PROPERTY, 121f.

[112] *Patton* v. *United States*, 281 U.S. 276 (1930).

[113] See *supra*, 69f.

[114] Carr, FEDERAL PROTECTION OF CIVIL RIGHTS, 195, takes issue with the argument of "a group of liberal and intelligent persons" who maintained: "It is as impossible to destroy prejudice and discrimination by law as it is to control opinions or morals." He writes: "Human nature may not be changed by law, but human behavior certainly can be controlled. Laws against murder have never resulted in the complete disappearance of this extreme form of antisocial conduct. But nearly everyone agrees that such laws help to keep the problem under control. Why should not the same result be achieved by a statutory attempt to curb racial and religious discrimination in employment?" The answer is plain: Because such discrimination is neither an "extreme form of antisocial conduct" nor often a *slight* form of such conduct. While discrimination in employment may lead to forms of antisocial conduct such as slander and murder from discrimination—the lesson of

The permission by the pre-Civil War Constitution of prejudice as a demonstration of freedom was not changed later on. The abolition of slavery can be considered an abolition of a constitutional anomaly rather than of a normal constitutional feature. Moreover, since the slaves were property, abolition legally merely amounted to the abolition of juristic objects toward which juristic subjects had been able to exercise prejudice. It did not proscribe those subjects from discriminating against their new colored fellow-citizens or juristic fellow-subjects, as much as against white people. Far from restricting discrimination, the Thirteenth Amendment merely expanded the circle of those who from now on had the right to discriminate, a right which was expanded by the Fourteenth Amendment.[115]

The modern civil rights program is dubious not only because of its degeneration into an aggressive "civil" rights program, but also on account of its nationalization. Although civil rights legislation in the states often was as dubious as national legislation, it was not always bad.[116] Moreover, had civil rights legislation oc-

---

the Hitler regime should never be forgotten—it usually will not do so. The pendulum ought not swing to the other extreme. While we would not discriminate in employment, we are reluctant to impose our opinion on others. The potential harm that may be done by discrimination does not seem to warrant actual restriction of employers. While we oppose discriminatory governmental practices, we would be reluctant to impose a nondiscriminatory behavior upon private individuals, unless such behavior is so antisocial that it can be considered a crime—and not merely a serious crime like murder. The naturalness of prejudice is stressed in Jerome Frank, LAW AND THE MODERN MIND (Anchor ed.; Garden City, N.Y., 1963), xxii.

[115] The increasing importance of the Fourteenth Amendment for the rights of the individual is pointed out by Corwin, THE CONSTITUTION AND WHAT IT MEANS TODAY, 251: "During the first ten years of the Fourteenth Amendment, hardly a dozen cases came before the Court under all of its clauses put together. During the next twenty years, when the laissez-faire conception of governmental functions was being translated by the Bar into the phraseology of Constitutional Law, and gradually embodied in the decisions of the Court, more than two hundred cases arose, most of them under the "due process of law" clause. During the ensuing twelve years this number was more than doubled—a ratio which still holds substantially." See also Charles W. Collins, THE FOURTEENTH AMENDMENT AND THE STATES (Boston, 1912), 188f., and Benjamin R. Twiss, LAWYERS AND THE CONSTITUTION, HOW LAISSEZ FAIRE CAME TO THE SUPREME COURT (Princeton, N.J., 1942), chs. 2–7.

[116] Konvitz/Leskes, A CENTURY OF CIVIL RIGHTS, discuss state law against discrimination with respect to public accommodations, to employment, education, and housing in chs. 6–9.

curred just in the states, the individual could have escaped civil rights perversions in one place by moving to another. Freedom of choice concerning civil versus "civil" rights would have existed. National civil rights legislation and for that matter, adjudication,[117] is restricting that freedom. National democracy, in an attempt to do away with what it considers the civil rights sins of the states, introduces such sins throughout the nation, and makes the protection of the individual from the government precarious.

While this precariousness is in large measure due to the growth of democracy, we wonder whether it perhaps jeopardizes democracy itself. Whereas a national civil rights program perhaps can best be realized by a national government, it appears open to doubt whether such a program can be genuinely democratic. The members of the national government often will be far away from the local communities and their specific conditions. And the very people who bear the brunt of national regulations—the people in the local communities—often will not be able to influence those regulations as much as they would if they were made at home.[118]

Modern civil rights legislation, opposed as it is to prejudice and discrimination, may be a step toward doing away with discriminations that can be considered the very essence of democracy, such as those exercised by the voter. For in a democracy, people have the right to vote not merely from considerations of reason, but also from those of sentiment. Voting is not only a judicious, but also a prejudicial act. It is not only in accordance with justice but also effects injustice, the latter often constituting the voter's own conception of justice. One of the devices of modern democracy, the secret ballot, is designed for the protection of the voter's prejudice. He can do secretly what he might not want to do openly. Not only the reasonable and unprejudiced dissenter from general opinion is to be protected by a voting procedure that stands in contrast to acclamation, but also the unreasonable and prejudiced voter. For democracy is based as much upon the passion as upon the reason of man, as much upon man's sense of

[117] See *supra*, 86f., 104n.
[118] See *supra*, 87ff.

justice as upon his proclivities for injustice and prejudice—the latter two being not necessarily identical.[119]

The Constitution confirms this way of thinking. Nowhere in that document is there any indication that the voter would not be free to act according to his predispositions and prejudices. As a matter of fact, the Constitution is not without prejudice when it prescribes that "no person shall be a Representative who shall not have attained to the age of twenty-five years, and been seven years a citizen of the United States," and establishes even more stringent qualifications for the offices of United States Senator and President.[120] As a democratic law, the American Constitution basically is a prejudicial document, and this fact was not changed by the Fifteenth and Nineteenth Amendments. While these amendments abolish constitutional prejudices concerning the ability to vote, they do not proscribe prejudice in the voting behavior. By expanding the number of voters, they expand the number of those who can exercise prejudice in the democratic process.

CONCLUSION

It has been said that it is "one of the interesting constitutional anomalies of the New Deal Era that the Supreme Court, even while it was engaged in sanctioning a tremendous expansion of federal and state power over economic and social matters, occupied itself at the same time with the formulation of an elaborate new constitutional law of civil liberties."[121] It would be more correct to speak of constitutional consistencies rather than anomalies. For the said expansion of governmental power was well in tune with the kind of civil liberties that were expanded. While economic rights were infringed upon, certain liberal rights were given a preferred status, and democratic rights proper, were expanded. "Civil" rights were promoted.

---

[119] A classic exposition of the fact that democracy is run by the passion as well as the reason of man is THE FEDERALIST.

[120] Art. I, sec. ii, clause 2; Art. I, sec. iii, clause 3; Art. II, sec. i, clause 5.

[121] Kelly/Harbison, AMERICAN CONSTITUTION, 796.

The elevation of certain rights to "preferred" freedoms was prompted mainly by the consideration that these rights are conducive to democracy.[122] Perhaps this elevation was prompted by the hope which originally led to the adoption of democracy—the hope that popular participation in government would guarantee the individual's protection from the government. But whereas at the beginning of the democratic era care was taken that democracy would remain a means and not become an end in itself, and liberal rights that were conducive to democracy were refused preference to other rights, the situation changed under the New Deal. Certain liberal rights were "preferred" because of their affinity to democratic rights and thus were actually downgraded from an end to a mere means.[123] The preference for certain rights for the sake of democracy jeopardized other rights through democracy. While it was perhaps hoped that a democracy that emphasized rights believed to be conducive to democracy, would protect freedom in general, this hope was not attached as a *conditio sine qua non* to the elevation of these rights to "preferred" freedoms. Therefore, their far-reaching protection actually could jeopardize freedom. For the more democracy became an end in itself through the degradation of liberal rights to democratic rights, the more it could become self-righteous, the more liberalism could become subservient to democracy. As it was, the democratization of liberal rights resulted in the deliberalization of democracy. Liberal rights were challenged by social rights.[124] The protective civil rights barrier was transgressed by an aggressive "civil" rights policy.

The question asked at the beginning of this chapter—whether the decline of economic rights and federalism was compensated for by the increased protection of civil rights through national power—must thus be answered in the negative. Aside from the fact that it is difficult to make up the decline of such important

---

[122] See *Palko* v. *Connecticut*, 302 U.S. 319, 323, 325, 328 (1937).

[123] See the author's IN DEFENSE OF PROPERTY, chs. 2, 5. For a critical review of the career of the doctrine of "preferred freedoms" and an attack upon that doctrine, see Justice Frankfurter in *Kovacs* v. *Cooper,* 336 U.S. 77, 89–97 (1949).

[124] For the basic antinomy between liberal and social rights, see Gerhard Leibholz, STRUKTURPRINZIPIEN DES MODERNEN VERFASSUNGSSTAATES (Karlsruhe, 1965), 15.

aspects of free government as federalism and economic rights, the promotion of civil rights through national power, which is a promotion of "civil," and not merely civil, rights, is complementary to rather than compensating for, that decline. The "nationalization" of civil rights, basically amounting to the promotion by the national government of social rather than liberal rights, had an effect similar to that of the "nationalization" of social legislation. It also derives from the same origin—the growth of democracy.

This growth thus resulted in what the Founding Fathers hoped to prevent—a challenge to free government. The major reason for this development is probably the growing belief in the infallibility of men and the increasing replacement by the democratic ruler of the *amor dei* through the *amor sui*. All of this is perhaps not surprising in view of the fact that prior to the American Revolution theistic natural law had become replaced by its deistic counterpart, and that the latter was generally accepted by the Founding Fathers. Still, everything might have worked out better than it did. Although deistic natural law is perhaps only a second best, it is perhaps the best kind of natural law of which a secular, individualistic society can conceive. Since the American Constitution was oriented toward higher law which under the doctrine of judicial review could be guarded by the judiciary from undue infringements by the democratic branches of government, there was hope that free government—implying the protection of civil rights in a democracy—would prevail as long as the courts fulfilled their mission as guardians of the Constitution and the higher law it embodies. As it was, the Supreme Court failed to fulfill this task. It has suffered the replacement of the *amor legis* through the *amor plebis*. It has sanctioned the increasing substitution of the protection of the individual from a federal liberal-minded government through the control of the individual by a national social-minded government. It has promoted the replacement of protective civil rights by aggressive "civil" rights. It has used judicial review to please rather than to check the national democratic majority and thus deprived that institution of its *raison d'être*.

142

5

CONGRESS ACTIVE
THE SUPREME COURT ACQUIESCENT

INTRODUCTION

The preceding chapters revealed fundamental changes in cherished principles of American constitutionalism, such as civil rights and federalism. Since these changes in large measure were due to congressional action, the question arises whether legislative activity is still adequately checked for its conformity with the Constitution. Free government will hardly work unless there is an institution which keeps it intact. This was recognized by Americans when they established judicial review.

The latter was an important contribution to political science. To curb the executive, Locke had advocated a separation of powers giving the legislature priority over the other branches of government. However, while he hoped that the government would do its duty and protect life, liberty, and property, he provided only for an extra-legal means of compelling it to fulfill its purpose, namely, the right of revolution or, rather, *diffidatio*. Blackstone elevated Parliament to virtual omnipotence. But while he trusted that the lawmakers would be guided by older law and respect life, liberty, and property, he provided for no machinery to keep them within constitutional bounds. Montesquieu, advocating a more genuine separation of powers and checks and balances, did not devise an institution which guaranteed his system. By announcing the doctrine of judicial review, the Americans took up Coke's idea on the rule of law as an ingredient of constitutionalism and filled the gap which existed in the political theories that came after him. They saw to it that the constitutionalism of the common law would continue.

The establishment of judicial review was not unnatural. Confronted as they were with the task of securing the individual's freedom under law, the Americans had to secure that freedom from the temporary lawmaker by subjecting him to the rule of law. For while the individual can be free only under law, his freedom exists only if the law is not oppressive. A limitation of the legislature could be auto-limitation, as suggested by Locke and Blackstone, and Justice Gibson in his answer to Chief Justice Marshall.[1] However, trusting a political institution with self-restraint is a dubious matter. And just as earlier those interested in freedom limited the executive by constitutionalizing it, they later saw the need of restraining the lawmaker. Since executive control of the legislature might have re-established monarchy, the only feasible way of controlling the legislature, while at the same time not jeopardizing popular government, appeared to be judicial review, which perhaps can be considered the institutional crown of free government.

In the following, we shall examine whether or not this supposition is correct. Remarks on the establishment of judicial review and its consequences for the rule of law and freedom will be followed by a discussion of its decline and the impact of that decline upon free government.

JUDICIAL REVIEW UNDER
TRADITIONAL CONSTITUTIONAL GOVERNMENT

The establishment of judicial review resulted from a desire to make the individual free from governmental oppression. The American colonists considered acts of the English Parliament to be an unjust infringement upon their rights. Naturally, they resorted to Lord Coke's words in *Dr. Bonham's Case* of 1610, that "the common law will controul Acts of Parliament, and sometimes adjudge them to be utterly void" as "against common right and reason."[2] James Otis invoked this argument in the *Writs of*

---

[1] *Eakin* v. *Raub,* 12 S. & R. 330 (Pa. 1825).
[2] 8 Co. Rep. 113b at 118a, 77 Eng. Rep. 646 at 652 (C.P. 1610).

Assistance Case.[3] The Supreme Court of Virginia in 1766 declared that the Stamp Act did not bind the citizens of that state "inasmuch as they conceived the said act to be unconstitutional."[4] In 1772 George Mason, who later drafted the Bill of Rights of the constitution of Virginia, applied the same doctrine to local legislation which was "contrary to natural right."[5] Shortly before the Declaration of Independence, Judge Cushing, who later became a judge on the original bench of the Supreme Court of the United States, advised a Massachusetts jury to ignore acts of Parliament as "void" and "inoperative."[6]

The lesson of legislative oppression which the colonists had learned in the years preceding independence was soon forgotten. As a result of the struggle during the colonial period between the royal governor and the colonial assembly, the early state constitutions, while professing a belief in Montesquieu's doctrine of the separation of powers, conceived of that separation primarily as a means for the restriction of the executive. Legislative power was undefined and fundamentally unrestricted, a vortex into which the other powers tended to be drawn.[7] As early as 1777, Benjamin Rush complained that under the constitution of Pennsylvania, "the supreme, absolute, and uncontrolled power of the State is . . . in the hands of *one body* of men. Had it been lodged in the hands of one man, it would have been less dangerous to the safety and liberties of the community. Absolute power should never be trusted to man . . . I should be afraid to commit my property, liberty and life to a body of angels . . ."[8] Five years later, Jefferson made a similar attack against the constitution of Virginia because of its concentration of power in the assembly. This was to him "precisely the definition of despotic government." He

[3] See Quin. 469 (Mass. 1761).

[4] John B. McMaster, A HISTORY OF THE PEOPLE OF THE UNITED STATES (New York, 1883–1913), V, 394f.

[5] Argument in *Robin* v. *Hardaway* in Jefferson, REPORTS 109 (Thomas Nicholson, Decisions of cases in Virginia by the High Court of Chancery, 1788–95).

[6] Corwin, DOCTRINE OF JUDICIAL REVIEW, 32.

[7] See Corwin, "Progress of Constitutional Theory."

[8] Benjamin Rush, "Observations on the Government of Pennsylvania," in Dagobert D. Runes (ed.), THE SELECTED WRITINGS OF BENJAMIN RUSH (New York, 1947), 57. See also pp. 68, 70.

added: "One hundred and seventy-three despots would surely be as oppressive as one . . . As little will it avail us that they are chosen by ourselves. An *elective despotism* was not the government we fought for."[9] The oppression was especially felt in states where the debtor element, the "rag money" party, passed acts fixing prices in paper money and making it a misdemeanor to refuse paper currency at its face value. Even though the notion of legislative sovereignty had come from the pages of Blackstone to influence American legal thinking, the spirit of an Otis, a Mason, or a Cushing was revived by Rhode Island judges who refused to enforce a rag money law because of its alleged repugnancy, that is, self-contradictory character, in the year Shays's Rebellion broke out.[10] It was not to die in the following decades.

A major reason for the Philadelphia Convention was to check the democratic despotism as it existed under the legislatures in the states. Motivated by a desire to protect the rights of the minority, most of the delegates favored judicial review.[11] Likewise, it is considered part of the Constitution in *The Federalist*.[12] And while the young Republic was recovering from its "critical period,"[13] judicial review was established in some of the member states.[14] Finally, in 1803, John Marshall declared an act of Congress void because of its incompatibility with the Constitution.[15] For the sake of the individual's protection from extreme democracy, judicial review was established on both the state and national levels. It was destined to become, "together with its juristic product, a body of 'constitutional law' . . . the most distinctive feature of the American constitutional system."[16]

Judicial review as conceived by the Founding Fathers demonstrated that the American Revolution was an event for the restitution rather than the replacement of the rule of law, and that the Constitution basically was a transmutation of that rule into written norms. The inhabitants of the New World trusted they would

[9] "Notes on Virginia," WRITINGS, II, 162f.
[10] *Trevett* v. *Weeden* (R.I. 1786).
[11] For a survey, see Corwin, DOCTRINE OF JUDICIAL REVIEW, 10ff.
[12] See THE FEDERALIST, No. 78.
[13] See *supra*, 73.
[14] See Corwin, DOCTRINE OF JUDICIAL REVIEW, 75f.
[15] *Marbury* v. *Madison*, 1 Cranch 137 (1803).
[16] Corwin, "Judicial Review," ENCYCLOPEDIA OF THE SOCIAL SCIENCES, VIII, 457.

remain free under old law. The significance of that "older" law[17] ought not to be overlooked. Of course, according to *The Federalist* judicial review was based upon the exceptional rejection of the sentence *lex posterior derogat priori,* through the acceptance of the principle that superior law cannot be superseded by inferior law; that superior law must invalidate inferior norms. Hamilton made it clear that "a constitution is . . . and must be regarded by the judges, as a fundamental law" which is superior to any statute. "No legislative act, therefore, contrary to the Constitution, can be valid." Essay seventy-eight depicts the Constitution as the sole source of justice. This, however, appears to be a rather narrow interpretation. A more careful reading reveals that for Hamilton the Constitution was not only the source, but also the recipient of superior law. It did not only distribute but it also received justice.[18] As distributor of law, the Constitution was superior; as a recipient of law, it had to be inferior. And just as it was superior to the younger law, the statute, it was inferior to the "older" law.

The acknowledgment of this older law became one of the characteristics of the exercise of judicial review by American judges. While many of them followed only the narrow interpreta-

[17] The term "older" law seems to be a happier expression than such terms as "higher," "natural," or "historical" law. Although it is not necessarily more precise than these expressions, it is more comprehensive, since it includes "higher," "natural," and "historical" law, even the law of an unwritten constitution. McIlwain uses that term in CONSTITUTIONALISM, ANCIENT AND MODERN, 39.

[18] This can be concluded from Hamilton's concept of a limited Constitution. Although he says in THE FEDERALIST, *78,* "[b]y a limited Constitution, I understand one which contains certain specified exceptions to the legislative authority, such, for instance, as that it shall pass no bills of attainder, no ex-post-facto laws, and the like," his use of the term "limited" instead of "limiting" suggests that also the Constitution itself is limited by certain principles which protect individual rights and that the restrictions upon the legislature, laid down in the written Constitution, are only declaratory of some of those supra-constitutional principles that rule the Constitution. This can also be concluded from the fact that Hamilton refers to the Constitution as "a fundamental law" (singular), but shortly, thereafter, he states that the judges ought to regulate their decisions by "the fundamental laws" (plural), thus again indicating that the Constitution is only a partial declaration of those supra-constitutional fundamental laws by which it is limited—and therefore ruled. While it thus follows from essay *78* that the Constitution is the recipient of superior law, there can be no doubt about this if one considers THE FEDERALIST as a whole. The Constitution appears here as nothing but the best possible—but by no means perfect—realization of the ideal of free government. It is thus inferior to that ideal and continually nourished by it. See the author's FEDERALIST, 118, 132ff., 148, 165ff.

tion of Hamilton's essay, others followed the broader one, realizing that since the Constitution as a source of law was superior to the statute, and as a recipient of law inferior to the older law, the older law had certainly to be as superior to the statute as it was to the Constitution. The result was that many judges, while making reference to the Constitution, hastened also to stress the incompatibility of the statute in question with the older law. Others even went so far as to mention only those older law principles. Two opinions of original judges of the Supreme Court may serve as illustrations to show how, from the start, the older law was tied up with the Constitution, and how it served, even though not expressly connected with the Constitution, as a guiding principle. As early as 1795, Justice Patterson, after referring to certain provisions of the constitution of Pennsylvania, maintained:

It is evident, that the right of acquiring and possessing property, and having it protected, is one of the natural, inherent and inalienable rights of man . . . . The legislature, therefore, had no authority to make an act divesting one citizen of his freehold, and vesting it in another, without just compensation. It is inconsistent with the principles of reason, justice and moral rectitude; it is incompatible with the comfort, peace and happiness of mankind; it is contrary to the principles of social alliance, in every free government; and lastly, it is contrary both to the letter and spirit of the constitution.[19]

Three years later, Justice Chase stated:

I cannot subscribe to the *omnipotence* of a *State Legislature,* or that it is *absolute and without controul;* although its authority should not be *expressly* restrained by the *Constitution,* or *fundamental law,* of the State . . . The *nature,* and *ends* of *legislative* power will limit the *exercise* of it. This *fundamental* principle flows from the very nature of our free *Republican* governments, that no man should be compelled to do what the laws do *not* require; *nor to refrain from acts which the laws permit.* There are acts which the *Federal,* or *State,* Legislature cannot do, *without exceeding their authority.* There are certain *vital* principles in our *free Republican governments,* which will determine and over-rule an *apparent and flagrant* abuse of *legislative* power; as to authorize *manifest injustice by positive law;* or to take away that security for *personal liberty,* or *private property,* for the protection whereof the government was established. An ACT of the Legislature (for I cannot call it a *law*) contrary to the *great first principles* of the *social compact,* cannot be con-

[19] *Van Horne's Lessee* v. *Dorrance,* 2 Dall. 304, 310 (1795).

148

sidered a *rightful exercise* of *legislative* authority. The obligation of a law in governments established on *express compact, and on republican principles,* must be determined by the *nature* of the *power,* on which it is founded. A few instances will suffice to explain what I mean. A law that punished a citizen for an *innocent* action, or, in other words, for an act, which, when done, was in violation of no *existing* law; a law that destroys, or impairs, the *lawful private* contracts of citizens; a law that makes a man a *Judge in his own cause;* or a law that takes *property* from A. and gives it to B: It is against all reason and justice for a people to entrust a Legislature with SUCH powers; and, therefore, it cannot be presumed that they have done it. The *genius,* the *nature,* and the *spirit,* of our State Governments, amount to a prohibition of *such acts of legislation;* and the *general principles of law and reason* forbid them. The Legislature may enjoin, permit, forbid, and punish; they may declare *new* crimes; and establish rules of conduct for *all* its citizens in *future* cases; they may *command* what is right, and *prohibit* what is wrong; but they cannot change *innocence* into *guilt;* or punish *innocence* as a *crime;* or violate the right of an *antecedent lawful private contract;* or the *right of private property.* To maintain that our Federal, or State, Legislature possesses *such powers,* if they had not been *expressly* restrained, would, in my opinion, be a *political heresy* altogether inadmissible in our *free republican governments.*[20]

Statements like these were frequently made throughout the nineteenth and the first decades of the twentieth centuries. It became characteristic of American constitutional development that it was not only maintained that the Constitution implied limitations that were derived from older law, but also that the older law implied limitations upon the Constitution itself and thus upon the legislature that acted under that Constitution.[21]

As can be gathered from the early decisions just quoted, the "older" law was of a most varied type. It ranged from the principles of the common law to those of natural law and the law of God; from such general maxims as the social contract and free government to those of natural rights and natural justice. This variety of values was not likely to create a clearly defined concept

[20] *Calder* v. *Bull,* 3 Dall. 386, 387–89 (1798).
[21] See, e.g., Justice Story in *Terrett* v. *Taylor,* 9 Cranch 43, 51–52 (1815), and *Wilkinson* v. *Leland,* 2 Pet. 627, 657–58 (1829); Justice Miller in *Loan Ass'n* v. *Topeka,* 20 Wall. 655, 663–64 (1874); Justice Brown in *Holden* v. *Hardy,* 169 U.S. 366, 389 (1898); Justice Lamar in *Simon* v. *Southern Ry.,* 236 U.S. 115, 122 (1915); See Corwin, "The 'Higher Law' Background of American Constitutional Law," HARVARD LAW REVIEW, XLII (1928–29), 149, 365; Charles G. Haines, THE REVIVAL OF NATURAL LAW CONCEPTS (Cambridge, Mass., 1930).

of the older law, in spite of the fact that some of these values were put down in so many words in documents such as the colonial charters and the Declaration of Independence. Since, in turn, the older law in various ways was intertwined with the Constitution, that Constitution was by no means the clear document which corresponded to the ideal of a Thomas Paine.[22] Consequently the body of constitutional law could not possibly become too precise either. Hooker said of law "that her seat is the bosom of God."[23] From what we have seen, it does not seem improper to apply that attribute to the American Constitution. Thus the whole body of constitutional law in this country became enshrouded in a certain mysticism. This resulted in the veneration of the Constitution as a civic gospel.[24] Its congregation was the American people; its high priests, the justices of the Supreme Court.

It is obvious that such a vague and mystical concept of a Constitution cannot fulfill one essential purpose of the law, namely, legal security. Therefore, it was necessary to make concrete the manifestations of the older law. Naturally, this task fell to those whose "proper and peculiar province" is to interpret the laws, the judges.[25] By applying the law to the case before them, they molded what was nothing but a mass of written and unwritten principles into a specific Constitution. And whereas their interpretation of the law would take into account the specific conditions of a specific time and thus be very much down to earth,[26] it would always indicate the values of the older law, and thus be close to heaven. The judges performed their task so admirably that American government came to be characterized as a "government of laws—not of men," a term which symbolizes the transmutation of the older law into concrete norms, emphasizing at the same time the superiority of the former over the latter. Like the sculptor who, when molding his clay into a piece of art, is guided by considerations of aesthetics, American judges, when

---

[22] Paine stated that "a constitution does not exist unless one can put it into one's pocket," quoted in Georges Burdeau, TRAITÉ DE SCIENCE POLITIQUE (Paris, 1949–56), III, 16.

[23] Richard Hooker, OF THE LAWS OF ECCLESIASTICAL POLITY (London, 1907), I, 232.

[24] See Bryce, AMERICAN COMMONWEALTH, I, 251, 304.

[25] THE FEDERALIST, No. 78.

[26] See *supra,* 60.

forming the law into legal decisions through an interpretation of the Constitution, were guided by considerations of an ethical justice. In order to preserve free government, they tested the acts of the national as well as state legislatures for their compatibility with the Constitution and the rule of law.

The power of judicial review, far-reaching as it was, did by no means imply to the judges a participation in the political process, as Chief Justice Marshall emphasized as early as 1824 and Justice Roberts as late as 1936.[27] The judiciary remained in the position attributed to it by Hamilton, i.e., "beyond comparison the weakest of the three departments of power."[28] In spite of great and tempting possibilities of self-aggrandizement, the judges made it clear that they did not intend to transcend the bounds that were imposed upon them by the law and decided to remain only interpreters of the law—and guardians of a Constitution which provided for the protection of the freedom of the individual, including his economic rights. This self-abnegation contributed to a growing admiration for the Bench. Though the weakest of the branches of government, the judiciary became the most respected. Foreigners have been impressed by this veneration ever since de Tocqueville.[29] An American writer could well speak of "The Cult of the Robe."[30] This high prestige, it should be

---

[27] "Judicial power, as contradistinguished from the power of the laws, has no existence. Courts are the mere instruments of the law, and can will nothing. When they are said to exercise a discretion, it is a mere legal discretion, a discretion to be exercised in discerning the course prescribed by law; and, when that is discerned, it is the duty of the Court to follow it. Judicial power is never exercised for the purpose of giving effect to the will of the Judge; always for the purpose of giving effect to the will of the Legislature; or, in other words, to the will of the law." *Osborn* v. *Bank of the United States,* 9 Wheat. 738, 866 (1824). "It is sometimes said that the court assumes a power to overrule or control the action of the people's representatives. This is a misconception . . . When an act of Congress is appropriately challenged in the courts as not conforming to the constitutional mandate the judicial branch of the Government has only one duty, to lay the article of the Constitution which is invoked beside the statute which is challenged and to decide whether the latter squares with the former. All the court does, or can do, is to announce its considered judgment upon the question. The only power it has, if such it may be called, is the power of judgment. This court neither approves nor condemns any legislative policy." *United States* v. *Butler,* 297 U.S. 1, 62–63 (1936).

[28] THE FEDERALIST, No. 78.

[29] De Tocqueville, DEMOCRACY IN AMERICA, I, 155ff.

[30] This term was first used by Jerome Frank as the title of an article which appeared in the SATURDAY REVIEW OF LITERATURE (Oct. 13, 1945), 12.

emphasized, was due to the judges' protection of freedom as it was guaranteed by the Constitution—including economic freedom. In large measure, confidence was vested in the judiciary because the Supreme Court was the confident protector of vested rights.

CONGRESSIONAL POWER UNDER MODERN DEMOCRATIC GOVERNMENT

For an observer of recent developments, the question must have arisen whether judicial review, this most idealistic feature of American governmental practice, is not becoming a mere ideal, and whether the cult of the Robe has been replaced by a cult of the popular vogue. There can be little doubt about that, as far as economic rights are concerned. Since 1936, the Supreme Court has been reluctant to declare acts of Congress dealing with economic matters, unconstitutional. While this reluctance does not in itself imply the disappearance of traditional judicial review,[31] recent developments indicate changes which warrant apprehensions concerning the very survival of customary judicial review. Throughout the years from *Marbury* v. *Madison* to *Dred Scott,* the acquiescence of the judiciary in acts of Congress neither implied a recognition of legislative supremacy nor of majoritarianism, in spite of the fact that this was the epoch of the great debates which saw Congress at the apex of its prestige, and witnessed a substantial progress of democracy through the broadening of suffrage.[32] The rigorous exercise of judicial review after the Civil War did not come as a surprise. It was not considered a usurpation of power by the judiciary. Rather, it seems to have been a natural corollary to the further increase of egalitarian

---

[31] The Supreme Court did not void an act of Congress between *Marbury* v. *Madison* (1803) and the *Dred Scott* decision (1857).

[32] It was during this very period that the great American jurists Joseph Story, James Kent, and Thomas M. Cooley advocated judicial review along the same lines as Chief Justice Marshall. See Joseph Story, COMMENTARIES ON THE CONSTITUTION OF THE UNITED STATES (Cambridge, Mass., 1833), 425ff.; Kent, COMMENTARIES 29ff.; Cooley, CONSTITUTIONAL LIMITATIONS. Story dedicated his work to Marshall.

democracy.[33] Today's judicial acquiescence in social legislation, by contrast, probably heralds the arrival of legislative supremacy. The Supreme Court seems to have abdicated its former position as the guardian of the Constitution and free government with its capitulation before the American *volonté générale* in 1937, when it permitted discrimination against economic rights.

This capitulation can be attributed to factors which are the result of the march of egalitarian democracy and the adjustment of juridical thinking to this march. Wilson's New Freedom held that for the sake of the majority the property-owning minority of the big manufacturers, the bankers, and the heads of the great railroad combinations should have their influence curtailed. He was the spokesman for those Americans who considered themselves underprivileged, whose ranks had been swelled, as Justice Lurton complained, by the recent "great influx of an enormous mass of immigrants . . . wholly unfamiliar with the American constitutional idea . . ."; people who increased "the number of those voters who object to any restraint upon the will of the majority . . ."; people who, arriving from nations which rejected judicial review, considered the "power to annul a law as the usurpation of legislative authority."[34] Hamilton, the builder of the American nation, the advocate of the protection of private property, and the originator of the doctrine of judicial review,[35] no longer was considered a great American because presumably "he did not think in terms of American life."[36] Wilson's New Freedom came close to the type of freedom that had been proclaimed by

---

[33] From 1789 to 1864, the Supreme Court declared an act of Congress void in only two cases; from 1864 to 1885 in sixteen, from 1886 to 1906 in twelve, from 1906 to 1924 in twenty-three, and from 1924 to 1935 in seventeen cases. During the first seventy-five years of the Court's existence judicial review was exercised only twice, whereas in the following seventy-one years this was done as often as sixty-eight times. The argument that this increased activity was largely due to the fact that "laissez faire came to the Supreme Court" (cf. Twiss, LAWYERS AND THE CONSTITUTION and Arnold M. Paul, CONSERVATIVE CRISIS AND THE RULE OF LAW [Ithaca, N.Y., 1960]), overlooks that laissez faire had been part of the constitutional credo ever since the Constitution was adopted. It is correct only in so far as the Court saw an increasing need for the protection of economic freedom when that freedom became increasingly threatened by social legislation.

[34] Horace H. Lurton, "A Government of Law or a Government of Men?" NORTH AMERICAN REVIEW, CXCIII (1911), 17.

[35] See the author's "Hamilton's Concept of Free Government."

[36] Wilson, NEW FREEDOM, 47.

Hichborn in 1777.[37] It was a decisive step toward the substitution of a limited democracy in which the legislative majority was restricted under law by an absolute democracy in which the majority reigned supreme. The New Deal was only a further step in this direction. It completed a development that had gotten its start at the end of the past century and was characterized by an opposition to judicial review.[38]

An opposition to judicial review by the majority of the people or by the political departments of government, no matter how vehement, does not necessarily amount to a disappearance of that institution. American history furnishes ample proof of this.[39] As long as no constitutional amendments prohibited its exercise, there could be no doubt that judicial review did exist, provided it was not renounced by the judges themselves. As a matter of fact, the Supreme Court for some time seemed little impressed by the growing tendency toward majoritarianism and legislative supremacy. A considerably greater number of congressional statutes or parts thereof were found to be unconstitutional during the first thirty-five years of this century, than in the same period preceding it.[40] The very threat of majoritarianism seemed to call upon the judiciary to stop legislative ambitions.[41] Stability was secured by testing what were conceivably expressions of a majoritarian

---

[37] See *supra,* 10.

[38] The forerunner of Wilson's New Freedom was Theodore Roosevelt's Square Deal. It is interesting to note that Theodore Roosevelt led the Bull Moose Party in a campaign that included a demand for the recall of judicial decisions. In 1912, he stated: "I contend that the people, in the nature of things must be better judges of what is the preponderant opinion than the Court, and that the Courts should not be allowed to reverse the political philosophy of the people." Roosevelt, "The Right of the People to Rule," THE OUTLOOK, C (1912), 620. Cf. Elihu Root, "The Importance of an Independent Judiciary," THE INDEPENDENT, LXXII (1912), 704; William H. Taft, POPULAR GOVERNMENT (New Haven, Conn., 1913), 162ff.

[39] For a few examples of animosity toward judicial action, compare Jefferson's letter to W. H. Torrance of June 11, 1815, WRITINGS, XIV, 302; Jackson's veto of the Bank of the U.S., Richardson, COMPILATION OF THE MESSAGES AND PAPERS OF THE PRESIDENTS, II, 582; Lincoln's attitude toward the *Dred Scott* decision, speech at Springfield, Ill., June 26, 1857, WORKS, II, 401.

[40] See *supra,* 153n.

[41] Indeed, it seems justified to speak here of reaction and counterreaction, *i.e.,* the rule that dangers of legislative majoritarianism are being matched by tendencies toward a more rigorous exercise of judicial review. Such a rule would, of course, correspond to what was originally considered the function of judicial review, namely, the restriction of the legislature representing the popular majority to within the limits set by constitutional law.

passion for their compatibility with the Constitution and those principles of the older law that were considered part of the American constitutional order.[42] But this attitude did not remain unchallenged. There came about a new form of juridical thinking which was ideally suited to the march of egalitarian democracy. Stimulated by contemporary developmentalist and pragmatist philosophy which considered stability an impossible—even an undesirable—condition and elevated the concept of change into a principle of social theory,[43] sociological jurisprudence questioned the Court's skeptical attitude toward legislative fiat and, thereby, the institution of judicial review itself.

The great man of sociological jurisprudence, Oliver Wendell Holmes, stated as early as 1881 that the law "should correspond with the actual feelings and demands of the community, whether right or wrong."[44] Three years later, he said: "Every one instinctively recognizes that in these days the justification of a law for us cannot be found in the fact that our fathers always have followed it. It must be found in some help which the law brings toward reaching a social end which the governing power of the community has made up its mind it wants."[45] The necessity of a law which reflected the mutability of social conditions was thus linked up with a rejection of older law. Present law was to be purged of "every word of moral significance,"[46] i.e., of a priori higher law

---

[42] For the fact that too much and too fast a lawmaking may lead to legal insecurity, see Madison's statement in THE FEDERALIST, No. 62, quoted *infra*, 170n. Hamilton made similar comments. Viewing the rule of the state legislatures under the Articles of Confederation with concern, he saw those bodies "tainted by the spirit of faction" and contaminated with "those occasional ill-humors, or temporary prejudices and propensities, which . . . beget injustice and oppression of a part of the community." He complained of "those practices . . . which have undermined the foundations of property and credit, have planted mutual distrust in the breasts of all classes of citizens, and have occasioned an almost universal prostration of morals." THE FEDERALIST, Nos. 27, 85.

[43] See Fred V. Cahill, JUDICIAL LEGISLATION (New York, 1952), 21ff.

[44] Holmes, COMMON LAW, 41f.

[45] Holmes, "Law in Science and Science in Law," in COLLECTED LEGAL PAPERS, 225. See also his statement, made in 1897: "It is revolting to have no better reason for a rule of law than that so it was laid down in the time of Henry IV. It is still more revolting if the grounds upon which it was laid down have vanished long since, and the rule simply persists from blind imitation of the past." "The Path of the Law," COLLECTED LEGAL PAPERS, 187.

[46] "I often doubt whether it would not be a gain if every word of moral significance could be banished from the law altogether, and other words adopted

standards. To make things complete, Holmes argued against judicial review. His famous dissent in *Lochner* v. *New York* maintained "the right of the majority to embody their opinions in law . . ." and cautioned the Court about its exercise of judicial review.[47] In 1913, the Boston Brahmin used more direct language when he remarked that the United States would not come to an end if the Supreme Court lost its power to declare an act of Congress void.[48] This meant that the Constitution and the older law were irrelevant if they conflicted with the wishes of the majority as reflected in the acts of Congress.[49] Here was a new concept of American government indeed. On the whole, it amounts to a recognition of the supremacy of the American *volonté générale*.

Sociological jurisprudence had a great impact upon constitutional development. Holmes came to occupy in great measure the position of official judicial philosopher for the modern age. Not only can he be considered "the starting point for almost all recent American legal writers . . . ,"[50] but also as the judge who brought about the fundamental shift in the attitude of the Supreme Court toward legislation and judicial review. His philosophy, originally confined to a small minority of the Court, advanced as consistently within that body as did the idea of absolute democracy with the American people. In the middle 1920s, the minority of Holmes and Brandeis was strengthened by Stone. By the middle of the 1930s, the minority favoring the Court's acceptance of New Deal legislation had increased to four judges.

---

which should convey legal ideas uncolored by anything outside the law. We should lose the fossil records of a good deal of history and the majesty got from ethical associations, but by ridding ourselves of an unnecessary confusion we should gain very much in the clearness of our thought." McKinnon, "The Secret of Mr. Justice Holmes: An Analysis," AMERICAN BAR ASSOCIATION JOURNAL, XXXVI (1950), 264.

[47] 198 U.S. 45, 75 (1905).

[48] See *supra*, 73n.

[49] For Holmes' derisive attitude toward the Court's testing of legislative acts for their compatibility with older and higher law, see his dissent in *Baldwin* v. *Missouri*, 281 U.S. 586, 595 (1930), where he complains that one can see "hardly any limit but the sky to the invalidation of . . . [legislative acts] if they happen to strike a majority of the Court as for any reason undesirable." The common law was for Holmes "not a brooding omnipresence in the sky but the articulate voice of some sovereign or quasi-sovereign that can be identified. . . ." *Southern Pac. Co.* v. *Jensen,* 244 U.S. 205, 222 (1917).

[50] Cahill, JUDICIAL LEGISLATION, 32.

Finally, the 1937 Court, faced with the threat of Roosevelt's court-packing plan, submitted to the demands of the popular majority. A landmark of American constitutionalism, the Court's traditional policy of protecting "the rights of the minor party" from "the superior force of an interested and overbearing majority"[51] through the invalidation of legislative fiat irrespective of the reaction of the other branches of government and the general public, had come to an end. Traditionally, majoritarian tendencies were matched by an increased exercise of judicial review. Consequently, one would have expected that throughout the New Deal the judiciary would continue to meet an increased majoritarian challenge with an increased activity in the exercise of judicial review. Instead, weakened by a judicial philosophy which bore the mark of majoritarian democracy, the Supreme Court capitulated.

Nothing the Court did in the ensuing years could minimize the importance of that capitulation, the decisive feature of which was the Court's abandonment of the individual's economic freedom to the dangers of majoritarianism. The Court, it is true, set out on an ambitious program to protect non-economic rights. In approaching these cases, the judges, often invoking older law, have tended to assume that statutes restricting such rights are unconstitutional. While the restrictive measures were usually the product of local and state legislation, the Court did not completely refrain from exercising judicial review over national legislation.[52] However, it is doubtful whether this can conceal the decline of judicial review. For the Court's fulfillment of "judicial duty" is basically confined to watching out for state legislation curtailing non-economic and democratic rights. Acts of Congress, especially those restricting economic rights, usually profit from "judicial self-restraint."[53]

The invalidation of state rather than national legislation leads one to ask whether the Court's activities are not prompted by the

---

[51] These words are taken from THE FEDERALIST, No. 10.

[52] A list of cases in which the Supreme Court voided congressional legislation can be found in Norman J. Small (ed.), THE CONSTITUTION OF THE UNITED STATES OF AMERICA (Washington, 1964), 1399ff.

[53] Cf. Alpheus T. Mason, "Understanding the Warren Court: Judicial Self-Restraint and Judicial Duty," POLITICAL SCIENCE QUARTERLY, LXXXI (1966), 523.

secure feeling of enjoying the support of the national majority, and raises doubts as to whether the Court would be able to muster the courage to seriously challenge that majority.[54] The fear of being unpopular is even more evident in the Court's invalidation of statutes which regulate non-economic rights as distinguished from laws that restrict the activities of economic minorities. But throughout American history the very essence of judicial review was its being exercised *in spite of* popular disapproval—even in the whole nation—and irrespective of criticism by economic or non-economic groups. Therefore, it is hard to believe that judicial review is emerging from its period of decline as long as the Court has not demonstrated its courage to face unpopularity not only in a few states, but throughout the nation by challenging legislative action not only for the sake of non-economic, but also for that of economic, rights. The different evaluation of non-economic and economic rights appears to be arbitrary. It is absurd to maintain that the rights of criminals are more important than freedom of contract and the right to work.[55] There is, aside from the Four Freedoms, a Fifth Freedom.[56] The latter occupies, quite symbolically, the position of a numerical minority vis-à-vis its four brethren. But this probably is a symbol of its importance above anything else. Its juxtaposition to the Four Freedoms could well mean that from a qualitative point of view the Fifth Freedom is as important as the Four Freedoms taken together and thus more important than any one of the four.

[54] While the Court has been willing to face intensive animosity throughout the nation, the fact ought not to be overlooked that this animosity is confined to a national minority.

[55] See Earl Latham, "The Majoritarian Dilemma in the United States Supreme Court," CONFLUENCE, II (1953), 22, and *supra,* 63. Perhaps the Court's zeal in the protection of non-economic rights derives from a bad conscience for neglecting economic rights.

[56] See *supra,* 132n. While there can be little doubt that modern corporations through laissez faire often gained enormous powers which could challenge the freedom of the individual (see Adolf A. Berle and Gardiner C. Means, THE MODERN CORPORATION AND PRIVATE PROPERTY [New York, 1932]), there also can be no doubt that governmental regulation of economic rights is more dangerous than that by private corporations. Adolf Hitler also denounced trusts and monopolies as oppressors of the individual's economic freedom and brought about governmental control of corporations. A serfdom greater than the German people had ever experienced before was the result. For a recent discussion, see Fritz Machlup, "Oligopoly and the Free Society," ANTITRUST LAW & ECONOMICS REVIEW, I (1967), 11.

While acquiescence in the legislative will resulted in an increase of the Court's popularity, it was likely to bring about a decline of its prestige, since that prestige was largely based upon the Court's practice of keeping the legislative body within the bounds set by the letter and spirit of the Constitution. It can hardly be doubted that the Court today no longer commands the respect it once did from friend and foe alike. It is no longer that "citadel of the public justice," functioning as an "excellent barrier to the encroachments and oppressions of the representative body"[57] Hamilton wished it to be, or the "stronghold and . . . battery" from which Jefferson thought "all the works" of egalitarian democracy would be "beaten down and erased."[58] This decline of the Court's prestige was enhanced by another factor. It is probably no mere coincidence that parallel to the Court's bowing to politics, politics entered the Court.[59] By 1941 the conservative judges of the pre-Roosevelt Court had been replaced. The rift within the Court, introduced by the dissents of sociological jurists, now had lost much of its *raison d'être,* since the new judges were in sympathy with the New Deal. A new unity of the Supreme Court, bolstering its waning prestige, could have been expected. "But peace and order, most unfortunately, did not come." Rather, the judges "turned to fighting one another as they and their liberal predecessors had fought the conservatives. They splintered in all directions in a riot of legalistic diversity to the accompaniment of what was hardly above the level of undignified name-calling."[60] The judges had not only capitulated before the legislative body; judicial behavior became similar to that displayed by the members of

---

[57] See THE FEDERALIST, No. 78.

[58] To John Dickinson on Dec. 19, 1801. WRITINGS, X, 302.

[59] It would indeed be worthwhile to study if and to what degree the behavior among judges of a tribunal is the result of the behavior of that tribunal as a whole vis-à-vis other institutions. There probably is such a connection. The loss of prestige of an institution like the Supreme Court through its capitulation in 1937 was likely to result in a loss of prestige for the individual judges, with the consequence that the judges lost their mutual esteem and adopted a behavior that was often not in tune with the dignity of their profession. (The fight between Justices Jackson and Black comes to mind immediately.) This behavior seems to substantiate the old truth that capitulators are not likely to act with as great dignity as do martyrs.

[60] Carl B. Swisher, "The Supreme Court—Need for Re-evaluation," VIRGINIA LAW REVIEW, XL (1954), 844f.

the most democratic branch of government. The reasons for these failures are similar and connected, which substantiates the thesis that the Court's capitulation before the political departments opened it up for politics. The internal disunity has been attributed to the fact that the new Justices were rebels against the earlier concept of the Court as a passive instrument of the law, a concept which for generations had contributed to the prestige of the judiciary—as well as to the Justices' belief, shaped by a sentiment inimical to judicial review, that the Court was merely another governmental institution molding public policy. This new attitude, it was said, prevented the judges from having "the reverence for the Court that had been inspired by the concept of the Court as virtually the instrument of a higher power."[61] This is quite correct. Once the judiciary was no longer conceived to be the protector of the "older" law of which the Constitution was a partial demonstration, it was likely to lose a great deal of its sublimity. This loss, in turn, was to reflect upon the morals of its members. But, at the same time, it should not be overlooked that the behavior failure, leading to the disunity among the judges, is nothing but a consequence of the fact that the Court, considering itself bound by legislative fiat rather than "older" law, no longer could be an instrument of a higher power because it had degenerated into a tool of the legislature. Thus, the struggle among the judges is of the same origin as the Court's capitulation before the lawmaker through the acquiescence in congressional fiat. To the reproach that the Court has become "an aggregation of prima donnas,"[62] there may be added the apprehension lest legislative majoritarianism has become the golden calf around which these prima donnas are dancing their legalistic steps.

THE CONSEQUENCES OF LEGISLATIVE SUPREMACY FOR FREE GOVERNMENT

The potential consequences of judicial acquiescence in acts of Congress can perhaps be best envisaged if we consider the situa-

---

[61] *Ibid.*
[62] *Ibid.*, 847.

tion in the major continental nations. In France, Germany, and Italy it was demonstrated that legislative supremacy and the rejection of judicial review helped to eliminate free government. That supremacy resulted not only in serious infringements upon the rights of the individual, but also in the abolition of democracy.

In Europe, the oppression of the individual originally was felt to derive from the monarch, not from the legislature. And since the monarch as a rule had been supported by subservient judges, liberation was sought in the replacement of the king's absolutism through an increase of the power of a representative legislature.

In France, the king under the *ancien régime* was not only the realm's chief administrator, but also, through his power of promulgation, the superior lawmaker. He was also the highest judicial authority. The Revolution transferred the sovereignty from the monarch to the people, by whom, in turn, it was delegated to their representatives in the Assembly. As in the early American state constitutions, the tribute paid to Montesquieu's doctrine of the separation of powers was more or less lip service.[63] Actually, the legislature was made omnipotent. The judiciary was accorded no important role. The revolutionaries remembered both the old courts' abuse of their right of *vérification et remontrance* and the judges' opposition to the reforms that were planned by the king in the last years of the *ancien régime.* Judicial review was not only omitted, but prohibited and put under penalty.[64] This remained so under subsequent governments from the Empire to the Third Republic.[65]

---

[63] Article 16 of the Declaration of the Rights of Man and Citizen of Aug. 26, 1789, maintains that "any society, in which the protection (*garantie*) of rights is not secured and the separation of powers not definitely accepted (*déterminée*), has no constitution." It is significant that neither the Bill of Rights of the Constitution of 1791, nor the Declaration of the Rights of Man of May 29, 1793, nor the Declaration of the Rights of Man and Citizen of June 23, 1793, nor the Declaration of the Rights and Duties of Man and Citizen of the Constitution of the 5th Fructidor of the Year III contained such a statement.

[64] See Law of Aug. 16–24, 1790, Arts. 10, 11; Constitution of Sept. 3, 1791, Tit. III, ch. 5, Art. 3; Constitution of 5 Fructidor, Year III, Art. 203; CODE PÉNAL, Art. 127.

[65] See Henri Desfougères, LE CONTRÔLE JUDICIAIRE DE LA CONSTITUTIONNALITÉ DES LOIS, (Paris, 1913), 94; Ho Hio Ky, LE CONTRÔLE DE LA CONSTITUTIONNALITÉ DES LOIS EN FRANCE (Diss. Paris, 1926), 135.

In Germany, under the *Justizstaat* of the First Reich, the judges tried to protect the individual's rights (*iura quaesita*) from the police power of the prince (*ius politiae*). Since, however, the princes would often disregard the decisions of the Reich courts, the prestige of the judges dwindled until finally in the police state of the eighteenth century, the courts lost their independence and became a means for the monarch's exercise of cabinet justice. The struggle against the absolute king was waged for popular participation in government, especially in the legislative process. And although under the *Konstitutionalismus* of the nineteenth century the judges were independent, that independence was one *under* the law, not one above legislative enactment. For the protection of the individual, the courts were permitted to test administrative acts for their legality. But, as the principle of *Gesetzmässigkeit der Verwaltung* implies, only the conformity of the administrative act with the statute could be tested, and by no means the statute itself. *Rechtsstaat* primarily meant the individual's protection from the executive through the legislative and judicial branches of government. It did not imply his protection from the legislature through the judges.[66]

In Italy, the Napoleonic invasion overthrew the absolute rulers in the different states, and liberated the people from the oppression of the princes, aristocracies, and the judges who were in their services. And although the old rulers could stage a comeback after the defeat of Napoleon, the desire for popular participation in government remained alive. In 1848, the King of Piedmont granted a constitution that vested legislative power with the representatives of the people and made the monarch and the judges subordinate to the law. This *Statuto* became, after unification, the Italian constitution. In the ensuing decades, the German concept

---

[66] The term *"Rechtsstaat"* (state of right) became a misnomer that came about "at the critical point at which the unproblematical law (*unproblematisches Recht*) was split up into legality and legitimacy." Carl Schmitt, DIE LAGE DER EUROPÄISCHEN RECHTSWISSENSCHAFT (Tübingen, 1950), 25n. It should be corrected into *"Gesetzesstaat"* (state of laws, i.e., man-made laws). The use of the term *Rechtsstaat* indicates the acceptance of the identity of the written norm and of right or justice. Significantly Stahl, who has been considered the creator of the concept of *Rechtsstaat*, was a positivist. See the author's "Rechtsstaat und Staatsrecht," in K. D. Bracher, C. Dawson, W. Geiger, Rudolf Smend (eds.), DIE MODERNE DEMOKRATIE UND IHR RECHT: FESTSCHRIFT FÜR GERHARD LEIBHOLZ (Tübingen, 1966), II, 17.

of *Rechtsstaat* was adopted in Italy.[67] For the protection of the individual, the public authority, executive and judicial alike, was restricted by legislative enactments. The courts had no right to question the constitutionality of such enactments. In Italy, as in other European countries, the legislature reigned supreme.

Unlike the Americans, the Europeans, not having experienced the shortcomings of legislative omnipotence, did not fill the gap in the philosophy of Locke. Indeed they were quite content with Rousseau. Unlike America where the individual was protected by a law superior to that made by Congress and thus remained an individual before the legislature, in Europe the individual, being absorbed by the *volonté générale,* was protected through the law made by the legislature and by nothing else. Europeans, believing in the Rousseauistic doctrine of the infallibility of the legislature which, somewhat in a mystical way, like the *volonté générale,* cannot err, thought this degree of protection quite adequate. Whether they were right, we shall partly answer in the following pages when we deal with some of the consequences of the rejection of judicial review in Europe.

In the Old World, where the *ancien régime* was rejected, the individual's freedom—so one hoped—was to be secured within the limits of any new law which was produced by the legislature and had not yet proven its value. The French Revolution rejected the older law of the *ancien régime* and replaced it by an entirely new law. It replaced the ancient, organically grown, natural constitution through formal constitutions which owed their existence to mere acts of the general will.

This general will was the ruthless purger of the older law and was considered infallible. Thus, the new constitution established

[67] See Vittorio E. Orlando, PRIMO TRATTATO COMPLETO DI DIRITTO AMMINISTRATIVO (Milano, 1900); Santi Romano, L'ORDINAMENTO GIURIDICO (2d ed.; Firenze, 1951). It was stated that in a *Rechtsstaat* "the law stands above all other activities; everything, including the state itself, must remain subject to the law, and must live and operate according to its norms. The state, inasmuch as it subjects itself to the law and guarantees law enforcement even with respect to itself . . . is a state governed by law!" Oreste Ranelletti, PRINCIPII DI DIRITTO AMMINISTRATIVO (Napoli, 1912), 142. The norms of which Ranelletti speaks are, of course, made by the legislature. For an account of the development of the concept of *Rechtsstaat* in Italy, see Caristia, "Ventura e avventure di una formola: Rechtsstaat," RIVISTA DI DIRITTO PUBBLICO, XXVI (1934), 388.

by the Convention appeared as the very embodiment of right. Sieyès could maintain that "the national will only needs its own reality in order to be always legal."[68] The glorification of the new constitution went so far as to lead one delegate to propose that anyone who dared to suggest an amendment should suffer capital punishment.[69] The distinction between older law and new positive law was cast aside. Whatever was legal, was considered legitimate.

This identity between legality and legitimacy was of even greater consequence in view of the fact that it was matched by an identity between constitution maker (*pouvoir constituant*) and ordinary law maker (*pouvoir constitué*). The French not only believed in the maxim that the new constitution was supreme and unhampered by considerations of higher law. Their constitution also declared supreme power vested in the representation of the people, the legislature. Not only the constitution made by the legislature had to be legitimate; in addition, any law made by the legislature had to be constitutional. This, of course, left no room for judicial review which is based upon the distinction between inferior and superior law. Its exercise was punishable as crime.

The voice of the people was identified with the voice of God and did not remain distinguished from it. The people, having discovered their own divinity, could derisively reject what they rightly considered a rather mystical concept of the supreme older law. It was replaced through a concrete, written law, which could be seen in black on white and whose reality was beyond any doubt: A law with mere "artificial reason" was discarded in favor of one which appeared to be the very embodiment of *raison* itself.[70] This conviction in the rightfulness of the general will resulted in sheer enjoyment of law-making. The legislator, drunk with power, indulged in the framing of more and more, and, in his opinion, better and better, constitutions and statutes. A wave of codification swept over the country, climaxing in the Napoleonic

---

[68] Sieyès, QU'EST-CE QUE LE TIERS-ÉTAT? (3d ed.; n.p., 1789), 114.

[69] See Jules Michelet, HISTORICAL VIEW OF THE FRENCH REVOLUTION (London, 1902), 3, saying: "The Revolution . . . was but the triumph of right, the resurrection of justice, the tardy reaction of thought against brute force."

[70] Cf. *supra,* 8.

legislation with its masterpiece, the Civil Code.[71] These laws were looked upon as the last and final demonstration of truth. Bugnet stated the sentiment of his time when he said that he did not know such a thing as the civil law, but only the *Code Napoléon*.[72]

The new ideas did not remain confined to France. The vision of Kant, who pressed to its extreme limits the opposition between natural and positive law and separated ethics from law, came true in spite of all attempts at restoration: The French Revolution, having "discovered in human nature an inclination and an ability to improvement," was "a phenomenon in human history which could never be forgotten."[73] Its impact upon the other nations of the continent was an immediate and enduring one. The hypnosis deriving from the French codifications was probably even stronger than that stemming from the military and political successes of Napoleon. At any rate, it was a more lasting one, being responsible for the wave of codification that was to sweep over Europe in the following generations.

The Heidelberg Romanist Thibaut pleaded for a codification of German law as early as 1814.[74] And although the influential Savigny, in his answer to Thibaut, at once sounded a warning on the danger of such an undertaking, and the Historical School founded by him rallied to his support, their efforts were of no avail.[75] Quite

[71] The Civil Code (or Napoleonic Code) was enacted in 1804, after various declarations of the rights of man and constitutions had been framed since 1789. It was followed by other codes, such as the Code of Civil Procedure (1807), the Commercial Code (1807), the Code of Criminal Procedure (1808), and the Penal Code of 1810. For a good survey on French codification after the Revolution, see Brissaud's contribution to A GENERAL SURVEY OF EVENTS, SOURCES, PERSONS AND MOVEMENTS IN CONTINENTAL LEGAL HISTORY (Boston, 1912), 274 (hereinafter cited as GENERAL SURVEY).

[72] Julien Bonnecase, ÉCOLE DE L'EXÉGÈSE EN DROIT CIVIL (2d ed.; Paris, 1924), 128. This attitude could hardly be found prior to the French Revolution, although there had come into existence some codifications of the law due to the then existing reform movements. But at that time the customary law was not yet rejected to the degree it was after the French Revolution and, consequently, the written norms were not considered as absolute law.

[73] DER STREIT DER FAKULTÄTEN IN DREI ABSCHNITTEN (Königsberg, 1798), 149.

[74] See A. F. J. Thibaut, ÜBER DIE NOTHWENDIGKEIT EINES ALLGEMEINEN BÜRGERLICHEN RECHTS FÜR DEUTSCHLAND (Heidelberg, 1814).

[75] Savigny's answer to Thibaut was published in Friedrich Karl von Savigny, VOM BERUF UNSERER ZEIT FÜR GESETZGEBUNG UND RECHTSWISSENSCHAFT (Heidelberg, 1814) and in "Stimmen für und wider neue Gesetzbücher," ZEITSCHRIFT FÜR GESCHICHTLICHE RECHTSWISSENSCHAFT (1816), No. 1.

a few of the German states adopted written constitutions that bear the mark of French liberalism. After unification, the process of codification that had been going on in the various German states was brought to a climax in a series of codifications for the Reich.[76] To the south of the Alps, the situation was similar. Neither the Historical School[77] nor the restoration of the Italian princes after the fall of Napoleon could prevent an increasing codification of the law. The laws of the Napoleonic Empire were welcomed and met with a better and more lasting fortune than the sovereignty of the Empire. After the battle of Waterloo, the Italians' desire for codification was felt so strongly that the restored governments made the cause of codification one of their first cares. If such legislation was in the beginning possible only in various petty states, there came about, after the political unification of the country, a codification of the law for the whole nation.[78] Other European nations experienced a similar growth of codified law.[79]

The consequences of these codifications upon the legal profession should not be underestimated. Whereas under the new relation between law and constitution the judges had no right to test legislative acts, the denial of such a right did not in the beginning necessarily imply their asquiescence in the new situation. The numerous laws providing for a punishment of judges exercising judicial review are the best proof of this. The important fact is that throughout the period of codification, there came about a change of mind with the judges. Soon, a denial of the right to test statutes no longer was considered an infringement upon judicial competence. On the whole, the judges lost the awareness that such a right was conceivable. Influenced by the new ideas, they became convinced that any one of the legislative fiats was a perfect embodiment of reason and beyond reproach. In their opinion, all

---

[76] For a survey see the writings of Brunner, Schröder, Stobbe, and Zöpfl, in GENERAL SURVEY.

[77] See Vanni, "I Giuristi Della Scuola Storica," RIVISTA DI FILOSOFIA SCIENTIFICA (1865); Brugi, "I Romanisti Della Scuola Storica," CIRCOLO GIURIDICO (1883).

[78] For a survey, see Calisse's contribution to GENERAL SURVEY, 187.

[79] For the extension of the Napoleonic Code to other countries, see Brissaud, supra, 165n. For a survey of codification in the Scandinavian countries, see Hertzberg's contribution to GENERAL SURVEY, 562; Glasson, "La Codification en Europe en XIXe siècle," REVUE POLITIQUE ET PARLEMENTAIRE, II (1894), 201.

laws were not only legal, but also legitimate. Judicial performance became nothing but a mere technique, largely concerned with a formalistic interpretation of the mere letter of the written norm whose validity was accepted at face value. The *quaestio juris juris* was not raised. The disaster which had been foreseen by Savigny came true.

In his famous answer to Thibaut, the founder of the Historical School had denied the "calling" of his time for codification. But, at the same time, he had stressed that there was a definite calling for jurisprudence (*Rechtswissenschaft*) to orient the positive written norms toward the values of higher, historically grown law, and thus to prevent those norms from degenerating into something merely nominalistic.[80] A short remark on the role of jurisprudence during the period of codification seems therefore appropriate, the more so since in European countries that science is as important for the development of the law as are the courts. Did European jurisprudence attempt to save the law from degenerating into positivism? On the whole, this question must be answered in the negative. European jurists became as much the slaves of the written laws as did the judges. With a few exceptions,[81] French jurists, through their conception of codification and its principles, were reduced to the part of mere interpreters. The Exegetical School was succeeded by the Dogmatic School, and what mainly distinguished the latter from the former was that it followed the order of the titles of the Civil Code rather than that of the articles. Another school was that of Laurent, who attached the highest importance to the study of the general principles which govern each subject.[82] But, as one author put it, "whether using exegesis, dogmatics, or governing principles, all these methods differed only in their way of arranging the material. At bottom they were identical in one respect: their absolute respect for the text, which served as a point of departure for their developments,

---

[80] See Savigny, VOM BERUF UNSERER ZEIT FÜR GESETZGEBUNG.

[81] See Batbie, "Révision du Code Napoléon," REVUE CRITIQUE DE LÉGISLATION ET DE JURISPRUDENCE, XXVIII (1866), 125. Émile Acollas, NÉCESSITÉ DE REFONDRE L'ENSEMBLE DE NOS CODES ET NOTAMMENT LE CODE NAPOLÉON AU POINT DE VUE DE L'IDÉE DÉMOCRATIQUE (2d ed.; Paris, 1866).

[82] For an account of legal science in this period, see Julien Bonnecase, LA THÉMIS (1819–31) SON FONDATEUR, ATHANASE JOURDAY (2d ed.; Paris, 1914).

and the logic of their deduction, which was their sole means of solving legal problems."[83] Clearly, juridical science in France was not likely to ask any question about the value of the law. The situation was similar in Germany. The Historical School did by no means succeed in preventing an extreme positivism, but, being itself detached from natural law, only delayed it. The whole bankruptcy of that school is symbolized by the ironical paradox that in 1842 their founder and acknowledged leader, Savigny, the great opponent of codification, became Prussian Minister for the revision of statutes. Five years later, the eminent jurist von Kirchmann denied the value of jurisprudence as a science because of the jurists' impotence toward and dependence upon legislative acts.[84] At the end of the century, Bergbohm could write that from the point of view of juridical positivism every law, even the basest legal norm, must be recognized as binding, as long as it came about in the prescribed forms.[85] He expressed the general opinion in a country where positivism had come to reign supreme. In Italy, juristic thinking was, during the nineteenth century, strongly influenced by French and German authors. Italian jurists, on the whole, also accepted the acts of the legislator at face value.[86] In the rest of Europe, the situation was not much different. Thus the representatives of the European schools of jurisprudence became as much enchanted with the concise norms that were showered upon them by the legislator as did their brethren of the Robe. Like the latter, they made no attempts to challenge the legitimacy of those norms.

If the nineteenth century witnessed a definite dependence of jurisprudence upon the legislature, that dependence turned into slavery the more the twentieth century advanced. This was due to a variety of causes. Owing to the march of egalitarian democracy, the legislature as the most democratic of the branches of govern-

[83] Alexander Alvarez, "Dominant Legal Influences of the Second Half of the Nineteenth Century," in THE PROGRESS OF CONTINENTAL LAW IN THE NINETEENTH CENTURY (Boston, 1918), 40.

[84] See J. H. von Kirchmann, ÜBER DIE WERTHLOSIGKEIT DER JURISPRUDENZ ALS WISSENSCHAFT (Berlin, 1848).

[85] Carl Bergbohm, JURISPRUDENZ UND RECHTSPHILOSOPHIE (Leipzig, 1892).

[86] See Arrigo Solmi, LA STORIA DEL DIRITTO ITALIANO (3d ed.; Milano, 1930), 851ff.

ment became more and more entrenched and increased its prestige. This development made unlikely a reversal of the jurists' respect for the legislative body and the resulting acquiescence in legislative fiat. Furthermore, the increase of legislation reduced the possibility of a change in the jurists' attitude. Already von Kirchmann had stated that jurisprudence would be overtaken by legislation and would never again be able to catch up with it.[87] The truth of this statement became more and more evident when legislative power was increasingly delegated to the executive, when the shower of legislative acts, as it had existed during the preceding century, became a veritable deluge of statutes and executive decrees.[88] Whereas previously the jurists, when accepting legislative acts, had acted voluntarily because they were genuinely impressed with the lawmaker's product, they now had virtually no alternative but that of acquiescence, because the enormous increase of norms simply overwhelmed them. Formerly only statutes were considered constitutional; now also decrees, being in conformity with statutes, would be so considered. Judicial subservience had progressed. The attitude of that time was expressed by Kelsen's dictum that "a wrong of the state must under all circumstances be a contradiction in terms."[89]

This statement, made in the 'twenties, sums up the predicament of Europe's legal profession. The main blame for that predicament goes, of course, to values of the French Revolution, such as the worship of the *volonté générale* and its representative, the legislature, and the ensuing veneration of the new codifications. But also, those who interpreted these codifications are to blame, although their attitude perhaps can be considered a tragic consequence of the French Revolution rather than ill will. It is not maintained that a political order can exist without a firm founda-

---

[87] See Kirchmann, WERTLOSIGKEIT DER JURISPRUDENZ.

[88] See Schmitt, LAGE DER EUROPÄISCHEN RECHTSWISSENSCHAFT.

[89] Hans Kelsen, HAUPTPROBLEME DER STAATSRECHTSLEHRE (Tübingen, 1911), 249. It is realized that from the point of view of his theory of law, Kelsen's dictum could not be different and did not amount to a denial of ethical values. Nevertheless, it afforded even the most despotic ruler a means for demanding obedience from his subjects, including jurists. It appears ironical that Kelsen should have been one of the first to feel the injustice (the "wrong of the state" that according to Kelsen could not exist) of the Hitler regime.

tion of positive law. Codification of the law may not be bad in itself. However one is tempted to wonder whether the supposed end of codification, legal security, was actually achieved, or whether the mass of codification that came about in the nineteenth and twentieth centuries did not rather create a state of permanent revolution resulting in legal insecurity.[90] Also, it is not denied that the interpretation of positive norms is the legitimate task of the judges and those trained in the law. Juridical positivism can thus fulfill an important role for the preservation of legal security, which is a prerequisite for the order in society. England furnishes an example that legal positivism in itself need not have bad consequences.[91] However, it is maintained that positivism might lead to disaster, and that in its extreme forms on the continent it did lead to the bankruptcy of the law itself, as soon as law made by the temporary lawmaker was considered the equivalent of right, as soon as *Gesetz* was conceived to be of necessity *Recht*, and the principle *loi, droit,* accepted.

Having arrived at this state of nihilism,[92] the final phase of the tragic development can only appear natural. The statement of a

[90] Jakob Burckhardt saw the most disastrous consequences of the French Revolution in the "authorization for a permanent revision" (*Vollmacht zur ewigen Revision*), saying that "the decisively new thing which was introduced by the French Revolution into the world is the possibility of and desire for changes for the public weal." HISTORISCHE FRAGMENTE, 205. Maurice Hauriou, PRINCIPES DE DROIT PUBLIC (2d ed.; Paris, 1916), xi, complained that the Revolution of 1789 amounted to the absolute introduction of the written law and the systematic destruction of customary institutions, that "it resulted in a perpetual state of revolution, because the mobility of the written law was not any longer neutralized by certain customary institutions, and because the forces of change were stronger than those of stability." It is interesting to note in this connection Madison's opinion on codification: "The internal effects of a mutable policy are . . . calamitous. It poisons the blessings of liberty itself. It will be of little avail to the people, that the laws are made by men of their own choice, if the laws be so voluminous that they cannot be read, or so incoherent that they cannot be understood; if they be repealed or revised before they are promulgated, or undergo such incessant changes that no man, who knows what the law is to-day, can guess what it will be to-morrow." THE FEDERALIST, No. 62.

[91] But see the warning voiced by the Lord Chief Justice in Lord Hewart, THE NEW DESPOTISM (1929). The situation in England strongly supports our thesis that too much emphasis upon the values of codified law is likely to result in a decline of right and justice. In England, the common law remained fundamentally intact in spite of various codifications. Codified law thus never superseded the historically grown law to the degree it did on the continent. Cf., however, H. R. Hahlo, "Here Lies the Common Law: Rest in Peace," MODERN LAW REVIEW, XXX (1967), 241.

[92] See Heinrich Mitteis, ÜBER DAS NATURRECHT (Berlin, 1948), 29.

Frenchman warning of the "legality that kills"[93] found its tragic confirmation, shortly after Schelling's lectures at Berlin during the winter of 1841–42 had ushered in the spiritual catastrophe of German idealistic philosophy and theology. Under the norms of the democratic and liberal constitutions of Italy, Germany, and France, supreme power was transferred to dictators,[94] who later, in a very legal manner, could proceed to purge the laws of their liberal and democratic features.[95] The continuation of dictatorship was, in turn, facilitated by a legal profession which had been brought up in a tradition of subservience to the legislator and his written norms. Possibly still unaware that sheer legality had now definitely killed legitimacy—for to most of them this was impossible in view of the accepted identity between these two values—the representatives of jurisprudence as well as the members of the judiciary continued to accept decrees and laws as they were used to doing, in spite of the fact that many of these laws obviously did not come up to that "ethical minimum" which Georg Jellinek, a positivist, had considered the essence of law.[96] Kant's idea of a right of resistance against the obviously unjust norm was forgotten.[97] The words *summum jus summa injuria* revealed their truth in a most terrible way. Europe's jurists, and especially the judges who applied terror law, had reached a low point in professional ethics. The individual was at the mercy of a dictator.

[93] Schmitt, LAGE DER EUROPÄISCHEN RECHTSWISSENSCHAFT, 31.

[94] The Italian constitution, the *Statuto,* was the old constitution of Piedmont of 1848. The Constitutional Laws of the Third Republic were adopted in 1875. The Weimar Constitution was adopted in 1919. Mussolini was appointed Prime Minister by the King on Oct. 30, 1922, and obtained a 306 to 116 vote of confidence in the Chamber on Nov. 18. A week later, the Chamber granted him plenary powers by a vote of 275 to 90. Hitler was appointed Chancellor by President Hindenburg on Jan. 30, 1933, and got plenary powers through the Enabling Act of March 24 by the comfortable majority of 441 to 94. (No votes were cast by 81 Communists and 26 Socialists, who were imprisoned or in hiding). Pétain received plenary power from the regularly constituted National Assembly on July 10, 1940, by a vote of 569 to 80. Even if the Communists, who were not present at the vote, had voted against this act, it would have passed by a comfortable majority.

[95] Formally, however, neither Mussolini nor Hitler ever abolished the old constitutions, the *Statuto* and the Weimar Constitution, but rather made use of the provisions which served their purposes.

[96] See Georg Jellinek, DIE SOZIALETHISCHE BEDEUTUNG VON RECHT, UNRECHT, UND STRAFE (2d ed.; Berlin, 1908), 45.

[97] See Mitteis, ÜBER DAS NATURRECHT, 30.

CONCLUSION

In the United States the individual, so far, has escaped this fate. On the other hand, Americans have ventured upon a road which may well lead to such an experience. That until now they have been spared could well be due to the fact that American constitutional evolution is slower than that of European nations.[98] Ignoring their own experience with legislative oppression and the disastrous consequences of legislative supremacy in Europe, Americans increasingly accepted the measures of Congress as final. Under the influence of political ideas which emphasized the rights of the majority rather than those of the individual, the Supreme Court, adjusting to rather than watching over congressional fiat, permitted judicial review to fade away. The traditional constitutionalist principle of a government of law and not of men was more and more replaced by the democratic dogma that the voice of the people—however unreasonable, transitory or distorted —is the voice of God. The Supreme Court developed from a constitutionalist to a democratic institution. Instead of preventing democratic sinning against the Constitution, it acquiesced and even participated in it, permitting the principle *non sub homine sed sub deo et lege*[99] to be superseded by the principle, *vox populi vox dei*. Strangely enough, all this occurred at about the time when the alarming results of juridical positivism reached their

[98] See *supra,* 93f.

[99] This is the inscription on Langdell Hall of the Harvard Law School. It seems to be representative of American constitutionalism prior to the change brought about by sociological jurisprudence. Contrariwise, the inscription on the Supreme Court Building seems to be representative of American government in the more recent period. "Equal Justice Under Law" can, of course, be interpreted to mean equal justice under higher as well as man-made constitutional and ordinary law. On the other hand, it may also be interpreted to mean equal justice under man-made law only, which would imply the subordination of the judiciary under all law that is made by men, irrespective of whether it is, from the point of view of older and higher law, acceptable or not. This latter interpretation does not appear to be possible in the case of the sentence *non sub homine sed sub deo et lege*. It is interesting to note that the construction of Langdell Hall preceded that of the Supreme Court Building by almost a generation, the time in which sociological jurisprudence came to the fore. Thus the two inscriptions can possibly be considered a symbol of the change of American constitutionalism.

climax in Europe and when the Europeans introduced judicial review in an effort toward reconstructing democracy as a constitutional government.[100]

The decline of judicial review in the United States must be viewed with apprehension. Ignoring experience, Americans increasingly have tended to believe that a rule made by the representatives of the people must be right by definition. As a result, they have become reluctant to question the rule of the national majority as it is exercised by Congress. However, the development during the past decades shows that there exists a present danger which, since it does not seem to be clear to many, must be pointed out. The decline of judicial review is the decline of the outstanding American guarantee for constitutional, limited, democracy, or free government, against the potential despotism of the majority. It is the decline of the institutional crown of the Constitution, of "the most distinctive feature of the American constitutional system."[101] It puts justice at the mercy of temporary and perhaps ill-conceived political desires. It can hardly be a blessing to the public. For not everything which appears to be good for the people is necessarily right, but only what is right is good for the people.[102]

Judicial acquiescence in congressional action tends to lead to the replacement of constitutional through congressional reason, of reason largely purged of passion through reason largely adulterated by passion, of law tested and approved by generations of jurists, through laws made by politicians—often on the spur of the moment. It will put us back to the kind of absolutism that was contested by Coke, the difference being that modern absolutism would be one of the popular majority which could not very well suffer the fate of a Charles I. Judicial review has often been denounced as a reactionary institution.[103] By standards of consti-

[100] See the author's "Judicial Review in Europe," MICHIGAN LAW REVIEW, LV (1957), 539.

[101] Corwin, "Judicial Review," 457.

[102] This was sadly stated by Radbruch after the experience of the Hitler regime. RECHTSPHILOSOPHIE, 335.

[103] Cf. Theodore Roosevelt, "The Right of the People to Rule," and Franklin D. Roosevelt's "Fireside Chat" of Mar. 9, 1937. The PUBLIC PAPERS AND ADDRESSES OF FRANKLIN D. ROOSEVELT (Samuel I. Rosenman [ed.], 1938–50), VI, 122. See also Charles G. Haines, THE CONFLICT OVER JUDICIAL POWERS (New York, 1909), and

tutionalism, it is more proper to say that its abolition would be a reactionary feat.

Judicial acquiescence in congressional action will be detrimental not only to the freedom of the individual by subjecting him to the power of the temporary majority, small as that majority may be, but also to popular government. An uncurbed Congress probably will be less constitutionalist and less reasonable than a Congress that must doubt whether its acts will be considered constitutional. It can afford to be more susceptible to temporary popular passions,[104] as well as to the designs of a popular President. The latter, having swayed his electorate, may also sway Congress. He may induce them to pass laws to his liking, including laws delegating power to him. In the end, that power may well be so great as to replace congressional by presidential government and make a farce of democracy.

the AMERICAN DOCTRINE OF JUDICIAL SUPREMACY (New York, 1914; 2d ed., Berkeley, 1932); Jerome Frank, "The Cult of the Robe," SATURDAY REVIEW OF LITERATURE (Oct. 13, 1945), 12; Edouard Lambert, LE GOUVERNEMENT DES JUGES ET LA LUTTE CONTRE LA LÉGISLATION SOCIALE AUX ÉTATS-UNIS (Paris, 1921).

[104] Hamilton's exposition of judicial review in No. 78 of THE FEDERALIST can be considered a complement to Madison's remarks on the value of representative government in No. 10: The probability that representatives will "refine and enlarge the public views" because their "wisdom may best discern the true interest of their country" and because their "patriotism and love of justice will be least likely to sacrifice it to temporary or partial considerations," can be increased through judicial review. On law in democracy, cf. Jerome Hall, LIVING LAW OF DEMOCRATIC SOCIETY (Indianapolis, 1949).

6

PRESIDENTIAL POWER ABUNDANT

INTRODUCTION

The possibility of an accumulation of power in the presidency —and its abuse—comes to mind in view of the fact that the American Constitution is said to provide for a "presidential system." Since "parliamentary government" denotes the supremacy of parliament,[1] the question arises whether "presidential system" implies the omnipotence of the President.

The term was coined merely to distinguish the American form of government from legislative supremacy. It meant that unlike the British Prime Minister or the French Premier, the President during his term was basically independent of the legislature. It was nothing but a reflection of the separation of powers.[2] Since the Founders had carried out that separation in a rather pure form, the presidency was about as strong as the other branches of government. From the point of view of power, then, the term "presidential government" originally was a misnomer.

This does not mean that it remained a misnomer. The preceding chapters have shown that important features of American government have undergone substantial changes. There is no reason why the presidency should not have. An absence of change in that aspect of government would make the United States a unique case also in comparison to other nations—including those with parliamentary governments—most of which experienced increases of executive power.

There is a provision in the Constitution which indicates a

[1] See Herman Finer, THE THEORY AND PRACTICE OF MODERN GOVERNMENT (rev. ed.; New York, 1949), Pts. IV–V; Robert Redslob, DIE PARLAMENTARISCHE REGIERUNG IN IHRER WAHREN UND UNECHTEN FORM (Tübingen, 1918).

[2] Cf. Bryce, AMERICAN COMMONWEALTH, chs. 20, 21, 25.

privileged position of the President vis-à-vis Congress and the courts. Whereas the members of the legislative and judicial branches shall "support" the Constitution, the President must "preserve, protect, and defend" it.[3] The President thus seems to be selected for the guardianship of the American system. And an institution designed to preserve, protect and defend a constitution is likely to be more powerful than one which is supposed only to support it. Lincoln might have felt this way.[4]

On the other hand, it could be argued that the guardianship of a constitution which provides for free government and its institutional guarantees must preclude the superiority of the executive or, for that matter, any other branch of government. It could be claimed that the very fact that the President must "preserve, protect, and defend," and not just "support" the Constitution, means that he has a greater obligation than the other branches of government to preserve the limiting aspects of it, and that he must go out of his way to prevent an increase of governmental power—including his own.

When the President, then, defends the Constitution, he must defend a constitution that provides for free government and governmental restraints. This raises the question whether in that defense he will exercise self-restraint or not, feeling that this restraint might jeopardize the Constitution. Even a President with no desire to increase the power of his office or his personal prestige may thus, by reason of the Constitution, overstep ordinary constitutional propriety.

To this constitutionalist possibility of increasing presidential power must be added a political one. The latter is not far from the former because the Constitution itself, aside from making the President a protector of the legal order, also makes him a political figure. As a matter of fact, the President probably is the most political figure in America. His office is the highest prize of politics. Therefore, whenever the political representative of the American nation defends the Constitution, he defends his own office. His office is staked more upon a successful defense of the Constitution than any other office. Under these circumstances,

[3] Art. II, sec. i, clause 8.
[4] See *supra*, 49.

can it be expected of a President to observe constitutional restraints? Can he be expected to deny himself power when even his constitutionalist obligation to defend the Constitution is basically undefined, when he virtually can hide political action under the cloak of constitutional duty, when his acts as a politician can be camouflaged by the prestige and reverence he enjoys as head of state?

As judicial review can be considered the institutional crown of American constitutionalism, the presidency can be considered the crown of American politics. And just as the more or less half-crowned political assembly in Congress has increased its power vis-à-vis the Supreme Court, it would be surprising if the President would not have done so, endowed as he is with the right to appoint the members of the judiciary. Furthermore, it would be surprising if the President would not have influenced Congress, especially if the latter is composed of men who rode into it on his coattails.[5]

In the following pages, we shall examine whether a constitutionalist, "weak" presidency has been superseded by a predominantly political, "strong" one, i.e., whether the political power of the office has narrowed down its constitutionalist features. This discussion will be followed by remarks on the implications of this development for free government.

THE WEAK PRESIDENCY OF TRADITIONAL CONSTITUTIONAL GOVERNMENT

Americans traditionally feared a strong executive. When James Bryce stated that in America great men are not chosen Presidents, he probably had in mind that fear.[6] While the United States can boast of great Presidents, their greatness was usually achieved in office. A strong man, even if, like General MacArthur, he is also a great man, does not stand much of a chance of entering the White House.

[5] See Malcolm Moos, POLITICS, PRESIDENTS, AND COATTAILS (Baltimore, 1950).
[6] Bryce, AMERICAN COMMONWEALTH, I, 73.

Fear of a strong executive existed in colonial times as well as during the formative period of the United States. Colonial history is characterized by fear of the royal Governor, whose power was continually curtailed by the colonies' legislative assemblies. At the end of the colonial period, the belief prevailed that the executive "was the natural enemy, the legislative assembly the natural friend of liberty, a sentiment strengthened by the contemporary spectacle of George III's domination of Parliament."[7]

Fear of the executive remained alive after independence. Madison remarked that "the founders of our republics . . . seem never for a moment to have turned their eyes from the danger to liberty from the overgrown and all-grasping prerogative of an hereditary magistrate."[8] In accord with this fear, most of the new state constitutions reduced the gubernatorial office "almost to the dimensions of a symbol."[9] Governors were elected by the legislature, usually for a period of one year. They were stripped of old prerogatives, such as the right to convene, prorogue, and dissolve the assembly, as well as of the right to veto legislative acts. Executive functions were subjected even more strictly to the advice of members of the legislature or of a council of state that was elected by the legislature. Often, executive power was left to legislative definition.[10] The principle of the separation of powers was mainly recognized as a means for curbing the all-powerful executive.[11] The Articles of Confederation established no formal executive at all.[12]

Fear of the executive remained alive during the framing and ratification of the Constitution. It is true that the Constitution provides for a stronger executive than the Articles of Confedera-

[7] Edward S. Corwin, THE PRESIDENT: OFFICE AND POWERS 1787–1957 (4th rev. ed.; New York, 1957), 5f.

[8] THE FEDERALIST, No. 48.

[9] Corwin, THE PRESIDENT, 6.

[10] See McLaughlin, CONSTITUTIONAL HISTORY OF THE UNITED STATES, 114; Nevins, THE AMERICAN STATES DURING AND AFTER THE REVOLUTION, 166; Charles C. Thach, THE CREATION OF THE PRESIDENCY 1775–1789 (Baltimore, 1922), ch. 2.

[11] See Carpenter, "The Separation of Powers in the Eighteenth Century"; THE FEDERALIST, No. 47.

[12] See J. C. Guggenheimer, "The Development of the Executive Departments, 1775–1789," in John F. Jameson (ed.), ESSAYS IN THE CONSTITUTIONAL HISTORY OF THE UNITED STATES (Boston, 1889), 116; Thach, CREATION OF THE PRESIDENCY, ch. 3.

tion and most of the state constitutions. But this is because legislative omnipotence in some of the states had generated a fear of the legislature,[13] rather than because of an absence of fear of the executive. While the latter was strengthened at Philadelphia, it is doubtful whether it was made as strong as the legislature.[14] It certainly was not made stronger. In the 1780s, the executive was not considered so much a protector against legislative usurpation as the legislature had been regarded as a liberator from executive oppression during the preceding decade. The shift in the constitutional theory of the framers of the Constitution from innate confidence in popular assemblies toward suspicion[15] was noticeable because legislative oppression had become evident, not because distrust in the executive had disappeared.[16] This is obvious in the debates of the Federal Convention. The advocates of a strong executive did not have their way. Only a moderately strong executive was established, and even this acceded to with reluctance.[17]

The institution of a hereditary monarchy seems to have been out of the question.[18] Even a single republican executive could not be easily agreed upon. Randolph considered it a "foetus of monarchy."[19] His advocacy of a plural executive was not without support. Only after James Wilson used his position as chairman of the Committee on Detail to incorporate his idea of a single executive into the preliminary draft of the Constitution did the acceptance of a single executive gain ground. But even then a "council of revision" was suggested as a check upon the President.

[13] See *supra*, 145ff.

[14] Rossiter, AMERICAN PRESIDENCY, 87. The Constitution deals with Congress before dealing with the President. In the first decades of the American republic, Congress was generally considered the more important of the two.

[15] See Corwin, "Progress of Constitutional Theory."

[16] Cf. Rossiter, AMERICAN PRESIDENCY, 75; Bryce, AMERICAN COMMONWEALTH, I, 219: "They [the Founders] were terribly afraid of a strong executive and desired to reserve the final and decisive voice to the legislature, as representing the people."

[17] Rossiter, AMERICAN PRESIDENCY, 76. For a description of the creation of the presidency, see Thach, CREATION OF THE PRESIDENCY, chs. 4–5.

[18] See Louise B. Dunbar, A STUDY OF "MONARCHICAL" TENDENCIES IN THE UNITED STATES FROM 1776 TO 1801 (Urbana, Ill., 1922); Max Farrand, THE FRAMING OF THE CONSTITUTION OF THE UNITED STATES (New Haven, Conn., 1913), 77, 88, 162, 173, 174; Warren, MAKING OF THE CONSTITUTION, 17ff., 43ff., 58, 378f., 436ff., 771.

[19] Farrand, RECORDS OF THE FEDERAL CONVENTION, I, 66.

Only toward the end of the Convention were efforts favoring such a council abandoned.[20]

The plans of Morris and Wilson, favoring direct election of the President by the people, a method believed to be conducive to executive strength, stood no chance of being accepted. Direct election smacked of elective monarchy. The delegates did not choose so much between direct and indirect election as between various types of indirect election. Originally most of them shared the view of Roger Sherman that the executive "ought to be appointed by and accountable to the Legislature."[21] Election by the legislature was provided for in the Virginia and New Jersey plans. It was agreed upon several times in the course of the debates. Only toward the end of the Convention was election by a special electoral college approved. And this was probably due largely to the fact that the matter had been turned over to the Committee on Unfinished Business, which happened to be chaired by an advocate of a strong executive, Gouverneur Morris.[22]

Reluctance to make the executive strong can also be recognized in provisions concerning presidential tenure. Advocates of a presidency for life, such as Morris and Hamilton, constituted an insignificant minority. The provision for a fixed term was qualified by the clause that an administration could be terminated by means of impeachment. Indefinite re-eligibility apparently was nothing but a by-product of mere re-eligibility.[23]

The Convention was also parsimonious with respect to the powers of the President. It is not hard to think of steps that could have been taken to strengthen the presidency further. The Convention "could have fixed a longer term, granted the President an item veto over appropriations, named four or five departments and made them clearly responsible to him, and required only a majority of the Senate for confirming treaties,"[24] and so on. Even some of the powers actually delegated to the President were given

---

[20] Corwin, THE PRESIDENT, 11; Farrand, FRAMING OF THE CONSTITUTION, 50, 70, 77, 79, 85, 157, 160, 171, 172, 202; Rossiter, AMERICAN PRESIDENCY, 77, 79.

[21] Farrand, RECORDS OF THE FEDERAL CONVENTION, I, 65.

[22] Corwin, THE PRESIDENT, 12f.; Farrand, FRAMING OF THE CONSTITUTION, 70, 77, 78, 85, 88, 115, 117; Rossiter, AMERICAN PRESIDENCY, 77f.

[23] Corwin, THE PRESIDENT, 13f.; Farrand, FRAMING OF THE CONSTITUTION, 77, 78, 88, 115, 117; Rossiter, AMERICAN PRESIDENCY, 78.

[24] Ibid., 80.

reluctantly. For instance, only two weeks before the end of the Convention was the President given the power to make treaties and to appoint ambassadors and judges, a power that until then had been reserved to the proposed Senate.[25]

To sum up, it can be said that the presidency proposed by the Convention was neither as strong as it could have been, nor enthusiastically made as strong as it was. It was strengthened, but only by the standards of the Articles of Confederation and most state constitutions. And its final strength was in no small measure due to the active participation of George Washington in the final debates[26] and to the general belief that this man of virtue would be elected President and to the hope that men like him would always be elected to the nation's highest office.[27]

The latter assumptions also played an important part in the struggle for ratification of the Constitution. For, in spite of the obvious caution employed by the Convention in creating the presidency, fears that the proposed executive was still too strong had to be overcome. Patrick Henry, expressing a widespread opinion, complained that the new Constitution "squints towards monarchy."[28] As Alexander Hamilton wrote, the opponents of the Constitution, calculating upon the aversion of the people to monarchy,

have endeavored to enlist all their jealousies and apprehensions in opposition to the intended President of the United States . . . He has been decorated with attributes superior in dignity and splendor to those of the king of Great Britain. He has been shown to us with the diadem sparkling on his brow and the imperial purple flowing in his train. He has been

[25] Corwin, THE PRESIDENT, 11; Farrand, FRAMING OF THE CONSTITUTION, 79, 85, 86, 88, 119, 157, 160; Rossiter, AMERICAN PRESIDENCY, 80.

[26] See Arthur N. Holcombe, "The Role of Washington in the Framing of the Constitution," HUNTINGTON LIBRARY QUARTERLY, XIX (1956), 317.

[27] Pierce Butler wrote to Weedon Butler on May 5, 1788, concerning the proposed President: "His powers are full great, and greater than I was disposed to make them. Nor, Entre Nous, do I believe they would have been so great had not many of the members cast their eyes towards General Washington as President; and shaped their Ideas of the Powers to be given to a President, by their opinions of his Virtue" (Farrand, RECORDS OF THE FEDERAL CONVENTION, III, 302).

[28] Henry's dictum can be found in Elliot, THE DEBATES IN THE SEVERAL STATE CONVENTIONS, III, 58. John Adams originally harbored similar fears (WORKS, VI, 430). Jacques Necker argued that the President of the United States had more power than the King of France had in 1789 (DU POUVOIR EXÉCUTIF DANS LES GRANDS ÉTATS [n.p., 1792], II, ch. 3).

seated on a throne surrounded with minions and mistresses, giving audience to the envoys of foreign potentates, in all the supercilious pomp of majesty.[29]

One of the major defenders of the new Constitution, and probably the major defender of the proposed presidency, Hamilton had his own strategy of defense. While stressing that the country needed an executive as strong as the one proposed, he went out of his way to emphasize that it was not actually as strong as it could have been and that it constituted no threat to freedom.[30] Historians still wonder how the champions of an executive as strong as the one proposed by the Convention were able to secure their victory. For strong indeed was the general feeling that executive power was dangerous to the rights of the individual.

THE STRONG PRESIDENCY
OF MODERN DEMOCRATIC GOVERNMENT

Today we write 1968—more than fivescore years after the only war America ever lost, the Civil War, less than onescore until 1984. These spans of years were not chosen arbitrarily. They are symbolic of the past and perhaps future increase of presidential power, for that power has increased by leaps and bounds since the Civil War. It may well continue to increase during the next sixteen years so as to bring about a situation similar to that described in George Orwell's sinister *1984*.

If we examine today's presidency in the light of Hamilton's statement just quoted, we must be surprised indeed at the enormous growth of its power and prestige. Today the American President is superior in dignity and splendor—not to mention power—to the King of Great Britain. He may wear no diamond on his brow and have no imperial purple in his train, but he is the symbol of the richest empire on earth even without these symbols of imperial might and wealth. The President's simple chair is more of a throne than the gilded throne of any reigning monarch. The President gives audience not only to the envoys of foreign

[29] THE FEDERALIST, No. 67.
[30] THE FEDERALIST, Nos. 67–77.

potentates but to these potentates themselves. These potentates, not to mention their envoys, can be received with supercilious majesty. The way in which the presidency is publicized often more than makes up for the pomp of majesty.

Comments by modern students of the presidency illustrate the great power of that institution. During the administration of President Hoover, when most people were not inclined to think of the presidency as strong, it was already noted that "nothing is more evident in the history of the Presidency than the steady accumulation of power in that office."[31] By 1940 presidential power had increased further as a result of the Depression, according to the outstanding American student of the institution.[32] His opinion was shared by the well-known British observer, Harold Laski, who called the range of the President's functions "enormous." To Laski, the President is not only the ceremonial head of state, "the final source of all executive decision" and "the authoritative exponent of the nation's foreign policy" but also "a vital source of legislative suggestion."[33] And yet presidential power continued to increase, partly as a consequence of World War II. In 1944 one author wrote that the President had "almost untrammeled power in time of war, rebellion or other high crisis."[34] Irrespective of whether we assume that the "high crisis" subsided after the war, the powers of the presidency were not reduced. The postwar presidency is "an inexhaustible fountain from which we may demand everything and anything that we desire." Its incumbent is not only "to manage our governmental business" but also "to engineer our national economy" and "to be the leader of . . . the nation, and even the world."[35] Another observer wrote that "the strong Presidency is an instrument and symbol of 1956."[36] A few years later the President was considered not only a "National

---

[31] Norman J. Small, SOME PRESIDENTIAL INTERPRETATIONS OF THE PRESIDENCY (Baltimore, 1932), 198.

[32] Corwin, THE PRESIDENT: OFFICE AND POWERS (1940 ed.).

[33] Harold J. Laski, THE AMERICAN PRESIDENCY (London, 1940), 26.

[34] George F. Milton, USE OF PRESIDENTIAL POWER, 3.

[35] Louis Brownlow, THE PRESIDENT AND THE PRESIDENCY (Chicago, 1949), 73. Sidney Hyman (THE AMERICAN PRESIDENT [New York, 1954], 239, 273) refers to the President as "manager of social justice and prosperity," as "manager of war and peace."

[36] Rossiter, AMERICAN PRESIDENCY (1956 ed.), 160.

Symbol," the nation's "Chief of State," "Chief Representative," "Chief Executive," "Commander-in-Chief," "Conservator-in-Chief of the Public Order and Safety," "Chief Diplomat," "Manager-in-Chief of External Relations," but also her "Chief Legislator" who, as "Party Chief," could dominate the legislature.[37] In short, the President has, by common consent, become The Chief. And whereas he can perhaps not yet be likened to the Latin American *El Jefe,* we wonder whether as a democratic tribune he has not actually become more powerful than Latin American dictators. Certainly there cannot be much doubt that "the history of the presidency is a history of aggrandizement" and that "the outstanding feature of American constitutional development has been the growth of the power and prestige of the Presidency."[38] After World War II that growth had become so obvious that the question whether it had not proceeded too far was asked not only by confessed foes of a strong executive but also by people who can hardly be accused of being prejudiced against presidential power.[39]

[37] Wilfred E. Binkley, THE MAN IN THE WHITE HOUSE (Baltimore, 1958), 114, 161, 185, 225, 245, 288; Richard F. Fenno, THE PRESIDENT'S CABINET (Cambridge, Mass., 1959), 159, 178, 216; Louis W. Koenig, THE CHIEF EXECUTIVE (New York, 1964), 91, 126, 158, 210, 237; Joseph E. Kallenbach, THE AMERICAN CHIEF EXECUTIVE (New York, 1966), 272, 285, 320, 375, 446, 482, 524. All of these authors discuss the President as legislator before discussing him as executive. The same was done by the U.S. President's Committee on Administrative Management, ADMINISTRATIVE MANAGEMENT (Washington, 1937), 2. This sequence is perhaps symbolic of the presidency's increasing role in legislation. Cf. E. Pendleton Herring, PRESIDENTIAL LEADERSHIP (New York, 1940).

[38] Corwin, THE PRESIDENT, 29f.; Rossiter, AMERICAN PRESIDENCY, 83.

[39] "Should one man have available the immense powers that are today the President's for the asking—indeed, for the taking? It seems to the authors that the time has arrived for us to recognize that crisis, and especially international crisis, has become a constant factor of national existence, and that reliance on intermittent recourse to presidential dictatorship is no longer the safe answer. What then is the safe answer? It seems to us that methods must be devised for making the national legislative powers available when need for important action arises. If . . . Nature abhors a vacuum, so does an age of crisis abhor a power vacuum. So, if the national legislative power is not at hand to assist in filling the vacuum, then it must be and will be filled by the power that is at hand at all times, that of the President. Most Americans, we may be sure, still desire to have legislation survive as an important technique of our national government." (Edward S. Corwin and Louis W. Koenig, THE PRESIDENCY TODAY [New York, 1956], viif.) Thus even Corwin, who throughout his life emphasized national and presidential power, in his later years became worried over the enormous increase of the latter. A similar change of attitude is evident in James M. Burns, PRESIDENTIAL GOVERNMENT (Boston, 1966).

Descriptions of the aggrandizement of the presidency can be found in nearly any study of that institution.[40] By and large, it can be said that this aggrandizement is due to the fact that the President has become the symbol of democracy and, as such, has been prompted by such factors as the decline of Congress, a series of emergencies, the increasing role of the United States in world affairs, and the rise of the "positive" state[41] to assume far-reaching legislative as well as executive powers. Significantly, this aggrandizement, which by the standards of the Founders can only be called revolutionary, was most obvious during the most revolutionary periods of American constitutional development, namely, during the administrations of Jackson, Lincoln, and "progressive" Presidents, periods that were characterized by a growth of democracy.[42]

The "Jacksonian Revolution" is to a large extent a reflection of revolutionary changes in the presidency. Clay's fear that that revolution was "rapidly tending toward a total change of the pure republican character of our Government, and to the concentration of all power in the hands of one man,"[43] was not unfounded. Election of the President by virtually universal white manhood suffrage as it came about with Jackson could hardly be squared with the Founders' concept of republicanism. It was likely to increase the power of the presidency. Jackson was well aware of

[40] As a matter of fact, it is hardly an exaggeration to say that all studies of the presidency are studies of its aggrandizement.

[41] Milton, USE OF PRESIDENTIAL POWER, 3; Rossiter, AMERICAN PRESIDENCY, 84ff. Cf. Rexford G. Tugwell, THE ENLARGEMENT OF THE PRESIDENCY (Garden City, N.Y., 1960).

[42] Herman Finer, THE PRESIDENCY: CRISIS AND REGENERATION (Chicago, 1960), 40. Milton, USE OF PRESIDENTIAL POWER, 3.

[43] CONGRESSIONAL DEBATES, vol. X, Pt. I, 60. Cf. Clay's address at Lexington, May 16, 1829, "The Beginning of Jackson's Administration," THE WORKS OF HENRY CLAY (fed. ed.; New York, 1904), VII, 369. On Apr. 11, 1834, James Kent wrote Joseph Story: "I look upon Jackson as a detestable, ignorant, reckless, vain and malignant Tyrant . . . This American Elective Monarchy frightens me. The Experiment, with its foundations laid on universal Suffrage and an unfettered and licentious Press is of too violent a nature for our excitable People. We have not in our large cities, if we have in our country, moral firmness enough to bear it." Quoted in Beveridge, LIFE OF JOHN MARSHALL, IV, 535n. Daniel Webster charged: "The President carries on the government; all the rest are sub-contractors . . . A Briareus sits in the center of our system, and with his hundred hands touches everything, controls everything." Quoted by Kallenbach, AMERICAN CHIEF EXECUTIVE, 567.

this. Considering himself a "tribune of the people,"[44] he stated: "The President is the direct representative of the American people; he possesses original executive powers, and absorbs in himself all executive functions and responsibilities; and it is his especial duty to protect the liberties and rights of the people and the integrity of the Constitution against the Senate, or the House of Representatives, or both together."[45] A solid foundation for a potentially omnipotent presidency was laid.

Lincoln, considering himself the executor of the will of the people, made full use of the presidential potential.[46] He raised the presidency "to a position of constitutional and moral ascendancy that left no doubt where the burden of crisis government in this country would thereafter rest."[47]

Whereas the immediate successors of Lincoln were content with exercising executive power, this did not remain so in the twentieth century. During the "progressive" era the President also became legislator.[48] Theodore Roosevelt, Woodrow Wilson, and Franklin D. Roosevelt, after having been successful legislative leaders in their home states, projected that type of activity onto the national scene. They no longer confined the President's legislative actions to what the Constitution expressly assigned to him. They no longer merely approved or rejected bills. They became instrumental in the initiation, framing, and passing of laws; making recommendations and proposals to Congress; and using their power of persuasion. The President became a sort of prime minister.

[44] Wilfred E. Binkley, AMERICAN POLITICAL PARTIES: THEIR NATURAL HISTORY (3d ed.; New York, 1958), 135.

[45] Quoted in Rossiter, AMERICAN PRESIDENCY, 97.

[46] See *supra,* 34ff.

[47] Rossiter, AMERICAN PRESIDENCY, 99. For a French report on the presidency under Lincoln, see Adolphe de Chambrun, LE POUVOIR EXÉCUTIF AUX ÉTATS-UNIS (2d ed.; Paris, 1896). Secretary of State Seward said of the presidency: "We elect a King for four years, and give him absolute power within certain limits, which after all he can interpret for himself." (Quoted in Corwin, THE PRESIDENT, ii.)

[48] This idea was first suggested by Howard L. McBain, THE LIVING CONSTITUTION (New York, 1927), 115: "The prime function of the Executive is not executive at all. It is legislative." Binkley (THE MAN IN THE WHITE HOUSE, 16) calls this "a statement of plain fact that would have been incomprehensible in the early days under the Constitution and indeed at almost any time before 1900." This seems to be borne out by Bryce, who observed that the President "does not sway the councils and guide the policy of those members of Congress who belong to his own side. The expression of his wishes conveyed in a message has not necessarily any more effect on Congress than an article in a prominent party newspaper" (AMERICAN COMMONWEALTH, I, 206).

This was complemented by an increase of "executive lawmaking" in a narrower sense, made possible through the delegation of legislative power to the President by Congress. Such delegation increased by leaps and bounds ever since World War I. It has reached proportions that justify the thought that the individual citizen is as subject today to executive proclamations, orders, ordinances, directives, rules, regulations, and what have you, as he is to acts of Congress and the laws.[49] Since the President is also exercising a great deal of influence in Congress, he can use that influence to encourage Congress to fortify his storehouse of powers by an ever increasing delegation of congressional functions. The President, as Chief Legislator, has the power to make himself by law the Big Controller and the Big Regulator.

This development is the more serious because it runs parallel to the increasing abolition of federalism. This means that the power of the President has enormously increased not only in relation to other branches of the national government but also in relation to the states. The presidency has become the predominant institution not only with respect to the institutional separation of powers but also with respect to the spatial, or territorial, division of governmental power. The President has not only become the chief of the federal government. He is chief of the nation.

The growth of democracy and the aggrandizement of the presidency are still continuing. The President is more of a democratic leader today than in the age of Jackson. He is elected by more people, including Negroes and women. He is better known to them. They not only read about him in more papers but hear him over the radio and see him on television. Presidential power is greater today than it was during the Lincoln administration. Theodore Roosevelt, who considered himself a "Jackson-Lincoln" President, employed his "stewardship theory" to expand that power in times of peace as Lincoln had expanded it in time of war.[50] The increase of presidential power went even further.

[49] For a discussion of these various forms of executive lawmaking, see Corwin, THE PRESIDENT, 392ff.

[50] "My view was that every executive officer, and above all every executive officer in high position, was a steward of the people, and not to content himself with the negative merit of keeping his talents undamaged in a napkin. I declined to adopt the view that what was imperatively necessary for the nation could not be done by the President unless he could find some specific authorization to do it. My belief was that it was not only his right but his duty to do anything that the needs

Franklin Roosevelt's conception of that power was reflected no longer in his cousin's stewardship theory, but in the Stuart theory, which John Locke described as the "Power to act according to discretion, for the publick good, without the prescription of the Law, and sometimes even against it."[51] The increase of presidential power did not come to an end with Roosevelt II.[52]

Although we tend to agree with the observation that the President is not omnipotent even today, we feel that this is not much of a consolation for people living under a constitutional government, for that government is based upon the assumption that no branch of government is powerful. But can we also observe that presidential power is not about to reach the limits of what is permissible under that form of government, that it is not about to reach the borderline of constitutionalism? The answer to that question is not very comforting, as is indicated in the literature on the presidency. Whereas the limitations upon the presidency have been mentioned only here and there, its powers have been stressed a great deal.[53] This is natural in view of the fact that the latter are

---

of the nation demanded unless such action was forbidden by the Constitution or by the laws. Under this interpretation of executive power I did and caused to be done many things not previously done by the President and the heads of the departments. I did not usurp power, but I did greatly broaden the use of executive power. In other words, I acted for the public welfare, I acted for the common well-being of all our people, whenever and in whatever manner was necessary, unless prevented by direct constitutional or legislative prohibition" (Theodore Roosevelt, THE AUTOBIOGRAPHY OF THEODORE ROOSEVELT [centennial ed.; New York, 1958], 197f.).

[51] Locke, TWO TREATISES, 393. Laski (AMERICAN PRESIDENCY, 12) writes: "Though Lincoln and Woodrow Wilson both exercised, in the pressure of wartime conditions, an almost dictatorial power, it is, I think, true to say that each wielded it with uneasiness." This can hardly be said of Franklin Roosevelt. Cf. ibid., 18; Lindsay Rogers, "Presidential Dictatorship in the United States," QUARTERLY REVIEW, CCXXXI (1919), 141; Rossiter, CONSTITUTIONAL DICTATORSHIP, Pt. IV.

[52] Rossiter, AMERICAN PRESIDENCY, chs. 4, 5.

[53] The precedent for this approach was perhaps set by William Howard Taft, OUR CHIEF MAGISTRATE AND HIS POWERS (New York, 1916), in which only the last chapter is devoted to "The Limitations of the President's Powers." Modern authors usually do not even devote a special chapter to the limitations on the presidency. Rossiter is an exception. Even in his AMERICAN PRESIDENCY, however, the chapter on "The Limits of the Presidency" is dwarfed by the other chapters that emphasize the increase of presidential power. Bryce called the presidency a "great office, the greatest in the world, unless we except the Papacy, to which any man can rise by his own merits" (AMERICAN COMMONWEALTH, I, 73). By contrast, today's presidency is perhaps the greatest office in the world without any of the qualifications mentioned by Bryce. The increase of the importance of the presidency was envisaged by a French contemporary of Bryce, Chambrun (POUVOIR EXÉCUTIF,

more prevalent today than the former, and that they continue to increase. But it should give us pause that even authors who emphasize the limitations upon the presidency admit that it has become the most powerful branch of the U.S. government.

The aggrandizement of that "most thoroughly American of institutions,"[54] the presidency, is *sui generis*. It differs substantially from the development in other nations, which by and large has tended toward diminution of executive power.[55] To begin with, there are only a few countries left where the offices of the head of state and the political executive are still combined. In these nations executive power has not increased as much as in this country.[56] The executive, be he monarch, as in Monaco, or president as in Latin America, has become more and more constitutionalized, whereas in the United States he has become more and more autocratic.[57]

In most countries, the offices of head of state and political executive are no longer combined. The head of state has become a figurehead who reigns but does not rule, who "can do no wrong." This is true of monarchies such as Belgium, Great Britain, the Netherlands, and the Scandinavian countries, as well as of republics such as Austria, France under the Third and Fourth

---

324ff.). Cf. also Woodrow Wilson, THE PRESIDENT OF THE UNITED STATES (New York, 1916).

[54] Rossiter, AMERICAN PRESIDENCY, 47. Cf. Laski, AMERICAN PRESIDENCY, 11: "There is no foreign institution with which, in any basic sense, it can be compared, because, basically, there is no comparable foreign institution."

[55] There is, of course, no straight line in the diminution of executive power in other states, just as there is no such line in the aggrandizement of the American presidency (Corwin, THE PRESIDENT, 30).

[56] Of the nations in which the offices of the head of state and of the political executive are still combined, the increase of executive power is probably most noticeable in Switzerland. This increase is not dangerous, however, because the Swiss executive is elected by the legislature and is plural, with one of its members serving as head of state for one year only. The first nation to adopt a federal constitution along the lines of the U.S. Constitution, Switzerland rejected a single executive in 1848 because one would "not think of proposing the creation of an office so contrary to the ideas and habits of the Swiss people who might see therein evidence of a monarchical or dictatorial tendency" and because Swiss "democratic feeling revolts against any exclusive personal preëminence" (*Rapport de la commission qui a élaboré le projet de constitution fédérale du 8 avril 1848* [1848], 65, trans. William E. Rappard in THE GOVERNMENT OF SWITZERLAND [New York, 1936], 76).

[57] Dictatorship in Latin America is on the wane. On the other hand Finer (THE PRESIDENCY, 40) speaks of the "autocratic evolution" of the American presidency.

Republics, the Federal Republic of Germany, and Italy. The political executive is usually more powerful. He is not as powerful as his American counterpart, however. In parliamentary systems the prime minister is elected by the legislature and remains dependent upon that body while he holds office. He can be dismissed any time, irrespective of whether he heads a one-party or a coalition government and of whether he can bring about a dissolution of the legislature. He is virtually nothing but the head of the executive committee of parliament. Unlike the American President, he hardly possesses constitutional prerogatives. He exists by the grace of parliamentary prerogative.

By and large, it can be said that the strength of foreign executives stands in striking contrast to that of the United States. Even if one disagrees with the often-made observation that the American President is the strongest executive in the world,[58] stronger even than his Russian counterpart,[59] it is still impossible to deny the unique and enormous growth of his office. The presidency can be compared to perpetually increasing concentric circles, each circle symbolizing a new addition to executive power. Is it a common target?

Perhaps this comparison is not too far-fetched, for the more conspicuous the executive office becomes, the more conspicuously must it become a target for attack.

The argument that the strength of the presidency depends upon the man who occupies it does not offer much consolation. The United States has had many "weak" presidents. Presidential power increased nevertheless. And just as weak presidents seem to have been unable or unwilling to halt the growth of that power,

[58] Here are a few samples: The presidency is considered "the highest political place held by any individual in the world" (Brownlow, PRESIDENT AND PRESIDENCY, 18), "the most important office on earth" (Rossiter, AMERICAN PRESIDENCY, cover). Harry S Truman said: "The Presidency is the most peculiar office in the history of the world. There's never been one like it, there's never been one as powerful, and there's never been any head of government who has had as much responsibility as the President of the United States now has, and has to assume" (TRUMAN SPEAKS [New York, 1960], 3).

[59] Ever since the nineteenth century, trends toward a decrease of monarchical power can be noted in Russia. The Communists made the legislature supreme. Although this supremacy stands more or less merely on paper, it can hardly be denied that since Stalin's death the power of the executive has decreased. Under Soviet constitutions, the offices of head of state and political executive are separated. Both are elected by the legislature.

there is a good chance that weak personalities entering the White House will be corrupted by it.[60] The probability of corruption appears to be even greater in the case of a strong personality who, with Machiavellian skill,[61] might use his power to the detriment of freedom.

PRESIDENTIAL POWER AS
A CHALLENGE TO FREE GOVERNMENT

The implications of the growth of presidential power for free government are plain. History has amply demonstrated that too much executive power is detrimental to liberal as well as democratic principles. The virtual absence of those principles constituted the most dubious feature of the *ancien régime,* and democratic revolutions were prompted by the hope that a replacement of executive through popular power would secure freedom. So great was the general antagonism toward the executive that Jefferson in the Declaration of Independence preferred to denounce the King rather than Parliament, although the struggle preceding the Declaration had been between the colonies and the Parliament which was more powerful than the King.

The democratization of executives has not changed the picture. It probably made things worse. Executives of the *ancien régime* were supported by the aristocracy, the military, the police, and the bureaucracy. Theirs was a minority government, always faced with an uprising of the majority. Modern executives are supported by the masses of people, as well as by the military, the police, and the bureaucracy. They are potentially more dangerous

[60] See *supra,* 14f. What a man can make of himself in the presidential office was expressed by Woodrow Wilson, who said of the President: "His office is anything he has the sagacity and force to make it . . . Some of our Presidents have deliberately held themselves off from using the full power they might legitimately have used because of conscientious scruples, because they were more theorists than statesmen . . . The President is at liberty, both in law and conscience, to be as big a man as he can . . . His is the vital place of action in the system, whether he accepts it as such or not, and the office is the measure of the man—of his wisdom as well as of his force." CONSTITUTIONAL GOVERNMENT IN THE UNITED STATES (New York, 1908), 69, 70, 73.

[61] This possibility becomes especially obvious in Richard E. Neustadt, PRESIDENTIAL POWER (New York, 1960).

because the minority must more or less suffer their actions without much hope for redress. Napoleon I gave the modern world the first inkling of what the rule of a powerful executive confirmed by plebiscite can mean for free government.[62] Mussolini, Stalin, and Hitler left no doubt that a democratically elected executive can deny not only the protection of the individual from the government, but also democracy itself. While the latter existed on paper, it was a farce in practice. It was replaced by democratic slogans.

Although American democratic slogans used by chief executives have been compared to their Communist and Fascist counterparts and American Presidents to Old World dictators,[63] such comparisons are perhaps unfair. Still, they point out dangerous trends. Whereas no American President can be compared to Hitler or Stalin, there have been "consensus Presidents"[64] who could carry out ambitious programs which not only jeopardized the individual's protection from the government, but also democracy. For the majority often were so much taken in by these programs or plans or deals that they were willing to follow the President as their plebiscitary leader in a way that made it doubtful whether the people controlled the President or the President the people.

Since executive omnipotence under the old regime was abolished by democratic revolutions, the question arises whether the American presidency, should its power increase to match that of modern dictators, will one day meet a similar fate. This appears improbable because the President is elected by the majority of the people and revolutionary movements usually succeed only if they enjoy the sympathy of a large part of the population.

This leaves the possibility of assassination. The personal tragedy involved in the death of President Kennedy makes this a delicate subject. However, it must not deter us from examining a problem that is relevant to a discussion of executive power.[65] Reason—not sentiment—must be our guide. And reason does not

---

[62] See Karl Loewenstein, "Opposition and Public Opinion under the Dictatorship of Napoleon the First," SOCIAL RESEARCH, IV (1937), 461; Harold C. Deutsch, THE GENESIS OF NAPOLEONIC IMPERIALISM (Cambridge, Mass., 1938).

[63] Raoul E. Desvernine, DEMOCRATIC DESPOTISM (New York, 1936).

[64] Burns, PRESIDENTIAL GOVERNMENT, sounds a warning against those Presidents.

[65] Napoleon I stated: *"Quand on veut se mêler de gouverner, il faut savoir se laisser assassiner."* LAROUSSE DU XXE SIÈCLE (Paris, 1928), I, 389.

preclude the assassination of Presidents, unreasonable as such assassinations often have been. An examination of the implications of presidential power for free government cannot omit an investigation of whether that power might incite assassination.

Assassination is not always an ordinary crime. It can be a political crime. Although the criminal aspect will often overshadow the political one, this need not be so. The latter may come to the fore to the degree that the former recedes. It is conceivable that the political aspect may be so predominant as to eliminate the criminal aspect. A crime may thus become a political act. As such, it may be ethical.[66] And, whereas we believe that the chances for a justification of political assassination are slight indeed, we are also aware that assassinations were undertaken for ethical motives—the bomb plots against Hitler in 1939 and 1944 being examples—and that they may be prompted by the conviction that they are legitimate by the standards of higher law or of the traditional constitutional order.[67]

---

[66] In distinction from ordinary criminals, persons who have committed political crimes are usually not extradited. In general, murder and other crimes are considered political crimes if they are connected with an attempt against the security of the state, its constitution, or organs of government. When assassins against Napoleon III had taken refuge in Belgium, Belgium in 1856 added an *attentat* clause to its law on extradition, which excluded assassination of a head of a foreign state or members of his family from the category of political crime. Although the Belgian attitude was adopted by other nations, including the United States, it is still the exception rather than the rule. For instance, after the assassination of King Alexander of Yugoslavia and the French Foreign Minister Barthou at Marseilles, Italy refused the extradition of the assassins on the grounds that they committed political crimes. The assassination of Ngo Dinh Diem and Ngo Dinh Nhu in South Vietnam only three weeks before the assassination of President Kennedy was considered by the Department of State a political rather than a criminal act, resulting in the recognition of those who were responsible for the killings as the new government of South Vietnam. On political crimes, see Herbert W. Briggs, THE LAW OF NATIONS (2d ed.; New York, 1952), 593, 597f.; Paul Guggenheim, TRAITÉ DE DROIT INTERNATIONAL PUBLIQUE (Geneva, 1953), I, 363ff.; Charles Cheney Hyde, INTERNATIONAL LAW, CHIEFLY AS INTERPRETED AND APPLIED BY THE UNITED STATES (2d ed.; Boston, 1945), II, 1019ff.; L. F. L. Oppenheim, INTERNATIONAL LAW (5th ed. by H. Lauterpacht; London, 1937), I, 561ff.; Wilhelm Sauer, SYSTEM DES VÖLKERRECHTS (Bonn, 1952), 211f.

[67] On the justification of tyrannicide, see Carl J. Friedrich, MAN AND HIS GOVERNMENT, ch. 34; Harold J. Laski, "A Defence of Liberty against Tyrants," an introduction to his edition of VINDICIAE CONTRA TYRANNOS (London, 1924); Oscar Jaszi and John D. Lewis, AGAINST THE TYRANT: THE TRADITION AND THEORY OF TYRANNICIDE (Glencoe, Ill., 1957); Hans G. Schmidt, DIE LEHRE VOM TYRANNENMORD (Tübingen, 1901); Hyman (AMERICAN PRESIDENT, 83) states that "America, unlike other nations, has never produced a doctrinaire justification for political murder."

Naturally, the growth of the presidency has invited criticism. Did it also invite assassination? The increase of assassinations ever since the aggrandizement of the presidency became obvious makes us wonder. Whereas before the Civil War none of fifteen Presidents was killed, four of twenty have been assassinated since then. We bewail the fact that over 11 per cent of American Presidents were assassinated. A more proper evaluation of this dilemma would be offered by saying that the percentage of Presidents killed was zero before the aggrandizement of the presidency had become conspicuous and rose to as much as twenty afterward.[68] Furthermore, it should give us pause that in recent decades the only objects of assassination were personalities such as Franklin Roosevelt, Truman, and Kennedy, whose strong desires to carry out ambitious social programs made the presidency appear in its full strength, while Presidents under whom the institution appeared relatively weak, such as Harding, Coolidge, Hoover, and Eisenhower, were not assassination objects. Increase of presidential power as well as assertion of that power thus seems to have whetted the appetite for assassination,[69] suggesting the possibility that past assassinations were political crimes and that future assassinations might be political rather than criminal acts, should the presidency degenerate from a constitutional to a despotic institution by further aggrandizement.

Be it first stated that this author considers such a possibility remote. He doubts that America will ever be ruled by a tyrant, although his doubts are tempered by the consideration that his parents had also doubted that Hitler's tyranny could exist in Germany and that the way for that tyranny was paved by an increase of executive power under a democratic constitution.[70]

---

[68] The picture does not change much if we include attempts at assassination. Significantly, the only attempt made against the life of a President prior to the Civil War was made against Jackson, who was probably the strongest President in the prewar period. After the Civil War, assassinations were attempted against President Truman, former President Theodore Roosevelt, and President-elect Franklin D. Roosevelt, all of whom favored a strong executive.

[69] The case of President McKinley is perhaps an exception which confirms the rule.

[70] See Carl J. Friedrich, "The Development of the Executive Power in Germany," AMERICAN POLITICAL SCIENCE REVIEW, XXVII (1933), 185; Grau, "Die Diktaturgewalt des Reichspräsidenten," in Gerhard Anschütz and Richard Thoma (eds.), HANDBUCH DES DEUTSCHEN STAATSRECHTS (Tübingen, 1932), II, 275; Jo-

However, this author also recognizes that his upbringing under a dictatorship might have made him less aware of oppression than Americans brought up in freedom or its image. He could well imagine that, while at some future date he might still consider the enlarged presidency constitutional and acceptable, Americans might find it to be dictatorial and unbearable, a temptation for political assassination. Such a temptation could be the more probable because it might be abetted by the cherished American belief in the rule of law and the right of revolution.

The latter combination is not as contradictory as it may appear. There is no discrepancy between the rule of law and the right of revolution, considering the way the latter is understood by Americans. Mind the sequence: rule of law and right of revolution, *not* right of revolution and rule of law. The rule of law is prior to the right of revolution. Under the American credo, a revolution is permissible only if it rests upon the awareness of the value of the rule of law, that is, of freedom. A right of revolution exists only if men are deprived of the freedom they enjoyed under such a rule. It is recognized only if government lost its legitimacy by abolishing the rule of law and freedom guaranteed by it, notwithstanding the legality of that process. The American concept of the right of revolution is thus oriented toward legitimacy and bound toward the reestablishment of a rule of law and the freedom of the individual ensuing from it. A revolution in that sense is conservative rather than destructive. It is revolution only by the standards of a state that came about as the result of a perverted evolution. By more normal standards, it does not really amount to a revolution. It is illegal only by the standards of a fraudulent legality. By more honest standards, it is legitimate. This accounts for its moral strength and general acceptance by a

---

hannes Heckel, "Diktatur, Notverordnungsrecht, Verfassungsnotand," ARCHIV DES ÖFFENTLICHEN RECHTS, N.S., XXII (1932), 257; Harlow J. Heneman, THE GROWTH OF EXECUTIVE POWER IN GERMANY (Minneapolis, 1934); Hugo Preuss, "Reichsverfassungsmässige Diktatur," ZEITSCHRIFT FÜR POLITIK, XIII (1924), 97; Rossiter, CONSTITUTIONAL DICTATORSHIP, Pt. I; Carl Schmitt, DER HÜTER DER VERFASSUNG (Tübingen, 1931); Richard Thoma, "Die Regelung der Diktaturgewalt," DEUTSCHE JURISTENZEITUNG (1924), 654; Frederick M. Watkins, THE FAILURE OF CONSTITUTIONAL EMERGENCY POWERS UNDER THE WEIMAR REPUBLIC (Cambridge, Mass., 1939).

nation that believes in a government of law and not of men.[71]

In view of this acceptance, could it be surprising if Americans also accepted the right of political assassination for the preservation of a government of law and freedom? Must not such an acceptance derive *a fortiori* from the acceptance of a right of revolution? Unlike a revolution, political assassination involves no war, no large number of casualties, no substantial destruction of property. It does not challenge the existing order. Whereas a revolution overthrows a political system with a view to re-establishing free government, political assassination merely eliminates a usurper. It could thus serve to prevent a perverted evolution toward an abolition of a government of law and thus make a revolution for the re-establishment of such a government unnecessary. It could prevent the sacrifices any revolution demands, which, aside from the risk of anarchy, are so great that the American document in defense of the right of revolution, the Declaration of Independence, permits that right only in case of repeated and serious abuses of governmental power and persistent refusals to rectify such abuses.[72]

These considerations might well prompt a political assassin. He might well have fewer inhibitions than revolutionaries, for his deed will not have the serious consequences of a revolution. He might not be patient enough to put up with many serious abuses of governmental power. A few less serious oppressions might trigger him into action. The American presidency, which we symbolized by ever increasing concentric circles reflecting the increase of presidential power, might indeed be a target. Could its occupant become a sharpshooter's target?

It may be argued that political assassination presupposes an unbearable President in an unbearable presidency, a combination which is unlikely to come about in this country. We tend to agree with this. On the other hand, it ought not to be overlooked that "unbearable" can mean different things to different people. A presidency endowed with certain powers and an autocratic Presi-

---

[71] Cf. Carl L. Becker, THE DECLARATION OF INDEPENDENCE (New York, 1922), 7ff.

[72] Cf. Locke, TWO TREATISES, 424ff., which obviously influenced Jefferson's defense of the right of revolution. Cf. Becker, DECLARATION OF INDEPENDENCE, 27.

dent might be acceptable to those who grew up under dictatorship but not to those who grew up in freedom. Even the latter might have different opinions on what is acceptable. People believing in the Founders' ideal of weak government might consider today's presidency less acceptable than those favoring strong government. They might feel that the presidency today is no longer compatible with a government of law and freedom.

Their suspicion is not unfounded. American government has more and more turned into a government of the laws made by the men in Congress and of proclamations, orders, ordinances, directives, rules, and regulations made by the man in the White House. It appears to be a government of men rather than of law. An abundance of laws can easily lead to abandonment of the law, of right and justice.[73] Since the presidency has played a decisive role in the increasing replacement of the government of law by a government of man-made laws, rules, and regulations, its occupant might well be held responsible for the decline of the rule of law.

Chances are that the President's vulnerability will further increase in the years to come. For he—the tribune of the people—will increasingly use the additional powers he will obtain with the further growth of democracy. Whatever his regulatory activities may be, and however beneficial they may be considered by some or even by many, they will engender the feeling that government by law, characterized by freedom, is being replaced by the government of one man, characterized by compulsion. Claims that presidential regulation is desired by the people will hardly comfort those who believe in the freedom of the individual. And claims that such regulation may be required by democratic reason of state will hardly impress individuals who, at best, are prepared to permit restrictions of freedom for constitutional reason of state.[74] In the years to come, presidential activities might well transgress the limits of what is permissible under the Consti-

---

[73] See *supra*, 155n., 170. The complaint against an excess of legislative lawmaking would, it seems, apply *a fortiori* to executive lawmaking, hardly envisaged by Hamilton and Madison.

[74] For the idea that an excess of democracy may be detrimental to constitutional government and the rights of the individual, see the author's IN DEFENSE OF PROPERTY, ch. 5. Cf. Carl J. Friedrich, CONSTITUTIONAL REASON OF STATE.

tution. The President could well become a target of political assassination.

It will be argued that assassination under a system that provides for impeachment and free elections every four years must be criminal and cannot be political. Such an argument is legalistic rather than realistic. "The cumbersomeness of the impeachment proceeding and the amount of time it is apt to consume"[75] make impeachment an ineffective means for removing a President from office. Only once was an American President impeached—and he was acquitted.[76] This occurred at a time when the presidency was just beginning to grow strong and when its occupant was not yet very influential in Congress. It would be considerably more difficult to impeach a President today. The chances of unseating a President through an election at the end of his first term are also slim. His office affords him enormous advantages over any opponent. Aside from orthodox advantages, there are new ones which are further demonstrations of how dangerous the man in the White House could be: The President could use the general fear of nuclear war to promote his re-election by creating an international crisis that would rally the nation behind him or by making concessions to the Communists, thus appearing as the man who preserved peace.

While we can hardly succeed in eliminating criminal assassination, we can perhaps reduce the probability of political assassination by eliminating possible sources of inducement to such assassination through a reduction of presidential strength, that is, through a regeneration of the presidency in the sense of constitutionalism.[77]

[75] Corwin, THE CONSTITUTION AND WHAT IT MEANS TODAY, 11.

[76] Although the acquittal was by only one vote, it was achieved by political maneuvers. Corwin, THE PRESIDENT, 65. See Benjamin P. Poore (ed.), TRIAL OF ANDREW JOHNSON (Washington, 1868); Chambrun, POUVOIR EXÉCUTIF, 299ff.; Howard M. DeWitt, THE IMPEACHMENT AND TRIAL OF ANDREW JOHNSON (New York, 1903).

[77] C. Perry Patterson (PRESIDENTIAL GOVERNMENT IN THE UNITED STATES [Chapel Hill, 1947]) suggested such a constitutionalist regeneration of the presidency at a time when other authors rejoiced in the authoritarian degeneration of that institution. Significantly, his work did not become well known, being like a voice in the wilderness. Recent literature on the presidency raises the question of scholarly

A decrease of presidential power through self-restraint can hardly be expected. The Supreme Court exercised such restraint occasionally out of an awareness of its judicial obligation, although even here it was asserted that the Court's "self-inflicted wounds" were tactical retreats for strategic gains.[78] However, the President is not a judicial but a political figure. His oath to "preserve, protect, and defend the Constitution of the United States" is qualified by the words, "to the best of my ability."[79] A politician will hardly find it within his ability to surrender power when power is considered the prize of politics.

Restraint of the presidency by the other branches of government is also improbable. During the past generations executive power has increased at the cost of legislative power. There is no reason to believe that this will change. The President's influence in Congress is likely to restrain that body from restricting presidential power. If Congress would pass an act to that effect, it would probably have to get the backing of the Supreme Court. This is unlikely to happen. For a long time, the Court has supported presidential ambitions and thus contributed to the increase of power in the presidency.[80]

Since the presidency has become the outstanding symbol of the people, it probably can be checked only by the people themselves, that is, by an amendment to the Constitution. Such an amend-

---

responsibility. It ought to be asked whether scholars advocating or sanctioning a strong presidency act in a responsible manner or promote dictatorship. The attitude of German scholars under the Weimar Republic ought to be a warning. These scholars accepted far-reaching presidential powers. As a result, parliamentary government degenerated into "presidential government" and the latter into the National Socialist dictatorship. Hitler virtually walked away with the power scholars had vested in the executive long before he became chancellor. Barry Goldwater considered himself a "constitutionalist" and denounced presidential power during his campaign. "My Case for the Republican Party, 1964," SATURDAY REVIEW, Oct. 17, 1964, 21ff.

[78] Cf. Robert G. McCloskey, THE AMERICAN SUPREME COURT (Chicago, 1960), 107f., 129f., 133f., 158, 178; John P. Roche, "Judicial Self-Restraint," AMERICAN POLITICAL SCIENCE REVIEW, XLIX (1955), 762.

[79] Const. Art. II, sec. i, clause 8.

[80] See Robert A. Horn, "The Warren Court and the Discretionary Power of the Executive," MINNESOTA LAW REVIEW, XLIV (1960), 669; Glendon A. Schubert, THE PRESIDENCY IN THE COURTS (Minneapolis, 1957); Patterson, PRESIDENTIAL GOVERNMENT, ch. 9; Leonard D. White, "Administration, Public," ENCYCLOPEDIA OF THE SOCIAL SCIENCES, I, 448.

ment could provide for specific restrictions of the powers of the President. However, as the fate of the Bricker Amendment seems to indicate, such an amendment may not stand much chance of ratification. The people seem to have accepted a strong presidency, not realizing the threat a tribune of the people may constitute to freedom. Perhaps an amendment that restricts the time of the President's tenure rather than his powers could more easily be passed. The Twenty-second Amendment could well point into the right direction. We suggest the consideration of an amendment restricting presidential tenure to one term of office.[81]

While this solution is not perfect in view of the fact that considerable power—a veritable arsenal for oppression—would remain in the hands of one man for four long years, it would attenuate the nightmare of a Machiavellian strongman in the White House for as long as eight and perhaps ten years. The democratic argument that the people have a new choice every fourth year would exist in fact, not just on paper. The anxiety of a prospective political assassin lest the President is perverting government of law and oppressing freedom would be decreased.

Since we are concerned with suggesting means for the prevention of assassination, this is no place for discussing the advantages of re-eligibility. This was previously undertaken by Hamilton.[82] It is open to doubt, however, whether Hamilton's arguments are still valid and whether he would advance them today in the face of enormously increased presidential power. It should be

---

[81] President Jackson, the only President to favor a one-term presidency, wrote that it was a subject "worthy of particular examination . . . to limit the service of the President of the U. States to a single term; whether of 4 or 6 years seems not material—the latter might perhaps be preferable, as corresponding with the term of service for which the senate are chosen. The chief magistrate of a free people, should never be found seeking and manoevoring to possess himself of the office. Full of care and responsibility, the merit of its possession is taken away, when obtained thro any channel or means, other than the voluntary expression of the people's will. When any shall be thus selected, and the constitution of the country, inhibit an extension of the trust beyond a single term, every thing of management and motive will be removed and an honorable, honest and faithful discharge of the duties confided, will alone have influence, and constitute his motive of action." ("Draft of the First Annual Message of December 8, 1829," in John S. Bassett, [ed.], CORRESPONDENCE OF ANDREW JACKSON [Washington, 1929], IV, 99.) Similar thoughts are expressed in de Tocqueville, DEMOCRACY IN AMERICA, I, 141ff. President Kennedy was assassinated on a campaign trip.

[82] THE FEDERALIST, No. 72.

kept in mind that the defender of judicial review was, above all, a believer in free government and property rights.[83] He advocated a strong presidency mainly in order to create a counterbalance to Congress, which he suspected of despotic designs.[84] Also, he probably backed the presidency out of the belief that George Washington would be the first President and that his successors would, like him, protect free government and property. In view of the increasing role modern Presidents have played in the regulation—and thus the restriction—of property and freedom, Hamilton, if he lived today, might well be an advocate of a weak presidency.[85] Certainly one of his arguments in favor of the President's re-eligibility is no longer convincing, namely, the argument that it was dangerous to have former Presidents who could not expect re-election "wandering among the people like discontented ghosts, and sighing for a place which they were destined never more to possess."[86] Former Presidents Herbert Hoover, Harry S Truman, and Dwight D. Eisenhower have not at all given the impression of being discontented ghosts sighing for the White House. They have supplied us with wisdom, amusement, and assurance. We prefer seeing them wandering among the people to seeing people sighing and wondering over assassinated Presidents.

[83] See the author's "Hamilton's Concept of Free Government," 351.

[84] See the author's FEDERALIST, 157ff. Hamilton's suspicion of the legislature, derived from his observation of the state legislatures under the Articles of Confederation (cf. THE FEDERALIST, Nos. 27, 81, 85), is evident in the numbers of the Federalist papers in which he defends the proposed presidency. He complains about "the tendency of the legislative authority to absorb every other," writing that "the representatives of the people, in a popular assembly, seem sometimes to fancy that they are the people themselves, and betray strong symptoms of impatience and disgust at the least sign of opposition from any other quarter; as if the exercise of its rights, by either the executive or judiciary, were a breach of their privilege and an outrage to their dignity. They often appear disposed to exert an imperious control over the other departments; and as they commonly have the people on their side, they always act with such momentum as to make it very difficult for the other members of the government to maintain the balance of the Constitution" (THE FEDERALIST, No. 71). See also THE FEDERALIST, No. 66.

[85] The threat to the rights of the individual from "the favorite of the people," the legislature, appeared to Hamilton as an American dilemma, perhaps *the* American dilemma (THE FEDERALIST, No. 66). That dilemma has grown in scope. Today, the rights of the individual are not only threatened by the legislature but also by what has more and more become another favorite of the people—the presidency.

[86] THE FEDERALIST, No. 72.

CONCLUSION

American government, originally called "presidential" to distinguish it from parliamentary government and not because of an accumulation of power in the presidency, has developed into a government in which such an accumulation exists. The "presidential system," in the beginning an aspect of the separation of powers, has become a serious challenge to that principle. In view of the corruptible nature of power, the increase of presidential power increasingly challenged free government. It seems to confirm the statement that power is evil.[87]

If power is evil, is it, like evil, inevitable? Evil can be inevitable. It is due not only to intentions, but also to circumstances. And although even evil circumstances need not bring forth the evil in men, they often do because, after all, men are not angels.[88] The increase of presidential power, then, may be due to intentions as well as circumstances.

The preceding pages mainly discussed how the presidency grew by virtue of intentions, be they the intentions of those who occupied the office, of those who delegated power to it, or of those who put up with the growth of its power. While these intentions may have been evil, they may also have been prompted by good faith. In politics, evil intentions are hard to tell from good ones because hypocrisy is not easily unmasked.

However, the intentional increase of presidential power, due in a large measure to the growth of democracy, does not explain the whole story. Whereas the first strongman in the White House, Jackson, was also the first "democratic" President, the first President who substantially enlarged presidential power, Lincoln, was considered a Whig. Be this as it may, Lincoln—whether prompted by good or evil intentions—probably would not have used his power the way he did had it not been for the Civil War.[89] Later on,

[87] See *supra,* 15n.
[88] See Benjamin F. Wright, "The Federalist on the Nature of Political Man," ETHICS, LIX (No. 2, Pt. II, 1949), 1.
[89] See *supra,* 34ff. Burckhardt: "Not every age finds its great man, and not every great endowment finds its time." REFLECTIONS ON HISTORY, 203. Alfred

the internal circumstances which contributed to the increase of presidential power during the Civil War were replaced by external circumstances. As the world shrank because of technical progress, as the United States became a world power which no longer could beware of entangling alliances, the power of the nation's representative in international affairs grew. It grew further on account of World War I, World War II, and the present Cold War.

Although even a circumstantial growth of presidential power appears to be justified only to the degree it preserves free government, it will often go further. The bigger the threat to the United States, the greater the probability that presidential power will transgress the limitations set to it by the principle of free government, limitations which especially in emergency situations are all too likely to become blurred. Furthermore, the blurring of those limitations often will obscure the distinction between circumstantial and intentional increases of presidential power. An incumbent President, seeing the possibility of enlarging the power of his office on account of circumstances, may use this opportunity to further his own designs toward enhancing that power—and his own prestige—beyond existing needs. He will often pretend to do so in the name of the people, and often actually be backed by the people.

Those interested in the preservation of free government, then, are faced with difficult tasks. They must prevent increases of presidential power which are due to an incumbent's ambitions whose evil features will often be shrouded by demagogic and hypocritical assertions of their good and altruistic nature. Furthermore, the friends of free government must prevent enlargements of the presidency which, while intentional, on the face of it are indeed of an altruistic nature in so far as they correspond to

Weber, DAS TRAGISCHE UND DIE GESCHICHTE (Hamburg, 1943), 34, writes that the "weltbedeutsame Genius"—he would not classify Lincoln as such—"since in turmoil he will always have to recognize what is essential, generally will receive his calling at the great turning points of history. He always will constitute a beginning as a founder, reformer, prophet, and also as a prophetic philosopher, and . . . put an end to, and destroy the old by establishing the new. As a statesman, he will sometimes personify a last culmination just before the decline, as did Pericles in classic Athens. In most cases, however . . . he will be a beginning even though he may personally perish, as in the case of Caesar."

the desires of the majority. This is already a more arduous task. For it means taking issue with prevalent conceptions of altruism by pointing out that the temporary good of the majority is not necessarily the long-range public good. Still more difficult is the task of preventing an undue circumstantial increase of presidential power. This task is complicated not only because circumstances may camouflage designs toward a growth of the nation's highest office, but also because the constitutionalist may be faced with a dilemma. When denouncing presidential power during an emergency, he may well denounce the very thing which may be necessary to master that emergency and to protect the United States. Just as Lincoln considered the preservation of the Union prerequisite to the survival of free government and enlarged presidential power in order to preserve the Union, modern friends of free government may consider the preservation of the United States from foreign aggression prerequisite to the survival of free government—and presidential power the proper means for that preservation. Again, in view of past experience, the latter may be answered that an exceptional restriction of freedom in times of war will lead to its regular restriction in normal times, that the dubious principle, *inter arma silent leges,* will be followed by the even more dubious principle, *inter bella silent leges* in the sense of *in pace silent leges,* and that free government will be the exception rather than the rule.

A way out of this dilemma might be a presidency which is weak as to internal matters, and strong with respect to foreign affairs. The power of the "internal" presidency could be measured by constitutionalist standards, and that of the "external" presidency, also by international exigencies. Constitutionalist restraints would then be prevalent in internal matters, and exceptional increases of power permitted for foreign affairs. The "internal" presidency would be more or less constant, and its "external" counterpart adjustable to international situations. However, such an arrangement is not without problems. Aside from the fact that nearly immeasurable power would remain in the hands of the President for the conduct of foreign affairs, it is open to doubt whether internal matters can be separated from foreign policy. In view of the generally accepted primacy of the latter, the "stronger" presidency would influence the "weaker" one and render the latter's constitutionalism illusory.

Since presidential power perhaps increased because a consultation of Congress often was unfeasible for reasons of national security, it might be advisable to substitute for unwieldy legislative chambers some smaller body to advise the President on, and consent to, foreign policy. Such a body could be composed, for instance, of the senior senators. Or a still smaller body could be elected by Congress. Even the latter, however, aside from being perhaps incompatible with federal and democratic principles, might be considered an impediment to speedy action required in certain emergency situations. All this might prompt people to leave things the way they are. The argument that the President, since he is elected by the people, might as well handle foreign affairs and emergencies the way he sees fit, will probably prevail. This takes us back to the truth that a democratic president is a potential dictator; to the argument that democratic checks upon the President's conduct of foreign affairs might frustrate an effective foreign policy and jeopardize the survival of the United States. It takes us to the dilemma of American foreign policy.

7

CONSTITUTIONAL FOREIGN POLICY THWARTED

INTRODUCTION

In the Cold War, the idea that American foreign policy is in a dilemma suggests tragedy. And tragedy makes us think of the Civil War. For somehow, tragedy in America seems to be insolubly connected with that event. As has been pointed out earlier, the Civil War was the beginning of a political tragedy we still experience. From that war on, a constitutionalist idyll characterized by federalism and the separation of powers as guarantees for the protection of civil rights, became increasingly replaced by a democratic *Machtpolitik,* a growth of national and executive power, and the emergence of new concepts of civil rights. The rule of law became replaced by that of men. Free government was challenged by democracy. Constitutionalist option was increasingly replaced by democratic action, and constitutional reason by democratic desire.[1]

Tragic as today's dilemma of American foreign policy is, is it similar to Lincoln's? Some parallels suggest that it is. In the Civil War, the survival of the Union was at stake; today, the survival of the United States is. Previously, presidential power was increased to save the Union and its type of government. Today, presidential power has been increased to preserve the United States and her type of government. We referred to Lincoln's constitutional dilemma. We may also consider the present dilemma of American foreign policy a constitutional one because that policy has raised questions of constitutionality.

However, these parallels could be misleading. Constitutional dilemmas may differ with the content of constitutions. The Con-

---

[1] See *supra,* 72ff., 83ff., 108ff., 127ff., 152ff., 160ff., 182ff., 191ff.

stitution facing Lincoln was predominantly liberal and only secondarily democratic. It was a "Whig" document that realized free government, a supreme law designed to check human passion and desire through reason. Lincoln's constitutional dilemma was a liberal dilemma. He was faced with the problem of keeping the Constitution liberal in the process of de-liberalizing it. In this pursuit, he was backed by a majority which, while it did not mind interfering with some Whig principles, basically accepted Whig doctrines. Today's situation is different. As a result of the growth of democracy, people not only became less convinced of the value of Whig principles, but in many respects became opposed to those principles. The Constitution to a large extent lost its liberal character and became predominantly democratic. Therefore, the present dilemma of American foreign policy is mainly a democratic one, because the President often will have to act undemocratically in order to preserve American democracy against foreign aggression. He will have to defend the democratized Constitution and the long-range national interest irrespective of the temporary desires of the people. In this effort, he is likely to be backed by a "Whig" minority because that minority recognizes even in the modern de-liberalized Constitution sufficient liberal values that merit its support of presidential policy.

We are thus confronted with the apparent paradox that in contrast to internal policy, modern foreign policy, although exercised by a popularly elected President in the name of the people, could be handicapped by popular demands. We are faced with the strange situation that as long as democracy had not yet outgrown free government, as long as constitutional option could still cope with democratic action, a more effective foreign policy was possible than today, when democracy inhibits constitutional reason.

In the following, it will be examined to what degree this kind of situation has come about and whether it really is a paradox. It will be investigated whether the growth of democracy, just as it has jeopardized democratic as well as liberal principles in internal affairs, also has jeopardized those principles with respect to foreign affairs. Remarks on the foreign policy of the United States up to the Cold War will be followed by an examination of changes in that policy and their impact upon national security.

CONSTITUTIONAL FOREIGN POLICY
UP TO THE COLD WAR

While as a result of the growth of democracy constitutionalism in America was on the way out, the American democracy, prior to the Cold War, was on the way in in world affairs. The preceding chapters demonstrated how the United States developed from a federal republic into a democratic nation, headed by a powerful President. They pointed out the dangers of this development for free government and the rule of law. One reason why these dangers may not have been recognized for a long time was that during this development there came about an enormous increase of American prestige in the world. Just as external glamor makes people overlook internal ugliness, so the glory of a nation in international affairs often overshadows her problems at home.[2] The loss of freedom on account of social legislation appeared insignificant due to the prestige Americans came to enjoy abroad. While it must not be overlooked that the latter would probably also have grown had freedom not been curbed inside the United States, it is understandable that under the circumstances the tightening of control, gradual and democratic as it was, went unnoticed by many. Americans abroad could count on the protection of a powerful—perhaps the most powerful—nation. The Western Frontier may have ceased in 1890,[3] but "New Frontiers" were opening up all over the earth.[4]

They opened up not only for individual citizens, but also for

---

[2] This is especially evident in the case of absolute regimes. Prussia's rise to power under Frederick II made people forget that the King arbitrarily incarcerated judges. The emergence of France as *La Grande Nation* overshadowed Napoleon's dubious plebiscites and his intolerance toward the judiciary. The rise of Germany under Hitler made people overlook the regime's cruelties. Historical appreciation seems to measure greatness by power rather than constitutionalism. This demonstrates how much constitutionalism has been on the defensive and unappreciated.

[3] Cf. Frederick J. Turner, THE FRONTIER IN AMERICAN HISTORY.

[4] The term "New Frontiers" was first used by Henry A. Wallace, NEW FRONTIERS (New York, 1934). Wallace, an important figure during the New Deal, had in mind the frontiers of social legislation inside the United States. In a polemic against Wallace, the author said in 1957 that "new frontiers" are wherever property rights are threatened in the world. "Benjamin Rush and the American Revolution," 89f.

the government. The constitutional idyll of a balance of spatial and institutional powers may have been ended. In international affairs, the United States became a weight in the balance of powers. She came to enjoy participation in the concert of nations, and often called the tune. That tune emphasized the grandeur of the American way of life, of freedom under democracy. It stressed the American burden to secure democracy for the realization of freedom. America's "manifest destiny,"[5] previously confined to the conquest of the American East, Midwest, and West, now spread to the world's West, Middle East, and East. Having marched with the sun, Americans now marched against the sun. The United States helped Cuba to become independent. She prevented European intervention in Venezuela. She became the dominant power in the Organization of American States.[6] She decided the outcome of World War I. Emerging from that war as the strongest creditor nation, she brought about the League of Nations.[7] By the time of the New Deal, few people doubted that this would be America's century.[8] The *Pax Americana* seemed close. At the end of World War II, it became a fact. As the strongest nation on earth, the United States was instrumental in bringing about the United Nations and became the leading power in that organization.[9] Never before had a people become so powerful in so short a time with so few setbacks.

At the end of World War II, Americans may well have reveled over their achievements. They may well have forgotten the tragedy of the Civil War. With delight, they may have remembered the prophesies of the founders of their nation—Federalists and Republicans alike—prophesies that envisaged American greatness. "I do believe we shall continue to grow, to multiply and

---

[5] Cf. Albert K. Weinberg, MANIFEST DESTINY (Baltimore, 1935).

[6] See Samuel F. Bemis, THE LATIN AMERICAN POLICY OF THE UNITED STATES (New York, 1943); Graham H. Stuart, LATIN AMERICA AND THE UNITED STATES (5th ed.; New York, 1955).

[7] See Samuel F. Bemis, A DIPLOMATIC HISTORY OF THE UNITED STATES (5th ed.; New York, 1965), chs. 33, 34.

[8] See Carroll D. Murphy and Herbert V. Prochnow, THE NEXT CENTURY IS AMERICA'S (New York, 1938).

[9] Cf. Ruth Russell, HISTORY OF THE UNITED NATIONS CHARTER (Washington, 1958); Clark M. Eichelberger, UN: THE FIRST TEN YEARS (New York, 1955); Lincoln P. Bloomfield, THE UNITED NATIONS AND UNITED STATES FOREIGN POLICY (Cambridge, Mass., 1960).

prosper until we exhibit an association, powerful, wise and happy beyond what has yet been seen by men,"[10] the author of the Declaration of Independence had stated, and added: "Not in our day, but at no distant one, we may shake a rod over the heads of all [European nations], which may make the stoutest of them tremble."[11] The major author of *The Federalist* complemented him: "Let Americans disdain to be the instruments of European greatness! Let the thirteen States, bound together in a strict and indissoluble Union, concur in erecting one great American system, superior to the control of all transatlantic force or influence, and be able to dictate the terms of the connection between the old and new world!"[12]

While the fulfillment of these prophesies must have given Americans pride, their satisfaction must have been augmented by the fact that American might had not been cherished for its own sake but for the good of men. "We are destined to be a barrier against the returns of ignorance and barbarism. Old Europe will have to lean on our shoulders, and to hobble along by our side, under the monkish trammels of priests and kings, as she can,"[13] Jefferson had stated, and John Adams added: "Our pure, virtuous, public-spirited, federative republic will last forever, govern the globe, and introduce the perfection of man."[14] It looked as if Americans had done even better than the sage from Monticello had prophesied. He had thought that the United States would become quite a colossus "when the southern continent comes up

[10] To John Adams, Jan. 21, 1812. WRITINGS, XIII, 123. (The word "grow" is printed there as "growl").

[11] To Thomas Leiper, June 12, 1815. WRITINGS, XIV, 308. He added: "But I hope our wisdom will grow with our power, and teach us, that the less we use our power, the greater it will be."

[12] THE FEDERALIST, No. 11. In an oration on the second anniversary of Independence, Dr. David Ramsay stated: "When I anticipate . . . the future glory of my country, and the illustrious figure it will soon make one [sic] the theatre of the world, my heart distends with generous pride for being an American. What a substratum for empire! compared with which, the foundation of the Macedonian, the Roman, and the British, sink into insignificance . . . We have laid the foundations of a new empire, which promises to enlarge itself to vast dimensions, and to give happiness to a great continent. It is now our turn to figure on the face of the earth, and in the annals of the world." Niles, PRINCIPLES AND ACTS OF THE REVOLUTION, 72.

[13] To John Adams, Aug. 1, 1816. WRITINGS, XV, 58f.

[14] John Adams to Jefferson, Nov. 15, 1813. (Jefferson's) WRITINGS, XIV, 6.

to our mark!" He had envisaged that this colossus would secure quite a stand "as a ralliance for the reason and freedom of the globe!"[15] As it was, the United States had become such a colossus all by herself.

The joy must have been enhanced by the fact that American achievements seemed to be unchallenged. Europe was in ruins; the British empire was disintegrating; the Soviet Union was devastated, the Red Army bled white. By contrast, the United States had hardly been touched by the war. She had suffered relatively few casualties. There was no destruction at home. She alone had the Bomb. The situation appeared bombastic. Peace seemed inevitable.[16] The *Pax Americana* looked like a *pax aeterna*. Kant's hope seemed to have been realized by America as it had been envisaged by Price.[17] *The Vision of Columbus,* as it was described by Joel Barlow, seemed to have come true.[18]

Since this development would hardly have been possible without a reasonable foreign policy, the thought occurs that this policy reflected constitutional reason rather than popular desire; that, in accordance with the principle of free government, it recognized democracy only in so far as that form of government did not jeopardize the security of the United States and her citizens from foreign aggression, that it must have been relatively untouched by the growth of democracy which brought about important changes in internal affairs.

For some time, this was indeed the case. While internally the United States became more democratic, foreign affairs were hardly affected by this development. Popular majorities were busy pushing democratic reforms inside the United States rather than trying to influence foreign policy. Democratic trends may have affected federalism, the separation of powers, the freedom of the individual, and the rule of law; they had not much impact upon foreign affairs. Foreign policy was democratic only in so far as major policy makers, such as the President and the senators,

[15] To John Adams on Aug. 1, 1816. WRITINGS, XV, 59.
[16] See Carl J. Friedrich, INEVITABLE PEACE (Cambridge, Mass., 1948).
[17] Immanuel Kant, ZUM EWIGEN FRIEDEN (Königsberg, 1795). On Price, see *supra,* 11.
[18] Joel Barlow, THE VISION OF COLUMBUS (5th ed.; Paris, 1793).

were elected. However, since they were elected for relatively long terms, and since their rationality was likely to be above that of their constituents,[19] the chances were that foreign policy would be made in the long-range national interest and not in the short-range interest of temporary majorities. The elected policy-makers could follow their reason and conscience rather than the often unreasonable and unconscientious clamors of the people. This applied *a fortiori* to foreign-policy-makers who were not elected. Coming from the richer strata of society, the members of the diplomatic service belonged to the very class that had been cool toward internal democratic reforms. They were hardly willing to let popular whims influence them. A long-range foreign policy in the national interest, unaffected by popular clamors which might have frustrated such a policy, was possible and was successfully pursued.

A foreign policy according to constitutional rather than democratic reason had been desired by the Founding Fathers. While the policy they had in mind was to be more democratic than that of other nations—it was to be made not by a monarch and his appointees, but by temporarily elected representatives[20]—it was not to be as democratic as it could have been. Just as internal policy was to be made by the representatives of the people who, it was hoped, would be more reasonable than the people themselves, foreign policy was to be made by such representatives. As a matter of fact, indirect democracy—implying a refinement of the public views—was to prevail in foreign policy to a larger degree than in internal affairs. Whereas those concerned with internal matters, such as state officials and members of the House of

---

[19] According to Madison, the purpose of representation is "to refine and enlarge the public views, by passing them through the medium of a chosen body of citizens, whose wisdom may best discern the true interest of their country, and whose patriotism and love of justice will be least likely to sacrifice it to temporary or partial considerations." THE FEDERALIST, No. 10.

[20] Sir Harry Johnston described foreign policy making up to the twentieth century as follows: "[A] country's relations with its neighbours or with distant lands were dealt with almost exclusively by the head of the State—Emperor, King, or President—acting with the more or less dependent Minister-of-State, who was no representative of the masses, but the employé of the Monarch. Events were prepared and sprung on a submissive, a confident, or a stupid people. The public Press criticized, more often applauded, but had at most to deal with a *fait accompli* and make the best of it." COMMON SENSE IN FOREIGN POLICY (London, 1913), 7f.

Representatives, were directly elected by the people, foreign policy makers, such as the President and the Senate, were elected indirectly by the presidential electoral college and the state legislatures. While the probability of a reasonable internal policy was good on account of representative government, the probability of a reasonable foreign policy was even better on account of a government that could be called super-representative. With respect to foreign policy, representative government was established in a second dimension to make doubly sure against the pitfalls of direct democracy.[21] The makers of internal policy were elected; those of foreign policy, selected.

This line of reasoning is evident in *The Federalist*. Aside from stressing the value of the more perfect Union for national security,[22] that work also praises the Constitution for facilitating a reasonable, long-range foreign policy, irrespective of transient popular desires. To Jay, the distinguished diplomat who in 1783 negotiated Independence, the Constitution delegated the treaty power "with such precautions, as will afford the highest security that it will be exercised by men the best qualified for the purpose, and in the manner most conducive to the public good . . . As the select assemblies for choosing the President, as well as the State legislatures who appoint the senators, will in general be composed of the most enlightened and respectable citizens, there is reason to presume that their attention and their votes will be directed to those men only who have become the most distinguished by their abilities and virtue, and in whom the people perceive just grounds for confidence." Since confidence in mere mouthpieces appears to be rather irrelevant, it follows that neither the President nor the senators are mere ministerial agents of the people, but representatives in the Burkean–Madisonian sense.[23] The conduct of foreign

[21] Madison in No. 14 of THE FEDERALIST referred to direct democracy simply as "democracy."

[22] See the author's FEDERALIST, ch. 8.

[23] Burke had stated: "Certainly gentlemen, it ought to be the happiness and glory of a representative, to live in the strictest union, the closest correspondence, and the most unreserved communication with his constituents. Their wishes ought to have great weight with him; their opinion high respect; their business unremitted attention . . . But his unbiased opinion, his mature judgment, his enlightened conscience, he ought not to sacrifice to you, to any man, or to any set of men living. These he does not derive from your pleasure; no, nor from the law and the constitution. They are a trust from Providence, for the abuse of which he is deeply

policy is entrusted to their sound judgment. Jay felt that age qualifications for the presidency and the Senate would guarantee that these offices will be held by "men of whom the people have had time to form a judgment, and with respect to whom they will not be liable to be deceived by those brilliant appearances of genius and patriotism, which, like transient meteors, some times mislead as well as dazzle." The young, flashy demagogue, the astute politician who knows how to charm the people and seduce them with promises, the publicity hero, the "image," was unsuited for the conduct of foreign affairs. Serious business like that was to be reserved for "wise" men, selected with "discretion and discernment," for men who "best understand our national interests . . . who are best able to promote those interests, and whose reputation for integrity inspires and merits confidence." Jay was glad that the treaty power was not lodged in "a popular assembly, composed of members constantly coming and going in quick succession," because "such a body must necessarily be inadequate to the attainment of those great objects, which require to be steadily contemplated in all their relations and circumstances, and which can only be approached and achieved by measures which not only talents, but also exact information, and often much time, are necessary to concert and to execute." He noted with satisfaction that the senators are elected for comparatively long terms during which they will have "an opportunity of greatly extending their political information, and of rendering their accumulating experience more and more beneficial to their country." He liked the idea that the Senate is changed only partially by new elections. This ensures "uniformity and order, as well as a constant succession of official information." He approved the President's authority to negotiate treaties with *"secrecy"* and *"despatch."* The independence of foreign policy makers from public opinion makes possible a policy that is the "most conducive to the public good."[24] The latter is not necessarily identical to the temporary desires of the

---

answerable." THE WORKS OF EDMUND BURKE (London, 1899), II, 12ff. See also his "Two Letters to Gentlemen of Bristol," *ibid.,* II, 249. See also *infra,* 243. For Madison's concept of representation, see *supra,* 213n.

[24] THE FEDERALIST, No. 64. According to THE FEDERALIST, democratic government is not necessarily conducive to the "public good," whereas free government is.

public. Foreign policy must conform to constitutional rather than democratic reason.

Hamilton agreed. Speaking of "the constitutional agency of the President" and "the constitutional representatives of the nation" in the Senate, he omitted the adjective "constitutional" when mentioning the House of Representatives. Obviously, he felt that the latter was all too democratic. "The fluctuating and, taking its future increase into the account, the multitudinous composition of that body, forbid us to expect in it those qualities which are essential to the proper execution of . . . a trust" the Convention saw fit to confer upon "constitutional" institutions like the President and the Senate. Hamilton was pleased that the House of Representatives is excluded from the treaty-making process. "Accurate and comprehensive knowledge of foreign politics; a steady and systematic adherence to the same views; a nice and uniform sensibility to national character; decision, *secrecy,* and despatch, are incompatible with the genius of a body so variable and so numerous."[25] For Hamilton, the genius of democracy could well conflict with the genius of the Constitution. However, constitutional provisions concerning the handling of foreign policy reduced the possibility that democratic reason would replace constitutional reason.

These provisions suggest something about the hoped-for substance of that policy. They indicate that the Constitution's blueprint for American foreign policy corresponds to its program for internal policy. When *The Federalist* rejects participation of the House of Representatives in treaty-making because the most democratic branch of the legislature, composed as it is of "members constantly coming and going in quick succession," is too "fluctuating" and too susceptible to temporary, popular desires; when it denies the young and flashy political genius a place among foreign policy makers; when it proposes that foreign policy be placed in the hands of the wise and mature who hold office for relatively long periods to ensure a "constant," "steadily contemplated" policy, characterized by "uniformity and order," by a "steady and systematic adherence to the same views" in order to succeed in the "attainment of . . . great objects;" then it pro-

[25] THE FEDERALIST, No. 75.

poses a foreign policy which reminds us of the steady rule of law, made by wise men over the ages out of respect for the rights of the individual, as distinguished from the mutable rule of laws, rules and regulations which are often made at the spur of the moment by less distinguished rulers from a desire to curtail those rights.[26] *The Federalist* proposes a foreign policy in the long-range national interest, a policy which corresponds to an internal policy favoring free government and the long-range public interest.[27] The national and public interests, identical as they may be, are not necessarily identical to the—more temporary—democratic interest. They are superior to it.

Since foreign policy corresponds to the rule of law, the thought occurs that the Founders of the United States also must have wanted that policy to possess something like an artificial reason, comparable to that of the rule of law.[28] They must have hoped that in time, wise men would build up a body of foreign policy in accordance with the principle of free government, to be respected by policy makers. While the latter's natural reason would add to that body, it would not be permitted to challenge its principal features. Foreign policy makers would have to act according to constitutional rather than democratic reason. Democratic reason would thereby not be excluded. Since the Constitution, by providing for a free government, provides for a popular government, democratic desires would be taken into account as long as they were compatible with the long-range national interest, or the constitutional reason of foreign policy that supposedly furthered that interest. While the more or less temporary natural reason of democracy was entitled to a hearing, it was to be subordinated to the more or less permanent artificial reason of foreign policy. Democratic desires, while they would ideally contribute to a

---

[26] Cf. *supra*, 155n., 170, 197.

[27] THE FEDERALIST leaves no doubt that the long-range public interest, or national interest, can be secured under a free rather than a democratic government as far as internal affairs are concerned. See the author's FEDERALIST, esp. chs. 4–6, 9. The situation is not different with respect to foreign policy: The "national interest" is the long-range public interest. Cf. Charles A. Beard's discussion of "National Interest in the Federalist" in his THE IDEA OF NATIONAL INTEREST (New York, 1934), 33ff. Recent studies include Hans J. Morgenthau, IN DEFENSE OF THE NATIONAL INTEREST (New York, 1951) and Robert E. Osgood, IDEALS AND SELF-INTEREST IN AMERICA'S FOREIGN RELATIONS (Chicago, 1953).

[28] See *supra*, 8.

long-range foreign policy in the national interest, were not to frustrate such a policy.

Here, then, were the principles of American foreign policy: Reflecting free government in the United States, that policy was to be in the long-range interest of the nation, and to favor free government abroad. To achieve this aim, it was to be made by carefully selected representatives who believed in free government and were relatively independent of public opinion.

For a long time, American foreign policy was in tune with these principles. The desires of the American people were generally in harmony with constitutional reason. Whenever they were not, the Constitution's safety-valve, providing for the conduct of foreign policy by carefully selected and presumably reasonable men, would go into effect. Foreign policy makers, supported by a diplomatic service that was generally in favor of free government and detached from democratic politics, would disregard popular clamors if such clamors challenged the long-range national interest.[29]

In spite of widespread desires that the United States help revolutionary France in her struggle with Britain, Washington issued a neutrality proclamation, "persuaded, that the happiness and best interests of the people of the United States, will be promoted by observing a strict neutrality . . ."[30] A few years later, Americans showed much sympathy for the fight of their Spanish American brethren for self-government, a fight that was sparked and nourished by the American Revolution. However, the United States government gave no active support to the Spanish Americans. It was even lukewarm in participating in a congress of the newly independent Spanish American states.[31] Later on, the admiration of the people of the United States for the Hungarians' attempt to regain their independence did not produce an official endorsement of that attempt.[32] The same was true when revolutionists in Poland made a desperate effort to cast off

[29] For popular reactions against official foreign policy, see Beard, IDEAL OF NATIONAL INTEREST, 390ff.

[30] To the Merchants and Traders of the City of Philadelphia, May 17, 1793. WRITINGS, XXXII, 460. See also Hamilton's "Pacificus" (1793) WORKS, IV, 432ff.

[31] See Joseph B. Lockey, PAN-AMERICANISM: ITS BEGINNINGS (New York, 1920), 313ff. and ch. 10.

[32] Cf. Lincoln's attitude in 1849 and 1852. WORKS, II, 62, 115.

the tyranny of the Tsar. Asked by Napoleon III to join France, Austria, and Great Britain in exercising a moral influence upon the Tsar, Secretary of State Seward wrote that there was "an insurmountable difficulty in the way of any active cooperation with the governments of France, Austria, and Great Britain." He explained: "Founding our institutions upon the basis of the rights of man, the builders of our republic came all at once to be regarded as political reformers and it soon became manifest that revolutionists in every country hailed them in that character, and looked to the United States for effective sympathy, if not for active support and patronage." Still, the United States preferred to yield to the counsels of Washington that "the American people must be content to recommend the cause of human progress by the wisdom with which they should exercise the powers of self-government, forbearing at all times, and in every way, from foreign alliances, intervention, and interference."[33] Toward the end of the century, President Cleveland regretted American attempts to protect the natives of Samoa against British and German authorities, although these attempts had substantial popular backing.[34] On the same occasion, referring to the pro-Cuban sentiment of the North American public in the Cubans' struggle for independence, he said that United States neutrality must prevail over "any shock our humane sensibilities may have received from the cruelties which appear to especially characterize this sanguinary and fiercely conducted war."[35] Throughout the period of isolationism, foreign policy was made according to constitutional rather than democratic reason. Irrespective of how much democratic movements abroad may have stirred the enthusiasm of

[33] Dispatch to the American minister in Paris of May 11, 1863. Department of State, PAPERS RELATING TO FOREIGN AFFAIRS, 1863 (Washington, 1864), 668.

[34] In his Third Annual Message of Dec. 2, 1895, President Cleveland declared "that our situation in this matter was inconsistent with the mission and traditions of our Government, in violation of the principles we profess, and in all its phases mischievous and vexatious." A COMPILATION OF THE MESSAGES AND PAPERS OF THE PRESIDENTS (New York, n.d.) XII, 6067.

[35] Ibid., 6068. Cleveland also observed: "Whatever may be the traditional sympathy of our countrymen as individuals with a people who seem to be struggling for larger autonomy and greater freedom, deepened, as such sympathy naturally must be, in behalf of our neighbors, yet the plain duty of their Government is to observe in good faith the recognized obligations of international friendship." The friendship toward monarchical Spain was more important than self-government for the Cubans.

Americans, they did not carry away the policy makers. Democratic reason was accepted only insofar as it did not conflict with constitutional reason.

The situation did not immediately change when foreign policy became internationalist. While the idea that the United States had a moral obligation to be concerned with what was going on in other nations gained ground,[36] "morals" were not so much conceived of in the sense of democratic, but rather of free, government. The United States would be active in world affairs not primarily for the sake of popular government, but for the sake of the ends of that government, for the protection of life, liberty, and property. This attitude basically reflected the desires of the American people. In 1898, President McKinley wanted the war in Cuba to end in "the name of humanity, in the name of civilization, in behalf of endangered American interests."[37] According to these interests, the protection of the rights of the individual was more important than self-government. A military government was established on Cuba "in the interest and for the benefit of the people of Cuba and those possessed of rights and property in that Island."[38] Similar considerations prevailed in United States policy toward the Philippines. Having gained their freedom from Spain, those islands were considered "unfit for self-government."[39] As a result, their government was to be exercised by the United States. A United States commission was instructed to establish order, uphold the law, and safeguard the rights of property and person "for the happiness, peace and prosperity of the people of the Philippine Islands."[40] An earlier proclamation issued by Major General Miles upon landing in

[36] See Beard, IDEA OF NATIONAL INTEREST, 364ff.

[37] Special Message to Congress of April 11, 1898. MESSAGES AND PAPERS OF THE PRESIDENTS, XIII, 6292. Cf. also President Cleveland's Fourth Annual Message of Dec. 7, 1896, *ibid.*, XIII, 6148ff.

[38] President McKinley's instructions to Major General Brooke, whom he designated Military Governor of Cuba. Charles S. Olcott, THE LIFE OF WILLIAM MCKINLEY (Boston, 1916), II, 197.

[39] President McKinley at a conference with a committee representing the General Missionary Committee of the Methodist Church, on Nov. 21, 1899. (Quoted in Beard, IDEA OF NATIONAL INTEREST, 368.) Cf. also Senator Platt's letter of Aug. 15, 1898. Louis A. Coolidge, ORVILLE H. PLATT (New York, 1910), 287.

[40] "Magna Carta of the Philippines," signed by President McKinley on April 7, 1900.

Puerto Rico contains a similar program. It did not promise self-government, but "to bring you protection, not only to yourselves, but to your property, to promote your prosperity, and to bestow upon you the immunities and blessings of the liberal institutions of our government . . . to give to all . . . the advantages and blessings of enlightened civilization."[41] The blessings of America's *liberal* institutions and of her *enlightened* civilization were the blessings of a government under which the liberal principle of the protection of the rights of the individual had priority over the democratic principle of popular participation in government. In the programing as well as execution of foreign policy, enlightened constitutional reason was superior to democratic reason, even if it meant intervention and war. The situation did not change under Presidents Theodore Roosevelt[42] and William Howard Taft.[43]

Under Woodrow Wilson, however, a shift of emphasis took

[41] Cited in Bailey W. and Justine W. Diffie, PORTO RICO: A BROKEN PLEDGE (New York, 1931), 3.

[42] Roosevelt often complained about the weakening of fiber that was becoming evident among sons of the upper class, especially in the East. He denounced the reluctance to go to war for the cause of free government. See the report of Ambassador Sternberg to the German Foreign Office, Nov. 15, 1898. GERMAN FOREIGN OFFICE MANUSCRIPTS, as mentioned in Beard, THE IDEA OF NATIONAL INTEREST, 372. In an address at the University of Paris on April 23, 1910, Roosevelt stated: "[T]he good man should be both a strong and a brave man; that is, he should be able to fight . . . to serve his country as a soldier, if the need arises. . . . War is a dreadful thing, and unjust war is a crime against humanity. But it is such a crime because it is unjust, not because it is war. The choice must ever be in favor of righteousness, and this whether the alternative be peace or . . . war. The question must not be merely, Is there to be peace or war? The question must be, Is the right to prevail? Are the great laws of righteousness once more to be fulfilled? And the answer from a strong and virile people must be 'Yes,' whatever the cost . . . no self-respecting individual, no self-respecting nation, can or ought to submit to wrong." THE WORKS OF THEODORE ROOSEVELT (nat. ed.; New York, 1926), XIII, 513. He considered "the whole flapdoodle pacifist and mollycoddle outfit" a moral disgrace and physical danger to the country. Nov. 27, 1915. SELECTIONS FROM THE CORRESPONDENCE OF THEODORE ROOSEVELT AND HENRY CABOT LODGE (New York, 1925), II, 464.

[43] In his First Annual Message to Congress, Dec. 7, 1909, Taft said, concerning his policy toward Nicaragua, that his administration was "intending to take such future steps as may be found most consistent with its dignity, its duty to American interests, and its moral obligation to Central America and to civilization." MESSAGES AND PAPERS OF THE PRESIDENTS, XV, 7418. This statement is another demonstration of how liberal rights, especially those of property, are put above democratic rights. Under Taft, Secretary of State Knox introduced "dollar diplomacy."

place. In the first year of his administration, Wilson proposed a foreign policy favoring "human rights, national integrity, and opportunity as against material interests," and promised to see to it "that from no quarter are material interests made superior to human liberty and national opportunity."[44] Property rights and material interests, ingredients of traditional foreign policy, are replaced by "human rights," "human liberty." "National integrity" seems to be more important than the national interest. Obviously, the inventor of "The New Freedom," a freedom implying a government of "the plain people" as distinguished from the well-to-do,[45] planned to emphasize the most human—but not necessarily the most humane—rights, namely, democratic rights. For the sake of democracy, he entered the war against Germany,[46] a nation that, on account of property qualifications for voting, was not very democratic, but highly constitutionalist.[47] Wilson's emphasis upon democracy was also evident in his advocacy of "self-determination." Under that program, what counted was that people determined their own way of life. It did not matter so much whether they chose a free government or an oppressive one. It has been said that Wilson "assumed that democracy, as practised in the United States, was a decided good and that other nations should be assisted in attaining it . . . The right of the peoples of the respective nations to choose their own government and determine their own fate he laid down as a fundamental postulate of international polity."[48] While this indicates that democracy had become an end in itself, this suspicion might go too far. Wilson's new accent on foreign policy probably did not yet elevate democracy above free government. For one thing, Wilson had constitutionalist inhibitions; for another, the Senate did not ratify his international commitments following World War I.[49]

[44] Mobile address of 1913. Quoted in David Y. Thomas, ONE HUNDRED YEARS OF THE MONROE DOCTRINE, 1823–1923 (New York, 1923), 240.

[45] Woodrow Wilson, NEW FREEDOM.

[46] See *supra,* 3.

[47] Most Germans think back to the Empire as "the good old days." On the *Rechtsstaat* in Imperial Germany, see the author's "Rechtsstaat und Staatsrecht."

[48] Beard, IDEA OF NATIONAL INTEREST, 377f.

[49] See Woodrow Wilson, CONSTITUTIONAL GOVERNMENT IN THE UNITED STATES (New York, 1908). Arguments that United States membership in the League of Nations could have prevented World War II are mere speculations. It appears

Thus, important innovations the President may have wanted to bring about for the sake of democracy were prevented.

While constitutional reason prevailed in the foreign policies of Coolidge, Harding, and Hoover,[50] the situation appears to be less certain in the case of Franklin D. Roosevelt. The fact that the New Deal was a second dimension of the New Freedom suggests that it favored a democratic government without the constitutionalist trimmings of the latter. We had seen that this was the case in internal policy, where free government became increasingly replaced by majoritarian democracy. However, this does not necessarily mean that democratic desire would have replaced constitutional reason in foreign policy. Inroads upon foreign policy are likely to occur only after they have been made successfully upon internal policy. Since democratic attempts did not altogether succeed in doing away with free government within the United States, it would not be surprising if they would have made no inroads upon foreign policy at all. As a matter of fact, they probably did not prevent a constitutional foreign policy until the end of World War II. There was not much of a problem. The Hitler regime was so stripped of constitutionalism and democracy that Roosevelt's animosity toward it was likely to be due to constitutional reason backed by the people. After Japan had attacked and Hitler had declared war upon the United States, American policy against those powers was in conformity with constitutional reason as much as with the desires of the American people. However, there exist doubts about Roosevelt's commitments to the Soviet Union toward the end of World War II. Here the barrier set by the artificial reason of foreign policy was crossed, and it was probably a crossing of the Rubicon. A democratic leader, having become a democratic autocrat, in the name of the majority committed the United States in a way that decried constitutional safeguards[51] and also was opposed to the long-range interests of the United States.

---

dubious whether American membership in the United Nations will prevent World War III. For the problems involved in membership of the United States in the United Nations, see *infra*, 249n.

[50] See Beard, IDEA OF NATIONAL INTEREST, 380ff.

[51] These measures prompted Senator Bricker to suggest an amendment restricting the power of the President to make treaties and executive agreements. Senator

DEMOCRATIC FOREIGN POLICY
AND COLD WAR PASSIVITY

Wilson's emphasis upon democracy and Roosevelt's commitments in the name of democracy suggest a progressive democratization of foreign policy. They prompt the question whether foreign policy came to follow the internal development which was characterized by the march of democracy, whether foreign policy became a reflection of democratic politics. This question can be answered in the affirmative.

This is obvious with respect to the execution of foreign policy. The executors of foreign policy, be they elected or appointed, were democratized. Throughout the nineteenth century, attempts to have the indirect election of senators replaced by a direct one were in vain. A constitutional amendment offered for this purpose in the House of Representatives as early as 1828 was not adopted. Forty years later, President Johnson suggested the reform in a special message to Congress. Nothing came of it. Still, the quest for a democratization of the Senate continued. In the end, it was crowned with success. What had not been achieved during the democratic Jacksonian revolution and during the democratic revolution brought about by the Civil War was attained in the democratic "progressive revolt."[52] The House of Representatives passed amendments providing for direct election of senators in 1893, 1894, 1898, 1900, and 1902, but the Senate either ignored or voted down these measures. In 1911, however, the Upper Chamber went along, prodded by the adoption in various states of preferential primaries which made the state legislatures ratify the popular choices and embarrassed by a scandal in Illinois where an election to the Senate was brought about through wholesale brib-

---

Andrew Schoepel of Kansas stated: "The Bricker amendment would restrain some future Roosevelt who might be tempted to indulge in another spree at Yalta." Quoted in Kelly/Harbison, AMERICAN CONSTITUTION, 863. See Felix Morley, TREATY LAW AND THE CONSTITUTION (New York, 1953). Cf. also Wallace M. McClure, INTERNATIONAL EXECUTIVE AGREEMENTS (New York, 1941).

[52] The expression is used by Kelly/Harbison, AMERICAN CONSTITUTION, 615. That work also brings a short discussion of the adoption of the Seventeenth Amendment. *Ibid.,* 625ff. A longer discussion is provided by George H. Haynes, THE SENATE OF THE UNITED STATES, ITS HISTORY AND PRACTICE (Boston, 1938).

ery in the state assembly. In 1913, the Seventeenth Amendment became part of the Constitution. It has been said that this amendment, combined with the growth of superior means of communication, created a "new type of political leader . . . one who secured election to public office through the techniques of democratic leadership and mass psychology rather than the craftsmanship of the conservative elder statesman."[53] It could be added that the popularly elected senator was likely to be the captive of mass psychology.

The situation is similar in the case of the President. Presidential candidates in the age of the press, radio, television, and jet secure election by techniques of democratic leadership and mass psychology—a combination which promotes demagoguery—rather than the craftsmanship of the elder statesman. As a result, they are likely to be more susceptible to becoming the captives of the psychology of the masses and mere executors of their will. It is true that the system originally designed by the Constitution providing for the election of the President through an electoral college still prevails formally. However, it is doubtful whether it prevails in the way in which it was conceived by the Founders. They had thought of the electors as men who were not bound by the desires of those who chose them—who were not necessarily the people themselves.[54] The first Presidents were selected accordingly. However, partisan considerations soon entered the picture, and electors were urged by party leaders to vote for certain candidates. The Twelfth Amendment "eased the way for further democratization of the process of selection . . . it carried with it an implication that the electors had become mere agents of the party's will and that they were no longer expected to exercise discretion."[55] This implication became general custom, was trans-

---

[53] Kelly/Harbison, AMERICAN CONSTITUTION, 628.

[54] During the first thirty years after the adoption of the Constitution, the states experimented freely with various methods of choosing electors. For instance, Massachusetts changed the method of choosing electors prior to every presidential election from 1796 to 1828. Selection of the electors by the legislature was not uncommon. See Herman V. Ames, THE PROPOSED AMENDMENTS TO THE CONSTITUTION OF THE UNITED STATES DURING THE FIRST CENTURY OF ITS HISTORY (Washington, 1897), 85.

[55] Kallenbach, AMERICAN CHIEF EXECUTIVE, 79. A general study is Lucius Wilmerding, Jr., THE ELECTORAL COLLEGE (New Brunswick, N.J., 1958).

muted into law, and "with rare individual exceptions, the electors have functioned as the automatons of their parties."[56] Soon generally elected by the people,[57] the electors up to the second decade of the twentieth century still had their names on the ballot and thus were at least formally presented to the electorate. The "presidential short ballot," introduced by Nebraska in 1917 and later adopted by approximately three-fourths of the states, did away even with this formal reminder of the original method. It omits the names of the candidates for the electoral college and only mentions the names of the presidential and vice-presidential candidates under the appropriate party caption.[58] Thus, in the majority of states, the people probably will not even know the names of the electors they are voting for. They simply vote for a presidential candidate. The fact that for purposes of filling the nation's highest office the national electorate is the sum total of the state electorates, seems to have merely formal significance. "With the choosing of electors taking place by popular action throughout the country on the same day, to all appearances and purposes the President is now chosen in a great mass action by the people of the nation."[59] This kind of election is exactly what the men who drafted the Constitution tried to avoid. High class themselves, the Founding Fathers wanted the Chief Executive to be selected by class rather than mass in order that he might be class independent of mass, class incorruptible by power, class that would intrepidly

[56] Louis W. Koenig, CHIEF EXECUTIVE (New York, 1964), 54. Koenig continues: "Custom, which dictates the electors' voting conduct, has been reinforced by legislation and court opinion. State statutes range from those calling for a party nomination of electors, which itself is a presumption of pledged electors, to the laws of two states prescribing that electors vote for the party nominees, regardless of personal preference. In *Ray* v. *Blair* (343 U.S. 214, 1952), the Supreme Court gave its blessing to these arrangements . . ." Kallenbach, AMERICAN CHIEF EXECUTIVE, 83, writes that under the law of Pennsylvania the presidential nominee of a party is required "to designate the slate of presidential elector candidates for his party—a very logical arrangement in view of the role the elector is expected to play."

[57] On the nomination of candidates for the elector post, see Robert G. Dixon, "Electoral College Procedure," WESTERN POLITICAL QUARTERLY, III (1950), 214; Ruth C. Silva, "State Law on the Nomination, Election and Instruction of Presidential Electors," AMERICAN POLITICAL SCIENCE REVIEW, XLIII (1948), 523.

[58] See L. E. Aylesworth, "The Presidential Ballot," AMERICAN POLITICAL SCIENCE REVIEW, XVIII (1923), 89; "The Presidential Short Ballot," *ibid.*, XXIV (1930), 966; S. D. Albright, "The Presidential Short Ballot," *ibid.*, XXXIV (1940), 955.

[59] Kallenbach, AMERICAN CHIEF EXECUTIVE, 82.

pursue the aims of a free, rather than democratic, government.

The democratization of the elected executors of foreign policy has been matched by that of the appointed executors in the diplomatic service. Significantly, that process got under way between the adoption of the Seventeenth Amendment and the short presidential ballot. Until World War I, the diplomatic service had been largely recruited from the social elite.[60] During and after the war, considered "the best possible guaranty that nothing of the sort shall happen again,"[61] this kind of recruitment came under attack. "The period's most important recommendation . . . was that the service should be democratized." In their suggestions for change, most writers were actuated by "the dangers inherent in recruiting a service from the social elite. The main danger was that the demands of the majority on foreign policy might be ignored."[62] With the passage of the Rogers Act of 1924, the desired changes came about. The "democratization" of the diplomatic service increased in the following decades. The recruitment base of that service was widened. The service become more representative of the majority.[63] As a result, diplomats were likely to reflect the wishes of the majority, possibly at the cost of free government and the long-range national interest.

[60] See "Our Diplomatic Service," FORUM LVI (Nov., 1916), 611; "Diplomatic and Consular Careers," NATION, C (Jan. 28, 1915), 97. Before Congress, Secretary of State Charles E. Hughes stated, "It is not a good thing for the diplomatic service to be recruited, even on a merit basis, exclusively from men of families of fortune." House Committee on Foreign Affairs, FOREIGN SERVICE OF THE UNITED STATES, Hearings on H.R. 12543, 67th Cong., 4th Sess. (Dec. 11–19, 1922), 8.

[61] "Responsible Diplomacy," NATION, CVII (Dec. 28, 1918), 793.

[62] Warren Frederick Ilchman, PROFESSIONAL DIPLOMACY IN THE UNITED STATES 1779–1939 (Chicago, 1961), 141. See also Graham H. Stuart, AMERICAN DIPLOMATIC AND CONSULAR PRACTICE (New York, 1936), chs. 7, 8; DeWitt C. Poole, THE CONDUCT OF FOREIGN RELATIONS UNDER MODERN DEMOCRATIC CONDITIONS (New Haven, Conn., 1924).

[63] See Ilchman, PROFESSIONAL DIPLOMACY, chs. 4, 5, which in their captions use the term "democratization." Drew Pearson stated in 1931 that the Foreign Service was "a social club whose members are selected from bluestocking Bostonians, wield thin forks with their left hands, and are no more representative of American life than the Redskins whom their ancestors pushed west." THE WASHINGTON MERRY-GO-ROUND (New York, 1931), 134. Ten years later, Robert Bendiner, THE RIDDLE OF THE DEPARTMENT OF STATE (New York, 1942), 111, wrote that the officers' backgrounds "tend in the main to reduce democracy to an abstraction." While the Foreign Service is probably not as much democratized as it could be, Ilchman's carefully documented study shows that since the First World War, the diplomatic resp. foreign service was considerably democratized.

The democratization of foreign policy makers was influenced by the Progressive movement and its egalitarian ideas. Changes in the diplomatic service were supported by the less well-to-do consular officers who felt that a fusion of the diplomatic and consular services and the democratization of the former would raise their own social prestige. Their attitude reflected the general argument that elitism in the recruitment of the diplomatic corps was a social injustice that had no place in a democracy.[64] The Progressives' ideas also influenced the democratization of the presidency. It was hoped that a directly elected President would be more of a man of the people and more responsive to their demands, that a chief executive elected "in a great mass action by the people of the nation" would be more active for the masses of the nation.[65] As to the Senate, it is undisputed that the Seventeenth Amendment in large measure was due to the advocacy of social reformers. True, the destruction by the Civil War of the idea that the states are sovereign entities, entitled to be represented by men who were elected by a branch of their governments, as well as the presence of corrupt state party bosses, contributed to its adoption. However, of greater importance probably were the attacks by Agrarian radicals and social reformers. They denounced the Upper Chamber for being composed of the representatives of moneyed interests. Populists, Bryan Democrats, and finally liberal Republicans and Progressives advocated the direct election of senators in the belief that the Senate by becoming more democratic would become more responsive to the forces favoring social reform, and would favor "the kind of social legislation so frequently sponsored after 1900 by Progressives."[66]

The democratization of foreign policy makers was likely to have the impact its advocates had hoped for. From now on, there was a good chance that foreign policy would reflect democratic rather than constitutional reason. Whereas previously it would be

[64] See Ilchman, PROFESSIONAL DIPLOMACY, chs. 4, 5.

[65] See *supra,* 185ff., 226.

[66] Kelly/Harbison, AMERICAN CONSTITUTION, 626. While this work stresses that the "majority of the senatorial Old Guard were honorable and upright men of high personal integrity," it adds that "from the standpoint of agrarian radicals and Progressives they were too generally associated with large business enterprise, too conservative, and too far removed from popular democratic influences."

made according to democratic desires only in so far as these desires corresponded to the Constitution, now it probably would be made just according to popular demand.

Democratization could affect the continuity of foreign policy. We had seen that the indirect selection of foreign policy makers resulted in a stable policy in the long-range national interest, a policy according to the Constitution, a policy which developed an artificial reason.[67] From now on, all this could change. Foreign policy could be made according to the more or less temporary desires of more or less temporary majorities. Made by the ruling majority which might disregard the artificial reason of foreign policy, it could be unstable. However, while as a matter of principle and technique foreign policy would be short-range and opportunistic, in practice it could still appear to be long-range if the democratic desires existing at various times happened to be identical or similar. In that case, the continuity of foreign policy would be more or less accidental owing to temporary conveniences and opportunities. It would no longer exist on account of principle, irrespective of temporary inconveniences. Basically, the long-range national interest would be subordinated to the short-range will of the majority.

Since the democratization of foreign policy makers in a large measure was brought about by a movement which favored social legislation over laissez faire, "liberalism" over liberalism, absolute majority rule over free government, there was also a good chance that the substance of foreign policy would change. This could mean that just as foreign policy previously favored liberalism, now it could favor foreign systems and movements that were akin to the programs of the Progressives, the New Freedom, the New Deal and the New Frontier. Since these programs emphasized social rather than property rights, "civil" rather than civil rights, national power rather than federalism, a concentration of power in the political branches of government rather than the separation of powers, foreign policy could well come to favor similar trends abroad. It could even become captivated by foreign movements that went further to the left, such as socialism and Communism. This would hardly be unnatural. History is full of

[67] See *supra*, 212ff.

examples which demonstrate how similar outlooks create mutual affections which prevent animosity among nations, bring about alliances, federations, and federal states.[68] Politics makes strange bedfellows only in exceptional cases. Usually, bedfellows in politics think of each other as good, not bad, fellows. To come to the crucial question: Could the political and social development in the United States have conditioned the American people so much in favor of the Soviet Union as to make an effective foreign policy toward that nation improbable?

A little over a generation ago, such a question would have been absurd. At that time, the free government of the United States in consequent application of its traditional policy of furthering liberalism abroad did not even recognize the Communist government of Russia.[69] Today, the question is imperative. For important changes have come about. The creator of the New Deal, Franklin D. Roosevelt, extended recognition to the Communist government of Russia.[70] This recognition, which occurred during the Depression, came, as far as Communist interests are concerned, at an opportune moment. At the very time when laissez faire was officially thrown out, Communism was officially helped along. For the recognition of the Soviet Union was likely to make her government respectable and perhaps create sympathy for Communism. From now on, the traditional friendship between the United States and Russia as well as the similarities between the U.S.A. and the U.S.S.R., were emphasized. Attention was

[68] For instance, the Catholic and Protestant alliances during the Thirty Years' War and the Swiss *Sonderbundskrieg;* the Holy Alliance; the Axis alliance between National Socialist Germany and Fascist Italy; the alliance between Communist countries. In the FEDERALIST, No. 2, Jay states: "With . . . pleasure I have . . . often taken notice, that Providence has been pleased to give this one connected country to one united people—a people descended from the same ancestors, speaking the same language, professing the same religion, attached to the same principles of government, very similar in their manners and customs . . ."

[69] Bemis, THE DIPLOMATIC HISTORY OF THE UNITED STATES, 729f., writes: "The fundamental reason for this [non-recognition] was the irreconcilability of the revolutionary communistic theory and practice of government with the theory and practice of American democracy and capitalism." See also M. W. Graham, "Russian-American Relations, 1917–1933; an Interpretation," AMERICAN POLITICAL SCIENCE REVIEW, XXVIII (1934), 387.

[70] See Bemis, THE DIPLOMATIC HISTORY OF THE UNITED STATES, 730f.; American Foundation (ed.), THE UNITED STATES AND THE SOVIET UNION; A REPORT ON THE CONTROLLING FACTORS IN THE RELATION BETWEEN THE UNITED STATES AND THE SOVIET UNION (New York, 1933).

drawn to the fact that both nations never had been at war; that the Soviet Union, like the United States, was a classless society; that the Soviet Union—the "workers' paradise"—was, like the United States, a haven for the oppressed; that like the United States, she was a young nation engaged in a great experiment of popular government. To many Americans, the Soviet Union was more "progressive" than their own country. She was considered an example to be followed if the misery of the Depression were to subside. The importance of the Communist revolution in 1917 was compared to that of the French Revolution.[71] The alliance during World War II cemented the friendship. The Soviet Union was considered a humanitarian nation, the victim of Hitler's aggression. Russia suffered enormous losses during the war. She won admiration for her heroism. Toscanini, having refused to play the Fascist *Giovinezza,* conducted the Communist International, and was loved for it by large segments of the American public. It is true that all of this sympathy for the Soviet Union did not make the United States a Soviet Union. However, did the U.S.A. perhaps become a U.S.S.R. in so far as she became a *United States Soviet* (or *Socialist*) *Raptured?* There can be no doubt that the fascination of many Americans with Communist Russia in many respects was similar to their forefathers' enchantment with France after the French Revolution. Did it have similar results?

Great as American enthusiasm for France may have been at the time, President Washington did not permit that enthusiasm to influence his foreign policy. He pursued a policy he considered to be in the long-range national interest. His successors acted similarly. They refused to support democratic movements abroad in spite of popular clamors to the contrary.[72] Foreign policy was given primacy before internal politics. This was possible because foreign policy makers were relatively detached from the people.

With the democratization of foreign policy makers, the situa-

---

[71] See Committee on Russian–American Relations, THE UNITED STATES AND THE SOVIET UNION (New York, 1933); National Council of American–Soviet Friendship, AMERICAN INDUSTRY COMMEMORATES THE TENTH ANNIVERSARY OF AMERICAN–SOVIET DIPLOMATIC RELATIONS, 1933–43 (New York, 1944); Pitirim A. Sorokin, RUSSIA AND THE UNITED STATES (New York, 1945).

[72] See *supra,* 218ff.

tion changed. Foreign policy was likely to become more responsive to temporary popular desires. Consequently, the impact of
popular sympathy toward the Soviet Union was greater than the
influence of popular enthusiasm for the ideals of the French
Revolution had been. There was a good chance that American
foreign policy would become all too friendly toward the Kremlin
and all too soft toward the latter's designs of world revolution and
imperialist expansion.[73]

On the other hand, such a development, probable as it was, was
not imperative. Irrespective of how much the American people
favored social legislation and admired the Soviet Union, they
might still have drawn the line between their internal and external
security, between the Soviet Union as a socialist nation and an
imperialist power. They might have realized that Russian foreign
policy endangered the United States, and effectively opposed that
policy. If the national interest of the United States demanded it,
the people, without the need of being brought to reason by another Pearl Harbor, might have been reasonable enough to rise to
the occasion and to sacrifice temporary desires for the long-range
national security.

Or, if the people would not do so, their representatives could.
Democratized as foreign policy makers had become, they still
were, for the period of their incumbency, formally independent of
the people. They still could do what they considered to be in the
national interest. They could ignore their democratic origin and
emphasize their constitutional status and duty. In Cold War
situations, they could rise to the occasion of putting constitutional
above democratic reason, of preferring the long-range national
interest over short-range popular desires.

As it turned out, the people were unable to rise to the occasion
and their representatives rose to it only occasionally. While for
some time the people respected a constitutional foreign policy and
refrained from putting it under democratic pressure, by the time

---

[73] While, upon pressure from the allies, Stalin dissolved the Comintern during
World War II, that organization was revived as the Cominform in 1948. The Soviet
government never renounced its aim of world revolution. A work without illusions
about Soviet imperialist aims is Salvador de Madariaga, THE BLOWING UP OF THE
PARTHENON; OR, HOW TO LOSE THE COLD WAR (London, 1960).

of the Cold War they had become so much influenced by pro-
socialist ideas that they exercised pressure and promoted a soft
policy toward the Soviet Union. Those who formally made and
executed foreign policy, while basically following popular desires,
would occasionally put constitutional above democratic reason.
However, for fear of popular reaction, often they would do so in a
lukewarm fashion which rendered their attempts ineffective.

At the end of World War II the United States probably could
have liberated all of Germany, Austria, Czechoslovakia, Hungary, and Yugoslavia, as well as the better part of Poland, Ruma-
nia, and Bulgaria. She could have taken Berlin, Prague, and
Vienna. As it was, the United States forces—after having fought
for over three-and-a-half years and having covered enormous
distances by crossing the Atlantic, the Channel, France, Belgium,
and large parts of Germany, Czechoslovakia, and Austria—
stopped a day's journey, a few miles short of Berlin, Prague, and
Vienna and let the Russians take these cities. To top it all,
American troops were withdrawn from large portions of territory for the liberation of which they had shed their blood so that
the Communists could have it without losing a man. General
MacArthur's keynote speech at the Republican convention of
1952 underscored this development: "We practically invited Soviet dominance over the free peoples of Eastern Europe through
strategic dispositions of Soviet force at the close of the European
war; we deliberately withdrew our armies from thousands of
square miles of hard-won territory, permitting the advance of
Soviet forces to the west to plant the red flag of communism on
the ramparts of Berlin, Vienna, and Prague, capitals of Western
civilization; we recklessly yielded effective control over areas of
vast uranium deposits without which the Soviet might never have
developed the threat of atomic power . . ."[74] In the year these
words were spoken, Eric Voegelin wrote that "politicians have
put the Soviet army on the Elbe, surrendered China to the Communists, at the same time demilitarized Germany and Japan, and
in addition demobilized our own army. The facts are trite, and yet

[74] Legislative Reference Service, Library of Congress (ed.), REPRESENTATIVE
SPEECHES OF GENERAL OF THE ARMY DOUGLAS MACARTHUR (Washington, 1964), 70.

233

it is perhaps not sufficiently realized that never before in the history of mankind has a world power used a victory . . . to its own disadvantage."[75] When these statements were made, Communist North Korea had already attacked South Korea, prompting American intervention according to the U.S. policy of containment.

Ten years later, the president of the American Historical Association asked whether that policy, by its very nature, does not yield the initiative to the revolutionary aggressor. His answer offered little comfort: "Really it has not contained all around the World Island of Eurasia. Meanwhile, time has been on the side of the Communists. They have crushed Hungary, with impunity. They have pushed into Laos, despite SEATO. They have jumped the Near East over NATO and CENTO and reached into Africa to compound chaos in the Congo. They have leaped the Atlantic over OAS to establish another Communist front in Cuba, a fourth front for the United States to defend at our very doorstep. In Eastern Asia the Open Door has closed. In the Western Hemisphere, is the Monroe Doctrine dead, as Khrushchev said?"[76] Obviously disillusioned with President Eisenhower who, upon the death of John Foster Dulles, invited Khrushchev only to be told by his guest a few months later that he was not welcome in the Soviet Union,[77] the same speaker expressed the wish that in spite of Communist strength, Americans would be "standing fast for the Rights of Englishmen and the Rights of Man, that is, for the Blessings of Liberty." Quoting John F. Kennedy, he stated that if "committed in every fiber of our being not merely to protect our nation but also to struggle for the cause of freedom on the world scene," Americans may still win. For "proud of our ancient heritage—we shall pay any price, bear any burden, meet any hardship, support any friend or oppose any foe in order to assure the survival and success of liberty."[78]

[75] Eric Voegelin, THE NEW SCIENCE OF POLITICS (Chicago, 1952), 172.

[76] Samuel F. Bemis, "American Foreign Policy and the Blessings of Liberty," AMERICAN HISTORICAL REVIEW, LXVII (1962), 303.

[77] Khrushchev's statement to opening session of Big Four Summit Conference in Paris, NEW YORK TIMES, May 17, 1960, 15.

[78] Bemis, "American Foreign Policy and the Blessings of Liberty," 305. The first statement by Kennedy is taken from his review of B. H. Liddell Hart, "Deterrent

As things turned out, Professor Bemis was as deluded by Kennedy's oratory as he was disillusioned by Eisenhower's feats. Under Kennedy, things went from bad to worse. His administration demonstrated that if old age is no guarantee of wisdom, youth is even less wise. The foreign policy of the New Frontier started out with a fiasco. The invasion in the Bay of Pigs made evident that the new United States government not only was unwilling to "pay any price, bear any burden, meet any hardship, support any friend, oppose any foe to assure the survival and the success of liberty," but was unwilling even to pay the low price and to bear the light burden of providing air cover for friends of liberty. As a result, Cuba—which a little over sixty years earlier had been aided by the United States to become independent—became a neo-colony, a Russian beachhead.[79] The story does not end here. In the missile crisis of 1962, the Russians may have been persuaded to withdraw weapons from Cuba. However, they did so only at the cost of an assurance that the United States would not attack Cuba. This assurance went far beyond a *de jure* recognition of the Communist regime ninety miles from American territory. It amounted to a legalization of illegitimate designs throughout the Western hemisphere. It gave Communism a sanctuary in the very center of the Americas. It provided Soviet imperialism with an ideal strategic base from which it could conquer Latin America and threaten the United States. Rather than paying any price for the success and the survival of liberty, the Kennedy administration paid a high price for the real and

---

or Defense," in the SATURDAY REVIEW, Sept. 3, 1960, 18. Kennedy added "that we are not men who can be pressed, by blackmail or by force, to accept the transfer of territories and peoples to Communist rule. In the 1960's it is our works, not our rhetoric, which constitute the real test of our survival." The second quotation is from Kennedy's Inaugural Address, quoted incorrectly. Kennedy's formulation according to PUBLIC PAPERS OF THE PRESIDENTS: JOHN F. KENNEDY (Washington, 1962), 1, can be found in the following paragraph.

[79] Prior to the invasion of the Bay of Pigs, Cuba had not yet definitely turned to Communism. This occurred only during the presidency of Kennedy. On the other hand the preceding administration ignored the well-known phenomenon of the pattern of revolution. It failed to recognize the probability that a revolutionary movement will fall prey to extremist elements. The development in Cuba demonstrates how cautious we must be in advocating "social change" in Latin America. This author expressed fears that the Castro movement might develop into Communism at a time when Castro was still fighting in the mountains. IN DEFENSE OF PROPERTY, 186.

potential subversion of liberty.[80] The Alliance for Progress was paralleled by a dalliance for recess.[81]

The failure of the New Frontier to hold the frontiers against Communism in the Western hemisphere was matched by its failures to prevent Soviet successes in other parts of the world. In 1961, Kennedy suffered the construction of the Berlin Wall, a clear violation by the Soviets of their commitments. Aside from permitting the elimination of West Berlin as a haven for refugees, Kennedy expressed a desire to negotiate the city's future status. In view of the fact that the legal status of West Berlin was clear, this could only be interpreted as a willingness to make further concessions to the Communists.[82] His attitude had serious consequences. It alienated Adenauer, a man known as much for his

[80] Salvador de Madariaga, LATIN AMERICA BETWEEN THE EAGLE AND THE BEAR (New York, 1962) points out the progress of Communist infiltration in Latin America ever since World War II. Agitation directed from Cuba, falling on fertile ground, will give momentum to Communist subversion. Some aspects of the missile crisis are peculiar. Why did the Russians not camouflage their missiles? Did they want to create a crisis that would overshadow the Chinese invasion of India? Did they want to create the crisis to extract an American assurance not to attack Castro's Cuba if the missiles were removed? Why did Kennedy react to the missiles only shortly before the elections of 1962, after his attention had been called to them throughout the preceding months by Senator Keating and Mrs. Luce? Did he want to use his "victory" in the missile crisis for the purpose of swaying the election?

[81] Cogent arguments have been advanced against economic planning in developing countries—a planning which the Charter of Punta del Este, establishing the Alliance for Progress, provides. See Peter T. Bauer, ECONOMIC ANALYSIS AND POLICY IN UNDERDEVELOPED COUNTRIES (Durham, N.C., 1957), and, with Basil S. Yamey, THE ECONOMICS OF UNDERDEVELOPED COUNTRIES (Chicago, 1957); Albert Hunold (ed.), ENTWICKLUNGSLÄNDER-WAHN UND WIRKLICHKEIT (Zürich, 1961). For a defense of the Alliance for Progress, see John C. Dreier (ed.), THE ALLIANCE FOR PROGRESS (Baltimore, 1962); Lincoln Gordon, A NEW DEAL FOR LATIN AMERICA (Cambridge, Mass., 1963). The latter title supports our thesis of the impact of internal social thought upon foreign policy. While the semi-feudalism in some Latin American nations is regrettable, the advocates of "social change" should ask themselves whether or not their advocacy might be water on the mills of the Communists, who also emphasize the need for social change and might take over in social revolutions, as they did in Cuba. If there is any hope for a disintegration of the Communist empire, it would be advisable not to risk Communist takeovers prior to such disintegration, or as long as there exists a danger that the Soviet Union might use such a takeover for establishing military bases, as in the case of Cuba.

[82] At that time, Ambassador Grewe of the German Federal Republic pointed out to President Kennedy that the rights of the Western allies in Berlin were so clear that there was nothing to negotiate. His arguments, considered all too legal, aroused the displeasure of Kennedy. As a result, Grewe was recalled.

inflexible opposition to Communism[83] as for his unwavering friendship toward the United States. It provided Adenauer's opposition with new arguments in favor of a German foreign policy that was less tied to the United States.[84] Kennedy's overtures to the Soviet Union created general distrust among America's allies. They affected de Gaulle's decision to quit NATO, and Adenauer's decision to knit Germany closer to France and less closely to the United States.[85] Kennedy thus furthered one of the major aims of Soviet policy since World War II,[86] namely, the destruction of Western unity and NATO.

The New Frontier ended with a dismal misjudgment of the situation in South Vietnam, a misjudgment which in no small measure contributed to the tragic development in that unfortunate country. A few weeks before his assassination, President Kennedy stated that a change in the government of South Vietnam might become necessary, encouraging opposition to President Diem, a staunch anti-Communist ally of the United States. Shortly thereafter, President Diem and his brother were assassi-

[83] Cf. Salvador de Madariaga, "Die deutschen Wahlen in weltpolitischer Sicht," leading article, NEUE ZÜRCHER ZEITUNG, Sept. 1, 1957. The fact that Adenauer during the past ten years had a continuous foreign policy prompted Madariaga to call him "the only living statesman of world class."

[84] At the time of the construction of the Wall, the author gained the impression that in the election campaign then being waged in Germany, the American government favored the candidate of the Social Democrats rather than her old ally, Adenauer, feeling the former would be more willing to go along with concessions to the Soviets. The American attitude backfired. While Adenauer lost his majority, the Social Democrats did not win either. The Free Democrats increased their strength and became Adenauer's coalition partners. They took a more rigid stand on Berlin than Adenauer did but were less pro-American.

[85] While Adenauer had always favored friendship with France, his foreign policy up to the Kennedy administration was hardly more pro-French than it was pro-American. Adenauer, who was close to John Foster Dulles, changed his attitude only because of Kennedy's policy toward Russia. That policy indicated that Khrushchev's congratulatory message to Kennedy upon his election, that relations between the U.S. and the U.S.S.R. would again follow the line along which they were developing in Franklin Roosevelt's time, might come true. In retirement, Khrushchev claimed that the Kremlin thwarted Nixon's election to the presidency by refusing his request to release U-2 pilot Francis Gary Powers, a release which would have given Nixon an extra 500,000 votes because it "would have shown that Nixon could have established better contacts with the Soviet Union." Khrushchev was full of praise for President Kennedy. PHILADELPHIA INQUIRER (July 12, 1967), 1.

[86] The Soviets here followed Lenin's advice, to prevent a united front of capitalist countries against the Soviet Union. See *infra*, 250n.

nated after their pleas to the American ambassador for help had been ignored. Those responsible for the assassinations were accepted as the new government of South Vietnam. The elimination of the generally recognized authority of President Diem created a political vacuum, brought about political uncertainty, and weakened the South Vietnamese military. All this aided the Viet Cong.[87]

In summary, Kennedy, contrary to his Inaugural Address which rebuked Eisenhower, not only failed to "begin" reasserting liberty against tyranny, but even failed to contain Communism. In less than three years under his presidency, Communism made greater progress throughout the world than during the full eight years under Eisenhower.[88]

Although we must be careful not to permit the personal tragedy involved in the assassination of President Kennedy to influence our evaluation of his administration, we do not want to appear as harsh in our judgment of him as he was toward Eisenhower. For one thing, he was probably too young for what has been considered "the highest political place held by any individual in the world."[89] Furthermore, his responsibility as well as that of his

[87] See Anthony T. Bouscaren, THE LAST OF THE MANDARINS: DIEM OF VIETNAM (Pittsburgh, Pa., 1965). This evaluation by a conservative was matched by the remark of the "liberal" Senator Mansfield at The Johns Hopkins University in 1966, that ever since the assassination of President Diem, things have gone from bad to worse in South Vietnam.

[88] Even an author partial to Kennedy, who emphasized Kennedy's good record, wrote of him: "He did not aim at anything so trite (or unachievable) as 'victory' in the cold war." Richard E. Neustadt, "Kennedy in the Presidency: A Premature Appraisal," POLITICAL SCIENCE QUARTERLY, LXXIX (1964), 325. According to William Manchester, Fidel Castro greeted the news that Kennedy had been wounded in Dallas with the cry, "Then he's re-elected!" On hearing that the wound had been fatal, he said uneasily: "Everything has changed." When Kennedy's widow heard that the killer was a Communist, she thought it "robs his death of any meaning." Russian Foreign Minister Gromyko, "one of the toughest of the hard-line Reds, was seen weeping as he left the U.S. legation in Moscow." THE DEATH OF A PRESIDENT (New York, 1967), 208, 249, 407, 498. In Europe, Kennedy's assassination was compared to that of Archduke Franz Ferdinand, a sympathizer of Serbian causes who was killed by a Serb.

[89] Brownlow, THE PRESIDENT AND THE PRESIDENCY, 18. For other comments on the importance of the office of the President, see *supra,* 190n. Statesmanship seldom goes with youth. Statesmanship requires wisdom, and wisdom usually comes with maturity and old age. Brilliance is a poor substitute for wisdom. To use Jay's words in THE FEDERALIST, Kennedy perhaps showed "those brilliant appearances of genius and patriotism, which, like transient meteors, some times mislead as well as dazzle." From what has been said in THE FEDERALIST Kennedy seems to have been unsuited for the handling of a serious matter such as foreign affairs. (See

predecessors was perhaps decreased by the democratization of foreign policy and the increasing conditioning of the American *demos* to the values of the New Freedom, the New Deal, and the New Frontier, resulting in sympathy for socialist experiments abroad, friendship for the Soviet Union, and naïveté toward her imperialist designs. Under these influences, American foreign policy became a policy of convenience, characterized by the quest for demobilization as long as the Soviet Union was relatively weak and the fear of a showdown as she grew stronger.

Toward the end of World War II, it would have been unpopular and inconvenient to follow Churchill's advice of putting the Soviet Union within proper bounds. As a result, Eastern Europe and parts of central Europe were ceded to her.[90] Since the American people "wanted their boys home," the administration demobilized when American forces were badly needed to prevent Communist expansion. In the Cold War, the United States mobilized, but only in so far as necessary for a policy of containment. To go farther would have been unpopular and inconvenient. People behind the Iron Curtain were encouraged to rise against their oppressors. When they did so in East Germany and Hungary, they were refused active support. Such support might have brought about a showdown with the Soviet Union. It was convenient to avoid it. As a result, the people behind the Iron Curtain were lost as allies, and the Soviet Union was relieved of one of her major problems.[91]

---

supra, 215.) The men at the Federal Convention in Philadelphia were wise when they made the age qualification for the chief executive higher than that for other federal officers. Although their country was uniquely immune from foreign aggression, they put the minimum age of the President at thirty-five, hoping that no President would come close to that minimum. Cf. *supra,* 181. Had the Founding Fathers lived in our day, and seen their country engulfed in international affairs, a nation whose security could, on account of the increase of presidential power, depend upon the acts of the President, they probably would have stipulated a considerably higher minimum age requirement. In modern times, statesmanship in the West seems to require age. The great statesmen of our century—Adenauer, Churchill, and de Gaulle—were all advanced in years. Failures in statesmanship— such as Mussolini and Hitler—were young when they came to power.

[90] See Winston S. Churchill, TRIUMPH AND TRAGEDY (Boston, 1953), Bk. 2, chs. 2–4; John L. Snell (ed.), THE MEANING OF YALTA (Baton Rouge, La., 1956); Herbert Feis, CHURCHILL, ROOSEVELT, STALIN (Princeton, N.J., 1957), chs. 51–60.

[91] See James Burnham, CONTAINMENT OR LIBERATION? (New York, 1952). Salvador de Madariaga, THE BLOWING UP OF THE PARTHENON, dedicated "to the memory of the Russian soldiers who, in October 1956, left the Red Army and fought and died for the freedom of Hungary," maintains that as long as the Soviet Union must

When the balance of power had shifted further in favor of the Soviet Union, Khrushchev was invited to the United States. Again, this step was in a large measure due to popular demand, prompted by the hope that an invitation would assuage Russia. Little concern was voiced that such an invitation might make Communism respectable throughout the world, an effect which in the long run could only be detrimental to American interests. Agreements for cultural exchange were prompted by similar short-sighted considerations. The very government which had supported proceedings against Richard Strauss and Wilhelm Furtwängler for having aided the National Socialist regime by performing classic works, now made the Communist regime respectable by having Communist artists not only perform classic but also Communist creations.[92] Again, this was done on account of the prodding of large segments of the American people, who often seem to be more anxious to applaud the representatives of a regime that persecuted Boris Pasternak and jailed his pallbearers than those of other nations.[93]

As to President Kennedy, he probably followed popular sentiment when he permitted the Bay of Pigs invasion to fail and paid

---

fear uprisings in Eastern Europe, she would be reluctant of pursuing imperialist aims elsewhere. Recent emphasis upon the disintegration of the Communist empire on account of indications of independence in some Communist nations, overlooks that these indications are given by governments which do not seriously challenge Moscow. When the chips are down, all Communist governments are likely to side with the Soviet Union. They so far seldom voted against the Soviet Union in the United Nations; they did not quit the Warsaw Pact. American overtures to Communist governments in Eastern Europe are no substitute for keeping the anti-Communist fire alive. For the risks involved in emphasizing disunity in the Communist world, see *infra,* 246ff.

[92] In view of the inhumanity of the National Socialist regime it certainly was disappointing that humanists like Strauss and Furtwängler did not raise their voices against the regime. On the other hand, these men were not "representative" of the regime. They were not members of the party. Strauss, who as Germany's outstanding composer early during the Hitler era had the presidency of the *Reichsmusikkammer* thrust upon him, soon got rid of that "honor." Furtwängler was attacked by Goebbels for performing the works of a "decadent" composer like Hindemith and left Germany in protest. Implored to return, he later claimed that performing Beethoven was more necessary under the Hitler regime than elsewhere. Strauss did not compose Nazi music, Furtwängler did not conduct Nazi compositions. In contrast, Shostakovich and Prokofiev composed for the Communist regime. Russian performers, often members of the Communist party, perform music representative of their regime.

[93] Cf. James Burnham, SUICIDE OF THE WEST (New York, 1964).

ransom for the liberation of the invaders. No war over Cuba. He probably followed that sentiment when he permitted the building of the Berlin Wall and agreed to negotiate the future status of West Berlin. No war over Berlin. He probably followed public opinion when in the missile crisis he gave the assurance that the United States would leave the Communist regime in Cuba alone if the Russians would remove their missiles. No war over Communism in Latin America—or the Western hemisphere. Kennedy's attitude toward the Diem regime in South Vietnam obviously was influenced by popular clamors.[94]

In Vietnam, again, the problem of a foreign policy prompted by temporary popular desires which favor socialism is evident. In the election of 1964, President Johnson denounced his opponent as trigger-happy because the Republican candidate advocated stepping-up the efforts against Communism in Vietnam and a harder line toward the Communists in Russia, realizing the absurdity of being friendly toward the latter while they were supplying the former. The incumbent President won an easy victory because many voters, though in their hearts they sensed that Goldwater was right,[95] voted for Johnson fearing that an election of Goldwater might lead to war. Upon this choice of convenience, President Johnson stepped up American efforts in Vietnam, being aware that abandoning South Vietnam to the Communists would be detrimental to the long-range interests of the United States. On the other hand, he did not step up those efforts in a way that could conceivably be as unpopular as Goldwater's suggestions. Thus, the United States became involved in a war that is waged half-

---

[94] Many of us remember the full-page advertisement in the NEW YORK TIMES, depicting a Buddhist monk who immolated himself out of protest against the Catholic rulers of Vietnam, and urging President Kennedy to curb persecution of the Buddhists. When, after the assassination of Diem and his brother and the overthrow of Catholic rulers other Buddhists immolated themselves, those who previously had demonstrated against the Catholic rulers of South Vietnam remained quiet.

[95] A campaign slogan for Goldwater was: "In your heart you know he is right." While expressing hope that people would vote according to their convictions of what is right, this slogan also indicated the fear that out of convenience they would not do so. Among American politicians, Barry Goldwater is one of the greatest profiles in courage. Here was a presidential candidate who told the voters what he believed in, irrespective of how many votes it might cost him. Cf. John F. Kennedy, PROFILES IN COURAGE (New York, 1956).

heartedly and which appears to be hopeless to many people. Rather than use her technical superiority, in large measure she permitted herself to become involved in the kind of war her adversary prefers, a kind of war which earlier had defeated the French. There is no doubt that President Johnson, when stepping up the American effort, tried to have constitutional reason prevail over contrary popular desires. However, he was reluctant to make that prevalence absolute. Perhaps the clamors of the people were too strong. Pull out of Vietnam now? "No," reply the people. Use nuclear weapons? "No," is the emphatic answer. The result is a gradual increase of the war effort—more troops, more bombing—with which the people are likely to go along, and a gradual, slight increase of casualties which the people are more likely to suffer than a sudden, big one because gradual though extended suffering to most men is more bearable than sharp, short pain. Be conciliatory toward North Vietnam and perhaps Red China? No! Get tough with the Soviet Union to make her stop aiding the enemy? No! The results are denunciations of Hanoi and perhaps Peking, and official friendliness toward Moscow, i.e., a gradual escalation which in all probability will not involve the Soviet Union.[96]

For as long as she can avoid it, the Soviet Union will not sacrifice one soldier. She will be content and happy to see the United States suffer as many casualties as possible by fighting other nations. Chances are that Russia will succeed in staying out of the war as long as her parade for peace will continue to have the effect of fostering the American desire to avoid a war with the Soviet Union at any cost. An escalation of the war in Vietnam to a point where it will involve Russia will be prevented by a Soviet

[96] Walter Lippmann, a critic of President Johnson's policy in Vietnam, in 1955 regretted that foreign policy is dictated by public opinion, and spoke of a "compulsion to make mistakes." Writing that "in matters of war and peace the popular answer in the democracies is likely to be No," he added that "the prevailing public opinion has been destructively wrong at the critical junctures. The people have imposed a veto upon the judgments of informed and responsible officials. They have compelled the governments, which usually knew what would have been wiser, or was necessary, or was more expedient, to be too late with too little, or too long with too much, too pacifist in peace and too bellicose in war, too neutralist or appeasing in negotiation or too intransigent. Mass opinion . . . has shown itself to be a dangerous master of decisions when the stakes are life and death." ESSAYS IN THE PUBLIC PHILOSOPHY (New York, 1955), 19f.

foreign policy which furthers escalation of such American desires as "no war over Berlin," "no war over Cuba," "no war over Communism in the Western hemisphere," into the desire "no war over the Communist world revolution." Better Red than dead.[97]

In 1951, General MacArthur criticized the foreign policy of the United States: "Is there wonder that men who seek an objective understanding of American policy thinking become completely frustrated and bewildered? Is there wonder that Soviet propaganda so completely dominates American foreign policy? And, indeed, what is our foreign policy? . . . I defy you or any other man to tell me what it is. It has become a mass of confused misunderstandings and vacillations. It has meant one thing today—another tomorrow. It has almost blown with every wind, changed with every tide. The sorry truth is we have no policy. Expediencies as variable and shifting as the exigencies of the moment seem to be the only guide."[98] He could have made this statement today. American foreign policy, having become democratized, is no longer a foreign policy in the traditional sense, implying a long-range program in the national interest irrespective of temporary, popular desires. Having become democratized, American foreign policy makers, to use the words of Burke who defended the American colonists in their struggle with Parliament irrespective of the opinions of his constituents, have increasingly become "a weathercock on the top of an edifice, exalted for . . . levity and versatility, and of no use but to indicate the shiftings of every fashionable gale."[99] A few exceptions only confirm the rule.

[97] For the idea that survival, not peace, is the supreme end of foreign policy, and the hope that after World War II Russia would not engage in a policy of aggrandizement and respect the freedom of her neighbors, see Walter Lippmann, U.S. FOREIGN POLICY: SHIELD OF THE REPUBLIC (Boston, 1943). Friedrich, CONSTITUTIONAL GOVERNMENT AND DEMOCRACY, 86f., takes issue with this view.

[98] Address in Boston, July 25, 1951. REPRESENTATIVE SPEECHES, 31.

[99] In a speech at Bristol, on certain points relative to his parliamentary conduct, Burke stated in 1780: "I did not obey your instructions. No. I conformed to the instructions of truth and Nature, and maintained your interest, against your opinions, with a constancy that became me. A representative worthy of you ought to be a person of stability. I am to look, indeed, to your opinions,—but to such opinions as you and I *must* have five years hence. I was not to look to the flash of the day. I knew that you chose me, in my place, along with others, to be a pillar of the state, and not a weather-cock on the top of an edifice, exalted for my levity and versatility, and of no use but to indicate the shiftings of every fashionable gale." WORKS, II, 382.

As a rule, these weathercocks seem to be cocksure only to turn with the gales of democratic opinion, an opinion that is often irrational, emotional, erratic, and in favor of social reform. Has the American *demos* become the demon of American foreign policy?[100]

TRAGEDY AND GUILT

In today's international situation, characterized by Cold War, this question amounts to asking whether or not the American people have been running into disaster. It raises the question of tragedy and guilt. That problem was discussed earlier in connection with Lincoln's war measures.[101] The tragedy we were concerned with then revolved around the replacement of free government by democracy. It was of a seemingly minor nature, because it basically consisted in the challenge of one American value, freedom, by another American value, popular government, and because the chances were that for a long time the latter would not absolutely do away with the former. The tragedy we worry over today is a major one. It involves the challenge of American democracy, a democracy that has not yet absolutely discarded liberal values and is still considered by many to be a free government, by a foreign power that stands for values that are neither liberal nor democratic. It involves the very survival of the United

[100] See de Tocqueville, DEMOCRACY IN AMERICA, I, 243f. He writes that "it is especially in the conduct of their foreign relations that democracies appear to me decidedly inferior to other governments . . . Foreign politics demand scarcely any of those qualities which are peculiar to a democracy; they require, on the contrary, the perfect use of almost all those in which it is deficient . . . [A] democracy can only with great difficulty regulate the details of an important undertaking, persevere in a fixed design, and work out its execution in spite of serious obstacles. It cannot combine its measures with secrecy or await their consequences with patience. These are qualities which more especially belong to an individual or to an aristocracy; and they are precisely the qualities by which a nation, like an individual, attains a dominant position." For discussions of democratic foreign policy, see DeWitt C. Poole, THE CONDUCT OF FOREIGN RELATIONS UNDER MODERN DEMOCRATIC CONDITIONS; Walter Lippmann, PUBLIC OPINION AND FOREIGN POLICY IN THE UNITED STATES (London, 1952); Max Beloff, FOREIGN POLICY AND THE DEMOCRATIC PROCESS (Baltimore, 1955); James B. Reston, THE ARTILLERY OF THE PRESS, ITS INFLUENCE ON AMERICAN FOREIGN POLICY (New York, 1967); Lester Markel (ed.), PUBLIC OPINION AND FOREIGN POLICY (New York, 1949).

[101] See *supra*, 50ff.

States and of her way of life. The tragedy following the Civil War turned around the question of whether free government, implying liberalism, would hold its own against the "liberalism" of a democracy[102] promoted by the Populist and Progressive movements and their successors, notably the New Deal and the New Frontier. Today's tragedy is that "liberal" democracy is in jeopardy of being annihilated by the Communists. In the case of Lincoln, we asked whether the French Revolution had descended upon him.[103] Today we must ask whether the Russian Revolution has descended upon the American people and their leaders. Formerly, we saw tragedy in the French Revolution's challenge to the ideas of the American Revolution. Today, we see tragedy in the fact that those ideas, adulterated as they have become through the influence of the French Revolution,[104] are about to be annihilated by the Russian Revolution.

A great friend and honorary citizen of the United States, Winston Churchill, gave the last volume of his history of the Second World War the title *Triumph and Tragedy*.[105] That title seems to especially fit the situation of the United States today. Hers was the greatest triumph; hers became the greatest tragedy. She—not England, not France, not Russia—emerged from the war as the undisputed strongest power on earth. She—not England, not France, not Germany, not Japan—became weaker and weaker, as far as her relative power, compared to that of the Soviet Union, is concerned. Here was a tragedy which occurred "never before in the history of mankind . . ."[106] In a period which, historically speaking, is minimal, the power of the United States became matched by that of the Soviet Union, a nation that has left no doubt about its antagonism to the American system on the inter-

---

[102] Significantly James Bryce entitled his classic on the United States THE AMERICAN COMMONWEALTH rather than "The American Democracy." A later work, including a discussion of the United States, he entitled MODERN DEMOCRACIES (New York, 1921).

[103] See *supra*, 55.

[104] See J. L. Talmon, THE ORIGINS OF TOTALITARIAN DEMOCRACY (London, 1952).

[105] The theme of the volume is: "How the Great Democracies Triumphed, and so Were able to Resume the Follies Which Had so Nearly Cost Them Their Life."

[106] Voegelin, NEW SCIENCE OF POLITICS, 172.

nal as well as international level. The security of the United
States, almost absolute in 1945, is now threatened at any moment,
from any place. Missiles carrying atomic warheads can reach the
United States at any time from the Soviet Union, perhaps from
Cuba, and from innumerable ships above and under the waters
that surround the United States.

Careless optimism prevailing during and after World War II
that Russia, aided by the United States against Hitler's on-
slaught, would be a friendly nation, in a large measure was due
to the fact that the U.S., while not becoming a U.S.S.R.,[107] had
become the United States Soviet Raptured. When it became evident that the Soviet Union was not so friendly after all, the
United States became the United States Soviet Reconciled. With
increasing Soviet might, the United States has increasingly become the United States Soviet Resigned. God only knows what all
this will lead to.[108] The careless optimism of twenty years ago has
been replaced by the anxiety that things will come out all right.
Since this hope may be against the odds, people have been seeking
consolation in dreams.

Since the dream that Russia would be friendly went up in
smoke, a new dream has come about. At the very time the Soviet
Union enormously increased her power, people began to dream of
the disintegration of the Communist empire. Our dreamers are
comforted by a variety of factors. Tito, during and after the war a
staunch Stalinist, broke with his master. Upon the death of Stalin,
other Soviet satellites spoke up to the Kremlin. To top it all, the
Soviet Union became challenged by Red China. One day, the
dream is, the U.S.S.R. will be engaged in a war with China,
perhaps having the United States as her comrade in arms, or,
better still, with the United States sitting it out. Disintegration in

---

[107] The possibility that the U.S. might become a U.S.S.R. was indicated by
Oliver Wendell Holmes in his dissent in *Gitlow* v. *New York,* 268 U.S. 652, 673
(1925): "If in the long run the beliefs expressed in proletarian dictatorship are
destined to be accepted by the dominant forces of the community, the only
meaning of free speech is that they should be given their chance and have their
way." For the dangers of becoming socialist resp. communist through evolution
rather than revolution, see the author's IN DEFENSE OF PROPERTY, 241n.

[108] Cf. Louis J. Halle, DREAM AND REALITY: ASPECTS OF AMERICAN FOREIGN POLICY
(New York, 1953).

the Communist empire is said to have been matched by that within various Communist nations. In Russia, the introduction of collective leadership after the death of Stalin, implying a struggle for power among the new leaders, means disintegration of Soviet leadership. This development is matched by other factors of disintegration, such as the quest for a higher standard of living and more consumer goods, the youth problem, and the liberalism of Professor Libermann. Yugoslavia offers a similar picture. Tito, busy defending himself against internal critics, agreed to decentralize the government. Similar situations exist in the other satellites of Eastern Europe. Even Red China, stronghold of Stalinism, is torn by internal struggles. Mao's Red guards have to fight to keep his opponents down. Everywhere, the dream is, the Communists are struggling for survival. One day, the people they now rule will overthrow them.[109]

All this may be true. Even in monolithic empires, there will always be some degree of diversity. Still, we do not really know its exact scope. Therefore, caution, extreme caution, is in order. Nearly everybody has emphasized the disintegration in the Communist world. Few people have asked how genuine and serious that disintegration actually is. Everything furthering the dream seems to be anxiously grasped and taken at face value. Nobody seems to want to look behind it. However, events may betray. Occurrences often are mere appearances. They are so in free nations whose governments usually go by the principle that honesty is the best policy. Must they not be so in nations whose governments frequently are inclined to cherish the rule, "the

---

[109] Zbigniew K. Brzezinski, THE SOVIET BLOC: UNITY AND CONFLICT (Cambridge, Mass., 1960), is representative of the majority of authors who emphasize disintegration. This author has the feeling that much of their evaluation might be prompted by wishful thinking and the desire to write what people like to hear because it gives them hope. Brzezinski, after enumerating his sources (official speeches and statements of Communist leaders, Communist newspapers and books, summaries and reports of Western agencies, secondary sources, his interviews with Communist officials, observations from travel, and statements by former Communist officials), writes: "Admittedly, such sources would not satisfy the rigorous archival standards of diplomatic history, but perhaps both the subject matter and its contemporary nature might be considered as legitimate justification" (xx). Madariaga speaks of Chinese Titoism as a "curious delusion." BLOWING UP OF THE PARTHENON, 24. That work exposes the dream world of Communist disintegration.

bigger the lie, the better?"[110] The reality, shunned by our dreamers, could well be that Tito's balking the Cominform was done on secret orders from Stalin, to give the West the dreamworld of Titoism. The advantages for the Communists of such a behavior are obvious. The West, seeing disunity in the Communist world, would be lulled into complacency, even give aid to Titoist countries and consolidate their regimes.[111] The split between Moscow and Peking may have been prompted by similar considerations, and actually be the product of a secret understanding between the leaders of both nations. The fact that this appears to be a split that involves the people themselves could only confirm the prescription of the big lie. For the argument that the Russian and Chinese governments could not very well tell their people about their disagreements, unless those disagreements were genuine, overlooks that the Russians and the Chinese are brought up to believe whatever the government tells them, and that both governments probably would not find it difficult at some later date to convince their citizens that after all, it is better to stick together against the capitalists.[112] At any rate, while Titoism and the rift between Moscow and Peking may be genuine, they do not appear to be too serious. When the chips are down in confrontations with capitalist nations, the Communist empire stands pretty united. Except for Yugoslavia, all the Eastern European satellites are tied to the Soviet Union by the Warsaw Pact. Yugoslavia may well have been left out in order to get her military supplies from the United States. All satellites, including Yugoslavia, have generally supported the Soviet Union diplomatically, as is demon-

[110] This principle was advocated by Hitler. A translation of the relevant passages from MEIN KAMPF (München, 1925–27) can be found in William Ebenstein (ed.), MAN AND THE STATE (New York, 1947), 302f.

[111] At the height of the crisis between Italy and Yugoslavia over Trieste, Italian arms received from the United States were pointed at Yugoslavian arms received from the United States.

[112] Until the conclusion of the Nonaggression Pact between Germany and the Soviet Union, the latter had been the *bête noire* of Hitler's propaganda machine, which was quite effective in creating anti-Russian and anti-Comintern feeling. Upon the conclusion of the Pact, that machine was as effective in convincing the Germans that the Pact was Hitler's greatest diplomatic victory and in the best interests of the German people. A similar situation must have existed in the Soviet Union. Communist parties in European nations, until then strictly opposed to Hitler's Germany, upon the conclusion of the Pact gave up their opposition.

strated by their votes in the United Nations.[113] In spite of Mao's denunciations of the Kremlin and the Kremlin's denunciations of Mao, the Russians have not ceased in their efforts to have Red China seated in the United Nations. They let her have Tibet. They let her spur on the Communists in Vietnam.

This takes us to another dream, the dream that the Russians want peace. Ever since World War II, they have staged international peace rallies and propagated peace. They would not have done so, our dreamers like to think, unless they meant it. That the Russians are a peaceful nation, it is argued, was demonstrated by their attitude in Korea and Vietnam. The North Koreans and the North Vietnamese went to war, prodded on by the Red Chinese. The Russians stayed out. As a matter of fact, so we are told, the rift between the Soviet Union and China is mainly due to the latter's militancy.

Again, all this may be true. But we do not know for sure. Therefore, caution is in place. The Soviet Union probably wants peace for herself. After her losses in World War II, she cannot very well want to go to war again. However, this does not mean that she wants peace for others. Soviet peace campaigns are basically made for the good of the Soviet Union. Involving capitalist nations in war would be in conformity with Lenin's advice. Civil wars—Americans burning America and killing Americans—would of course be ideal. Even engaging some Asian Communists in war would be conceded as a tactical retreat to further

---

[113] American hope in the United Nations seems to be another dream. That organization, originally conceived by the United States to preserve the status quo existing in 1945, i.e., the *Pax Americana,* no longer serves that purpose. The admission of new states which often became independent with American support (see Grayson Kirk, "Declining Empires and American Interests," SURVEY, LXXXV [1949], 254; Henry A. Byroade, "The World's Colonies and Ex-Colonies: a Challenge to America," UNITED STATES DEPARTMENT OF STATE BULLETIN, XXIX [1953], 655), resulted in a growth of nations which are tending to side with the Soviet rather than the Western bloc. See Clark M. Eichelberger, UN: THE FIRST FIFTEEN YEARS (New York, 1960), 133. In the General Assembly, which seems to have become the most important branch of the organization (Sydney D. Bailey, THE GENERAL ASSEMBLY OF THE UNITED NATIONS [New York, 1960], 253ff.; Benjamin V. Cohen, THE UNITED NATIONS [Cambridge, Mass., 1961], 16ff.), a combination of the "uncommitted" and Communist nations can now outvote the United States and her allies. See also "New Era of Change for UN," BUSINESS WEEK (Oct. 22, 1960), 95; "Changing World, Changing UN," COMMONWEAL, LXXIII (1961), 400.

the strategic aim of sapping the strength of the nation that can challenge Communism the most, namely, the United States, and of preserving the power that can promote Communism and hurt capitalism the most, the Soviet Union.[114] But, our dreamers will argue, what about the loss of prestige that is bound to result from the unusually publicized[115] rift between the two major Communist powers? The answer is simple. Aside from the fact that strong nations need not worry about prestige,[116] such a loss will be more than made up for by the enormous prestige the Soviet Union stands to gain as an advocate of peace. If the major Communist power denounces Communist as well as capitalist warmongers, then she must be an honest advocate of peace, a nation to be trusted. Again, we do not know whether we are right in our skepticism toward the peace aims of the Soviet Union. Still, the following facts are undisputed. The North Koreans received Russian weapons after they had invaded South Korea. The Viet Cong

[114] For Lenin's advice that Soviet foreign policy should foster war among capitalist nations and that tactical retreats are permissible if they further strategic ends, see his statements in Stefan T. Possony, LENIN READER (Chicago, 1966), chs. 9, 10. Cf. also de Madariaga, BLOWING UP OF THE PARTHENON, 20ff. In the Middle East, the Soviet Union encouraged Arab animosity toward Israel, probably hoping for either a protracted war among those capitalistic nations, a war which perhaps would involve the United States and permit the Soviet Union to exploit misery, or for a fast victory of her Arab friends, which also would increase Soviet influence. She was not willing to sacrifice one soldier for the Arabs. Recognizing the U.S. as the only power that at present constitutes a threat to Russian security, the major aim of Soviet foreign policy has been to weaken the United States. It has not so much been concerned with other free nations. On the other hand, while American security is mainly threatened by the Soviet Union, American foreign policy has not been directed mainly toward that nation, but rather has permitted itself to be engaged by Communist small fry, such as the Koreans and Vietnamese.

[115] Usually, the Soviet press refrains from publishing unpleasant news. The fact that it not only publishes, but literally publicizes, news on the rift between Moscow and Peking emphasizing publicity features such as Chinese demonstrations against the Russians and vice versa (for instance, the Chinese attempt to storm the Russian embassy in Peking, resulting in the Russian withdrawal of personnel from China; the Russians' denouncing of the Chinese at gatherings in Russia which resulted in the Chinese delegation's ostentatious walk-out in protest, etc.) shows a peculiar deviation from past practice.

[116] That the Soviet Union does not care about a loss in prestige was demonstrated in the winter war against Finland, when she apparently could not win. The purpose of her poor showing in that war could well have been to convince Hitler that he need not fear the Soviet Union and could concentrate his war efforts against the West. Perhaps the maneuver backfired. It perhaps prompted Hitler to invade the Soviet Union. Later, he referred to the Soviet showing in the winter war as "the greatest deceit in world history."

and North Vietnamese fight with such weapons. If Russia would cut off her supply to North Vietnam today, the war would probably stop tomorrow. Russian supplies, continually increasing, keep the war going, and Vietnamese and American blood flowing.

In 1951, General MacArthur said: "There is no slightest doubt in my mind but that the Soviet has been engaging in the greatest bulldozing diplomacy history has ever recorded. Without committing a single soldier to battle, he has assumed direct control over a large part of the population of the world. His intrigue has found its success not so much in its own military strength, nor indeed in any overt threat or intent to commit it to battle, but in the moral weakness of the free world . . . It is a weakness which has caused our own policymakers, after committing America's sons to battle, to leave them to the continuous slaughter of an indecisive campaign by imposing arbitrary restraints upon the support we might otherwise provide them through maximum employment of our scientific superiority, which alone offers hope of early victory."[117] The same words could be spoken today, although things look worse than seventeen years ago. The Communist empire and its military strength have grown.

This takes us, then, to the question of guilt. It is an anxious, harrowing question. For it involves the guilt not of one man, but of many, the guilt not only over a short period, but over an era. It involves collective and protracted guilt. A satisfactory answer is more difficult to reach than in Lincoln's case. In that case, the question simply was whether one man, during a brief period of clear and present danger, committed contempt of a Constitution which unequivocally embodied free government. One man's clear actions in a clear situation, measurable by a clear Constitution,[118] facilitated the answer. Today, the question is whether foreign policy makers since World War II, during a protracted period which to many did not present a clear and present danger because "people never had it so good" and the war was merely cold, have contravened a Constitution that no longer set the un-

[117] Speech in Austin, Texas, June 13, 1951, REPRESENTATIVE SPEECHES, 22.
[118] We have in mind only a relative clarity. As the discussion in ch. 1 has shown, a determination of Lincoln's guilt was not easy.

equivocal standards by which guilt could easily be measured. For the Constitution, relativized and democratized as it has become through formal amendments and judicial interpretation, has increasingly embodied democratic values at the cost of liberal ones and facilitated softness toward international Communism. This degradation General MacArthur probably had in mind when he spoke of the "moral weakness" that spawned a blunderous American foreign policy. His statement prompts us to examine guilt against the background of moral weakness and to find out whether this weakness mitigates the guilt involved in the "deliberate"[119] behavior of American politicians. The question basically is whether foreign policymakers can be blamed for behaving the way they did under the circumstances they were in and the conditioning they were under.

In view of the democratization of policymaking, we shall first examine the guilt of the American *demos*, always aware of the dubious nature of collective guilt.[120] As was shown, the American people in large measure prompted a foreign policy that aided international Communism. To the detriment of the long-range national interest, unwilling to curb egoistic temporary desires, they acted irresponsibly. The fact that their behavior may have been produced by the agitations of their leaders does not change this truth. For whereas it is one of the peculiar features of the growth of democracy that the people, supposedly getting more and more power, often actually get less and less because they fall prey to persuasive demagogues, they remain, as long as their freedom is not seriously restricted, responsible. Seduction does not absolve the seduced.

On the other hand, it appears doubtful whether these objective facts, suggesting guilt, are matched by subjective ones, confirming

---

[119] Voegelin, NEW SCIENCE OF POLITICS, 172.

[120] As long as only one out of a thousand or more is not guilty, it is unfair to consider all thousand or more guilty. *A fortiori,* this must be so, when those not guilty comprise a substantial part of the population which, in conformity with the rules of the democratic game, goes along with the guilty majority, as has been the case in the United States. When in the following we examine the people's guilt, we have in mind mainly those who prompted foreign policy. We think less of those who indifferently went along and even less of those who opposed foreign policy, although even in the case of the last group the degree of opposition will determine the degree of absolution.

guilt.[121] We do not know whether the people thought their behavior was wrong, whether they were aware that it was, or might be, detrimental to the national interest. After World War II, the Soviet Union was weak. Why not demobilize? When the Soviet Union grew stronger she did not expand. Why not just pursue a policy of containment? When she took Cuba, why not just resign to the fact rather than risk a nuclear war that would destroy more than it would gain? These arguments, shortsighted as they may be, are not far-fetched. It would be unfair to maintain that they were made in bad faith, and it will be difficult to prove that they were. Therefore, the people must be given the benefit of the doubt. *In dubio pro reis.*

Whether the American people will come off so easily before the bar of history is a different question. Here they may well be condemned for having committed some of the greatest blunders in the evolution of America and of freedom. The verdicts of history are made on account of objective facts and their consequences. History—in distinction to historians—usually does not ask why people acted the way they did, but only how people acted. History is peculiarly immune from considerations of right and wrong. The fighting among historians over what is right and wrong in history is perhaps the best proof of this.[122] For that fighting does not change the objective facts of the making of great empires—and of their unmaking. When history will render its verdict on the decline of the American empire, the greatest empire the earth had known until then,[123] the New Generation of Americans that since World War II have increasingly determined American policy, will not come off lightly.[124]

While that generation will be burdened with a severe moral guilt, it cannot well be burdened with guilt in the legal sense. To begin with, when people prompted a foreign policy that was detrimental to the long-range national interest, they acted according to the ordinary laws. Did they also act in conformity with the

---

[121] Cf. Jerome Hall, PRINCIPLES OF CRIMINAL LAW (Indianapolis, 1947), ch. 5.

[122] Cf. Jakob Burckhardt, JUDGMENTS ON HISTORY AND HISTORIANS (Zohn, trans.; Boston, 1958).

[123] See Dr. Ramsay's statement, *supra,* 211n.

[124] For the concept of the New Generation, see the author's IN DEFENSE OF PROPERTY, 5.

superior law in which morals and ordinary laws meet—the Constitution? The answer is in the affirmative. There was no contempt of Constitution. When influencing foreign policy since World War II, the people exercised their constitutional rights, notably that of free speech. Free speech has been denied in a clear and present danger;[125] it has not been denied for the creation of such danger, although such danger might prove fatal. Furthermore, the people can hardly be expected to draw the line between constitutional and democratic reason. They cannot very well be expected to ask to what degree their temporary desires might conflict with the artificial reason of foreign policy and the long-range national interest, especially in view of the fact that the democratization of the Constitution probably made them believe that democratic reason was constitutional by definition. The people, as a rule, do not think ahead, but only of the immediate future. For them, the idea of a constitution does not imply what is implied for America's greatest Chief Justice.[126] The people are interested not so much in the survival of their living Constitution, but in surviving and living well under it. They do not ask what, in the long run, they can do for America, but what America can do for them, now. For that reason, the Founding Fathers wisely entrusted the care of foreign policy not to the people themselves, but to their selected representatives.

Did these representatives fulfill that trust since World War II? We do not think so. While what was said about the moral guilt of the American people also applies to their representatives, what has been said about the legal guilt of the people does not. The elected policymakers contravened the Constitution in so far as they usually did not act in the long-range national interest. Furthermore, conditioned as they may have been by the prevailing intellectual climate, they still committed their blunders "deliberately," for "phenomena of this magnitude cannot be explained by ignorance or stupidity."[127] While doubts have been raised whether today's representatives are of as high caliber as they used to be,[128]

---

[125] *Schenck* v. *United States,* 249 U.S. 47 (1919).

[126] Marshall's statement that a constitution is destined to last for ages can be found *supra,* 60.

[127] Voegelin, NEW SCIENCE OF POLITICS, 172.

[128] Cf. *ibid.,* 175.

and while they probably do not constitute as much of an elite as Madison had hoped, they still are some kind of an elite. Their intellectual level is well above average.[129] They could be expected to recognize the long-range national interest and to let that interest prevail over short-range popular desires if those desires were detrimental to that interest. However, with a few exceptions—we think of the decisions to halt Communist aggression in Korea and Vietnam[130]—they failed to do so.

Are there extenuating circumstances? That question revolves around the problem of whether the democratization of policymakers has changed representative government from one approaching the Burkean–Madisonian ideal to one which makes the representatives mere spokesmen of their constituents. Without any doubt, constitutional innovations have pointed in this direction. Perhaps they mitigate the guilt of those who have been all too willing to follow popular desires. Still, these innovations, while changing the mode of election, have not changed the legal status of the elected. Presidents and senators still have their fixed terms during which they are legally immune from their constituents, during which they can act according to their own conscience, irrespective of the wishes of those who elected them, and fulfill their constitutional trust. That trust requires putting the long-range national interest above the short-range personal interest of getting re-elected.

As to the degree of a possible mitigation of guilt, the election of Presidents for four years and of senators for six seems to favor the former. However, this is debatable in view of the fact that Presidents seem to be surer of re-election than senators.[131] Even if the Presidents were granted more extenuating circumstances than senators on account of their shorter official terms, their guilt

[129] In European literature, the U.S. Senate is usually considered a high caliber legislative chamber, an evaluation that is matched by American authors. Although the United States in the period following World War II has had no statesman in the presidency of the caliber of an Adenauer, Churchill, or de Gaulle (men unique in their respective nations throughout this century), American Presidents in general have been able men.

[130] Cf., however, with respect to the war in Vietnam, *supra,* 241f., and, concerning the Korean War, MacArthur's speeches before Congress, April 19, 1951; at Austin, June 13, 1951; at Boston, July 25, 1951; at Miami, Oct. 17, 1951.

[131] See *supra,* 198. While some senators, on account of re-elections, hold office for considerably longer periods than Presidents, senators, as a rule, do not seem to be as certain of re-election as Presidents.

would still be greater than that of other policymakers. They, and not others, have been the major architects of foreign policy.[132]

CONCLUSION

The idyll of national security and a steady growth of American might, as it existed under free government, has been destroyed by the march of democracy. While the American people perhaps have a moral guilt for this development, guilt in a legal sense is confined to those governing them. Since that guilt increases with the amount of power held, it is greatest with the Presidents. These are the facts. Are there remedies?

The safest remedy probably would be a restitution of classic representation. However, such restitution presupposes undoing many things brought about by the growth of democracy. It is improbable. In spite of occasional setbacks, democracy marches on as long as it remains basically intact.[133] The representatives of the people are likely to remain under pressure from the *demos*. They won't dare to follow their own free will, if such a will still exists and has not been brainwashed by popular clamors.

Lincoln tried to save the Constitution by being unconstitutional. Could today's government perhaps try to save the American democracy by being undemocratic? The Civil War was won by disregarding certain provisions of the Constitution.[134] Could the Cold War be won by denying certain aspects of modern democracy? Could rulers use their power to forestall future blunders that might be prompted by an irresponsible multitude, by putting that multitude in its place? This question basically amounts to asking whether or not the President as the major depository of

---

[132] This development in large measure may be due to the growth of the membership of the Senate, making that body too clumsy for the exercise of an effective foreign policy Cf. THE FEDERALIST, Nos. 64, 75. On the responsibility of Presidents since World War II, see the author's IN DEFENSE OF PROPERTY, 196ff.

[133] Chancellor Kent made this statement (see *supra*, 3) without the qualification added here when the basic freedom of democracy—and the continued existence of free democracy—was taken for granted. While Kent recognized that an increase of democratic rights might decrease liberal rights, he did not yet envisage—at least for the United States—a situation in which democracy could cause the defeat not only of free government, but of itself.

[134] See *supra*, 34ff.

popular power could use his office to deny aspects of democratic life in order to save the American democracy from foreign imperialism.

It is a touchy question. For such a use of power could easily be an abuse. It would not only be undemocratic, but also go far beyond the Constitution's concept of representation. Still, a President, faced with the annihilation of the United States, might see no other way out. The democratization of the Constitution and subsequent popular determination of foreign policy made obvious the improbability of classic representation on the one hand and the danger of plebiscitary representation on the other. Since classic representation wouldn't work and plebiscitary government has jeopardized the very existence of the United States, a President might well feel a need for existential representation in the sense of Hobbes.[135] As the existential representative of the people, he might well assume despotic powers in order to successfully lead the American democracy through crises threatening her very existence. Presidential dictatorship could assume a variety of forms. It could start out by promising the people some kind of millennium or great society. Later on, the President, seeing the security of the United States threatened and aware of the people's proclivity for immediate comfort, knowing that they do not want to recognize this danger, might do things he considers imperative for national survival, assuage the people by white lies, or take recourse to oppression. A slight credibility gap might be widened into a gulf between the ruler and the ruled, which by ordinary democratic standards is incredible. All this could conceivably come about under Presidents who are prompted by the mere desire to save the United States, just as Lincoln, when contravening the Constitution, may have been prompted by the desire to save the Union. If there can be no security through the freedom of the people,[136] a President might feel, perhaps security can be

---

[135] The concept of existential representation is dealt with by Voegelin, NEW SCIENCE OF POLITICS. For a discussion of Hobbes and Voegelin, see Heinz Laufer, "Homo homini homo," in Alois Dempf, Hannah Arendt, Friedrich Engel-Janosi (eds.), POLITISCHE ORDNUNG UND MENSCHLICHE EXISTENZ: FESTGABE FÜR ERIC VOEGELIN (München, 1962).

[136] Cf. Alpheus T. Mason, SECURITY THROUGH FREEDOM (Ithaca, N.Y., 1955); Woodford Howard, "Constitutional Limitation and American Foreign Policy," in Dietze, ESSAYS ON THE AMERICAN CONSTITUTION, 159; Harry H. Ransom, CAN AMERICAN DEMOCRACY SURVIVE THE COLD WAR? (Garden City, New York, 1964).

achieved by his own freedom to restrain and suppress the people. For reason of democratic state, he might argue, policy must be determined by his own reason rather than that of the *demos*.

Does this make the President the demon of foreign policy? Not necessarily. He might well secure national survival. His dictatorship might even be backed by those friends of free government for whom the American democracy, in spite of its curtailments of freedom, still contains sufficient liberal elements to warrant its defense from foreign aggression. These liberals, blaming the majority for having curbed liberal rights within the United States and for having brought about the decline of the United States as a world power, might well feel that a restriction of the *demos* is a *conditio sine qua non* for national security. Since the very survival of the United States has become jeopardized through popular license, presidential license might be considered justified, a risk worth taking.

While existential representation might not make the President the demon of foreign policy,[137] it might well make him the demon of democracy. History has shown that an increase of executive power in times of emergency does not necessarily diminish when the emergency is over. The assumption of dictatorial powers by President Lincoln had serious consequences for free government long after the Civil War.[138] There is no reason to believe that the result of presidential dictatorship in the Cold War would be less serious. Such a dictatorship might ensure the existence of the United States. Whether it will save democracy is open to doubt. To judge from the experience with constitutionalism since the Civil War, it will not. The constitutional tragedy spawned by that war might well be followed by a democratic tragedy brought forth by the Cold War, a war which sometimes has not been, and in the future may not be, so cold. Five-score years after the survival of the Union faced Lincoln with a constitutional dilemma, the question of the existence of the democratic nation he helped to build faces Americans with a democratic dilemma.

[137] Perhaps the word "might" ought to be emphasized. Our optimism is based upon the premise that an existential President will ensure the existence and the freedom of those whom he represents, from foreign powers. It is, of course, possible that such a President will make undue concessions to a foreign power and thus bring about an annihilation of national existence.

[138] See *supra*, 55ff.

8

AMERICA'S DEMOCRATIC DILEMMA

The American Dream envisaged a great challenge: The American people were to perpetuate the values of the American Revolution. That revolution, by abolishing monarchy, topped a long evolution toward popular government and, by adopting written constitutions, formalized the protection of the individual under the rule of law. It was not only the climax of English constitutional development, but, from a liberal point of view, also superior to the French Revolution. The American Revolution was the only modern revolution which unequivocally established free government. It was not supposed to be merely a static event. It was supposed to be dynamic and permanent. Americans would not rest on their laurels. They would expand free government. They would ensure the growing protection of the individuals from their rulers by broadening the popular basis of government. Living up to their challenge, the American people could make the United States the strongest power on earth. As the representative of the new world of free government, the United States would use her power for the emancipation of the world. She would spread freedom through self-government. The *Pax Americana* would not only be more extensive than the *Pax Romana*. It would be a higher, nobler dimension of its predecessor. Unlike Roman law, American law was not marred by the idea, *quod principi placuit legis habet vigorem*.[1] America was not only staunchly republican, but also subordinated the *ratio plebis* to the *ratio legis*. *Homo homini homo: non sub homine sed sub deo et lege.*[2]

---

[1] Justinian, DIGEST, I, 4, 1; INSTITUTIONS, I, 2, 6. A similar statement is Ulpian's *princeps legibus solutus est,* DIGEST, I, 3, 31. The thesis that the authoritarian features of the Roman law have been overrated is advanced in Charles H. McIlwain, CONSTITUTIONALISM ANCIENT AND MODERN, ch. 3, discussing the "constitutionalism" of Rome.

[2] The first sentence was coined by Laufer, "Homo homini homo"; the second can be found in Henry Bracton, DE LEGIBUS ET CONSUETUDINIBUS ANGLIAE, folio 5.

So far, the American Dream has not come true. This has been due in large measure to the fact that the *ratio plebis* increasingly was permitted to replace the *ratio legis*. The American Constitution has become democratized to a degree that makes people wonder whether it still embodies free government—implying the subordination of the democratic principle of popular government to the liberal principle of the protection of the individual from the government—or whether it stands for absolute democracy. This democratization had in its wake a *Relativierung* of constitutional values and the determination of these values by those in power. Property rights have been diminished, and "social" rights, promoted; democratic rights have been emphasized at the cost of liberal rights; "civil" rights have been elevated over civil rights. The *demos* has striven toward a more "active" government regulating individuals, and rejected Jefferson's ideal of a government which basically leaves the citizens "free to regulate their own pursuits of industry and improvement."[3] It has curtailed constitutional safeguards such as federalism, the separation of powers, and judicial review. Flexing its muscles, the American majority has conceived of the flexibility of the Constitution not so much in the sense of John Marshall, who wanted the principle of free government to be immune from change, but in that of Oliver Wendell Holmes, who made plain that even free government could be altered if the people wanted it.[4] Holmes indicated that democratization might result in proletarianization. It could be added that it might end up in vulgarization. Modern students of the United States wonder not only whether the U.S. might become a U.S.S.R. but also whether the principle, *lex, rex,* is about to be replaced by the principle, *sex, rex.*[5] The pursuit of temporary

---

[3] First Inaugural Address, WRITINGS, III, 321.

[4] See *supra,* 60, 69, 73f., 155f., 246n.

[5] Max Lerner, AMERICA AS A CIVILIZATION (New York, 1957), 679, speaks of the "American absorption with sex." Indeed one often gains the impression that the empire of laws of which Harrington spoke is being replaced by the empire of sex. Pitirim A. Sorokin, THE AMERICAN SEX REVOLUTION (Boston, 1956), considers the American preoccupation with sex the climactic expression of the disease of "sensate culture" which is spread throughout the Western world. He sees American sexual freedom leading to the inner collapse of the West and the conquest of America by outer barbarians, as in the case of the Roman empire.

pleasures and conveniences rather than of the long-range happiness that was desired by the Founders,[6] made illusory not only the hope that Americans would increase their freedom from their own government, but also jeopardized the survival of the United States from foreign aggression. So far, Americans failed to make the most of the rendezvous with destiny their Founding Fathers had. Indeed, their modern "rendezvous with destiny" may have destined them to an *après-vous* with the Soviet Union.[7]

Democracy, supposed to promote freedom from the government, has increasingly challenged that freedom. The more the democratic component of free government was permitted to grow, the more tenuous its liberal component became. The greater the democratic action, the smaller the constitutional option.[8] Democratic action frustrated a constitutionalist internal policy. It prevented a foreign policy according to constitutional reason. It thus seriously threatened the survival of freedom. But this has not been its only ill effect. It also jeopardized democratic principles themselves and may well turn out to be self-defeating. History has demonstrated that absolute democracy often ends up in monarchy. The United States need not be an exception to that rule. She could start out with an elected monarch. She could also accept an elected dynasty which could evolve into a hereditary monarchy.[9] After Lockean free government has been challenged by Rousseauistic democracy, Hobbesian monarchy could well be around the corner.

---

[6] On the meaning of the "pursuit of happiness" see *supra,* 64f.

[7] Eric F. Goldman, RENDEZVOUS WITH DESTINY (New York, 1952), lauds the New Deal. It matches the optimism of Harry L. Golden, ONLY IN AMERICA (Cleveland, Ohio, 1958) and ENJOY! ENJOY! (Cleveland, 1960). The author's doubts about Golden's optimism (IN DEFENSE OF PROPERTY, 3) also apply to Goldman's.

[8] Cf. *supra,* 83ff., 127ff., 160ff., 191ff., 212ff., 224ff.

[9] Cf. Stephen Hess, AMERICA'S POLITICAL DYNASTIES FROM ADAMS TO KENNEDY (Garden City, N.Y., 1966). Amaury de Riencourt, THE COMING CAESARS (New York, 1957), advances the opinion that the presidency eventually will develop into an American version of the Roman emperor. He traces this trend back to the Jacksonian era, when the presidency began to derive its power and influence from the masses of people. Jefferson resented the "perpetual re-eligibility of the President. This I fear, will make that an office for life, first, and then hereditary." To Washington on May 2, 1788. WRITINGS, VI, 454. Franklin D. Roosevelt was a President for life. The Twenty-second Amendment precludes a presidency for life. It does not preclude a presidency in the hands of a dynasty.

An inquiry into the causes for this development raises the question of the rationality of American government and takes us to the problem of representation. America's Founders had hoped that the representative government they designed, a government which to Madison, the "father of the Constitution," implied a refinement of the public views, would create a democratic challenge which would realize the American Dream. As it was, this kind of government in practice became increasingly replaced by some sort of plebiscitary democracy which had been advocated by Rousseau, who considered representation an adulteration of the general will.[10] Now a refinement is an alteration. Without doubt, representative government is an alteration of direct democracy. From the democratic point of view, it even is an adulteration. However, since according to the *ratio* of constitutionalism, the rationale for democracy is the protection of the individual, it is not democracy but only *rational* democracy which can be the yardstick.[11] What matters is mainly the degree to which democracy can be expected to secure the protection of the individual from internal and external attacks. It is not the sheer rule of the general will that counts, but that will's reasonable protection of freedom.[12] Reputed for their wisdom,[13] the Founding Fathers formed a government which they hoped would ensure for the people a maximal use of their abilities under the rule of law. They preferred a refined to a rudimentary popular government—a representative, predominantly rational, to a direct, more emotional democracy. Feeling that representation would provide for rational government, the Founders thought they could afford a system which, on account of its checks and balances and divisions of power, was rather sophisticated and complicated. Such a government was ill suited to a plebiscitary democracy which was likely to resent and to diminish its major features as impediments

---

[10] CONTRAT SOCIAL, Bk. III, ch. 15. POLITICAL WRITINGS, II, 95ff.

[11] The *ratio constitutionalis*, or *ratio legis* of constitutionalism, corresponds to Coke's artificial reason of the law. Cf. *supra*, 8.

[12] The individual thus cannot be forced to be free, as Rousseau would have it. Had Rousseau lived to see the cruelty of the French Revolution, he might well have gotten second thoughts on some of his statements. His writings must be understood against the background of monarchical and aristocratic absolutism. See Cobban, ROUSSEAU AND THE MODERN STATE.

[13] See *supra*, 12.

to democratic action. The free government framed at Philadelphia was a tender fabric which could be run only by reasonable men, which the representatives of the people hopefully were. Rousseau had argued that classic representation adulterated democracy. In the United States, the representative popular government as it was defended in *The Federalist*[14] has been adulterated by democracy.

It is conceivable that the diminution of rational government which was likely to result from the replacement of classic representation by a more plebiscitary one, could have been made up by creating a more reasonable electorate. An improvement of the public's rationality probably was in Jefferson's mind when he stressed the value of education for the democratic process.[15] Although education is no substitute for common sense and intelligence, it will generally promote the rationality of democracy. While, in view of the fact that "human nature does not change,"[16] education perhaps cannot change "human action"[17] so as to guarantee the preponderance of reason over emotion, it usually will further that preponderance. Has it increased the reason of the American people to a degree that would justify the replacement of classic by plebiscitary representation? In answering this question, we must keep in mind that the rationality of a government is relative to its present circumstances. Although less rationality is required for running a simple, small, agricultural society than for ruling a complicated, large, industrial one, the government of the former, even if from an absolute point of view it is less saturated with rational features than that of the latter, can still be more rational and successful than its modern counterpart. Since American society has become very complex, a replacement of representative by plebiscitary government could thus be justified only if the education of the electorate has considerably improved.

[14] Cf. THE FEDERALIST, Nos. 9, 10, 14, 35, 52–64, 68.

[15] To John Adams, Oct. 28, 1813. WRITINGS, XIII, 394, esp. 399ff. This letter also contains Jefferson's remarks on natural aristocracy. While Jefferson favored a rule of the majority, he stipulated that it be reasonable. First Inaugural Address, WRITINGS, III, 318.

[16] Voegelin, NEW SCIENCE OF POLITICS, 165.

[17] Ludwig von Mises, HUMAN ACTION (3d rev. ed.; Chicago, 1966), is an exposition of individualism which supports our argument against democratic action.

This is hardly the case. Today's electorate is not much better educated than its counterpart during the eighteenth and early nineteenth centuries. Today's voters may know more about more things; their knowledge probably is not as deep. Even if it is, it probably has not increased in proportion to the complexities of the society. To judge by the growth of these complexities, the general knowledge of the American public, like that of other societies, has probably fallen farther and farther behind. The trend toward specialization proves this. A little knowledge is a dangerous thing. It decreased the possibility of a rational understanding of the present and future life of the United States. It made the American people a "lonely crowd"[18] that has lost touch with—and wants to get away from—the realities of rational existence and seeks refuge in an emotional, often "rationalized," dream world.

While the impact of popular emotions upon the government was not decreased by education, it was increased by the extension of the suffrage.[19] Even if one agrees with the generally accepted opinion that there ought to be no property qualifications,[20] one can hardly deny that their abolition watered down the rationality of the electorate. As a rule, property owners are more reasonable than those who have no property, for it generally takes more brains to acquire and keep property than not to acquire or lose it. Even if one agrees with the generally accepted opinion that suffrage should not be restricted on account of race, color, or previous condition of servitude, one can hardly deny that the Fifteenth Amendment extended the right to vote to a relatively uneducated part of the population whose rationality was likely to be affected by their want of education.[21] The same applies to the

[18] Cf. David Riesman, THE LONELY CROWD (New Haven, Conn., 1950).

[19] Cf. Kirk H. Porter, A HISTORY OF SUFFRAGE IN THE UNITED STATES (Chicago, 1918). More general treatises are W. J. Shepard, "Suffrage," ENCYCLOPEDIA OF THE SOCIAL SCIENCES, XIV, 447; Georg Meyer, DAS PARLAMENTARISCHE WAHLRECHT (Berlin, 1901).

[20] For risks involved in the abolition of property qualifications, see the author's IN DEFENSE OF PROPERTY, 146ff.

[21] Regrettably, this has not been changed to this day. There is a long way to go toward the realization of Jefferson's plan of giving every citizen that minimum of education which is necessary for a rational democracy. Educational tests for the right to vote, impartially administered to *all* citizens, could increase the rationality of popular government.

bulk of immigrants. Leaving the old country because they could not make a satisfactory living, they usually were ignorant of American government and national interests, and often were influenced by the emotional appeal of political machines.[22] Although on the European continent, democracy has been safest in Switzerland which has not permitted women to vote to this day, the Nineteenth Amendment is fair enough. Still, it decreased the rationality of the electorate. Women generally are less rational than men. It was in large measure the emotionalism of American women in 1945 which prompted the demobilization of American military forces, a demobilization that turned out to be detrimental to the national interest. It has been said that education for all is no education at all. It could be added that suffrage for all, i.e., suffering all, means suffering for all—the kind of suffering we described.[23]

The preceding paragraphs indicate that America's democratic challenge has turned into a democratic dilemma. The extension of

[22] Cf. Lurton, "A Government of Law or a Government of Men?," 17.

[23] Perhaps it ought to be added that the extension of the suffrage, implying a stronger emotional impact upon the government, resulted not only in a growing replacement of classic representation through plebiscitary democracy—something formal—but also in the increasing substitution of free government through social democracy,—something substantive. This was natural, for social democracy is as suited to plebiscitary democracy as free government is to classic representation. While the extension of the suffrage gave the vote to more and more individuals, it favored collectivism rather than individualism. Much as those to whom suffrage was extended wanted to become free, they in a large measure were people who would profit from collectivism rather than individualism. Those who had no property, and perhaps debts, having been used to lean on their fellow men to provide them with a living and not to collect debts, now were likely to lean upon the state for providing them with a living, annulling their debts and giving them property. Having been taken care of by their former masters, the emancipated slaves were likely to want to be taken care of by society. The immigrant, often a servant, pauper, or debtor in the old country, was likely to lean on the collective that emancipated him. Women, naturally leaning on men, were likely to expect more things from the government than men. While it cannot be denied that the extension of the suffrage to the groups mentioned set many individuals free who pursued their own aims at their own risk, the percentage of individualists in these groups is probably rather small. As a consequence, the extension of the suffrage contributed toward developing the United States from an individualistic to a more collectivistic society, from a laissez faire economy to that of a welfare state. Rather than taking care of themselves, more and more people trusted the government to take care of them. The New Freedom, the New Deal, and the New Frontier may have promoted collectivism and the welfare state; they also resulted from popular desires toward such a development.

265

the suffrage cannot well be criticized. It corresponds to the American Dream which provides for an increasing protection of freedom through a broadening of democracy. And yet that extension, by diminishing the rationality of the government, prevented the realization of the Dream because it not only failed to increase, but actually decreased, the protection of the individual from his own as well as foreign governments. Also, one cannot find fault with the growth of the United States. That growth is part of the American Dream. And yet, the complexities it brought about made rational government less probable and jeopardized constitutionalist features such as federalism, the separation of powers, and judicial review, and thus again frustrated the Dream. These trends will continue. American society will become even more complex, and the suffrage will be extended even further.[24] Government will become even less reasonable. Attempts to compensate for this by an increasing "rationalization" of the government will render the latter more and more monolithic to the detriment not only of freedom, but also of democracy.

Since the march of democracy seems to make this development inevitable, it is difficult to pinpoint responsibility and guilt. To be sure, to be is to be guilty. Somehow humans, who as reasonable beings are responsible for their actions, live always in guilt, and the ethical man will always worry about this guilt. This must be kept in mind if people are not considered guilty for what they have been doing or have permitted to be done by others. For, as far as American political development over the generations is concerned, a verdict of "not guilty" is generally in order.[25]

The people themselves hardly can be blamed for what has happened. It is a paradox that while in a democracy power is vested in the people, no responsibility can usually be pinned upon them. America's development from a free to a democratic govern-

---

[24] A reduction of age qualifications for voting would diminish the rationality of the electorate further. Youngsters generally are less educated, less mature, less reasonable than their elders. So far American parents often suffer from the irrational demands of their children. Should suffrage be extended to a younger age group, the whole nation might suffer from these immature demands. The Nineteenth Amendment increased the chances of a political candidate with good looks irrespective of brains. The lowering of the voting age increases the chances for the election of bobby soxers' idols.

[25] Our emphasis in the following will be on the *general* development, as distinguished from that over short periods.

ment, while it was due to democratic action, did not incriminate the *demos*. The people trusted that the extension of the suffrage, the replacement of classic by a more plebiscitary representation, their requests for curtailments of federalism, the separation of powers and judicial review, for the welfare state and a democratic foreign policy, were as legitimate as they were legal. Even moral guilt hardly can be said to exist. The democratic component of free government increased at the expense of the liberal component only gradually, over the generations. Since this took place under a popular government which supposedly was to expand, it was unlikely to stir up controversy. Those responsible probably hoped that emphasis upon broadening democracy would increase freedom. At any rate, they generally felt sure that such emphasis was well within the bounds of free government. Like the New Generation that permitted American power to wane since World War II, the Old Generation at times may have had a moral guilt for certain specific events. It cannot well be blamed for the gradual, extended process of the replacement of free government by social democracy.

Caution also must prevail concerning the guilt of the ordinary representatives of the people. While those men may be guilty for specific actions during short spans of time, such as the blunders in foreign policy since World War II, the situation is different with respect to the over-all development in the United States. The representatives cannot well be blamed for extending the suffrage and for complying with popular demands in other respects. To be sure, under the Constitution they were supposed to follow their own conscience rather than those demands. On the other hand, the growth of democracy and the growing pressure of an increasingly irrational electorate probably made it increasingly difficult for them to keep their heads clear, especially since the judges— supposedly the most rational interpreters of the Constitution— developed from platonic guardians of the rule of law to courtiers of the *demos*. Again, while we do not want to diminish the responsibility of the judiciary,[26] it would be unfair not to consider exten-

---

[26] See *supra*, 152ff.; Hayek, CONSTITUTION OF LIBERTY, ch. 16. Goldwater, "My Case for the Republican Party," 23, stated that "of all three branches of government, today's Supreme Court is the least faithful to the constitutional tradition of limited government, and to the principle of legitimacy in the exercise of power."

uating circumstances. Under pressure from the popular majority, the judges for a long time held out for the protection of the individual from the government. When the Robe finally capitulated before the popular vogue, it was only under the duress of Roosevelt's court-packing plan.

This leaves the question of the guilt of a few democratic leaders who perhaps were seducers of the people. It takes us to the innovators of whom the young Lincoln had warned when he admonished his countrymen to abide by the law of the Constitution.[27] Lincoln himself became an innovator during the Civil War, and the question of his guilt has been raised. The problem of guilt must also be raised in the case of Presidents who explicitly favored the "New"—be it in the form of a New Freedom, or a New Deal, or a New Frontier. They made the people believe that perhaps only the new was true and that traditional free government was false. While it cannot be denied that their programs were geared to the proclivities of the people, the question arises whether they exploited these proclivities, especially in emergencies, and whether they unduly overstepped the Constitution by emphasizing democracy at the cost of free government. The New Freedom sowed a dangerous seed. However, Wilson probably did not want democracy to extend beyond the principle of free government. His administration was one of constitutional government.[28] On the other hand, Roosevelt's administration in many respects was detrimental to free government and was, not without justification, denounced as democratic despotism.[29] Kennedy continued Roosevelt's program. Had he remained alive, there might have been a Kennedy dynasty.[30] But again, mitigating circumstances must be considered. The fact that Roosevelt and Kennedy ruled during the emergencies of the Depression,

[27] *Supra*, 51f.

[28] The author of CONGRESSIONAL GOVERNMENT (Boston, 1885), attacking Congress, also wrote CONSTITUTIONAL GOVERNMENT IN THE UNITED STATES, praising the latter.

[29] Desvernine, DEMOCRATIC DESPOTISM.

[30] Hess, AMERICA'S POLITICAL DYNASTIES, 528, writes that upon winning the Democratic nomination, John F. Kennedy gave his brother Robert a cigarette box with the inscription: "When I'm through, how about You?" Robert Kennedy, when asked about the meaning of that inscription, answered that it did not imply a succession in the presidency, but rather the general idea of what he planned to do as a human being.

World War II, and the Cold War, could decrease their guilt, although that guilt could increase if they took advantage of those situations. Also, their guilt might be lessened—small as this possibility seems to be—if they merely considered themselves obligated to execute the will of the majority under the new, democratized, Constitution. Thus perhaps even those who can be blamed for America's political plight the most may be allowed some benefit of the doubt. While they probably exploited the march of democracy and unduly accelerated it, they also may have been driven by the democratic thrust.

Guilt or no guilt: there is not much doubt about the tragedy of American political development. This development runs in a cycle of stages of about one hundred years' length. The first stage, beginning with the American Revolution, was characterized by free government. The second stage, starting with the Civil War, brought democracy. The 1970s and 1980s may well initiate the third, monarchical, stage.[31] Today, the United States perhaps is "halfway to 1984."[32] The tragedy is obvious: the two hundredth anniversary of the American Revolution may turn out to witness the abolition of the major values of that revolution. Lincoln's sad expression, visible in his last photographs, may have been due to his evisaging tragedy for the Constitution he said he cherished. Americans today, captured in the truthfulness of their tragic existence by America's greatest painter,[33] probably see tragedy

---

[31] This does not deny that democracy may have increased already during the first stage, that aspects of free government may have persisted in the second stage, and that some features of democracy and free government may exist in the monarchical stage. Perhaps the American development can also be seen in the framework of the English evolution which witnessed constitutionalist revolts in the thirteenth and seventeenth centuries. If the four-hundred-year cycle holds, there will be a new *diffidatio* during the next century.

[32] Gladwyn Jebb, HALFWAY TO 1984 (New York 1966), asserts this of the world in general. According to Hess, AMERICA'S POLITICAL DYNASTIES, 528, a joke during the Kennedy administration was: "We'll have Jack for eight years, Bobby for eight, and Teddy for eight. Then it'll be 1984." This is no laughing matter.

[33] It has been said that upon a tragic experience in 1945, Andrew Wyeth changed from impressionistically depicting "the exuberance of life and joy" to "more austere" works that were a "clear, objective vehicle of expression." (Edgar P. Richardson in Pennsylvania Academy of the Fine Arts [ed.], ANDREW WYETH [New York, 1966], 10, 20). Perhaps this change is symbolic for the change in the United States during that year from the exuberance of life and joy following the successful conclusion of World War II to the recognition of the harsh truth that from now on America would decline and that the American Dream would come to an end. A

ahead not only for their own existence, but also for a democratic way of life which to many of them—lonely as they find themselves to be in, and against, the crowd—no longer makes sense.

The fact that America's democratic challenge has turned into her democratic dilemma does not mean that a democratic challenge would no longer exist. Quite to the contrary. That challenge is greater now than it ever was before not only because what will happen in the United States could determine the fate of the earth, but also, because the task ahead is far more difficult. Previously, the democratic challenge implied the natural development of broadening democracy for the sake of freedom. Today, it implies the artistic undertaking of curtailing, or at least containing, democracy for the sake of freedom. Difficult as the latter may be in view of the democratic tide, it is not impossible. Wisdom can defy historical rules. It did so during the American Revolution which brought forth the American Dream. The Founding Fathers restricted majority rule for the sake of minority rights. This could happen again, for many people recognize their plight.[34] The task will be more arduous than during the formative period, although it was hard enough then. Today's electorate is less rational. People are less imbued with free government and the idea that democracy is a mere means for the protection of the individual and not an end in itself. They do not generally believe that the majority can be wrong. Not a few people in a few states but the whole mass of the population of a big Nation—a democratic majority that is more firmly entrenched than it was during the revolutionary era—must be coped with and convinced. On the

---

similar change took place earlier in Europe. The impressionist painters, while indicating disintegration and yet trying to smooth it over by impressing upon the spectator the illusion (Wickoff) that things were pleasant enough (see José Ortega y Gasset, "Meier-Graefe," "Del realismo en pintura," and "Tiempo, distancia y forma en el arte de Proust," OBRAS COMPLETAS [Madrid, 1946–47], I, 96, 560; II, 699), were followed by the more realistic expressionists who depicted existential tragedy. European painters thus are representative of the *fin de siècle,* as Wyeth perhaps is of the end of the American century. Although he was preceded by American impressionists and expressionists, the "truth of the object" (Richardson, ANDREW WYETH, 10) in tragedy is the most evident in his work.

[34] The general recognition Wyeth gained in spite of his refusal to please his more fashionable critics, inspires confidence. It shows that a substantial portion of the American people resist being lulled into a dream world.

other hand, the fact that in our day democracy has advanced to a stage in which it is ready to degenerate into monarchy, may provide the friends of free government with an additional stimulus that perhaps could achieve the wonder of convincing the majority that democracy, much as it is a *forma formarum,* still is nothing but a form that derives its justification from having freedom for its substance.

The American people basically have a great deal of common sense.[35] Emotional and passionate as the American *demos* may have become, it still is composed of rational beings who might again prefer the permanent public good to temporary conveniences. The opportunistic egoism of the masses, often camouflaged by dubious appeals to the "public good," still could make room for a truly altruistic policy that will further the rights of the individual and thus serve the public good in the long run. Reason might again prevail over emotions and passions. As during the formative period, political science might again purify politics.[36] It could restore those typical American features of constitutionalism—federalism, the separation of powers, and judicial review. It could reconfirm free government with its inherent protection of all the rights of the individual from the government. It could invigorate the rule of law which in the democratic era has been damaged not only by the kind of lawlessness of which the young Lincoln complained,[37] but also by a fraudulent legality as it became reflected in democratic laws, rules, and regulations. It could revive the vital center of free government by repudiating trends which from the point of view of the American heritage, have gone off center.[38] To use an expression by Jefferson, it could steer the

[35] See MacArthur's speech in Cleveland on Sept. 6, 1951 (REPRESENTATIVE SPEECHES, 39), and Courtney Whitney, MACARTHUR (New York, 1956), 503ff.

[36] Regrettably, more and more political scientists believe in a "value-free" science. Content with describing and analyzing politics, they sanction the latter. Against this trend are Friedrich, MAN AND HIS GOVERNMENT, and Voegelin, NEW SCIENCE OF POLITICS.

[37] *Supra,* 24f.

[38] The vital center we have in mind is to be distinguished from that advocated in Arthur M. Schlesinger, Jr., THE VITAL CENTER (Boston, 1949), which favors social democracy. Schlesinger, a prominent member of the Americans for Democratic Action, advised President Kennedy. While without doubt the center of American politics has moved toward social democracy, we feel that this trend has devitalized the center. This devitalization in a large measure is due to

American "argosy"[39] safely into port to be ready for new exploits. In the preceding pages, we crossed a lot of sea, and the reader may often have wondered whether America might go down. However, "they are ill discoverers that think there is no land, when they see nothing but sea," wrote Bacon, the great antagonist of Coke.[40] Ships sink, but there always is land. And while America may founder in the turbulences of democracy, there is firm ground to be regained. It is the *terra firma* of a Constitution which embodies the reason of the common law as it matured over the ages, an artful, and not just artificial, reason which stands in strong contrast to the often irrational actions of the living and their leaders, actions which are comparable to the ever shifting and often turbulent waves of the sea. While America's free polity has been jeopardized by those that sought (as they termed it) the reformation of the laws, it may still be saved.[41] Free government may still prevail in the United States and even become the common law of the world, a world which probably cannot remain half slave and half free.[42]

So far, the American Dream has not come true. This in no way discredits Americans who are—and basically want to be—like

---

the disparagement of property rights, implying men's reluctance to work because they feel the government will take care of them anyway. The transfer of power from the oldest President ever to leave office to the youngest President ever to assume office, is perhaps symbolic for the taking over of the New Generation from the old. The latter basically believed in getting things through effort. The New Generation more and more expects things without effort. Perhaps this explains Kennedy's popularity among that generation. Here was a man who—in contrast to the self-made man, Eisenhower—got far without much effort, as he was born to riches. One of his favorite plays was HOW TO SUCCEED IN BUSINESS WITHOUT REALLY TRYING. This more and more is becoming the dream of the New Generation. See the author's IN DEFENSE OF PROPERTY, 187ff.

[39] To John Dickinson, March 6, 1801, WRITINGS, X, 217. In his First Inaugural, Jefferson also indicated the course to be taken: "Let us, then, with courage and confidence pursue our own federal and republican principles, our attachments to our union, and representative government." WRITINGS, III, 320.

[40] ADVANCEMENT OF LEARNING, II: vii, 5. The quotation is the *leitmotif* of Lippmann's THE PUBLIC PHILOSOPHY, a book which in many respects supports the ideas here expressed.

[41] On Coke's concept of the artificial reason of the law, see *supra*, 8. Hooker's words, quoted *supra*, vi, can be found in LAWS OF ECCLESIASTICAL POLITY, I, 77.

[42] Cf. Lincoln's "House Divided Speeches," *supra*, 42. Should the values of constitutionalism prevail, Locke's words that "in the beginning all the World was *America*," TWO TREATISES, 319, could become complemented by the fact that in the end all the world became America.

other people. Their first President, while hoping for a realization of the Dream, also stated that this aim might not be achieved and that democracy in America could well develop the way it usually did in other parts of the globe.[43] As a matter of fact, the American Dream has faded away. A need has been seen for reclaiming it.[44] Whether it will be reclaimed remains to be seen. Whether its realization was doubtful from the beginning because it was, after all, a dream, is another question.[45]

[43] In 1789, Washington, reflecting on the system set up by the Constitution, stated: "I . . . cannot undertake to decide . . . what may be its ultimate fate. If a promised good should terminate in an unexpected evil, it would not be a solitary example of disappointment . . . If the blessings of Heaven showered thick around us should be spilled on the ground or converted to curses, through the fault of those for whom they were intended, it would not be the first instance of folly or perverseness in short-sighted mortals." Proposed Address to Congress, WRITINGS, XXX, 301.

[44] Cf. Richard C. Cornuelle, RECLAIMING THE AMERICAN DREAM (New York, 1965). After expressing hope that the United States would be a rallying point for the reason and freedom of the globe, Jefferson had written: "I like the dreams of the future better than the history of the past,—so good night! I will dream on . . ." To John Adams on Aug. 1, 1816. WRITINGS, XV, 59. Hayek, believing in the liberal civilization, addressed his CONSTITUTION OF LIBERTY "To the unknown civilization that is growing in America," obviously feeling that the known civilization America had when liberalism was the essence of the American way of life, has been fading away.

[45] See Voegelin, NEW SCIENCE OF POLITICS; ORDER AND HISTORY (Baton Rouge, La., 1956–   ); SCIENCE, POLITICS AND GNOSTICISM (Chicago, 1968).

.

SELECTED BIBLIOGRAPHY

SOURCES

Charles Francis Adams (ed.), THE WORKS OF JOHN ADAMS (Boston, 1850–56).

Roy P. Basler (ed.), THE COLLECTED WORKS OF ABRAHAM LINCOLN (New Brunswick, N.J., 1953).

Edmund C. Burnett (ed.), LETTERS OF THE MEMBERS OF THE CONTINENTAL CONGRESS (Washington, 1921–36).

Henry Steele Commager (ed.), DOCUMENTS OF AMERICAN HISTORY (7th ed.; New York, 1963).

Richard K. Cralle (ed.), THE WORKS OF JOHN C. CALHOUN (New York, 1853–59).

Jonathan Elliot (ed.), THE DEBATES, RESOLUTIONS AND OTHER PROCEEDINGS IN CONVENTION ON THE ADOPTION OF THE FEDERAL CONSTITUTION (Washington, 1876).

Max Farrand (ed.), THE RECORDS OF THE FEDERAL CONVENTION (New Haven, 1911).

John C. Fitzpatrick (ed.), THE WRITINGS OF GEORGE WASHINGTON (Washington, 1931–44).

Paul Leicester Ford (ed.), PAMPHLETS ON THE CONSTITUTION OF THE UNITED STATES (Brooklyn, 1888).

Worthington Chauncey Ford (ed.), JOURNALS OF THE CONTINENTAL CONGRESS 1774–89 (Washington, 1904–37).

Alexander Hamilton, James Madison, John Jay, THE FEDERALIST (Modern Library ed.; New York, 1937).

Gaillard Hunt (ed.), THE WRITINGS OF JAMES MADISON (New York, 1900–10).

Henry P. Johnston (ed.), THE CORRESPONDENCE AND PUBLIC PAPERS OF JOHN JAY (New York, 1890–93).

Andrew A. Lipscomb (ed.), THE WRITINGS OF THOMAS JEFFERSON (Washington, 1903–4).

Henry Cabot Lodge (ed.), THE WORKS OF ALEXANDER HAMILTON (New York, 1904).

William S. Myers (ed.), THE STATE PAPERS AND OTHER PUBLIC WRITINGS OF HERBERT HOOVER (New York, 1934).

Hezekiah Niles (ed.), PRINCIPLES AND ACTS OF THE REVOLUTION (Baltimore, 1822).

Office of the Federal Register (ed.), PUBLIC PAPERS OF THE PRESIDENTS (Washington, 1961–   ).

SELECTED BIBLIOGRAPHY

James D. Richardson (ed.), MESSAGES AND PAPERS OF THE PRESIDENTS (Washington, 1897–1927).

Samuel I. Rosenman (ed.), THE PUBLIC PAPERS AND ADDRESSES OF FRANKLIN D. ROOSEVELT (New York, 1938–50).

Francis N. Thorpe (ed.), THE FEDERAL AND STATE CONSTITUTIONS, COLONIAL CHARTERS, AND OTHER ORGANIC LAWS OF THE STATE, TERRITORIES, AND COLONIES NOW OR HERETOFORE FORMING THE UNITED STATES OF AMERICA (Washington, 1909).

SECONDARY WORKS

Randolph G. Adams, POLITICAL IDEAS OF THE AMERICAN REVOLUTION (Durham, N.C., 1922).

Association of American Law Schools (ed.), SELECTED ESSAYS ON CONSTITUTIONAL LAW (Chicago, 1938).

Charles A. Beard and Mary Beard, THE RISE OF AMERICAN CIVILIZATION (New York, 1927–39).

Carl L. Becker, THE DECLARATION OF INDEPENDENCE (New York, 1922).

H. Hale Bellot, AMERICAN HISTORY AND AMERICAN HISTORIANS (London, 1952).

Daniel J. Boorstin, THE IMAGE OR WHAT HAPPENED TO THE AMERICAN DREAM (New York, 1962).

Orestes A. Brownson, THE AMERICAN REPUBLIC, ITS CONSTITUTION, TENDENCIES, AND DESTINY (New York, 1865).

James Bryce, THE AMERICAN COMMONWEALTH (2d ed.; London, 1891).

John W. Burgess, RECENT CHANGES IN AMERICAN CONSTITUTIONAL THEORY (New York, 1923).

Roger Burlingame, THE AMERICAN CONSCIENCE (New York, 1957).

Edward McNall Burns, THE AMERICAN IDEA OF MISSION (New Brunswick, N.J., 1957).

Andrew Carnegie, TRIUMPHANT DEMOCRACY (New York, 1886).

William S. Carpenter, THE DEVELOPMENT OF AMERICAN POLITICAL THOUGHT (Princeton, N.J., 1930).

Zechariah Chafee, HOW HUMAN RIGHTS GOT INTO THE CONSTITUTION (Boston, 1952).

John Chamberlain, FAREWELL TO REFORM (New York, 1932).

Thomas C. Cochran and William Miller, THE AGE OF ENTERPRISE (New York, 1942).

Thomas I. Cook and Malcolm Moos, POWER THROUGH PURPOSE (Baltimore, 1955).

Thomas M. Cooley, A TREATISE ON THE CONSTITUTIONAL LIMITATIONS WHICH REST UPON THE LEGISLATIVE POWER OF THE STATES OF THE AMERICAN UNION (5th ed.; Boston, 1883).

———— THE GENERAL PRINCIPLES OF CONSTITUTIONAL LAW IN THE UNITED STATES OF AMERICA (Boston, 1880).

Archibald C. Coolidge, THEORETICAL AND FOREIGN ELEMENTS IN THE FORMATION OF THE AMERICAN CONSTITUTION (Freiburg i. B., 1892).

Richard C. Cornuelle, RECLAIMING THE AMERICAN DREAM (New York, 1965).

Edward S. Corwin, LIBERTY AGAINST GOVERNMENT (Baton Rouge, La., 1951).

Edward S. Corwin, THE CONSTITUTION OF THE UNITED STATES OF AMERICA: ANALYSIS AND INTERPRETATION (Washington, 1953).

William W. Crosskey, POLITICS AND THE CONSTITUTION IN THE HISTORY OF THE UNITED STATES (Chicago, 1953).

Merle Curti, THE GROWTH OF AMERICAN THOUGHT (3d ed.; New York, 1964).

Donald Davidson, THE ATTACK ON LEVIATHAN (Chapel Hill, N.C., 1938).

Raoul E. Desvernine, DEMOCRATIC DESPOTISM (New York, 1936).

Joseph Dorfman, THE ECONOMIC MIND IN AMERICAN CIVILIZATION (New York, 1946–59).

Norman Dorsen, Thomas I. Emerson and David Haber, POLITICAL AND CIVIL RIGHTS IN THE UNITED STATES (3d ed.; Boston, 1967).

Georges Duhamel, AMERICA THE MENACE (Boston, 1931).

Durand Echeverria, MIRAGE IN THE WEST (Princeton, N.J., 1957).

Paul H. B. d'Estournelles de Constant, AMERICA AND HER PROBLEMS (New York, 1918).

Sidney Fine, LAISSEZ FAIRE AND THE GENERAL-WELFARE STATE (Ann Arbor, Mich., 1956).

Herman Finer, AMERICA'S DESTINY (New York, 1947).

Carl J. Friedrich, CONSTITUTIONAL GOVERNMENT AND DEMOCRACY (rev. ed.; Boston, 1950).

——— MAN AND HIS GOVERNMENT (New York, 1963).

Daniel R. Fusfeld, THE ECONOMIC THOUGHT OF FRANKLIN D. ROOSEVELT AND THE ORIGINS OF THE NEW DEAL (New York, 1956).

Ralph H. Gabriel, THE COURSE OF AMERICAN DEMOCRATIC THOUGHT (New York, 1940).

John A. Garraty (ed.), QUARRELS THAT HAVE SHAPED THE CONSTITUTION (New York, 1964).

J. A. C. Grant, OUR COMMON LAW CONSTITUTION (Boston, 1960).

John Gunther, INSIDE U.S.A. (rev. ed.; New York, 1951).

Robert J. Harris, THE QUEST FOR EQUALITY (Baton Rouge, La., 1960).

Louis Hartz, THE LIBERAL TRADITION IN AMERICA (New York, 1955).

Friedrich A. Hayek, THE ROAD TO SERFDOM (London, 1944).

——— THE CONSTITUTION OF LIBERTY (Chicago, 1960).

Homer C. Hockett, POLITICAL AND SOCIAL GROWTH OF THE AMERICAN PEOPLE 1492–1865 (3d ed.; New York, 1940).

Richard Hofstadter, SOCIAL DARWINISM IN AMERICAN THOUGHT (rev. ed.; Boston, 1955).

John C. Hurd, THE THEORY OF OUR NATIONAL EXISTENCE (Boston, 1881).

Thomas Paul Jenkin, REACTIONS OF MAJOR GROUPS TO POSITIVE GOVERNMENT IN THE UNITED STATES, 1930–1940 (Berkeley, 1945).

Paul G. Kauper, CONSTITUTIONAL LAW (3d ed.; Boston, 1966).

Alfred H. Kelly (ed.), AMERICAN FOREIGN POLICY AND AMERICAN DEMOCRACY (Detroit, 1954).

Edgar Kemler, THE DEFLATION OF AMERICAN IDEALS (Washington, 1941).

James Kent, COMMENTARIES ON AMERICAN LAW (3d ed.; New York, 1836).

Harold J. Laski, THE AMERICAN DEMOCRACY (New York, 1948).

Max Lerner, AMERICA AS A CIVILIZATION (New York, 1957).

E. R. Lewis, A HISTORY OF AMERICAN POLITICAL THOUGHT FROM THE CIVIL WAR TO THE WORLD WAR (New York, 1937).

Walter Lippmann, PUBLIC OPINION (New York, 1922).

Charles H. McIlwain, THE AMERICAN REVOLUTION, A CONSTITUTIONAL INTERPRETATION (New York, 1923).

Andrew C. McLaughlin, A CONSTITUTIONAL HISTORY OF THE UNITED STATES (New York, 1935).

—— THE COURTS, THE CONSTITUTION AND PARTIES (Chicago, 1912).

Frederick W. Maitland, THE CONSTITUTIONAL HISTORY OF ENGLAND (Cambridge, 1908).

Dumas Malone and Basil Rauch, EMPIRE FOR LIBERTY (New York, 1960).

Alpheus T. Mason, FREE GOVERNMENT IN THE MAKING (3d ed.; New York, 1965).

—— THE STATES RIGHTS DEBATE: ANTIFEDERALISM AND THE CONSTITUTION (Englewood Cliffs, N.J., 1964).

André Maurois, THE MIRACLE OF AMERICA (New York, 1944).

Charles E. Merriam, A HISTORY OF AMERICAN POLITICAL THEORIES (New York, 1903).

John C. Miller, ORIGINS OF THE AMERICAN REVOLUTION (Stanford, 1957).

Edwin Mims, THE MAJORITY OF THE PEOPLE (New York, 1941).

James Monroe, THE PEOPLE THE SOVEREIGNS; BEING A COMPARISON OF THE GOVERNMENT OF THE UNITED STATES WITH THOSE OF THE REPUBLICS WHICH HAVE EXISTED BEFORE, WITH THE CAUSES OF THEIR DECADENCE AND FALL (Philadelphia, 1867).

Samuel E. Morison and Henry S. Commager, THE GROWTH OF THE AMERICAN REPUBLIC (5th ed.; New York, 1962).

Felix Morley, THE FOREIGN POLICY OF THE UNITED STATES (New York, 1951).

Gunnar Myrdal, AN AMERICAN DILEMMA (rev. ed.; New York, 1962).

Allan Nevins, THE EMERGENCE OF MODERN AMERICA, 1865–1878 (New York, 1927).

Vernon L. Parrington, MAIN CURRENTS IN AMERICAN THOUGHT (New York, 1927–30).

Dexter Perkins, FOREIGN POLICY AND THE AMERICAN SPIRIT (Ithaca, N.Y., 1957).

Ralph B. Perry, PURITANISM AND DEMOCRACY (New York, 1944).

Florence A. Pooke, FOUNTAIN-SOURCES OF AMERICAN POLITICAL THEORY (New York, 1930).

Édouard Portalis, LES ÉTATS-UNIS (Paris, 1869).

Roscoe Pound, THE DEVELOPMENT OF CONSTITUTIONAL GUARANTEES OF LIBERTY (New Haven, Conn., 1957).

Arthur M. Schlesinger, POLITICAL AND SOCIAL GROWTH OF THE AMERICAN PEOPLE 1865–1940 (3d ed.; New York, 1941).

Arthur M. Schlesinger, Jr., THE AGE OF ROOSEVELT (Boston, 1957–60).

André Siegfried, AMERICA AT MID-CENTURY (New York, 1955).

Norman J. Small (ed.), THE CONSTITUTION OF THE UNITED STATES OF AMERICA. ANALYSIS AND INTERPRETATION (Washington, 1964).

J. Allen Smith, THE SPIRIT OF AMERICAN GOVERNMENT (New York, 1907).

John Steinbeck, AMERICA AND AMERICANS (New York, 1966).

Joseph Story, COMMENTARIES ON THE CONSTITUTION OF THE UNITED STATES (2d ed.; Boston, 1851).

Carl B. Swisher, AMERICAN CONSTITUTIONAL DEVELOPMENT (2d ed.; Boston, 1954).

——— THE SUPREME COURT IN MODERN ROLE (rev. ed.; New York, 1965).

Alexis de Tocqueville, DEMOCRACY IN AMERICA (Bradley ed.; New York, 1954).

Henry van Dyke, THE SPIRIT OF AMERICA (New York, 1910).

Eric Voegelin, THE NEW SCIENCE OF POLITICS (Chicago, 1952).

——— ORDER AND HISTORY (Baton Rouge, La., 1956–).

Charles Warren, CONGRESS, THE CONSTITUTION, AND THE SUPREME COURT (2d ed.; Boston, 1935).

H. G. Wells, THE FUTURE IN AMERICA (New York, 1906).

Woodrow Wilson, CONSTITUTIONAL GOVERNMENT IN THE UNITED STATES (New York, 1908).

Benjamin F. Wright, AMERICAN INTERPRETATIONS OF NATURAL LAW (Cambridge, Mass., 1931).

INDEX

Absolutism, 20
  aristocratic, 162, 262
  democratic, viif., 7–9, 14, 44, 87,
    90f., 128f., 146, 154, 156, 173,
    229, 261
  monarchical, viii, 88, 161f., 173,
    189, 209, 259, 262
  see also Despotism
Acollas, Emile, 167
Acton, Lord, 15
Adams, James T., 100
Adams, John, 4, 15, 67f., 181, 211
Adamson Act, 76
Adenauer, Konrad, 236f., 239, 255
Adkins v. *Children's Hospital of*
  District of Columbia, 76
Aggressive protection of civil rights,
  98, 129f., 138, 141f.
Albright, S. D., 226
Alexander, King of Yugoslavia, 193
Allgeyer v. *Louisiana,* 70
Alliance for Progress, 236
Alvarez, Alexander, 168
Ambition, 50–54, 129, 154, 203
Amending power, *see* Constituent
  power
Amendments to Constitution, 39, 98,
  104f., 109, 122, 154, 199, 251
  see also under the respective num-
  bers of the amendments
American century, 210
American credo, viif., 3–10, 12–16,
  64, 84, 106
American Dream, vii, 16f., 259f.,
  262, 266, 269f., 272f.
American growth, 210–12, 266
American Revolution, 5–10, 14, 17,
  25, 64–68, 87, 99f., 105–7, 142,
  146, 218, 245, 259, 269f.

American Revolution (*Continued*)
  a *diffidatio,* 8f., 12, 14
  meaning for the world, 10–13,
    15–17, 19f., 211, 219, 259, 273
  permanent, dynamic, 13
American tradition, viii, 3–16, 40–42,
  64–83, 93, 98–108, 115, 129, 134,
  143–53, 177–82, 193, 209–23,
  234, 243, 267f., 271
Ames, Herman V., 225
Amy v. *Smith,* 106
Anarchy, 24f., 129, 170, 196
Ancien régime, 20, 86, 161, 163, 191f.
Annapolis Convention, 65f.
Anschütz, Gerhard, 91–93
Antisocial conduct, 137f.
Argentina, 20
Aristocracy, 162, 191, 262
Articles of Association, 32
Articles of Confederation, 4, 65, 86,
  89, 100f., 106, 112, 155, 178f.,
  181, 201
Assassination, 18, 44, 192–201, 237f.,
  241
Attorney General of the U.S., 124,
  126, 129
Austria, 189, 219, 233
Autolimitation, 144, 151, 199
Axis Berlin-Rome, 230
Aylesworth, L. E., 226

Bacon, Francis, 272
Bailey, Sidney D., 249
Baldwin v. *Franks,* 117
Baldwin v. *Missouri,* 156
Barère, Bertrand, 87
Barlow, Joel, 13, 212
Barron v. *Baltimore,* 105
Barthou, Jean-Louis, 193

Designed by Gerard A. Valerio

Composed in Linotype Old Style #7 by Kingsport Press

Printed letterpress by Kingsport Press
on 60 lb. Warren's '1854'

Bound by Kingsport Press in G. S. B. S/711